CONCEPTUALIZING 21ST-CENTURY ARCHIVES

ANNE J. GILLILAND

SOCIETY OF American Archivists

CHICAGO

Society of American Archivists
www.archivists.org

Printed in the United States of America.

Cover design by Paula Ashley, Next Year's News, http://www.nyninc.com/.
Interior graphic design by Sweeney Design, kasween@sbcglobal.net.

Library of Congress Cataloging-in-Publication Data

Gilliland, Anne.
  Conceptualizing 21st-century archives / Anne J. Gilliland.
      pages cm
  Includes bibliographical references and index.
  ISBN 978-1-931666-68-8
  1. Archives—Technological innovations—History. 2. Archives—Automation—History. I. Title.
  CD973.D3G45 2014
  025.17'140285—dc23
                            2013048094

Table of Contents

LIST OF TABLES:

LIST OF FIGURES:

Preface

Much has been made of the constant technological and sociocultural change associated with the digital age. This book contemplates how records, archives, and the archival and recordkeeping[1] fields have developed conceptually as a result of or in response to that change and where archival and recordkeeping ideas, practices, and research are positioned in the early twenty-first century. The subject of technology and archives still makes some working archivists nervous, even after more than seventy years of interaction with computing and information technology. The accelerating pace of change, the increasing number of areas and activities in which archivists could or should be engaged, and the constant learning curve involved contribute to this understandable nervousness. At the same time, as someone who works with budding generations of new archivists who enter our graduate education programs, I am also very aware of and encouraged by the excitement, energy, and sense of tremendous optimism among those entering this field as it turns digital.

In 1992 at the University of Michigan, I developed and taught the first regularly scheduled graduate archival course in the United States on what was then referred to as the archival administration of electronic records. I became interested in how to approach this kind of topic, with its technical and business-oriented content, in a way that students and archival professionals would understand, would be able to place within the context of wider archival ideas and contributions, and would hopefully also enjoy. In 2004, with funding from the Institute of Museum and Library Services, Elizabeth Yakel and I began the Archival Education and Research Initiative with the aim of strengthening archival education and scholarship. This initiative includes the Archival Education and Research Institutes (AERI) which, for one week each year, bring together archival faculty and doctoral students from around the globe to present their research, develop new curricula and pedagogy, learn about new methodological approaches in research, and, overall, nurture an academic community and a research front. AERI provides the opportunity to expose this community in depth to several of the emergent areas of research that I discuss in this book. I hope that this exposure will in turn encourage further integration of the outcomes of this work into archival education, ultimately enhancing the professional knowledge base, as well as increasing research attention. Among AERI's curricular activities is a collective endeavor to develop more conceptual approaches to archival education. The rationale underlying this effort is that by developing a sound conceptual base and also by understanding the lineage of those concepts as well as of developments in the field, future archivists will be better equipped to move across media, technologies, settings, and cultures in ways still fundamentally archival in perspective and role.

I wrote this book from a similar impulse. Drawing upon archival sources, scholarly literature, recordkeeping research outcomes, and professional archival discourse, I sought to synthesize the interactions of the archival field with technology over the past century to address several questions: what lessons can the archival field learn from its history about ideas tried and abandoned? Which ideas and practices are truly new, and which continue to hold good, regardless of technological shifts? In what ways do archivists need to expand their thinking and their practices to fulfill their "glocal" roles? And, how should archivists approach working across the boundaries of their individual institutions, traditional and new constituencies, and national archival traditions and practices in the twenty-first century?

This book traces the lineage of descriptive systems development, as well as of the creation and management of computer-generated records and the curation of all sorts of digital materials with which archivists are engaged. These lineages attest that many of the phenomena that so preoccupy us today people experienced or contemplated in other forms and in other times. By understanding how archival practices and thinking were challenged or how archivists responded at different points over the past century, we can begin to discern how and why ideas rise, fall, and resurge. Indeed, for a profession that prides itself on looking backward to look forward, the disregard for and loss of its own memory relating to technological and related conceptual developments over the past century is surprising. Generations of pioneers have now passed on or retired, and their seminal work and its legacy are largely transparent. This memory loss is exacerbated because, in the American archival literature at least, too much of this historical context has been fragmented or is absent altogether. This makes it hard for archivists to look at archival developments holistically, to place themselves and their role within them, and to obtain the crucial insight to support decisions that need to be made for the future. In this book, therefore, I attempt to collate and synthesize this history and legacy as well as to review key developments up to the present day with a view to laying out the knowledge base upon which the future of the field is constructed and to acknowledging those whose work supports or builds upon each key development, model, or idea.

A final note about how the book is organized: each chapter addresses either the historical development or the current state of an area within archival science that information and communications technology have significantly affected, with a primary emphasis upon the experiences of the archival field in the United States and the ways in which these relate to developments elsewhere. The chapters build upon and reinforce each other to construct a picture of how archives arrived in the twenty-first century and to suggest where they might be going in the foreseeable future. I included substantial footnotes to point readers to additional literature so that they may pursue individual topics in greater depth and to present any supplemental commentary or associated information. Inevitably, however, in a book with such a broad scope, there may be omissions in coverage, instances where I did not treat all aspects with equal depth, and instances where future developments will move beyond what I have covered here.

Note

1   Both "recordkeeping" and "record-keeping" are terms of art within the archival field, but connote different conceptual approaches. In this book, "recordkeeping" will be used to indicate the broader and more inclusive conceptualization first used in the Australian Records Continuum, and "record-keeping" will be used to indicate the creation, management, and use of active records.

Acknowledgments

I am profoundly grateful to the many people who contributed intellectually and personally to the writing of this book. The students with whom I have worked over the years have introduced me to more perspectives, experiences, and knowledge than I would ever otherwise have encountered. In particular, I would like to thank Amelia Acker, Kimberly Anderson, Michelle Caswell, Andrew Lau, Lori Lindberg, Kalpana Shankar, Ciaran Trace, Michael Wartenbe, Deborah Weissman, and Eunha Youn, whose own scholarship and passion have pushed me over the years to reflect and respond—for that my work is the richer. I also wish to pay tribute to the intellectual stimulation, inspiration, and friendship of my colleagues, in particular Marcia Bates, Jonathan Furner, Robert Hayes, and Ellen Pearlstein at UCLA; Maynard Brichford at the University of Illinois at Urbana-Champaign; Terry Cook at the University of Manitoba; Richard J. Cox at the University of Pittsburgh; Luciana Duranti at the University of British Columbia; Luiz Mendes at California State University–Northridge; Mirna Willer at the University of Zadar; Frank Upward at Monash University; Elizabeth Yakel at the University of Michigan; and most especially, my longtime friend, mentor, and research collaborator, Sue McKemmish at Monash University.

I would like also to thank the U.S. Institute for Museum and Library Services, the U.S. National Historical Records and Manuscripts Commission, and the U.S. National Science Foundation for their generous funding support of several of the projects discussed in this book; the Library of Congress Manuscript Division, The National Archives (U.K.), the U.S. National Archives and Records Administration, and the University of Wisconsin–Milwaukee Archives Department for providing me with access to relevant archival materials; Brad Miles for his assistance with archival research in Milwaukee; Cal Lee and Nancy McGovern for their contributions to and reflections on chronologies of relevant events that draw heavily upon their own pioneering work with electronic records; Kimberly Anderson for helping with the collation of relevant media materials; Marcia Bates, Michael Buckland, Jonathan Furner, Peter Hirtle, Luiz Mendes, Joshua Sternfeld, and Kelvin White for their input and careful readings of various drafts of this manuscript; and especially Eunha Youn, not only for her invaluable assistance in gathering bibliographic materials for this book, but for her patient and scrupulous reading and rereading of, and many insightful suggestions about, multiple versions of the manuscript.

Finally, I would like to thank Peter Wosh and Teresa Brinati of the Society of American Archivists for their immensely patient encouragement and support during the writing and publication of this book.

Anne Gilliland
Los Angeles, October 2012

CHAPTER 1

Introduction

This chapter introduces the book's scope and main themes. It reviews the components of the traditional archival paradigm and identifies several constructs emerging from technological developments, intellectual and community movements, and archival scholarship that expand and challenge the paradigm to move beyond physically bound thinking and to become more inclusive of multiple ways of knowing and practicing.

The Archival Role in Digital Timespace

Places, people, and cultures geographically distant from us have become evermore present in our lives through technological advancements. Over the past two centuries, first locomotives, automobiles, and airplanes made rapid travel across long distances possible for migration and emigration, business, curiosity, and pleasure. Then rockets and satellites awed and inspired us with their capacity to gaze at the earth and its neighbors from outside our own atmosphere and to place the earth within its astronomical and cosmological contexts. Local and remote communities became better informed about each other and more interactive by means of the telegraph, telephone, and television. Governing and doing business, as well as remembering, voicing, capturing, storing, and disseminating personal and community experiences within and across generations and geography were augmented dramatically when visual and audio recording technologies, and then electronic mail, cellular telephones, the Internet, and the cloud entered everyday life. The Web revolutionized citizen interaction with government and citizen access to public records, fundamentally altering citizen relationships with the state. At the same time, however, the amount of data gathered and maintained by governments and for-profit organizations on individual citizens is at an all-time high. Our perceptions of time and events have also progressively morphed. Work, learning, sports, leisure activities, and, indeed, our daily routines, have become more granular and precise with the adoption first of the pocket-, then the wristwatch, and finally the split-second clock. Even the finality of death seems to have been affected as we contemplate the digital afterlives of our Facebook pages and Twitter accounts. We are left with a world simultaneously more fragmented and more integrated, a world bigger and more diverse and yet smaller, a world where control over how and when information is created and used has been democratized and yet those information patterns are increasingly exploited or under surveillance.

These developments fundamentally change how we conduct our lives, how we relate to other people and places, how we become informed, and how we conceive of the passing of time, of past events, and of the very act of remembering. They have become so transparent and embedded that it is hard to remember that the majority occurred only across the course of six or seven generations and that pervasive digitality supported by developments such as the World Wide Web, high-speed IP data networks and mobile broadband, and the cloud emerged only in the last twenty years. Today's digital technologies transcend the limitations of space, refashion the parameters of time, and blur boundaries not only between official and personal, public and private, corporate and public domains, but also between material and nonmaterial. They make possible not only physical, but virtual societies and communities; support collaborative work practices; optimize digital capacity; and spawn innovative genres and altered literacies. As events during the "Arab Spring" that began in 2010 illustrate only too well, digital technologies can play an important role in supporting democratization and liberation in the present, as well as in rescuing, reconciling, and repatriating the legacy and knowledge of the past. All the while, changes in modes of creation and transmission can alter the resulting form, nature, and capacity of the record. They can also generate new forms of societal documentation—the digital residue of our lived lives—that capture complex, diverse, and distributed; often sensitive; and sometimes highly personal aspects of our existence, much of which in the past was absent from the official records and even from collections of personal papers that filled the world's archives. The personal is increasingly inextricably embedded in the official record, and the private in the public.

Archives are a critical component of how many societies remember, are held accountable, and generally conduct their affairs. They are ancient entities. Although they have taken on many forms, archives have always been concerned with the human record and how it can bridge time and space and remain meaningful and useful. Many fields and institutions view themselves as integrally associated with information, memory, and evidence in one form or another. However, among them, the recordkeeping professions—archival science and records management—are, first and foremost, the professions of the record. Archives are predicated on an understanding of the power of the record in bureaucratic, societal, community, and individual lives. Over time, they have played key roles as trusted witnesses and correctives to the records and narratives of events, actions, communities, and lives. They have also, however, been complicit in the promulgation and preservation of centralized power and control, and the perpetuation of official narratives that silenced, ignored, or misrepresented countless other perspectives and experiences. They are, in the words of law and commerce scholar Doris Long, both the "sword and the shield," not only for governments and other big institutions, but also for cultures, communities, and individuals.[1] At the same time, archives and the professions of the record have themselves evolved. Canadian archival scholar Terry Cook suggests that over the past 150 years, the archival identity has been shifting across four different frameworks or mindsets: juridical legacy, cultural memory, societal engagement, and community archiving. He sees these as being cumulative rather than completely replacing each other. As a result, he argues, the archivist "has been transformed . . . from passive curator to active appraiser to societal mediator to community facilitator. The focus of archival thinking has moved from evidence to memory to identity and community, as the broader intellectual currents have changed from pre-modern to modern to postmodern to contemporary."[2] Chinese scholars Xiaomi An and Wang Wang, who have been engaged in developing metasynthetic approaches to records and knowledge management in business and government settings, posit that there are five levels of consciousness at work today: egocentric, ethnocentric, sociocentric, world centric, and planet- or cosmocentric.[3] The archival ideas, practices, and research discussed throughout this book support Cook's argument that archival thinking has evolved and grown increasingly complex. They also evidence that multiple different mindsets or consciousnesses are indeed at work today, sometimes interactively and sometimes independently.

Thinking and Acting "Glocally"

The twenty-first century is synonymous in many people's minds with the digital age, an era when digitally empowered change has tremendous implications for archives and recordkeeping—how we secure rights and responsibilities; develop individual and collective senses of the present and of posterity; and inscribe, analyze, preserve, make accessible, and repurpose the data, records, artifacts, and other aspects of cultural heritage that comprise our societal memory. As if this were not sufficient food for thought as the archival field contemplates its role and its future in this century, the digital age has also been a prime facilitator of another critical shift toward *glocalization*. Sociologist Roland Robertson famously defined glocalization in 1997 as "the simultaneity—the co-presence—of both universalizing and particularizing tendencies."[4] In other words, while national, sector, and institutional interests and perspectives often set the agenda in the past, today the focus on simultaneously addressing local and global needs and perspectives, as well as on understanding the effects of interaction between the two, is growing. Archives should be concerned about glocalization for several pressing reasons. Indigenous, local, and colonial recordkeeping and memory systems and practices that developed out of particular national and cultural traditions and worldviews are simultaneously grappling with their tangled and often still traumatic colonial legacy, and interfacing and negotiating with other traditions and worldviews in whole new digital ways. New and reconstituted nations are working to develop their national identities and strengthen their own bureaucratic, scholarly, and professional infrastructures internally, while seeking visibility and recognition on the world stage. In devising standards, best practices, regulations, and terminology for international implementation, developers need to consider that recordkeeping can take place and data can be exchanged effectively and equitably across national, cultural, linguistic, and ideological boundaries, as well as among different technological environments. Major archival traditions, while necessarily evolving to address digital considerations, nevertheless remain rooted in specific national, legal, political, cultural, and historical contexts and assumptions. Furthermore, not every national recordkeeping tradition has historically been represented during the processes associated with creating international standards, best practices, regulations, and terminology. For example, even with opportunities for wider professional commentary, international records management and archival description standards remain strongly rooted in certain European, North American, and Australian conceptualizations. Asian epistemologies, Indigenous protocols for working with archival materials, as well as the blossoming community archives movement empowering ethnic, racial, and grassroots communities often on the margins of mainstream institutional archival activity, further challenge these traditions. These challenges require the archival field to take local cultural and community practices and ontologies into account, to engage in participative and consultative approaches, and to contemplate the very real possibility that some community archives will not have the necessary resources to implement or comply with standards and best practices, or may decide not to implement them for philosophical, political, or other reasons.

At the same time, little is new about progressive technological change, per se. It is easy to forget the accelerating number of transformations in recording and communications technologies as well as the multiple and shifting epistemologies with which archives have had to cope over the past three or more millennia. In this sense, the digital age is but one more era in the archival temporal continuum. The perpetual challenge for archives has been to respond in thoughtful and constructive ways to new developments and to address those yet to come. Such responses require of archivists and archives today a glocal orientation and a careful balancing of continuity with innovation, of responsibility with responsibilities, and of reflexivity with principled rigor.

The Evolving Archival Paradigm

As chapter 2 discusses in more detail, discourses not only within the archival profession but also within information technology and management communities and disciplinary scholarship locate the archival role in varying places along a spectrum that ranges from bureaucratic practice to cultural heritage to identity construction to human rights concerns, with all shades in between. These discourses tend to take on their own trajectories, often passing each other by with only nominal nods, rather than pausing to contemplate what kinds of cross-formations might be possible or useful in understanding and advancing archives and their roles in an increasingly technologized and glocal society. A little over a decade ago, I authored a report for the Council on Library and Information Resources titled *Enduring Paradigms,*[5] *New Opportunities: The Value of the Archival Perspective in the Digital Environment,* arguing that the various paradigms that historically guided each of the information professions come up short when compared with the scope of the issues continuously emerging in the digital environment. Instead, an overarching dynamic paradigm—that adopts, adapts, develops, and sheds principles and practices of the constituent information communities as necessary—needs to be created. Such a paradigm may possibly be taking shape through recent work in digital and data curation.

First defined by American physicist and philosopher of science Thomas Kuhn, a *paradigm* is a formal model or pattern of beliefs, outlooks, assertions, values, and practices regarding a particular activity or phenomenon.[6] The archival paradigm (or paradigms, if one views the different frameworks and traditions within which archivists have operated as distinct paradigms rather than as different manifestations and phases of a unifying paradigm) with which this book is primarily concerned first took shape in a series of regulations and manuals published in France, Prussia, the Netherlands, Spain, Italy, and elsewhere in Western Europe in the eighteenth and nineteenth centuries. Emanating chiefly out of the experiences of those working principally in archives holding state and municipal records, it supports an evidence-based approach to the management of those records. It is fundamentally concerned with the organizational and individual functions, processes, and contexts through which records and knowledge are created and preserved as well as the ways in which records individually and collectively reflect those functions, processes, and contexts in and over time. The paradigm operates on multiple conceptual, functional, and professional levels as a framework for archival theorizing as well as for archival practice. In this framework, theory develops out of practice (inductive) and practice develops out of theory (deductive). It represents both a particular perspective on information and knowledge management and a distinctive professional ethos. Table 1.1 outlines several of the traditional and emergent components of the paradigm.[7]

Table 1.1. Components of the archival paradigm

Component	Examples
Core concepts (interdependent)	Record, recordkeeping, archives, evidentiality, transactionality, accountability, memory, identity
Subconcepts and ancillary concepts (interrelated)	Authority, creatorship, document, original/copy, power, reliability/authenticity
Canonical precepts	*Respect des fonds* and the principle of provenance (keeping materials generated by the same organization, person, or activity together and not intermixing them with materials of a different provenance), the sanctity of original order, the notion of hierarchy in records
Characteristics inherent in records due to the circumstances of their creation	Naturalness, organic nature or interrelationship, impartiality, authenticity, uniqueness
Constituent parts of records	Documentary form (intrinsic and extrinsic elements), annotations, context, and medium; digital bitstream
Records and recordkeeping models	The records life cycle, the records continuum model, the Open Archival Information System (OAIS) Reference Model
Emergent constructs	The archival multiverse, archival reconciliation, archivalization, co-creatorship, community archives, digital components, functional requirements for recordkeeping, living archives, postcustodialism, risk management
Recordkeeping contexts	Juridical-administrative, provenancial, procedural, documentary, technological, historical, sociocultural
Recordkeeping mandates	Laws, regulations, standards, best practices, institutional mission
Recordkeeping processes	Records creation, capture, organization, disposition, pluralization

Archival professional practices	Appraisal, preservation, collective and hierarchical arrangement and description, dissemination of records, outreach
Professional ethics and values statements	Society of American Archivists *Core Values Statement and Code of Ethics*, International Council on Archives *Code of Ethics*

In *Enduring Paradigms*, I argued that the traditional paradigm, and especially archival ideas about provenance, authenticity, collective description, and preservation, offers powerful approaches for grappling with problems of volume, heterogeneity, trustworthiness, and persistence that dog the entire world of information preservation, description, retrieval, and use.

Kuhn argues, however, that paradigms undergo periodic shifts, such as the shifts and phases identified by Cook, and that these shifts open up new ways of thinking within a field.[8] While this book argues for the continuing relevance of fundamental paradigmatic ideas to the twenty-first-century archival field as well as to areas of information and knowledge management that have emerged or grown over the past decade, therefore, it is also concerned with each of Cook's paradigmatic phases and the ways in which the different approaches they represent continue to interact, spurred on by technological developments and the missions of the organizations and initiatives under which archivists operate. This book delves more deeply and critically into the history of how the archival paradigm took on its distinctive shape in American archival practice and thought. It also examines how the paradigm has evolved over the past century and needs to continue to evolve in response to technical and sociopolitical movements, to international developments and collaborations in the field, and now to the forces of glocalization.

In 1994, Australian archival scholar Sue McKemmish observed that

The loss of physicality that occurs when records are captured electronically is forcing archivists to reassess basic understandings about the nature of the records of social and organisational activity, and their qualities as evidence. Even when they are captured in a medium that can be felt and touched, records as conceptual constructs do not coincide with records as physical objects. Physical ordering and placement of such records captures a view of their contextual and documentary relationships, but cannot present multiple views of what is a complex reality. The traditional custodial role takes on another dimension when it is accepted that the record is only partly manifest in what is in the boxes on the repository shelves.[9]

A recurring theme in the chapters that make up this book is the debate over the nature of some key archival concepts, principles, and practices in a postphysical, postcustodial, and postmodern world. This discourse does not call for abandoning archival ideas, even though the continuing relevance and viability of particular archival and recordkeeping practices such as records retention scheduling and appraisal have been challenged. It does, however, point up the need for the conceptualization of those ideas to become simultaneously more expansive and more rigorous to encompass and address wider social, geopolitical, technological, and ontological realities. While research in practice is slowly increasing, the theory building of key individuals such as Cook, Upward, and McKemmish and the findings of prominent research collaborations that bridge sectors and disciplines drive much of the discourse. At the same time, ideas and methods emanating out of scholarship in other fields influences this research. As Figure 1.1 indicates, the past twenty-five years witnessed unprecedented growth, diversification, and increasing complexity in archival research. Although some of the highest profile research resulted from the prioritization of electronic records concerns in national funding agendas and by major government archives, the growing size and scope of graduate archival education and the expanding cohorts of faculty opened up more areas of research and encouraged more research in practice. Notable growth in the published research literature parallels this expansion, not only in professional journals and reports, but also in research journals, conference proceedings, and monographs.[10] Couture and Ducharme analyzed forty articles from five North American and international archival professional journals between 1988 and 1998 to identify major research themes.[11] Figure 1.1 juxtaposes Couture and Ducharme's findings with a review conducted by Gilliland and McKemmish of recent thematic trends in archival scholarship based upon research presented by participants at the 2009 through 2011 annual meetings of the Archival Education and Research Institute (AERI), currently the largest international forum for archival researchers, educators, and doctoral students.[12]

Research topics, 1988–1998 (Couture and Ducharme, 1998)	Research topics, 2008–2012 (Gilliland and McKemmish, 2013)
<ul><li>Archives and archival science—the nature of the Archive, archival goals, and the usefulness of archives</li><li>Archives and society—the role and place of archives, archival science and the profession</li><li>Archival issues—ethics, access, privacy</li><li>Archival functions</li><li>History of archives and archival science</li><li>Management of archival programs and services</li><li>Technologies</li><li>Types of media and archives; electronic records</li><li>Types of archival institutions</li></ul>	<ul><li>Anthropological data collection and repatriation</li><li>Archaeological recordkeeping</li><li>Archival description and recordkeeping metadata</li><li>Archival education, training, and pedagogy</li><li>Archival implications of social media</li><li>Archives and human rights</li><li>Archives and postcoloniality</li><li>Arts and performing arts archives</li><li>Business records and recordkeeping</li><li>Community recordkeeping practices</li><li>Community-based archives and community-centric archival policy</li><li>Criminal justice, counterterrorism and recordkeeping</li><li>Decolonization of the Archive</li><li>Diasporic and expatriate records and identity concerns</li><li>Digital curation</li><li>Digital forensics</li><li>Digital heritage convergences</li><li>Digital humanities convergences</li><li>Digitization and associated policy concerns, e.g., copyright</li><li>Electronic recordkeeping systems and approaches</li><li>Evidence studies</li><li>Globalization and other global concerns</li><li>Health records and recordkeeping</li><li>History of archives and archival practices</li><li>Indigenous knowledge, culture and the Archive</li><li>Legislative analysis</li><li>Memory and identity studies</li><li>Metadata modeling</li><li>Moving image archives (analog and digital)</li><li>Museum archives</li><li>Personal recordkeeping and digital archives</li><li>Scientific recordkeeping and data archives</li><li>Social justice, human rights, truth and reconciliation commissions</li><li>The social life of records and documents</li><li>Transformative research by and with Indigenous and other communities partners</li><li>Trusted digital repositories</li></ul>

Figure 1.1. Expansion of the scope of archival research in the twenty-first century

Some Resonating Emergent Constructs

Within this discourse, several convergent constructs relate to sometimes intersecting, sometimes competing ideas, models, frameworks, and imperatives. Because they emanate out of different archival, juridical, and intellectual traditions, it is often possible to identify certain constructs, movements, and initiatives with specific geographic regions, as well as with particular individuals or formative collaborations between individuals. Figure 1.2 lists some of the key contributions over the past fifty years, as well as prominent associated individuals and organizations. Unfortunately, it is not yet possible to fully acknowledge or integrate similar contributions

USA
  AERI (Gilliland, Yakel)
  Archives and museum informatics (Bearman)
  BitCurator (Lee, Woods, Kirschenbaum)
  Community archives (Bastian, Alexander)
  DICE Group (Moore, Marciano, University of
    North Carolina, Chapel Hill)
  DigCCurr (Tibbo, Lee)
  EAD (Pitti, SAA)
  Electronic Records Research Agenda (NHPRC)
  The Internet Archive (Kahle, Prelinger)
  MARC AMC/APPM (Hensen, SAA, RLIN)
  OAIS (CCSDS)
  Pittsburgh Project (Cox, Bearman, Duff)

Canada
  Contemporary archival informatics (Duranti,
    MacNeil)
  InterPARES (Duranti)
  Macroappraisal (Cook)
  Postmodern constructions of archives (Cook)
  RAD (BCA, CCA)
  Total archives (Smith)

U.K.
  CAMiLEON (Hedstrom, Rusbridge, Wheatley)
  CEDARS (CURL, Universities of Cambridge,
    Leeds, and Oxford)
  Community archives (Flinn, Stevens,
    Shepherd)
  DCC
  JISC

Europe
  Collective memory and archives (Ketelaar)
  DLM Forum
  Erpanet
  EU Framework Programme
  MoReq

Australia
  Archival reconciliation (McKemmish,
    Faulkhead, Russell)
  Australian Series System (Scott)
  AS4390-1996
  CRKM (Monash University, NAA, SR
    NSW, ASA CDS, McKemmish, Gilliland,
    Cunningham)
  Continuum thinking (Scott, Upward,
    McKemmish, Reed, Hurley)
  RKMS (McKemmish, Acland, Cumming, Reed,
    Ward)
  Relationships in records/simultaneous
    multiple and parallel provenance (Hurley)
  VERS (PROV)

China
  Metasynthetic strategies for recordkeeping
    (Feng, An, Liu, Wang)

South Africa
  Archives, justice, and reconciliation (Harris)

Figure 1.2. Some key contributions to evolving archival ideas, practices, standards, and technologies by region

to archival thought and practice that occur in other regions due to inadequate mechanisms for exchanging information across the global archival community, for example, robust programs for translating scholarly and professional literature, terminology, and semantics, and support for professional and scholarly exchanges.

These contributions and the strands of discourse that surround them indicate a growing intellectual and practical complexity of the status, role, and practices of archives in society. They interweave theoretical models of recordkeeping, discussions about the nature and import of archival concepts and practices in a "post-" world fraught with contemporary glocal challenges, and contemplation of how new technological capabilities open up new possibilities and new ways of thinking about them.[13] To prepare readers for discussions in the following chapters, I outlined some emergent constructs central to discussions about the potential nature and roles of the twenty-first century.

Archives as a Place and Post-custodial Approaches

The construct of archives as physical places of custody that can be trusted to protect the evidence value of the records they hold and to maintain a professional neutrality in the face of how and why those records were created or could be used lies at the heart of the modern archival paradigm. As already mentioned, that paradigm had its roots in European practices. Luciana Duranti eloquently uses historical warrant to demonstrate how, from Roman times onward, archives occupied physical places that take custody of bureaucratic documents, transforming them as they cross the archival threshold into "testimony of past actions."[14] She argues that the preservation of that testimony and the evidence it implies is endangered once it is no longer in active use unless it is physically removed from its creators and those with a direct interest in its content and transferred across the archival threshold into archival custody.[15] However, archivists working with born-digital materials are only too aware today of how technological complexities, policy concerns, and economic costs may result in those materials never being physically stored within a physical archives. Instead, they might remain with their original creator, be placed together with nonarchival materials within an institutional or other digital repository, or stored remotely in the cloud.

One of the first major challenges to the traditional custodial paradigm came in 1981. F. Gerald Ham, in a plenary address to the annual meeting of the Society of American Archivists, argued that archivists had entered the "post-custodial era," when "the revolution in information processing" was resulting in an unprecedented abundance of hard-to-preserve records. This abundance, he asserted, was forcing archivists out of their introspective proclivities and excessive proprietaryness toward their holdings and into a more active role in which they "must make crucial decisions—or decide by not deciding—about the future of the historical record."[16] In other words, archivists could no longer conduct themselves as passive recipients and custodians of old, but still valuable, records. Instead, they would need to be proactive. In the same speech, Ham noted several other ways in which this revolution challenged traditional archival ideas—how databases compiled from multiple sources confound the notion of aggregations of records with a single provenance; and how the mutability of materials created and maintained electronically renders the principle of retaining records according to their original order irrelevant, challenges the uniqueness of records that could so easily be reproduced, makes it difficult to distinguish between an original and a copy, and raises new questions about how to ensure that records are not altered in any way. He argued that, as a result, archivists would need to rethink what would constitute appropriate archival "processing" when working with these materials.

Ham set out a five-point agenda for how archivists should proceed in the post-custodial era. First, they should develop coherent and comprehensive programs for acquiring archival materials locally, regionally, and nationally. Second, they should focus on providing easy and centralized access to materials becoming increasingly complex and dispersed. Third, they should address the ways in which materials are created by information technology and devise how to appraise and preserve them for future use. Fourth, they must become involved in resolving the conflicts between freedom of information and privacy in terms of how these affect the quality and content of the archival record and access to it. Fifth, they should make better use of available national resources for archival activity. In

1992, Australian archivist Glenda Acland was particularly emphatic in her support for a post-custodial perspective:

> A change in the traditionally perceived archival mindset is needed here to manage the records and their continuum, not the relics at the end stage in the record life cycle. . . . With the spotlight clearly on the record rather than the relic, the equilibrium can be adjusted to provide efficient, effective and innovative public record management with an intellectual control not custody axis, safeguarding and making accessible archival resources for good government, public accountability and future research needs. [17]

In 1996, fellow Australians Frank Upward and Sue McKemmish, influenced by, among others, the work of sociologist Anthony Giddens and archives and museum informaticist David Bearman,[18] brainstormed a set of "structural principles" for recordkeeping in a late modern society that add a more conceptual approach to Ham's agenda:

1. A concept of "records" which is inclusive of records of continuing value (= archives), which stresses their uses for transactional, evidentiary and memory purposes, and which unifies approaches to archiving/recordkeeping whether records are kept for a split second or a millennium.

2. A focus on records as logical rather than physical entities, regardless of whether they are in paper or electronic form.

3. Institutionalization of the recordkeeping profession's role requires a particular emphasis on the need to integrate recordkeeping into business and societal processes and purposes.

4. Archival science is the foundation for organising knowledge about recordkeeping. However, this knowledge should be combined with relevant knowledge and skills from other fields.[19]

Much from these agendas has been taken up in a variety of different ways in the past thirty years, both nationally and internationally, as the chapters in this book demonstrate, although many archivists still fail to understand that what is called for here is a conceptual shift in how records are thought of, regardless of the media in which they present themselves. They do, however, recognize that it may be technologically, politically, and economically impractical, unsound, or even impossible to physically acquire, preserve, and provide access to the massive volume of digital materials being generated by organizations and individuals today. Archival theorists and institutions alike have built on the notion of post-custodialism with arguments and programs that view centralized archives as "an archives of last resort."[20] Upward, however, cautions that "post-custodial approaches to archives and records cannot be understood if they are treated as a dualism. They are not the opposite of custody. They are a response to opportunities for asserting the role of an archives—and not just its authentication role—in many re-invigorating ways."[21]

Archivists are increasingly encouraged and professionally educated to become actively engaged with the management and intellectual aspects of the keeping of records. Examples of this engagement include articulating functional requirements for recordkeeping systems design, devising and implementing policies for the appropriate management of active records and archives stored by third-party vendors, undertaking business process analyses to understand where records are or should be created, brokering user access to materials of archival value such as large-scale databases that remain in the custody of the original creator, and developing automated ways to validate permitted users as well as to provide online users with customized digital information in response to their queries.[22]

Notwithstanding all these developments, bricks-and-mortar archives endure, at least for the moment, as the primary repositories for preserving records. More importantly, perhaps, mainstream archival practices remain profoundly physically oriented. If they are to transition into a more thoroughly digital conceptualization and set of functions, archives will need a clear sense of which characteristics of the physical archives ensure and demonstrate security and trustworthiness and how they achieve those characteristics. Their efficacy needs to be rigorously evaluated, and then the functionality of those characteristics of demonstrated continuing value must be translated and operationalized for the digital environment.

Some digital proponents argue that the physical orientation of archives might only be sustainable for a handful of years, at which point everything worth keeping will either be born digital or digitized. While such statements inevitably raise critical questions about what functions and capabilities might be omitted or lost if this were indeed to be the case,[23] unquestionably it is time for the archival field to move beyond its physical orientation not only to remain relevant and viable in the digital age, but also to take on new functions associated with shifts in the archival paradigm and to take advantage of new capabilities associated with changes in information technology and knowledge development.

Archivization and Archivalization

The constructs of *archivization* and *archivalization* were not part of the traditional archival paradigm. Rather, they are critical constructs that emerged out of shifting intellectual approaches in the arts and humanities, enhancing the reflexivity of professional archival thought. In 1995, French philosopher Jacques Derrida argued that "the technical structure of the archiving archive also determines the structure of the archivable content even in its very coming into existence and in its relationship to the future . . . the archivization produces as much as it records the event."[24] Influenced by Derrida, Foucault, and a growing number of postmodern and postcolonial scholars, several prominent archival thinkers have in recent years called the field's attention to the many historical ways in which archives have been active agents in shaping their future holdings and thereby, public perceptions about historical events.[25] Coining a related term, *archivalization,* Eric Ketelaar discusses "the conscious or unconscious choice (determined by social and cultural factors) to consider something worth archiving . . . influenced by social, religious, cultural, political and economic contexts."[26]

Bearing in mind Ham's agenda for post-custodial archives and the kinds of activities that post-custodial archivists have begun to take on, such critiques invoke important questions about whether it is possible to undertake such roles and activities without increasing the archivization and archivalization effects. While these questions certainly have philosophical and theoretical dimensions, the same critical scrutiny needs to become embedded in archival practice, continuously analyzing how archivists approach their work, the degree of reflexivity archivists evidence about that work, and the impact of the work on archival inclusivity and pluralization that a glocal orientation demands.[27]

Communities of Memory and of Records

The past decade also saw increasing interest on the part of scholars in archival studies in the relationships between memory and communities, and records and archives. Some of this emanates out of the influence of postmodernism and postcolonialism upon archival thought, but it also overlaps considerably with human rights considerations relating to records and recordkeeping in diverse contexts around the world.[28] It is useful to juxtapose several recent statements by archival scholars that point to different aspects of these relationships. Drawing upon the work of political scientist James Booth on the concept of a community of memory,[29] Ketelaar writes:

> Collective identity is based on the elective processes of memory, so that a given group recognises itself through its memory of a common past. A community is a "community of memory." That common past is not merely genealogical or traditional, something which you can take or leave. It is more: a moral imperative for one's belonging to a community. The common past, sustained through time into the present, is what gives continuity, cohesion and coherence to a community. To be a community, a family, a religious community, a profession involves an embeddedness in its past and, consequently, in the memory texts through which that past is mediated.[30]

McKemmish, Gilliland, and Ketelaar further discuss the archival implications of this assertion:

> Societies institutionalise their collective archives according to their own evidence and memory paradigms. These paradigms influence what is remembered and what is forgotten, what is preserved and what is destroyed, how archival knowledge is defined, what forms archives take, how archives are described and indexed, and who has ownership, custodial and access rights relating to them. They also shape archival notions of reliability, authenticity, and trustworthiness. . . . Available technologies and prevailing literacies also play a formative role in shaping the archives and the formation of collective memory.[31]

In a similar vein, Jeannette Bastian coined the term "community of records" when discussing her research in the Virgin Islands. She writes:

> The effect of the loss of access to their archives on the ability of the Virgin Islands' people to write their own history and construct their collective memory. . . . In a wider sense, this story of colonial memory also concentrates our attention on the general relationships between records and the communities that create them, between

records and memory and between memory and access. . . . It suggests that, in order to use records as reliable indicators of an entire society, both the subjects as well as the creators of the records must be seen as active participators in a process in which record creating is defined as much by place, people, and community as it is by the act of creation itself.[32]

These statements emanate out of the authors' research with regard to particular historical or cultural communities but prompt the reader to consider how the characterizations associated with communities of memory and/or records might transfer into digital environments such as social media sites or digital community archives.

Community Archives

Community archives have received increasing attention from both archival scholars and working archivists over the past decade, especially in the United States, the United Kingdom, and Canada.[33] The increasing prominence and prevalence of community archives, as well as the attention they receive from archival repositories and scholars, resulted in the ad hoc designation of this as the "Community Archives Movement." The United States, the United Kingdom, and Canada all project strong national identities but also have substantial or key populations of diverse ethnic and racial heritages and histories. Community archives in themselves are not new to those nations, nor are they limited to ethnically or racially based communities. Archives and historical societies have existed since the nineteenth century, and folk-life and oral history collections have been seeking to capture and recover disappearing or unrecorded history since the 1930s. The emergence of such entities addressed not only the contributions of immigrant communities, but also, in the case of the United States, the experiences and contributions of African Americans, including former slaves, the legacy of the Confederacy in the Southern states after the Civil War of the 1860s, and the impact of the Great Depression in the 1930s—all aspects of American history that community members, historians, and folklorists believed were not well represented in mainstream institutional archives.[34] In the United Kingdom, the "history-from-below" movement, in concert with the rise of social or people's history,[35] was also influential, especially in documenting labor and women's movements in the 1970s and 1980s.[36]

In Canada, Total Archives, formally articulated by Wilfred Smith in 1972 but with much older roots,[37] sought to document all of Canadian society through the acquisition of all forms of documentary media, both publicly and privately generated; to control that documentation from creation to final disposition; and to develop archival networks.

However, community archives, variously conceived of or referred to today as community-led, -centric, or -based archives; DIY (do-it-yourself), grassroots, oppositional, participatory, or independent archives;[38] and archives from-the-bottom-up, are no longer a phenomenon predominantly of countries with a significant colonial, immigrant, slavery, refugee, or labor history or with a tradition of independent or private archives. They are increasingly emerging around the globe in physical, digital, and hybrid forms due, in part, to a compelling contemporary mix of political, professional, and technological factors that go far beyond these earlier forms of community heritage and documentary efforts. Political factors include community organizing in support of democratization efforts and social justice activism, and responding to tensions between national and community identities and narratives that pivot around debates over assimilation and pluralization, recognition of rights and obligations, and self-determination. Concerns about historical and contemporary asymmetries in power and the ways in which archives of different types might reinforce or redress those asymmetries often bind these particular factors together. Professional factors include the blurring of distinctions between archives and other kinds of information, memory, and heritage institutions and their associated professions and practices, and a growing realization on the part of the archival profession that many kinds of disciplinary, cultural, and community expertise beyond that of the professional archivist might be relevant. Finally, technological factors include the opportunities for community voices to be recorded, stored, presented, disseminated, accessed, and augmented, often independently of physical archives by employing social media, mobile technologies, and cloud computing. The technological factors, coupled with a social justice orientation that occurs in many grassroots community archival efforts, also bring the community archives movement into a new dialogue with the field of community informatics.[39]

British archival scholar Andrew Flinn, one of the leading researchers examining the community archives phenomenon, reminds us that while the term "community" can and does take on many different meanings depending upon the context, the application of the term "archives" to an entity that might bear few, if any, of the hallmarks of a professionally run institutional archives (for example, a physical repository with a permanent collection, professionally trained archival staff, and adherence to archival standards and best practices) is also contested.[40] Such variation and contestation can make it difficult to pin down the exact parameters of community archives and thus to talk about them in generalities. Flinn himself uses the term "community archives" broadly and inclusively, stressing that "the definition of the community is one which is based upon self-identification by the participants and that in terms of the motivation behind and ownership of the archival activity, the community should play a significant, even dominant role."[41] He makes a distinction between communities that are largely inspired by interest, leisure, or antiquarianism (as was the case in many of the early efforts referenced above) and those driven by a more political agenda (be that educational, commemorative, empowering, or transforming).[42] Indeed, he notes that "independent and community-led archival endeavors" are often "explicitly identified with a political agenda and purpose."[43]

The Voice, Identity, and Activism (VIA) Framework depicted in Table 1.2, which I developed based on research and other forms of community engagement of faculty and students at the University of California–Los Angeles, identifies, although not exhaustively, factors and considerations that can come into play relating to recordkeeping, documentation, and archives from the standpoint of and in accordance with the interests of communities and groups seeking to organize, to project, or to protect their identities, issues, and rights; to pursue social justice agendas; and to have their beliefs and experiences acknowledged.[44] The framework has three guiding principles:

1. The interests, needs, and well-being of the community are central. Robust and recognized recordkeeping and archives are as critical to the empowerment and profile development of grassroots, identity- and issue-based, and activist communities as they have

traditionally been to high-power organizations and bureaucracies such as governments, corporations, religious organizations, and academic institutions, even if their manifestations may not take on the same forms as those found in more "mainstream" settings. They are, therefore, a fundamental component of social justice, civil rights, and democratic movements and have direct impact upon the lives and well-being of communities and their constituents.

2. Community records and heritage materials should not simply be approached by archives and collecting institutions external to the community as collectibles, "rescue" or "salvage" projects, or means to diversify or "round out" existing documentary sources. Instead, the place and meaning of community archives and their contents need to be clearly understood in any potential archival relationship between the community and an external collecting institution and a mutually beneficial partnership approach devised.

3. A community-centric framework for approaching archives and recordkeeping should recognize that important and constantly evolving community interests, epistemologies, demographics, and emotions must be addressed in recordkeeping and archives activities and that these will present challenges necessitating a rethinking of "mainstream" archival practices as well as a heightened understanding of those of the communities in question.

It should be noted that not all factors and considerations are present in each context, and the VIA Framework is not meant to be a checklist or to conflate distinct concerns that exist within individual communities. Rather, the framework seeks to raise consciousness of the presence of such factors and considerations within communities, within archivists and archival researchers from noncommunity institutions seeking to partner with those communities, and within students preparing for professional careers that may involve them with community archives.

Table 1.2. Voice, Identity, Activism (VIA): A community-centric framework for approaching archives and recordkeeping

VIA-relevant communities:	Examples:
	• Activist groups, e.g., antidevelopment/urban redevelopment; antimilitarism, civil rights, environmental, economic action, organized labor, prodemocracy activists. Alternative movements. • Arts and music communities, e.g., artists' collectives, community arts and murals projects, and music festivals. • Ethnically or racially based immigrant and diasporic communities. • Gender-, gender-identification-, or sexual-orientation-based communities. • Genocide survivors and victims of ethnic cleansing. • Hidden or invisible communities, e.g., undocumented immigrants or students, gangs, mental health patients. • Homeless populations. • Human trafficking victims and their families and descendants. • Incarcerated individuals (current and former). • Indigenous/aboriginal/native communities. • Migrant worker and day laborer populations. • Military veterans. • Religious communities. NOTE: Communities may overlap in membership, and boundaries may be both fuzzy and fluid. They will usually have subcommunities, hierarchies, and power dimensions, may not necessarily be cohesive, and are always dynamic.
Motivations for archives and recordkeeping:	**Examples of related activities:**
To have voice	• Promoting and communicating community-centric narratives, perspectives, and experiences. • Maximizing or exposing the amount, type, and limitations of voice available to community members.
Community and pan-community identity development (inward and outward orientation)	• Community organizing and agenda development. • Communicating. • Sharing. • Displaying. • Individual and joint programming. • Educational, cultural, and memorialization activities. • Fund-raising and asset identification. • Networking information resources. • Reaching or acknowledging consensus (explicit or tacit) about what history has to be remembered, communicated, passed down, or otherwise saved.
Community activism and struggles in support of social justice objectives	• Collection and mobilization of evidence and information in support of achieving human, civil, moral, and other rights, equity, dignity, and reconciliation. • Repatriation, recovery, and obviation of appropriation of cultural goods, traditional knowledge, and community places. (cont.)

	• Coalition and alliance-building through shared concerns, experiences, or knowledge, or in solidarity. • Consciousness-raising.
Conflict resolution/ postconflict recovery	• Collection and mobilization of evidence, information, and cultural goods in support of special tribunals and other legal bodies as well as of rights to reparations and compensation and the determination of geographic boundaries and traditional lands. • Statements in support of community, religious, and national identity. • Development of new national identities.
Commemoration, celebration, affirmation, recovery, therapy, and mourning	• Collective and individual remembering of persecution, liberation, disasters, epidemics, acts of defiance, and other defining events in the history of the community. • Commitment "never to forget." • Recovery of community memory, heritage, culture, belief systems, traditional practices, lands, and language.
Recordkeeping	• Addressing internally and externally imposed administrative, legal, fiscal, knowledge management, accountability/transparency, and access needs and requirements for records. • Ensuring appropriate access, privacy, and security regimes for records. • Tracking rights and responsibilities, e.g., regarding reparations, compensation, and benefits due to community members. • Ensuring acknowledgment of authors and co-creators and addressing their rights. • Documenting land and property ownership, e.g., traditional lands, community or personal property seized or confiscated during military actions.
Community characteristics:	**Examples, manifestations, and considerations:**
Resiliency	• Sustainability. • Health and well-being. • Ability to grow and change. • Ability to form, become dormant, and be reactivated as needed. • Depth as well as breadth of engagement.
Location or place	• Physical and/or virtual places and spaces. • Single or distributed location. • Mobile archives. • Unlocatedness/lack of place. • Dislocatedness. • Affective (emotional and/or aesthetic) places and spaces. • Sacred/spiritual places and spaces. • Diasporic/dispersed locations. • Invisible or hidden communities. • Inward and outward orientation of communities. • Landscapes of memory. (cont.)

	• Voluntary vs. involuntary locations. • Stable vs. unstable locations. • Accessibility and proximity to community members.
Affective aspects (emotions)	• Anger. • Aspiration. • Compulsion. • Dignity. • Disappointment. • Distrust. • Excitement. • Exclusivity. • Fear. • Feelings of "otherness." • Grief. • Guilt. • Hope. • Independence. • Inspiration. • Intimacy. • Low self-worth. • Pride. • Regret. • Reification of memory. • Resilience. • Self-deprecation. • Sentimentality. • Shame. • Spirituality. • Thankfulness. • Trauma.
Affective aspects (manifestations)	• Desire or imperative to tell or celebrate one's story inside and outside the community, with or without anonymity or pseudonymity. • Concealing one's story from all but trusted insiders. • Fear that stories needing to be heard by community members would not be available to them, or would be inappropriately made available if in the hands of external institutions. • Fear that external institutions would expose vulnerable individuals (e.g., "preserving the closet," victims of persecution). • Fear of obliteration or alteration of documentation or exposure to persecution if documentation is all gathered in one place and/or name indexes or dossiers are compiled and made widely available. • Sense that one's life doesn't merit archival attention and preservation. • Desire to forget. • Conflicted emotions about recordkeeping, e.g., concerns about or memories of external tracking or surveillance of community and its members, aversion to externally imposed recordkeeping or reporting requirements. • Hoarding vs. storing (cont.)

	• Importance of viewing and listening, playing and displaying. • Material objects serving as memory triggers.
Generational considerations	• Changing community demographics and dynamics. • Multigenerational communities • Intergenerational memory transfer and cultural and protocol barriers thereto. • Attitudes and affects relating to inherited documentation. • Changes in attitudes toward the past and the present resulting from generational and attitudinal shifts, sociopolitical gains, and cultural assimilation. • Differences between communities regularly replenished by immigration and those made up of successive generations of children born in the adopted country. • Shifts in identity due to assimilation, intermarriage, or deliberate dispersion of community members (e.g., through relocation or rehousing programs). • Community rules and sentiments about eligibility for membership such as tribal blood quantum requirements. • Shifting emphases between forgetting and remembering of defining or iconic events or experiences in community memory (e.g., Holocaust survivors and their descendants).
Conceptual, epistemological, and belief systems	• Understandings of power, ownership, time, stewardship, trust, what is secret or sacred, and what can be said and which stories told or recorded and what not, when, and under what circumstances. • Community ontologies. • Protocols for knowledge transmission inside and outside the community. • Protocols for handling sensitive objects, for ritual performance, or for behaviors within sacred spaces. • Protocols regarding language and specifics words.
Required specialized or insider knowledge, insight, experience, or personal attribute	• Need for insider knowledge to "explain" the records to others and to "read" what the records say and don't say or to pick up on community "markers." • Understanding language/vocabulary/community semantics, rituals and protocols and community protocols for learning, hearing, describing, preserving, performing, or otherwise handling or transmitting certain knowledge or documentation, for example, relating to gender, age, community affiliation. • Understanding the roles of and respecting and working with community elders, tribal councils, and other community bodies, and with community ethics review boards.
Documentation characteristics:	**Examples of archival and recordkeeping considerations:**
Perceived or actual paucity of records and textual documentation	• Loss or lack of textual and bureaucratic records and other documentation presenting community perspectives and experiences, especially in comparison to records and other documentation externally created about the community. • Investment of "recordness" in disparate, often otherwise commonplace objects, including "what they carried with them" and "what they were given." (cont.)

	• Purposive creation of documentation, often in multimedia or performative forms. • Fugitive documentation.
Perceptions of quality or value of records and various forms of documentation	• Personal mementos, "what they carried with them," and "what they were given." • Inability to establish reliability and/or authenticity of records, either because of inability to trace their provenance or because of a lack of formal recordkeeping processes and forms. • Incidental, accidental, or nonexpert photography, or oral or video recordings. Materials in poor preservation state. • "Saving what survived." • Attributing other values to materials, e.g., associative, recovery/reconstruction, sentimental. • Performative qualities. • Representational limitations of different forms of documentation. • Affective value/value as affect.
Nature of recordkeeping, records, and archives	• Recordkeeping based in oral, music, dance, or other kinetic and/or ritual traditions. • Designated or trusted living recordkeepers or storytellers, e.g., griots, community elders, family history-keepers, heritage language speakers, avocational community archivists. • Survivors and witnesses. • No physical archives in a traditional professional sense. • Community language as a living archives. • Social networks as living archives. • Reliability, authenticity, originality, and even long-term sustainability of materials may not be primary preoccupations. • The knowledge of interest to the community may reside as much, if not more, in context about the content than in the content itself.
Nontextual forms of records and recordkeeping processes; Nontraditional sites of creation of documentation	• Winter counts, barks, stories and storytelling, music forms such as Native American drum beats, jazz and hip hop. • Jewelry. • Spoken language. • Site-specificity. • Indigenous "keeping places." • Planning meetings. • Political events. • Cultural festivals. • Performances. • Lectures • Artists and writers' collectives and workshops. • Development/redevelopment projects. • Informal gatherings. • Restaurants. (cont.)

	• Shops. • Churches and other religious spaces. • Places or moments of testifying. • Social media sites and other "unlocated" locations. • Coconstitution between authors and audiences.
Distributed or networked documentation	• Dispersion through diaspora, war, disaster, theft/looting, or community relocation. • Documentation linked through websites and portals. • Materials generated through social media. Networked genealogical information/genealogy networks. • Hierarchical and nonhierarchical production.
Policy considerations:	**Examples:**
Indigenous and other cultural protocols	• Implications of sovereignty or legal guarantees of self-determination for the creation, preservation, description, ownership, and access of records and traditional or community knowledge and cultural practices? • Are professional best practices best for the community? • Are community protocols an empowering and feasible approach for a community/for multiple communities? • Oversight, participation and processes for developing community protocols. • How community protocols of one community might interact with those of another community or with the practices of noncommunity institutions (including professional and international best practices and standards)? • Processes for and implications of the evolution, updating, and promulgation of community protocols.
Ownership	• Community understandings about ownership, e.g., that materials are of community rather than individual provenance or authorship, that some kinds of records or documentation cannot be owned, or that records created about the community with or without its consent might belong to the community. • Combating physical, intellectual, and cultural appropriation of community materials. • Replevin actions. • Repatriation and/or digital repatriation and recovery initiatives. • Determining those aspects of a documentary object to which notions of ownership pertain. • Specifying protocols and policy regarding the commodification/commercialization of community heritage or legacy by the community and by other parties.
Ethics	• Implementing community ethics review boards or processes. • Ensuring equal or equitable voice in all aspects of partnership projects with noncommunity groups and individuals. • Balancing the political and public nature of empowerment and recovery with individual privacy or personal or community vulnerability concerns. • Protecting sacred and secret knowledge. (cont.)

Preservation	• Ensuring that conservation and restoration practices are in accordance with community beliefs and practices, e.g., for recordings of heritage language or traditional storage, for preserving ritual items, and for keeping materials "alive." • Identifying preservation priorities and mechanisms for materials in an environment of very limited resources. • Ensuring that digital preservation practices are in accordance with community beliefs and practices. • Exploring the potential for sharing preservation facilities and other resources across multiple communities. • Understanding preservation implications of repatriated materials, as well as of digital repatriation and recovery.
Description	• Importance of organizing and providing access points to meet community needs, e.g., key topics, forms of expression, language, appropriate disclosure of information and stories. • Ensuring that descriptive tools and their accessibility/dissemination address concerns about privacy and vulnerability, e.g., avoiding "dossier compilation" and "outing" individuals. • Who should/can describe? Who is the expert? • Identifying and addressing co-creator roles and interests through description. • Developing models and policies for exporting or linking descriptive metadata to wider information systems.
Access	• Who may and who may not access a community's archives or documentation, and under what conditions and legal requirements? • How should that access be facilitated? • Does the community have a priority constituency, agenda, or critical issue or event that would influence access and/or digitization considerations? • Ensuring accessibility to the community of community materials held within noncommunity institutions. • Addressing access concerns regarding images and recordings of community materials created and disseminated by noncommunity institutions and individuals. • Identifying digitization priorities and mechanisms for materials in an environment of very limited resources. • Ensuring that digitization practices are in accordance with community beliefs and practices.
Agency	• Who may speak for the community? • Who should be consulted within the community on records and archival matters? • What kind of archival role(s) might exist within the community and who performs or should perform those roles? • What is the background (e.g., insider/outsider, "double-insider") and positionality of the archivist? • What language and vocabulary are or should be employed? • To whom, if anyone, is the community or its organizations accountable or beholden? • Who supports archival endeavors, politically, financially, emotionally, and in what ways? (cont.)

	• What kinds of partnerships or relationships exist within or between communities that might be relevant to their archives and recordkeeping? • Are there identifiable moments when or reasons why community archives and records might reasonably be given to or placed within more mainstream archives, e.g., a political agenda has been achieved; community documentation is at demonstrable risk?
Compliance with external recordkeeping requirements	• Reporting requirements to receive recognition, aid, or benefits. • Maintenance of dual recordkeeping systems, e.g., according to community practices as well as external legal, regulatory or professional requirements, for accountability, funding, industry, judicial, military, educational, or other reasons.
Admissability of records	• Demonstration of trustworthiness of records, e.g., circumstances of creation and preservation, chain-of-custody, transparency. • Admissibility of nontextual records in courts as evidence.

Co-creatorship

Co-creatorship and the closely related constructs of *multiple simultaneous* and *parallel provenance* have arisen in archival research (particularly records continuum research) concerning the genesis of records and how this should best be described,[45] and from archival work in postcolonial and gender studies contexts. These propositions argue that traditional notions of provenance are oversimplified. With their emphasis on a single creating entity, those notions fail to acknowledge that multiple parties with different types of relationships to each other can be involved in the genesis of records. The propositions maintain, for example, that subjects as well as creators of records should be acknowledged as participants in that genesis and that archivists have an ethical imperative to pursue descriptive mechanisms for representing both creator and co-creator worldviews and experiences, and supporting diverse user needs and concerns, within and relating to a given community of records.[46] As the Pluralizing the Archival Curriculum Group (PACG) points out,

> They challenge existing constructs of the archive itself, as well as ownership and other rights in record. They point to the need to take into account the multiple perspectives and requirements of the co-creators of records in appraisal decisions; capture their multiple perspectives and contexts in archival description; and reflect and negotiate a matrix of mutual rights and obligations in archival policy making and in the development of professional codes of ethics.[47]

In a physical world, much of archival arrangement and description is bound by the facts that materials can be in only one place and one arrangement at a time, and that archival descriptive tools are resource intensive and cumbersome to create and update. All of these practical considerations support using single provenance as the dominant mechanism for arranging and describing archives. In a digital world, however, it can become much easier to discern multiple and simultaneous provenance from the traces left behind, such as audit trails, routing information, and data stamps. It is also easier to support multiple arrangements of the same materials; to make evident their documentary relationships to materials from other series or *fonds*; to provide alternate, or alternative, views of finding aids and other descriptive tools; and to open those tools up to others for annotation and emendation.

An important point not to be lost in this discussion is that archival theory is frequently the result of a rationalization of practice, or of what is practically possible when working with archives (i.e., it is inductive), rather than of theorizing first (i.e., deductive reasoning) and then implementing that theory. While Hurley's theorizing involves contemplating the provenancial complexities of actual record series, how multiple simultaneous and parallel provenance might be practically implemented in archival arrangement and description stymies its impact on archival thinking. If what is practically possible expands, however, the corresponding theory also has the potential to take hold and even to expand to contemplate a wider range of possibilities.

Digital Repatriation

In a somewhat different vein of discourse about custody, archives engage increasingly in repatriating their holdings (either the original materials or digital versions thereof) to the communities about which they were created or from whom they were removed, often without consent. A constant limitation in debates about repatriation is the physicality of the materials involved. Sometimes those materials are legitimately or perforce the records of two different countries, but they could only physically reside in one. Sometimes they have been removed or appropriated during wars or other conflicts or even by collectors and researchers from other countries.

Sometimes the physical safety of materials in their current location raises concerns, and a movement begins to relocate them, but relocation can result in them being separated physically (and sometimes intellectually, culturally, or emotionally) from their originating community. Microfilming was often used to provide surrogate copies to those who did not have the original materials. Today, digital repatriation offers a wider range of possibilities for overcoming the physical considerations of keeping records but raises others about what constitutes "giving back," what is given back, the degree of physical and intellectual control over either the original or the digitized materials that any of the parties involved may or should actually have (including the conditions under which they are preserved, copyright concerns, and the adequacy and perspectives of any descriptions that are also transferred or shared), and the accessibility and usability of repatriated materials by the community to which they were repatriated.

Repatriation can occur as a result of redress, reparations, and replevin actions, in response to approaches articulated in community or Indigenous protocols, as negotiated in peace treaties or through the work of tribunals, or in circumstances where a former colonial power holds archives containing the historical records of a now-independent nation. These communities usually recognize that keeping the materials somewhere is important for a variety of reasons, but they may not have the physical facilities necessary to preserve them and make them accessible. They also do not always trust archives associated with state and academic institutions elsewhere and sometimes even in their own nations to provide stewardship of these materials in ways that take into account their needs and perspectives. They may wish to host, disseminate, and augment a digital community archives of repatriated digitized materials, to annotate materials provided online by mainstream archival repositories, or to negotiate protocols with mainstream repositories for the care and dissemination of holdings relating to them. By the same measure, however, universal, equitable access is not always the objective of community-based or grassroots archives where addressing community interests and identity needs might take priority. Understanding the underlying emotional and spiritual as well as political and social factors at play may make a big difference to the extent and scope of a repatriation effort, as well as to decisions regarding whether original, digital, or other surrogates of materials are to be repatriated or shared. For example, do the communities seeking repatriation always want the original materials, or are they more interested in what the act of repatriation, even if of digital copies, symbolizes in terms of acknowledging and respecting their rights and worldviews? Do they desire the materials for what they say or contain or for what they represent in the minds of the community?

The Archival Multiverse

The concept of the *archival multiverse* emerged in the past two years from the Pluralizing the Archival Curriculum Group (PACG), an international working group of faculty and doctoral students who have been participating in the annual AERI, and it has been gaining traction in the archival field. American philosopher and psychologist William James originally conceptualized the multiverse in 1895, and fields as wide-ranging as physics, psychology, and literature use the term today to refer to a hypothetical set of multiple possible universes.[48] The archival multiverse is arguably the metaconstruct that overarches the above-referenced concepts, most of which attempt to introduce relativist or additional community and international perspectives to a paradigm at heart positivist, nation oriented, and modern in its conceptualization. It refers to "the plurality of evidentiary texts, memory-keeping practices and institutions, bureaucratic and personal motivations, community perspectives and needs, and cultural and legal constructs with which archival professionals and academics must be prepared . . . to engage."[49] A recent report authored by the PACG focuses on the role of archival education and research within archival studies, articulating the central challenge the archival multiverse presents to the traditional archival paradigm:

> How do we move from an archival universe dominated by one cultural paradigm to an archival multiverse; from a world constructed in terms of "the one" and "the other" to a world of multiple ways of knowing and practicing, of multiple narratives co-existing in one space? An important related question is, How do we accept that there may be incommensurable ontologies and epistemologies between communities that surface in differing cultural expressions and notions of cultural property and find ways to accept and work within that reality?[50]

Notes

1 Doris Estelle Long, "The Impact of Foreign Investment on Indigenous Culture: An Intellectual Property Perspective," *North Carolina Journal of International Law and Commercial Regulation* 229 (1998): 240. Cited in Rehka Ramani, "Note and Comment: Market Realities v. Indigenous Equities," *Brooklyn Journal of International Law* 26 (2001): 1147.

2 Terry Cook, "Evidence, Memory, Identity, and Community: Four Shifting Archival Paradigms," *Archival Science*, DOI 10.1007/s10502-012-9180-7.

3 Xiaomi An and Wang Wang, "Towards Comprehensive Integration Management of Business Continuity, Records and Knowledge," in *Proceedings of the 6th International Conference on Networked Computing and Advanced Information Management,* Seoul, South Korea, August 16–18, 2010, 5–9.

4 Roland Robertson, "Comments on the 'Global Triad' and 'Glocalization,'" Institute for Japanese Culture and Classics, Conference on Globalization and Indigenous Culture, 1997, http://www2 .kokugakuin.ac.jp/ijcc/wp/global/15robertson.html. See also Robertson, "The Conceptual Promise of Glocalization: Commonality and Diversity," *ART-e-FACT: Strategies of Resistance,* no. 4, http:// artefact.mi2.hr/_a04/lang_en/theory_robertson_en.htm.

5 Anne J. Gilliland-Swetland, *Enduring Paradigms, New Opportunities: The Value of the Archival Perspective in the Digital Environment* (Washington, D.C.: Council on Library and Information Resources, 2000).

6 Thomas S. Kuhn, *The Structure of Scientific Revolutions* (Chicago: University of Chicago Press, 1962).

7 It should be noted that the structure of this table reflects an American perspective on the archival paradigm. Other archival traditions, particularly those based in records continuum ideas might order or group some of the components differently.

8 Cook, "Evidence, Memory, Identity, and Community," 2012 preprint.

9 Sue McKemmish, "Are Records Ever Actual?," in *The Records Continuum: Ian Maclean and Australian Archives First Fifty Years*, ed. Sue McKemmish and Michael Piggott (Clayton, Aus.: Ancora Press in association with Australian Archives, 1994), 187–203.

10 Anne J. Gilliland and Sue McKemmish, Introduction and "Building an Infrastructure for Archival Research," *Archival Science* 3–4 (2004): 143–47, 149–99.

11 Carol Couture and Daniel Ducharme, "Research in Archival Science: A Status Report," *Archivaria* 59 (2005): 41–67. The article was first published in French as "La recherche en archivistique: un état de la question," *Archives* 30, nos. 3–4 (1998): 11–38.

12 Anne Gilliland and Sue McKemmish, "Archival and Recordkeeping Research: Past, Present and Future," in *Research Methods: Information Management, Systems, and Contexts* (Prahran, Aus.: Tilde University Press, 2013).

13 See, for example, Cook, "Evidence, Memory, Identity, and Community"; Fiona Ross, Sue McKemmish, and Shannon Faulkhead, "Indigenous Knowledge and the Archives: Designing Trusted Archival Systems for Koorie Communities," *Archives and Manuscripts* 34, no. 2 (2006): 112–49; and Anne J. Gilliland and Sue McKemmish, "Recordkeeping Metadata, the Archival Multiverse, and Societal Grand Challenges," in *Proceedings of the International Conference on Dublin Core and Metadata Applications 2012,* Kuching, Malaysia, September 2012, 106–15, http://dcpapers.dublincore.org/ pubs/article/view/3661.

14 Luciana Duranti, "Archives as a Place," *Archives and Manuscripts* 24, no. 2 (1996): 242–55. Republished in *Archives and Social Studies: A Journal of Interdisciplinary Research* 1, no. 1 (2007), Archivo Municipal Cartagena, http://tinyurl.com/2dbasvb.

[15] Duranti, "Archives as a Place." See also Terry Eastwood, "Should Creating Agencies Keep Electronic Records Indefinitely?," *Archives and Manuscripts* 24 (November 1996): 256–67.

[16] F. Gerald Ham, "Archival Strategies for the Post-custodial Era," *The American Archivist* 44 (Summer 1981): 207.

[17] Glenda Acland, "Managing the Record Rather Than the Relic," *Archives and Manuscripts* 20, no. 1 (1992): 58–59.

[18] For example, David A. Bearman, "Record-keeping Systems," *Archivaria* 36 (1993): 16–37.

[19] Frank Upward, "Structuring the Records Continuum Part One: Post-custodial Principles and Properties," *Archives and Manuscripts* 24 (1996): 268–85.

[20] Charles M. Dollar, *The Impact of Information Technologies on Archival Principles and Method* (Macerata, Italy: University of Macerata Press, 1992), 75–76; and Linda J. Henry, "Schellenberg in Cyberspace," *American Archivist* 61 (Fall 1998): 319.

[21] Upward, "Structuring the Records Continuum Part One."

[22] David Bearman, "An Indefensible Bastion: Archives as a Repository in the Electronic Age," in *Archival Management of Electronic Records*, ed. David Bearman (Pittsburgh: Archives and Museum Informatics, 1991): 14–24; Kenneth Thibodeau, "To Be or Not to Be: Archives for Electronic Records," in *Archival Management of Electronic Records*, 1–13; Sue McKemmish and Frank Upward, "Somewhere Beyond Custody," *Archives and Manuscripts* 22, no. 1 (1994): 138–49; Steve Stuckey, "Keepers of the Fame? The Custodial Role of Australian Archives–Its History and Its Future," *Archives and Manuscripts* 22, no. 1 (1994): 35–48; Greg O'Shea and David Roberts, "Living in a Digital World: Recognizing the Electronic and Post-custodial Realities," *Archives and Manuscripts* 24, no. 2 (1996): 286–311; Adrian Cunningham, "Commentary: Journey to the End of the Night: Custody and the Dawning of a New Era on the Archival Threshold," *Archives and Manuscripts* 24, no. 2 (1996): 312–21; and Jeannette Bastian, "Taking Custody, Giving Access: A Post-custodial Role for a New Century," *Archivaria* 53 (2002): 76–93.

[23] For example, Sentilles observes that when researching for a cultural biography on U.S. Civil War actress Adah Isaacs Menken, "had I relied on digital archives, I would have missed nonverbal clues in my search. What surrounds the materials found? How is it placed within the larger document? What does the cover of the item suggest about the target audience and how it was being packaged for sale? Does the quality of paper or print suggest something valuable about its production that changes the way we interpret the words on the page? For scholars of the history of the book and many historians using material culture, digital reproductions are not adequate substitutions for artifacts." Renée M. Sentilles, "The Archives of Cyberspace," in *Archive Stories: Facts, Fictions and the Writing of History*, ed. Antoinette Burton (Durham, N.C.: Duke University Press, 2005), 146.

[24] Jacques Derrida, *Archive Fever: A Freudian Impression*, trans. Eric Prenowitz (Chicago: University of Chicago Press, 1996).

[25] See, for example, Tom Nesmith, "Still Fuzzy, But More Accurate: Some Thoughts on the 'Ghosts' of Archival Theory," *Archivaria* 47 (Spring 1999): 136–50; Joan M. Schwartz and Terry Cook, "Archives, Records and Power: The Making of Modern Memory," *Archival Science* 2 (2002): 1–19; and Sue McKemmish, "Placing Records Continuum Theory and Practice," *Archival Science* 1 (2001): 333–59.

[26] Eric Ketelaar, "Archivalisation and Archiving," *Archives and Manuscripts* 27 (1999): 54–61.

[27] Anne Gilliland, "Afterword: In and Out of the Archives," in *Interdisciplinary Essays on European Knowledge Culture, 1400–1900*, ed. Randolph Head, special issue, *Archival Science* 10, no. 3 (September 2010): 333–43.

[28] Jeannette Bastian, *Owning Memory: How a Caribbean Community Lost Its Archives and Found Its History* (Westport, Conn.: Libraries Unlimited, 2003); Andrew Flinn, Mary Stevens, and Elizabeth Shepherd, "Whose Memories, Whose Archives? Independent Community Archives, Autonomy and

the Mainstream," *Archival Science* 9 (2009): 71–86; Kelvin L. White, "*Meztizaje* and Remembering in Afro-Mexican Communities of the Costa Chica: Implications for Archival Education in Mexico," *Archival Science* 9, nos. 1–2 (2009); Michelle Caswell, "Khmer Rouge Archives: Accountability, Truth, and Memory in Cambodia, *Archival Science* 11 (2011); and Ruth Bayhylle, "Tribal Archives: A Study in Records, Memory and Power," (PhD diss., University of California–Los Angeles, 2011).

[29] W. James Booth, "Communities of Memory: On Identity, Memory, and Debt," *American Political Science Review* 93 (1999): 249–63.

[30] Eric Ketelaar, "Sharing: Collected Memories in Communities of Records," *Archives and Manuscripts* 33 (2005): 50.

[31] Sue McKemmish, Anne Gilliland, and Eric Ketelaar, "'Communities of Memory': Pluralising Archival Research and Education Agendas," *Archives and Manuscripts* 5 (2005): 146–75.

[32] Bastian, *Owning Memory*, 1–2.

[33] See, for example, Flinn et al., "Whose Memories, Whose Archives?," 71–86; Andrew Flinn, "Archival Activism: Independent and Community-led Archives, Radical Public History and the Heritage Professions," *InterActions: UCLA Journal of Education and Information Studies* 7, no. 2 (2011), eScholarship, University of California, http://escholarship.org/uc/item/9pt2490x; and Jeannette A. Bastian and Ben Alexander, eds., *Community Archives: The Shaping of Memory* (London: Facet 2009).

[34] See, for example, John J. Appel, *Immigrant Historical Societies in the United States, 1880–1950* (New York: Arno Press, 1980); Faith Davis Ruffins, "Mythos, Memory, and History: African-American Preservation Efforts, 1820–1990," in *Museums and Communities: The Politics of Public Culture*, ed. Ivan Karp, Christine Mullen Kreamer, and Steven D. Lavine (Washington, D.C.: Smithsonian Institution, 1992); and John Higham, "The Ethnic Historical Society in Changing Times," *Journal of American Ethnic History* 13, no. 2 (1994): 30–44.

[35] See Howard Zinn, *A People's History of the United States* (New York: Harper and Row, 1980).

[36] See, for example, Ben Blake, "The New Archives for American Labor: From Attic to Digital Shop Floor," *The American Archivist* 70, no. 1 (2007): 130–50; and Graham Smith, "The Making of Oral History: Sections 1–2," in *Making History: The Changing Face of the Profession in Britain* (London: Institute of Historical Research, 2008), Making History, http://www.history.ac.uk/makinghistory/resources/articles/oral_history.html.

[37] Wilfred I. Smith, *Archives: Mirror of Canada Past* (Toronto, Ont.: University of Toronto Press, 1972).

[38] By "independent archives," I am referring to archives that are not aligned with government, academic, or other mainstream archives, and that often are not publicly funded, but whose existence is one hallmark of a democratic, pluralistic state.

[39] Sawyer and Rosenbaum define "social informatics" as a problem-driven "interdisciplinary study of the design, uses and consequences of information and communication technologies (ICTs) that takes into account their interactions with institutional and cultural contexts. Social informatics research may be done at group, departmental, organizational, national and/or societal levels of analysis, focused on the relationships among information, information systems, the people who use them and the context of use." See Steve Sawyer and Howard Rosenbaum, "Social Informatics in the Information Sciences: Current Activities and Emerging Directions," *Informing Science* 3, no. 2 (2000): 1, http://www.inform.nu/Articles/Vol3/v3n2p89-96r.pdf. Williams and Durrance describe "community informatics" as a field that encompasses both study and practice aspects, one that emerged relatively recently out of library practice and that operates at a nexus between digital information and communication technologies and historical local communities. Community informatics is strongly influenced by social informatics and is largely concerned with the transformative effects of digital information technology upon these communities as well as inequities that might be created or reinforced relating to the accessibility and usability of information technology and

digital information resources. See Kate Williams and Joan Durrance, "Community Informatics," *Encyclopedia for Library and Information Science*, 3rd ed. (New York: Taylor and Francis, 2009), 1.

[40] Flinn, "Archival Activism," 6–7.

[41] Flinn, "Archival Activism," 7.

[42] Flinn, "Archival Activism," 8.

[43] Flinn, "Archival Activism," 1.

[44] The VIA Framework is being used by archival researchers at UCLA and Monash University in ongoing research that is contemplating how key professional concepts and practices, e.g., record, recordkeeping, archives, creatorship, appraisal, description, and access, could be pluralized in ways that could take into account the needs, beliefs, practices, and concerns of grassroots, identity- or issue-based, and activist communities. It was developed based on analyses of several sources: the mission, scope, and activities of community-based archives in the United States; partnership projects, case studies, and service learning conducted by faculty and students at UCLA's Department of Information Studies and elsewhere over the past decade in multiple grassroots, identity- or issue-based, and activist communities; and characteristics and themes emerging out of the work of scholars of these fields and movement leaders. For more information on these activities, see Andrew Lau, Anne Gilliland, and Kim Anderson, "Naturalizing Community Engagement in Information Studies: Pedagogical Approaches and Persisting Partnerships," *Information, Communication and Society*, 15 no. 7 (2012): 991–1015.

[45] Chris Hurley, "Parallel Provenance: (1) What, If Anything, Is Archival Description?," *Archives and Manuscripts* 33, no. 1 (2005): 110–45; and Hurley, "Parallel Provenance: (2) When Something Is *Not* Related to Everything Else," *Archives and Manuscripts* 33, no. 2 (2005): 52–91, http://www.info-tech.monash.edu.au/research/groups/rcrg/publications/parallel-provenance-combined.pdf; Ketelaar, "Sharing."

[46] Anne J. Gilliland, "Contemplating Co-creator Rights in Archival Description," *Knowledge Organization* 39, no. 5 (2012): 340–46.

[47] Archival Education and Research Institute (AERI) Pluralizing the Archival Curriculum Group (PACG), "Educating for the Archival Multiverse," *The American Archivist* 74, no. 1 (2011): 68–102.

[48] See, for example, Rajni Kothari, D. L. Sheth, and Ashis Nandy, eds., *The Multiverse of Democracy: Essays in Honour of Rajni Kothari* (Thousand Oaks, Calif.: Sage Publications, 1996); Ananta Kumar Giri, "Cosmopolitanism and Beyond: Towards a Multiverse of Transformations," *Development and Change* 37 (November 2006): 1277–92; and Helge Kragh, "Contemporary History of Cosmology and the Controversy over the Multiverse," *Annals of Science* 66 (October 2009): 529–51.

[49] AERI PACG, "Educating for the Archival Multiverse."

[50] Ibid.

CHAPTER 2

∞

Reframing the Archive in a Digital Age: Balancing Continuity with Innovation and Responsibility with Responsibilities

This chapter reviews societal ideas about archives and the complex of technological, political, and ideological pressures and imperatives to which they have been subject. It argues the ongoing need to re-examine traditional understandings of core archival concepts such as record, recordkeeping, evidence, and even archives, and the nature and activities of archives and archivists in the twenty-first century in light of digital and social change.

Authors in the Nineteenth century who sought to give a more precise meaning to the word archives gave contradictory definitions of it because they followed preconceived ideas, like Ménage and Le Duchat before them. We have seen that in the predominant thought of the first of these etymologists his conception of archives was that of ancient documents; for the second, it was the idea of precious documents. Several modern authors attach to the word archives other conceptions just as little satisfactory in themselves, e.g., that of official documents, of historical documents, of authentic documents, of documents in substantiation of rights.

In actual practice, if archives are in fact composed above all of documents in great part in one or another of these categories and sometimes in all of these, it does not mean that there may not be found in the archives documents which are neither ancient nor precious nor official nor authentic nor such as substantiate rights. Let us disregard the term historical, which seems to us not to have any concrete meaning. . . . Thus we come to recognize in the term archives two meanings: one broad and vague, generally used in ordinary language, and the other narrow and precise, on which the specialists are beginning to agree. . . .

—Charles Samaran, professor of bibliography and archivistics, École Nationale des Chartes, Paris; future director general of the National Archives of France; and first chairman of the International Council on Archives; "Archives," February 1938.[1]

Archives, Power, and Politics

The stereotype of archives as dark, dusty, socially removed, and relatively unchanging physical spaces has arguably helped them to remain unthreatening, low-budget presences to those whose activities they document or from whom they request resources. Frequent allegorical and fantastical allusions in literature indicate yet more popular conceptions and misconceptions of archives.[2] Like Charles Samaran in 1938, archivists today still find themselves constantly explaining to records creators, users, resource allocators, and the general public what they do and why it is important. This has become even more necessary in a century when the Internet Archives and Googles of the world seem, in popular perception, to be putting traditional archives out of business.

However, peeling away the stereotypes and looking back over archival history, one readily discerns that archives have always been dynamic, their content and its meanings accumulating and inevitably changing in media and format as recording technologies evolved over decades and centuries. Even if archives are at times physically removed, as entities they remain socially embedded, their rationales, contents, processes, and activities directly reflecting the contingency of archives upon their own juridical, political, social, cultural, and technological contexts. Moreover, archives have historically been closely and unabashedly associated with the exercise, structures, and worldviews of power. While archives and the records they contain generally do not explicitly intend to be unrepresentative of different perspectives, experiences, and epistemologies, they inevitably and inexorably reflect and legitimize how, when, why, and by whom those records were generated and preserved. Furthermore, different recordkeeping and archival systems, regardless of the power associated with them, are also predicated on differing worldviews that may well be in contestation with one another.

The term "archive" derives from the Greek *arkhé* ("government" or "order") and *arkheion* ("the home of the archons"). In classical Athens, the archons headed civic, military, and religious affairs and also presided over the Metroon, built around 140 BCE on the site of the old senate house that had previously housed the city's records. The Metroon not only served as the state archives, it was also a sanctuary for Meter, the mother of the gods. The archons controlled access to the records within the Metroon.[3] The power of the archons and of the Metroon was evident not only in terms of their offices and functions, but also in the prominent sandstone architecture and central placement of the Metroon within the Agora at the front of the house of the council and facing the towering Acropolis. Decrees passed by the assembly or council of Athens were first written on papyrus or wooden tablets and then transcribed onto stone steles placed on public display in the Agora, which was the seat of Athenian administrative bodies and public offices, or, if particularly important, on the Acropolis.

This close association between official authority and archives extends throughout the history of archives in the Western world,[4] where the power of official recordkeeping has been explicitly applied not only in the administrations of governments and other large religious and mercantile bureaucracies, but also in the promulgation of official epistemologies, especially within colonial machinery. For example, the sixteenth-century Spanish court developed a new cosmography to incorporate the previously unknown (to the Spanish) human, biological, and physical phenomena they encountered in the colonies of the Indies. Ordinances and instructions were issued on how everything was to be documented and reported back to Spain and then retained within official archives.[5] Collins and Blot write of the resulting "colonial scriptural economy" in Mexico, where "the colonizers write their histories, *relaciones*, *cartas*, using the rhetorical frameworks and within the worldview of the dominant society, within the episteme of the dominant world." Thomas Richards, writing of Victorian knowledge organization and the British Empire's need for an archives for "keeping track of keeping track," makes the important point that "it was much easier to unify an archive composed of texts than to unify an empire made of territory."[6] Ann Laura Stoler, in her research relating to the archives of the Dutch East Indies, writes of how "the colonial order of things [can be] seen through the record of archival productions . . . archives as condensed sites of epistemological and political anxiety rather than as skewed and biased sources. These colonial archives were both transparencies in which power relations were inscribed and intricate technologies of rule in themselves."[7]

Challenges posed by digitality are not the only set of issues confront-
ing archives today. Archives are increasingly caught up in an intellectual milieu largely characterized by "post-" discourses and with a strong
focus on how history is understood, managed, and represented. In his
1897 travel account, *Following the Equator: A Journey around the World*,
Mark Twain's Pudd'nhead Wilson states that "the very ink with which all
history is written is merely fluid prejudice."[8] Postmodernism, postcolonialism, postethnic, postwestern, and postgenderism movements and cultural
projects (among others) seek in varying ways to expose power structures
and prejudices at work in society and its institutions and technologies.
They also challenge commonly accepted notions of objective reality and
scientific and other forms of truths, high culture, and grand and metanar-
ratives frequently projected through historical and other memory institutions such as archives. For several decades now, multifaceted critiques
have been building that, until recently, have largely taken place outside
the world of professional archivists—in critical theory, philosophy, sociology, anthropology, literature, new media, and other arts fields. Repudiating
modern-era beliefs, values, theories, structures, and methods, as well as the
historical, cultural, and bureaucratic evidence at the heart of the professionally constructed archives, these critiques focus on the concept of the
Archive in society and its shifting mandates;[9] on what it means *to archive*,
and the *power* and *authority* associated with the Archive that wields it
and how, and its effect on individuals and groups over time;[10] on the
basis for value judgments;[11] and, as a result, on *what the Archive contains*,
the narratives or "truths" it supports or reinforces,[12] and how the Archive
can affect our epistemologies, lives, and self-knowledge.[13] Obviously, the
critiques do not concur with more traditional professional archival theory
and practices that uphold the notion of the Archive (often expressed with
a capital A to denote it as a societal rather than a professional concept)
as a trusted and disinterested repository of records and other documentary materials that can support accountability and historical scholarship.
Rather, they tend to view the Archive, and by implication, the Archivist
and Archival processes, as key players in the exercise and control of power
and knowledge, as colonial agents, and as arbiters of values in society.

In so doing, these academic movements became a prime target of
conservative politics in some countries, such as the United States, regarding the nature, role, value, and explication of the arts, education, heritage, and culture. Pervasive in the intellectual, educational, and cultural
debates are tropes such as *culture wars, the past as contested terrain, identity politics, ontological incommensurability, dominant* and *counternar-
ratives,* and *ethical* and/or *liberal pluralism.* These movements, however,
also contributed a vocabulary and important conceptual and emancipatory
frameworks and rationales for social justice activism such as redress and
reconciliation actions and for nonelite community memory initiatives such
as community-based archives and the new museums movement that began
in the 1980s and 1990s.[14] Moreover, the new digital technologies and social
media greatly enhanced the ability of groups under- or misrepresented
in the historical record to organize, document, collect, narrate, annotate,
exhibit, and publicize their own histories independent of traditional institutions and structures. These movements also inspired a rich academic
focus on nontextual and intangible or nonmaterial heritage, especially in
areas such as memory, identity, and performance studies; for example,
on "embodied memory" that is either inscribed or incorporated through
social practices (e.g., Connerton[15]); performance as an "act of transfer" of
social memory and cultural identity (e.g., Taylor[16]); landscape and sites
of memory (e.g., Schama[17] and Nora[18]); virtual culture (e.g., Jones[19]); oral
documents (e.g., Turner[20]); and Indigenous and other community storytelling (e.g., Faulkhead[21]). Such a focus broadens notions of "texts" as objects
of study and objects that effect action, and also heightens awareness of
the kinds of communities and community practices and texts that need
to be included in discussions about cultural heritage, collective memory,
national historical narratives, recordkeeping, community empowerment,
and so forth.

Although much postmodern scholarship originated in Europe—also the
cradle, in the eighteenth and nineteenth centuries, of the body of modernist ideas underlying contemporary archival theory and practice—it is in
postcolonial settings such as Canada, Australia, and South Africa that this
critique has begun to show the most influence on archival thinking. In
such settings, populations tend to be racially and ethnically diverse and

their histories intertwined and often interdependent (it should be noted that this is true in former colonizing nations also). Colonial practices often still reside in living memory, and the roles played by archives in supporting such administrations and by the record in perpetuating particular world-views to the detriment of the less empowered can be more apparent. In recent years, archival scholars such as Cook, Harris, Stoler, and Wareham added their voices to the postmodern and postcolonial critiques emanating out of other disciplines and situated them in the sphere of actual archives, that is, the places or repositories or systems and their processes, holdings, and accessibility. By so doing, they created something of a bridge between external critiques and professional practice. They acknowledged that archival repositories worldwide identify and preserve materials that relate primarily to the elites and their interests—governments, monarchs, churches, corporations, academic institutions—and that the archival paradigm descends overwhelmingly from European conceptualizations. Thus, both archives and the archival paradigm could be identified as agents in the proliferation of a grand Western-centric historical and political narrative. Seen from this view, archives might be criticized for promulgating hegemonic practices that potentially appropriate, underrepresent, and ignore, or worse, repress, distort, or even obliterate, the narratives and experiences of the "other."

Such critiques may have most apparent relevance in the so-called New World, but the entire world is changing with globalization and ubiquitous digital media. Among their most important implications is their challenge to the archival field and to the creators of archives everywhere to think more about what exactly they consider to be "the record" and to engage more parties in assisting them in making that determination. They challenge the field to articulate better to the general public, to scholars, and to the creators of the materials they seek to preserve and make available why and how it does what it does. They challenge the field, through its metadata and curatorial practices, to make more evident the complexities and hierarchical and myriad other relationships inherent in the content of the archive, as well as the absences, silences, and trauma it reflects. And they lead society as a whole to contemplate how digital technology can help.

Archives, Pluralism, and Activism

In light of these critiques, several archivists have argued for the importance
of increased reflexivity and activism on the part of archivists, including a
sounder understanding of the intellectual lineage of archival science and
of its own politics of memory.[22] For example, Terry Cook writes:

> How, for example, have archivists reflected these changing societal realities and power
> struggles as they built their "houses of memory"? How have archival assumptions,
> concepts, and strategies reflected the dominant structures and societal ethos of their
> own time? Upon what basis, reflecting what shifting values, have archivists decided
> who should be admitted into their houses of memory, and who excluded? To answer
> these questions, we need an intellectual history of our profession. We need to under-
> stand better our own politics of memory, the very ideas and assumptions that have
> shaped us, if we want our "memory houses" to reflect more accurately all components
> of the complex societies they allegedly serve.[23]

Dutch archival scholar Eric Ketelaar warns of the power of the archive
to support what he calls the "total registry."[24] And indeed, one could argue
that standardization of electronic record-keeping practices and metadata
schemas, effected through such things as ISO standards, the Sarbanes-
Oxley Act in the United States,[25] and professional best practices to support
global information and business exchange and digital interoperability,
has tremendous power to create conformity and facilitate oversight. Such
developments are promoted to support not only effective and accountable
government and business practices, but also the participation of all nations
in the global economy. But, at the same time, as discussed in chapter
1, it can be argued that such standardization, developed predominantly
through the participation and in accordance with the worldviews and
priorities of the archival and recordkeeping communities of large nations,
especially Western ones, may overwhelm or further marginalize regional
or Indigenous practices, epistemologies, and ontologies.

Archives reframed and optimized in light of these shifting public and
scholarly expectations, needs, and behaviors, as well as the imperatives
and opportunities associated with digital information and communications
technology, have the potential to tell more stories and to support new types
of users and new ways of doing research on archival holdings of all kinds
and of any provenance. They can actively contribute to the empowerment

and examination of and redress for underrepresented communities and experiences—those whose stories are not told, or whose perspectives historically have not been represented within the record. American intellectual historian Louis Menand reminds us that "the universe is plural: it hangs together, but in more ways than one."[26] Archives can work toward such pluralism, not by trying to represent every possible viewpoint—such efforts inevitably lead to new reifications, marginalizations, and omissions—but by acknowledging overtly in their practices their own stance and its limitations as applied in the gathering and description of archival holdings and by striving to ensure that multiple perspectives on history and memorykeeping as well as differing disciplinary approaches and belief systems can and should simultaneously exist and be represented within the archive. Related to this, archives can also serve as loci for action, witnessing controversial events, and preserving or rescuing fugitive testimonies (as in the cases of archivists working with the United Nations Peacekeeping Mission in Darfur and with truth commissions around the world); supporting the public in gaining access to records that are concealed or repressed (as in the case of the South African History Archive [SAHA]); and intervening to prevent the illegal destruction of records worldwide.

Archives and Human Rights

If all of this seems somewhat academic and idealistic, especially in light of the ever-accumulating backlogs of materials that archives continuously need to manage, there can be no doubt that many archives worldwide face a very real set of social memory and human rights issues arising directly out of those records and an unprecedented confluence of events. The openings of formerly inaccessible government archives because mandatory closure periods have expired, the advent of new democracies, and the work of truth and reconciliation commissions (TRCs) in Europe, Africa, Latin America, and Asia coincide for the first time with the ability to disseminate information about the contents of those archives over the Internet and by other digital means.[27] Shocking, traumatic, misleading, but often meticulously kept records relating to official acts carried out by the Third Reich before, during, and after World War II; by the Khmer Rouge in Cambodia;

in the former Soviet Union and apartheid South Africa; and in many other locations around the globe are coming to light. And it has become apparent that sometimes the best way to safeguard the documentary record is to export it digitally (rather than physically) out of the country, as did archivists working with United Nations peacekeeping missions in Darfur. But such strategies also raise challenges for archivists in terms of how to ensure the intellectual and physical accessibility of these records for those who need to use them locally and globally, while at the same time balancing the advantages of online dissemination and delivery against considerations of the privacy and security of those mentioned in the records and the often disturbing or lurid nature of the materials.

In responding to these kinds of contested memory and human rights concerns, archives are now able to do some things, especially in partnerships between archivists and with the affected communities themselves, such as "reconstructing" archives and creating alternative archives[28] that were previously unimaginable given the limitations of the traditional archives. Today, many more community efforts in several countries and transnationally are developing community-centric archives, especially digital archives, that incorporate a diversity of materials gathered and presented from the community's own perspectives.[29] An example of such an initiative is the Koorie Heritage Archive in Australia, where the Indigenous Koorie people's oral history, related official records, images of Koorie artifacts, and moving images are digitized and made accessible online from a database.[30] Designed to be taken out into communities on a laptop computer, it is a living archives that uses technology to enable Koorie people to add their own stories and information and give their perspectives on other records in the societal Archive. Parts of the system related to content sacred or secret for Koories, or for their Elders, are restricted accordingly.[31]

Building Digital Archives

As this brief review of recent discourse indicates, stereotypes notwithstanding, conceptualizations of archives have evolved over the past hundred years, as have those of the "records" archives contain or might contain and of the "archivists" responsible for their management over time. In the digital realm, as in the postmodern one, even the word "archives" is subject to challenge. It can mean something quite different to computer scientists, systems administrators, or digital librarians. Today, entities referred to as archives may be physical or virtual; they may be institution- or community-based;[32] or they may be personally created and retained. They may be stand-alone repositories or housed within a special collections unit within a research library; they may be digitally distributed across many locations but collated as a single or transparently federated virtual archives on the Internet; they may be placed in the cloud; or they may reside only on a digital storage device and be disseminated through a personal Web page. What they all have in common, however, is that they exist intellectually at points of convergence between accountability, memory, and identity, and individual, community, and cultural concerns. Classically, archives would contain primarily, if not exclusively, original bureaucratic records. Increasingly, they include multiple versions and formats of those records, as well as a host of nonbureaucratic historical, documentary, and other nonpublished or primary materials, many of which do not come in traditional textual forms and whose status as records archivists widely debate. These might include oral and visual histories; scientific data such as satellite images, read-outs from digital instrumentation, and digital lab notebooks; virtual re-creations of architecture or performances; and nontangible community records such as Indigenous stories, songlines, winter counts, and barks.

Today's professional archivist is not just a historian or custodian of records, but a highly trained archival expert who advocates for the record and who may also take on roles as a record-keeping systems analyst, metadata architect, digital curator, digital asset manager, videographer, oral historian, ethnographer, or community activist. However, there have always been individuals who are not archivists by virtue of professional education and experience, but rather by avocation or perforce, such as the designated family or community historian, the high school yearbook committee chair, or the rescuer of unwanted film or home movies.[33] Even in cyberspace, they are the individuals who recognize the imperative to archive and who operate at many different levels recording, capturing, and preserving–for example, the manager of the social networking site or the archiver of the listserv.[34]

As the discussion in subsequent chapters of this book illustrates, defining and modeling core concepts such as the *archive*, the *record*, and *evidence* when these have a substantial or even purely virtual existence might seem a comparatively simple task, until one actually tries to do it. The rootedness of the archival paradigm in physicality only really started to become evident in the twentieth century, first with the need to cope with various new audiovisual recording technologies and then with computing and networked technologies. As the pre-eminence of the physicality of the archive declines, it should provoke archivists to contemplate more closely several questions associated with that physicality. For example, what exactly is the *affect* of the physicality of the archive? Or of the record, for that matter? And what is the nature of the relationship between that affect and the physicality of the materials held in the archive, their housing and description, and their power? What happens when the physicality goes away, as it surely will in the near future as the amount of born-digital materials increases and materials in more traditional forms are digitized? What are the implications of disbinding and other forms of deconstruction of the physical arrangement of archival materials to facilitate digitization for how users understand and experience those materials? Will dematerializing the arrangement of archival materials result in a less tight coupling between arrangement and description than is traditional? Does dematerialization increase society's need for other means to establish trust in a record? At the same time, it is important to be cognizant that the infrastructure supporting our digital world, even the cloud, is still profoundly physical. It relies upon a complex of physical components such as hard drives and servers that must be physically located somewhere. Powering this infrastructure and maintaining all the data it contains require vast amounts of energy and result in the emission of vast amounts of heat. Information technology manufacturers and storage and service providers will be increasingly challenged to diminish its environmental and community impact, and when it does, new archival considerations will undoubtedly arise.

It is unlikely, and, it could be argued, undesirable, even in a future where all production is digital and all materials not born digital are digitized, that all archives will become repositories solely of digital materials. At the same time, there is no doubt that digital content and capabilities will transform physical archives and that the conceptual as well as the practical aspects of the archival paradigm will require some reframing. For traditional, and traditionally underresourced, archives, however, a future that incorporates responsibility for an exponentially increasing volume of digital materials and associated new tasks, while exciting, can seem overwhelming. Table 2.1 provides examples of activities that have been added to the portfolio of the traditional institutional archives over the past five decades.

Table 2.1. Examples of multiplying areas of archival engagement over the past fifty years

Activity	1970s	1980s	1990s	2000s	2010s
Advocating for archives, explaining what they do and why they should matter in their lives	X	X	X	X	X
Identifying specifications for digital recordkeeping systems		X	X	X	X
Disposition scheduling of paper records	X	X	X	X	X
Disposition scheduling of machine-readable/electronic/digital records	X	X	X	X	X
Appraising paper records	X	X	X	X	X
Appraising machine-readable/electronic/digital records	X	X	X	X	X
Selecting "manuscript" materials, e.g., photographs, personal papers, literary manuscript drafts, audiovisual materials	X	X	X	X	X
Identifying and acquiring digital "manuscript" materials, e.g., social media, personal web pages, digital video				X	X
Developing strategies and programs for increasing documentation of underdocumented groups and phenomena		X	X	X	X
Preserving traditional media	X	X	X	X	X
Preserving analog sound and visual media	X	X	X	X	X
Preserving electronic records and other born-digital media	X	X	X	X	X
Preserving and curating digitized archival materials			X	X	X
Arranging and describing traditional materials	X	X	X	X	X
Arranging and describing analog sound and visual materials	X	X	X	X	X

[Arranging and] describing electronic/digital materials	X	X	X	X	X
Staying abreast of changing metadata schemes and mappings and associated descriptive software and updating all descriptions			X	X	X
Selecting nondigital materials for digitization			X	X	X
Digitizing and describing at the item or within-item level, mounting digitized materials online, and integrating them into other online resources			X	X	X
Providing physical reference services	X	X	X	X	X
Providing digital reference services			X	X	X
Managing and ensuring the continued trustworthiness of digital and digitized holdings and all the associated metadata, including assuring compliance for those stored in the cloud	X	X	X	X	X
Identifying how to use new developments like social networking to document or support the activities of communities that were previously absent or underdocumented in the archives, and to support archival outreach				X	X
Lobbying against unduly restrictive records closures and copyright protections, while also protecting the needs and interests of affected individuals and communities	X	X	X	X	X
Ensuring that archives support human rights concerns related to recordkeeping and records accessibility	X	X	X	X	X
Accommodating changing needs, communication modes, and methodological practices of existing archival users		X	X	X	X
Reaching out to potential nontraditional and often unseen users of archives globally and accommodating their modalities, motivations, competencies, languages, and worldviews			X	X	X
Partnering with diverse communities on the development of community archives and archival protocols, and on digital repatriation activities			X	X	X
Engaging in practice and community-based research to learn how to do all of the above more effectively			X	X	X

Practically speaking, archives need to find ways to integrate, in an organic and effective manner, born-digital as well as digitized archival content and to rethink records creation, information retrieval, and end-user services within a comprehensive archival regime, as well as within a plural and glocal world. Definitions, practices, and workflow for managing nondigital materials will need to be rethought to address a host of emergent questions. For example, when it comes to working with digital records or building digital archives, who or what is in the driver's seat? Is it archivists, technological advances, external funding priorities, current events, policy requirements, intellectual movements, or the various and shifting needs of users? Which archival approaches continue to work in the digital age, which need to be enhanced, and which might even be abandoned? How might archival notions of the record, evidence, fixity, permanence, uniqueness, authenticity, ownership, and custody be shifting? Who should or will be the archivist (for example, do self-archiving or corporately administered archival escrow services for digital materials have appropriate and viable roles)? Should the academic scientist, archaeologist, anthropologist, or ethnomusicologist, to name but a few, who gathers the documentation as part of his or her own research take on responsibility also for archiving it, and, if so, under what preservation and access conditions and ethical regimes? What might developments such as self-archiving services mean for the trust we place in the archived record? Can archives be kept in the same digital repository as research data and bibliographic materials? If so, according to what kind of management regime? How much of our digital heritage should actually be preserved? If we were able to preserve it all, should we? On what basis should we make those decisions? How can archives protect the interests of the individual associated with a record when that record, and many more related to it, go online?[35] Are there profession-specific practices or approaches that information and memory institutions such as libraries, museums, and archives can learn from or share, especially in the areas of metadata creation, content curation, and programming for users?[36] What economic and policy structures might best support the long-term development and ongoing management of digital archives?

Conclusion

This book cannot possibly answer all of these questions, but they indicate the kind of reflexivity and knowledge of prior experiences and strategies with which the twenty-first-century archivist must be equipped.

Indubitably, new forms of cooperation between archival repositories and, more broadly, across information and memory professions and the public and private sector, are needed, but new ways of thinking about what often turn out to be old or pre-existing questions and challenges are also necessary.

The archives of the digital age, which are also the archives of today, know no media limitations and are quite able to transcend their physical housing. They are also society's continuity with its past. As in Samaran's day, archives hold the ancient, the precious, the official, the historical, and the authentic. But, increasingly, they are also enabled to capture and make available the unofficial, the social, the personal, the ethnographic, and the witnessing that undergird rights, obligations, and memory of all people in all places.

Digital developments allow archives to span time and space in new ways. Virtual archives and archival services offer users, both local and remote, more granular and customized access, even if, at present, to less content, than can the physical archive and its services. The Internet is a vehicle that the archive can use to capture more and more candid materials created through digital communications and the World Wide Web, as well as to support shared responsibility for documenting and collecting, for federating collections online, and for opening up the archive for a variety of types of use and user interactions.

For all of these exciting developments, however, archivists still need to understand where there is continuity with, and where change is needed in, traditional practices. Even more important, as new activities are layered on top of existing backlogs, archivists must figure out how to balance day-to-day responsibilities with their overarching responsibility as the profession of the record to that record, to society, and to all of humanity whose lives are somehow caught up in that record.

Notes

Portions of this chapter were previously presented in a keynote speech, "The Construction of the Archive and the Representation of Alternative Pasts," at the Summer School on Memory, Power and the Alternative Pasts, Helsinki, Finland, May 2011; and at the Summer School for Old Books, University of Zadar, September 2009.

1   Subject Files of Solon J. Buck Relating to Archival Principles, Practices and Institutions, 1789–1956, Box 1, RG 64 Records of the United States National Archives and Records Administration, National Archives and Records Administration.

2   See, for example, John Bunyan, *The Pilgrim's Progress* (London, 1684); Arthur Conan Doyle, *The Maracot Deep* (London, 1929); Sylvia Townsend Warner, *Kingdoms of Elfin* (London, 1972); and José Saramago, *All the Names* (London: Harcourt, 1999).

3   James P. Sickinger, *Public Records and Archives in Classical Athens* (Chapel Hill: University of North Carolina Press, 1999); Diskin Clay, "Epicurus in the Archives of Athens," in *Studies in Attic Epigraphy, History and Topography*, Hesperia Supplement 9 (Princeton, N.J.: American School of Classical Studies at Athens, 1982), 17–26.

4   Luciana Duranti, "Archives as a Place," *Archives and Manuscripts* 24, no. 2 (1996): 242–55. Republished in *Archives and Social Studies: A Journal of Interdisciplinary Research* 1, no. 1 (2007), Archivo Municipal Cartegena, http://tinyurl.com/2dbasvb.

5   Maria Portuondo, *Secret Science: Spanish Cosmography and the New World* (Chicago: University of Chicago Press, 2009).

6   Thomas Richards, *The Imperial Archive: Knowledge and the Fantasy of Empire* (New York: Verso, 1993), 3–4.

7   Ann Laura Stoler, *Along the Archival Grain: Epistemic Anxieties and Colonial Common Sense* (Princeton, N.J.: Princeton University Press, 2009), 20.

8   Mark Twain, *Following the Equator: A Journey around the World* (Hartford: American Publishing Company, 1897), 699.

9   See, for example, Michel Foucault, *The Archaeology of Knowledge and the Discourse on Language* (New York: Pantheon, 1972).

10 See, for example, Jacques Derrida, *Archive Fever: A Freudian Impression*, trans. Eric Prenowitz (Chicago: University of Chicago Press, 1996).

11 See, for example, Pierre Bourdieu, *Distinction: A Social Critique of the Judgment of Taste*, trans. Richard Nice (Cambridge, Mass.: Harvard University Press, 2000).

12 See, for example, Jean-François Lyotard, *La Condition Postmoderne: Rapport sur le Savoir* [The Postmodern Condition: A Report on Knowledge] (Paris: Editions de Minuit, c. 1979).

13 See, for example, Linda Tuhiwai Smith, *Decolonizing Methodologies: Research and Indigenous Peoples* (London: Zed Books, 1999).

14 For example, the theme for the MINOM-ICOM International Movement for a New Museology 14th Annual Conference held in Cape Verde in October 2011 was to reflect on "*Altermuseology* with those who seek a world with justice and solidarity far beyond the perspective of cooperation between rich and poor, which has marked relations between north and south," http://www.minom-icom.net/.

15 Paul Connerton, *How Societies Remember* (Cambridge: Cambridge University Press, 1989).

16 Diana Taylor, *The Archive and the Repertoire: Performing Cultural Memory in the Americas* (Durham, N.C.: Duke University Press, 2003).

17 Simon Schama, *Landscape and Memory* (New York: Vintage Books, 1995).

[18] Pierre Nora, *Rethinking France: Les Lieux de Mémoire*, vol. 1, trans. David P. Jordan (Chicago: University of Chicago Press, 2001).

[19] Steve Jones, *Virtual Culture: Identity and Communication in Cybersociety* (Thousand Oaks, Calif.: Sage Publications, 1997).

[20] Deborah A. Turner, *Conceptualizing Oral Documents* (PhD diss., University of Washington, 2009).

[21] Shannon Faulkhead, *Narratives of Koorie Victoria* (PhD diss., Monash University, 2009).

[22] See, for example, AERI PACG, "Educating for the Archival Multiverse," 68–102 (see chapter 1, n. 47); McKemmish et al., "'Communities of Memory,'" 146–75 (see introduction, n. 31); Frank Upward, Sue McKemmish, and Barbara Reed, "Archivists and Changing Social and Information Spaces: A Continuum Approach to Recordkeeping and Archiving in Online Cultures," *Archivaria* 72 (Fall 2011): 197–238.

[23] Terry Cook, "What Is Past Is Prologue: A History of Archival Ideas Since 1898, and the Future Paradigm Shift," *Archivaria* 43 (Spring 1997).

[24] Eric Ketelaar, "Archival Temples, Archival Prisons: Modes of Power and Protection," *Archival Science* 2, nos. 3–4 (2002).

[25] The Sarbanes-Oxley Act of 2002, Pub. L. No. 107-204, 116 Stat. 745, also known as the Public Company Accounting Reform and Investor Protection Act of 2002.

[26] Menand describes such pluralism as "an attempt to make a good out of the circumstance that goods are often incommensurable. People come at life from different places, they understand the world in different ways, they strive for different ends. This is a fact that has proved amazingly hard to live with, and the reason is that as associated beings, we naturally seek to find our tastes, values, and hopes reflected in other people. It would be one thing, in other words, if each individual simply had his or her own spin and there were no way to get groups of people spinning in the same direction. But individuals do belong to groups, they take their identities from groups, and it tends to be as members of groups that they pursue the goods they desire. To the extent that one group perceives its goods as incompatible with the goods of another group, there are collisions." Louis Menand, *The Metaphysical Club: A Story of Ideas in America* (New York: Farrar, Strauss, Giroux, 2001), 377.

[27] For example, Svärd and Sundqvist discuss the challenges of disseminating information on the TRC findings in Sierra Leone using information and communication technologies (ICTs). They find, however, that lack of access to ICTs as well as of information skills impeded the ability of women and children in that country to empower themselves and hindered sustainable development. They cite the Sierra Leonean TRC Act as calling for the commission "to create an impartial historical record of violations and abuses of human rights and international humanitarian law related to the armed conflict in Sierra Leone from the beginning of the conflict in 1991 to the signing of the Lomé Peace Agreement, to address impunity, to respond to the needs of the victims, to promote healing and reconciliation and to prevent a repetition of the violations and abuses suffered." Proscovia Svärd and Anneli Sundqvist, "IT, the Most Revolutionary Issue Globally: But Is It for All?," *INFOtrend: Nordic Journal for Information Specialists* 62, no. 3 (1997): 71–78.

[28] For example, after an appeal to researchers who had made copies of their materials, it was possible to reconstruct virtually, at least in part, the unique holdings of the National and University Library in Sarajevo, which were destroyed by war during the 1990s. "Activist" archivists in South Africa, South America, and elsewhere, seek out and then describe or digitize and make available online archival evidence in the form of hidden records and personal testimonies relating to the persecuted and the disappeared to provide a counterpoint to the official record. See the South African History Archive, http://www.saha.org.za/about_saha.htm.

[29] Elizabeth Crooke, "The Politics of Community Heritage: Motivations, Authority and Control," *International Journal of Heritage Studies* 16 (January–March 2010): 16–29; Dominique Daniel, "Documenting the Immigrant and Ethnic Experience in American Archives," *The American Archivist* 73 (Spring/Summer 2010): 82–104; Flinn et al., "Whose Memories, Whose Archives?," 71–86 (see

chapter 1, n. 28); Mary Stevens, Andrew Flinn, and Elizabeth Shepherd, "New Frameworks for Community Engagement in the Archives Sector: From Handing Over to Handing On," *International Journal of Heritage Studies* 16 (January–March 2010): 59–76; Andrew Flinn, "Independent Community Archives and Community-Generated Content: 'Writing, Saving and Sharing our Histories,'" *Convergence: The International Journal of Research into New Media Technologies* 16, no. 1 (2010): 39–51; Helen Klaebe and Marcus Foth, "Capturing Community Memory with Oral History and New Media: The Sharing Stories Project," in *3rd International Conference of the Community Informatics Research Network (CIRN)*, ed. Larry Stillman and Graeme Johanson, October 9–11, Prato, Italy, http://eprints.qut.edu.au/4751/; Horacio Roque Ramirez, "A Living Archive of Desire: Teresita la Campesina and the Embodiment of Queer Latino Community Histories," in *Archive Stories: Facts, Fictions, and the Writing of History*, ed. Antoinette Burton (Durham, N.C.: Duke University Press, 2005), 111–35; Joel Wurl, "Ethnicity as Provenance: In Search of Values and Principles for Documenting the Immigrant Experience," *Archival Issues* 29, no. 1 (2005): 65–76; and Lynette Russell, "Indigenous Records and Archives: Mutual Obligations and Building Trust," *Archives and Manuscripts* 34, no. 1 (2006): 32–43.

[30] "Koorie" is the term that many Indigenous Australians use to refer to themselves.

[31] See Koorie Heritage Trust, "Collections," http://www.koorieheritagetrust.com/collections; see also Monash University, "Trust and Technology Project," http://www.infotech.monash.edu.au/research/centres/cosi/projects/trust/.

[32] An increasingly over-used yet nuanced term, "community," as used here, refers to any kind of group, whether special interest, regional, ethnic, racial, or gender-based, that has archival needs and materials, but that functions outside the parameters of traditional or mainstream institutional environments.

[33] For example, Rick Prelinger, collector of the Prelinger Archives of sixty thousand advertising, educational, industrial, and amateur films; or public participation in the Home Movie Day initiative, "More About Home Movie Day," http://www.homemovieday.com/about.html.

[34] Of course, on the grandest scale, there is Brewster Kahle and the Internet Archive and its Wayback Machine, http://www.archive.org/.

[35] Italian journalist and novelist Italo Calvino once wrote that "biographical data, even those recorded in the public registers, are the most private things one has, and to declare them openly is rather like facing a psychoanalyst." Italo Calvino, *The Literature Machine* (London: Vintage, 1997), 339.

[36] For some examples, see Gilliland-Swetland, *Enduring Paradigms* (see chapter 1, n. 5); Anne J. Gilliland-Swetland, Layna White, and Robin L. Chandler, "We're Building It, Will They Use It? The MOAC II Evaluation Project," in *Proceedings of Museums and the Web 2004, Arlington, Virginia, March 31–April 3, 2004*, http://www.archimuse.com/mw2004/papers/g-swetland/g-swetland.html; Layna White and Anne J. Gilliland-Swetland, "Museum Information Professionals as Users and Providers of Online Resources: Museums and the Online Archive of California II Study," *ASIST Bulletin* (June/July 2004): 23–26.

CHAPTER 3

The Quest to Integrate the World's Knowledge: American Archival Engagement with the Documentation Movement, 1900–1950

The International Congress of Libraries and Archives held in Brussels in 1910 is widely regarded as a seminal moment in the development of information science. Yet, its centrality to the development of archival science as well as the national and international interactions between archivists and the documentation movement out of which information science was to grow are less appreciated. This chapter explores these early interactions and why they were abandoned. It also establishes historical context for documentary and metadata ideas central to much of the subsequent discourse regarding archival descriptive standards and archival automation, digital libraries and archives development, cyberinfrastructure-building, and, most recently, community-based archives and digital curation.

The story of American archives—is one to craze the historians, to amaze the layman, and to leave the law-maker unconcerned as ever. . . . This country, which has so completely out-distanced other countries in the development of Library Science, is immeasurably behind them in all that pertains to archives. In general our archives are neglected if not completely ignored.
—Waldo Gifford Leland, 1912[1]

Introduction

We tend today to think that archival descriptive standards, integrated multimedia information systems that traverse national and disciplinary boundaries, effective management of administrative records created in new formats, documentation strategies, and collaboration of archives, libraries, and museums are integrally tied to technological, intellectual, and professional developments that have occurred over the past five decades. In fact, these were all central preoccupations of visionary individuals convening as part of the documentation movement in Europe and the United States in a complex of international and interdisciplinary forums in the first half of the twentieth century, just at the point when the American archival profession was beginning to organize. While recording, information, and communication technologies continued to generate new capacities for creating, managing, and disseminating information of all kinds, the documentation movement faded, in part because of the historical context in which it occurred. International interactions between individuals and forums could not be sustained in the face of the devastation and disruptions caused by two world wars, economic depression, and the start of the Cold War. However, professionalization of the information and cultural fields, reinforced by developments in graduate education and sometimes coupled with sentiments of national exceptionalism, also led to increasing emphasis on distinctive professional identities and roles and differences in philosophy and practices within different national contexts and traditions, thus creating increasing divisions between fields and jurisdictions.

Waldo Gifford Leland and the Introduction of European Ideas about Archival Arrangement and Description into the United States

Waldo Gifford Leland was one of several remarkable men instrumental in the development of the archival profession in the United States in the first part of the twentieth century. Among his many contributions to the field, Leland was an important figure in early discussions about U.S. archival descriptive practices because of his role in introducing the ideas and principles enunciated by late nineteenth- and early twentieth-century European archivists, librarians, and documentalists to the nascent archival community in the United States. Leland received his graduate degree in history from Harvard in 1901, and in 1903 began what was to be twenty years of work for the Bureau of Historical Research of the Carnegie Institution in Washington, D.C., which was directed from 1903 until 1928 by social historian and prominent advocate for a national archives, J. Franklin Jameson.[2] Compared to European countries, America was in a disadvantaged position in the first several decades of the twentieth century when Leland made his most important contributions, having no substantive archival tradition, no national archives, and no formal archival education programs. The American Historical Association had been formed in 1884, followed, in 1895, by the formation of the Historical Manuscripts Commission, the Public Archives Commission in 1899, and, in 1909, the Conference of Archivists that itself would evolve, in 1936, into the Society of American Archivists.[3] This was a period when American historians such as Leland and Jameson,[4] to support the new academic field of American historical scholarship, were campaigning hard for a national archives and for more robust archival repositories around the country. They were also investing considerable efforts in developing documentary guides to archival materials dispersed across the country, as well as to materials relating to the colonial history and revolutionary struggles of America held in repositories in other nations such as England, France, and Spain. In trying to organize the profession, American historians looked to Europe, not only for materials relevant to the history of the United States, but also for conceptual definitions and ideas about best practices for applying a scientific approach to the management of archival materials at home.[5]

    Through his work with the Carnegie Institution, Leland became intimately familiar with the development of guides for archival holdings. The *Guide to the Archives of the Government of the United States in Washington*, which he coauthored with Claude Halstead Van Tyne, was published in 1904, and Leland subsequently revised and expanded a new edition published in 1907. He then traveled to repositories throughout the eastern United States to collect letters of Continental Congress delegates.

In 1903, when Leland undertook the *Guide* at Jameson's behest, Jameson wrote to him with advice about how to go about doing such a survey:

> My hope is that you and Van Tyne will prepare an archive report which shall not only surpass everything heretofore accomplished in that way in this country, but shall be a model of accurate workmanship and utility to historical students. I have two general suggestions which I venture to make now: First, that you should make every endeavor to find and read all the previous and partial surveys of the material. . . . In the second place, archive reports in this country have really been made without any observation of the admirable archive reports common in Europe, where this sort of thing has been much more completely elaborated than with us. If you never had much occasion to use Langlois and Stein: Archives de l'Histoire de France, I advise you to make a thorough study of that book. It is quite a model in its way.[6]

Also in 1903, with a grant from the Carnegie Institution, Leland began to study European archival practice in French repositories.[7] His interaction with France continued from 1907 to 1914, and even included taking a course at the École des Chartes on archival theory and methods following the 1910 International Congress of Libraries and Archives, and then again from 1922 to 1927, when he served as the Carnegie Institution's principal representative in that country. He began work on what was to become a multivolume *Guide to Materials for American History in the Libraries and Archives of Paris*, the first two volumes of which were published in 1932 and 1943, with drafts of the remaining three forming part of Leland's personal papers, which today are held by the Library of Congress. He also directed the foreign copying program of the Library of Congress for French manuscripts relating to the United States and started work on what became the institution's two-volume *Calendar of Manuscripts in Paris Archives and Libraries Relating to the History of the Mississippi Valley to 1803*.[8]

Most influentially for the development of archival arrangement and description in the United States, and undoubtedly himself influenced by the European archivists and librarians he encountered in the course of his work in France as well as proponents of progressivism whom he met in Washington, D.C.,[9] Leland was persuaded against the application of bibliographically oriented manuscript approaches to archival management. In his keynote address, "American Archival Problems," presented at the first Conference of Archivists in 1909, he argued in favor of the principles articulated in 1898 by the Dutch archivists Muller, Feith, and Fruin in their now famous *Handleiding Voor Het Ordenen En Beschrijven Van Archieven* or *Manual for the Arrangement and Description of Archives*. These principles, derived from the authors' observations and experiences regarding the characteristics and properties of Dutch government records, included maintaining and describing the archival *fonds* as a whole and preserving the original order of the materials in the *fonds*.[10]

Leland did not question, however, the validity of applying principles thus derived to American records, even though significant differences existed between the recordkeeping practices of the United States and those of European countries, most notably, the absence of registry systems to ensure the creation and maintenance of meaningful order of records of specific activities. Archival historian Peter Wosh argues that Leland's championing of internationally recognized best practices involved other problematic aspects. In particular, he maintains that the promotion of objective standards and shared principles that today might appear unexceptional created a new and narrow orthodoxy in American archival practices that excluded the history and experiences of minority groups and cultures and disparaged inferior repositories and individuals, especially those of the South that addressed Confederate and African American history.[11] As a result, the newly formed Society of American Archivists was exceedingly homogeneous, and diversity largely disappeared.[12] Separate documentation movements emerged, which could validly be considered the precursors of the documentation strategy approach proposed in the 1980s, especially in relation to African American and Afro-Latin history.[13] Such a critique presages a well-recognized issue that contemporary metadata standards developers face in devising universal descriptive schemes; that is, how to balance the precision and prescriptiveness required to ensure consistency and quality control in descriptive practices and facilitate data exchange between different parties, tolerating or including alternate cultural practices and understandings and specific community needs necessary to support diverse creators and users.

1910 International Congress of Libraries and Archives

Jameson personally introduced Leland to the Belgian archivists, also in 1909.[14] In 1910, Leland was one of four representatives of the American

Historical Association (AHA) who attended (at their own expense) a historic first meeting of European and American archivists at the International Congress of Libraries and Archives.[15] The congress was a very grand affair held in Brussels during the world's fair and organized by the International Institute for Bibliography (IIB). The presence of Americans surprised some.[16] In his draft report for the AHA, Leland remarked that

> One of the officials attending the congress . . . said, "But I thought there were no archives in America." He was told that there were indeed archives in America, but that these men were [there] due mainly to the benevolence of Providence, and not to the sagacity and foresight of government.[17]

In his brief talk at the congress, Leland discussed the nascent and disparate state of archives in the United States and his work on the survey of the states. He expressed the hope that the situation would be better systematized in ten years.[18] He also mentioned his 1909 speech at the first Conference of Archivists where, at his urging, it had been agreed that American archivists should look to implement European methods and practices.[19] He later noted in a letter to his wife that he had "got a great many ideas" at the congress.[20]

Dunbar Rowland, director of the Mississippi Department of Archives and History, another of the American attendees at the 1910 congress, provided some more insight for the European attendees into American thinking and the clear desire of U.S. archives to be part of an international uniform initiative in his presentation titled "The Importance of the Concentration and Classification of National Archives":

> . . . it is for us at the beginning of the twentieth century to seriously direct our attention to the duty of making national archives more accessible and more usable. There is an impetus in that direction, and it is very gratifying to think that the present century may be marked by the adoption of a great international plan for the concentration and classification of public archives.[21]

It was clear that an initiative he envisaged to develop a "uniform method of classification" would be European led:

> . . . careless and unscientific methods prevail in the United States, and an acknowledgment of this fact relieves us of the imputation that we come to you as advice-givers . . . we wish, by the confession of our own short-comings, to emphasize our

interest in any progress on this side which will enable us to solve the archive problems on our side of the water.[22]

Interestingly, when Dunbar Rowland wrote to Jameson seeking background data on European practices for his paper, Jameson had responded that he did

> not know of any book in which the subject is comprehensively treated, except one in Swedish and one in Dutch, and I do not know that you read these languages. . . . I have here, however, a German translation of the Dutch one—Anteilung zum Orden und Beschreiben von Archiven by Muller, Feith and Fruin, translated by Kaiser—and will cheerfully lend it to you if it will be useful, although, being rather the standard book, its facts will be pretty well known to your audience.[23]

The Association des Archivistes et Bibliothécaires Belges (Association of Belgian Archivists and Librarians), founded by Joseph Cuvelier at the turn of the century in Brussels, promoted the Brussels congress. Cuvelier, who had published extensively on classification of *fonds* and the publication of finding aids, was also particularly interested in the role of archival education in preparing archivists in the more technical aspects of archival practice. As secretary of the congress, he was influential in determining the content of the Brussels discussion, which focused, therefore, on the development of archival education in countries with no existing formal programs. The keystone of the system of Belgian archival education, which Cuvelier believed to be exceptionally rigorous, was its Cours Practique d'Archivéconomie, which included the new science of arrangement and description delineated in Muller, Feith, and Fruin's *Manual*. The *Manual* had been translated from Dutch into French in the same year as the Brussels congress by Cuvelier and Henri Stein of the Archives Nationales in Paris. Muller, Fruin, and Stein all attended the 1910 congress, and the concept of provenance advocated by the *Manual* was adopted as "the basic rule" of the profession[24] and formally endorsed by the congress.[25]

The background of the *Dutch Manual* (as it came to be known), and its subsequent widespread adoption, is well known today. It was produced for the Dutch Association of Archivists, in cooperation with the State Archives of the Netherlands and the Ministry of the Interior. It drew predominantly on the kinds of records found in Dutch archives in an attempt to develop a single methodology that could be used to standardize arrangement and description across Dutch archives and historical collections and support Dutch colonial infrastructure.[26] French archival theory also influenced it as a result of Muller's 1873 attendance at the École des Chartes in Paris, as did the adoption by some Dutch archives of the Prussian concept of provenance.[27] For the first time, a text clearly and concisely delineated and elaborated upon concepts and principles of archival arrangement and description, such as *respect des fonds* and provenance, that had been progressively institutionalized and codified through a series of regulations and manuals as bureaucratic practices and the national historical consciousness of European nation-states evolved.[28] According to Theodore Schellenberg, the *Dutch Manual* was fast adopted as the "bible for modern archivists," and over the next two decades it was translated and published in countries across Europe. The *Dutch Manual* was finally published in the United States in 1940, coinciding with the initiation of the first recurring course in the history and administration of archives, taught by German émigré and former Prussian state archivist Ernst Posner at American University in Washington, D.C.

The International Institute for Bibliography and the Documentation Movement

Most librarians and library scholars with any background in library classification history and theory are probably familiar with the documentation movement centered in Belgium around the turn of the twentieth century, as well as with the ferment of ideas surrounding the development of cataloging and classification schemes that characterized that period. The movement's relationship to the archival field at the time, however, is less well known.[29] For archivists, one of the most interesting aspects of the documentalist or documentation movement was its inclusion of archival ideas and principles, as well as those of library, museum, bureaucratic, and other documentation practices. The movement's founders, prominent lawyers Paul Otlet and Henri-Marie Lafontaine, sought to develop a classification scheme to serve as the architecture for a master bibliography of the world's accumulated knowledge in all documentary forms, regardless

of its professional context and to support the goals of social democracy
and pacifism prevalent among intellectuals in Belgium and elsewhere at
the time. According to W. Boyd Rayward, a scholar of classification history,

> The collaboration between the two founders began in the early 1890's. In 1893 they
> transformed the bibliographical section of the Société des études sociales et poli-
> tiques, in which they were both active, into an International Institute of Sociological
> Bibliography. The following year Otlet obtained a copy of Melvil Dewey's Decimal
> Classification and in March 1895 he wrote to Dewey seeking permission to translate
> the classification and to use it for bibliographical purposes.[30]

Otlet subsequently created the Universal Decimal Classification,
one of the most prominent examples of faceted classification, and, in
1913, Lafontaine received the Nobel Peace Prize for his work with the
International Peace Bureau.[31]

The International Institute for Bibliography, which was to undergo
several subsequent renamings until it eventually became the International
Federation for Information and Documentation (FID), was established in
Brussels by the International Conference on Bibliography in 1895. The
International Conference met in Brussels from September 2 to 5 to "study
matters of classification and the international organisation of bibliography
generally."[32] In the same decade that the IIB was established, several archival treatises were published in Europe,[33] the most influential being Muller,
Feith, and Fruin's *Manual,* regarding the arrangement and description of
archival materials, a subject in which Otlet became greatly interested.[34]
Prior to the International Congress of Librarians and Archivists in July
1910, Otlet had participated in the Congress for Administrative Sciences
also held in Brussels. According to Rayward:

> [Otlet] regarded its work as primarily documentary, administrative documentation
> being a subject of long-standing interest to him. As President of the Congress's section
> for documentation, he had . . . assembled an enormous documentary exhibit.[35]

The scope of the documentalist perspective on administrative documentation in many ways presaged ideas about the integration of recordkeeping functions, activities, and practices not fully expressed within the
archival community until the development of the records continuum in
the 1990s:[36]

By far the greatest number of resolutions taken by this congress dealt with documentation. . . . It was resolved that "all the theoretical and practical knowledge relating to
general documentation should be brought together and co-ordinated" . . . [and] that
"there should be a general method for administrative documentation. This method
should embrace the various operations to which documents are submitted (creation,
conservation, classification, communication, publication, retirement, transferral to
archival depots)."[37]

Otlet visited America in early 1914 and received some expression of
interest from the secretary of state. However, U.S. participation would
have required the country to join the Union of International Associations
(UIA), the research institute and documentation center founded in 1907 in
Brussels by Lafontaine and Otlet, which was not possible since the United
States government could only belong to organizations formed by official conventions.[38] According to Otlet, "The United States Government
would gladly consider supporting 'any international agreement which the
governments supporting these organisations may agree on.'"[39] There was,
of course, no time to pursue these matters as the First World War swiftly
enveloped Europe.

As historian of information science Michael Buckland notes, the term
"documentation" was increasingly accepted from about 1920 onward as
generically encompassing "bibliography, scholarly information services,
records management, and archival work."[40] It is not surprising, therefore,
that Leland wrote to Otlet in 1925, stating his deep interest in the IIB and
the Committee on Intellectual Cooperation with which it was associated in
various ways, and advising him that an American Committee on Intellectual
Cooperation was to be formed at a conference to be held in March 1925. He
also asked for more information about the status and work of the IIB, and,
sending his regards to Senator Lafontaine, said that he hoped to see Otlet
when he visited Brussels in May.[41] In his response, Otlet included a plea to
the Americans that essentially spoke of the need to reverse the past flow of
influence from Europe to the United States, drawing upon American cooperative impetus, expansive thinking, and energy.[42] Such American leadership did not occur until the second half of the twentieth century, however,
when staff of the young U.S. National Archives pushed for the formation
of the International Council on Archives (ICA) following World War II and

later still in the form of American-developed information and communications technologies, as well as extensive federal support for research and development of cyberinfrastructure and digital libraries.

The Archival Legacy of the 1910 Congress of Librarians and Archivists

A decade after the 1910 congress, a report at the twenty-fifth annual meeting of the AHA relating to the work of the Public Archives Commission stated that "the Commission has been able, through participation in the Congress of Archivists in Brussels and through the annual conferences of archivists which it initiated in 1909 to inculcate and encourage in this country the best methods of archive administration."[43] The future of the international movement that brought together archivists, librarians, and documentalists was never secured, however. While a permanent committee had been established with the aim of holding international congresses every five years, a second congress of librarians and archivists never occurred because of the outbreak of World War I. Disillusionment followed the war. The growing and increasingly territorial information and cultural professions that had come together across nations in the documentation movement around notions of universality of description, integration of types of information resources, and the potential of new technologies moved apart and became more distinct in their specializations, more reified, and more nationally based.[44] While they served as umbrella organizations to bring their members together across international lines, the formation first of the International Federation of Library Associations (IFLA), and then, after World War II, of the International Council of Museums (ICOM) and the International Council on Archives, reinforced the silos developing among the different professional areas and interests.

While documentalists might have lost their international focus between the two world wars, archivists remained understandably preoccupied with international issues. Foremost among their concerns was how to recover and make available records that had been displaced. This involved both international cooperation and contemplation of common methods of arrangement and description. Solon J. Buck, arguing in 1946 in his role as

U.S. national archivist in favor of creating an archives as part of the newly formed United Nations Educational, Scientific and Cultural Organization (UNESCO), noted the shift to archival concerns. He wrote that the legacy of the 1910 congress was that "subsequently the librarians withdrew from the committee, which then continued its existence only to represent the archivists. Plans were several times made for an international congress of archivists, the last time for one to be held in Italy in 1935, but it was not possible to bring any of these to fruition."[45] Buck mentioned a third effort for international cooperation among archivists that also had its roots in the 1910 congress and was underway at the time of his writing:

> The Technical Committee of Archivists [was] set up in 1931 by the International Institute of Intellectual Cooperation, the operating agency of the League of Nations' International Committee of Intellectual Cooperation. This was to be a sort of advisory board of archival experts from different countries, which was to meet annually to draw up resolutions and plans for presentation to the International Institute of Intellectual Cooperation. . . . It studied such questions as the international exchange of photographic facsimiles, the standardization of archival terminology, the durability of modern types of records, and the archivists' concern with motion-picture film. . . . The fate of this committee is bound up with that of the International Institute of Intellectual Cooperation and probably lies now in the hands of the United Nations Educational, Scientific, and Cultural Organization.[46]

Noting how the FID had "given much attention to archives as an important phase of the larger subject of documentation," Buck expressed his hope that the FID's first postwar conference in Paris in November 1946 would align with the activities and interests of the young UNESCO.[47] Leland attended that meeting in Paris (the 16th International Documentation Conference) as a representative of the American Council of Learned Societies (ACLS). Final resolutions at that conference expressed a strong desire to work closely with UNESCO, for cooperation with ISO on the standardization of documents, and for FID to remain in charge of the development of Universal Decimal Classification. A final recommendation called for training in documentation to be developed in educational institutions; it was assumed this was particularly directed at a role that UNESCO might play (and later did in archival education).[48]

The American Documentation Institute

While the documentation movement declined in Europe between the two world wars, it was on the rise in the United States. Perhaps even less well known than American archival involvement with the IIB/FID is the role that U.S. National Archives staff and SAA members played in the early days of the American Documentation Institute (ADI), the organization that eventually evolved into today's Association for Information Science and Technology (ASIS&T).

In 1937, Buck attended "by invitation, a conference on documentation under the auspices of *Science Service*, at which a resolution was adopted favoring the organization of a Documentation Institute and requesting the chairman of the meeting, Mr. Watson Davis, to arrange for a meeting of delegates from national scholarly agencies to bring about such an organization."[49] Watson Davis, the visionary behind the American Documentation Institute, was director of Science Service, a nonprofit institution founded in 1921 to increase and improve the public dissemination of scientific and technical information. Science Service sponsored early innovation in microphotography and also established a Documentation Division and a Bibliofilm Service.[50] In 1935, it set up the Documentation Institute.

Science Service's trustees were nominated by the National Academy of Sciences (where Science Service was housed), the National Research Council, the American Association for the Advancement of Science, and the E. W. Scripps Estate—many of the same entities that pushed for the recent development of cyberinfrastructure to support digital scholarship. In the 1920s, Davis began to wonder whether it would be possible to develop "some method for putting books and manuscripts into compact and portable form by some miniature photographic process similar to motion picture films."[51] He became a major proponent of microfilm for revolutionizing the management of data and information, promoting it in terms that reverberate with much of the enthusiasm in recent years from proponents of emergent digital information technologies:

> One of the newer and most promising tools of documentation is the microfilm. Compact, to an extraordinary degree, promising to outlast our omnipresent paper, and capable of reproducing anything the eye can see, even in natural colors, microfilms

promise to hurdle some of the present barriers to easy and effective interchange of intelligence in many fields.[52]

As a reporter, Watson Davis encountered how Europeans were talking about documents and documentation, and he wanted to bring those ideas to America, noting that "'documentation' is being used because it includes all phases of issuance, use and interchange of recorded information."[53]

Buck represented the National Archives on the organizing committee that met to establish the American Documentation Institute on March 13, 1937, a meeting that he also chaired.[54] He was elected a trustee and treasurer of the new organization and served along with Watson Davis and Ludvig Hektoen as one of the three incorporators. On November 1, 1937, after Davis, the president of the institute, requested that the Archivist of the United States nominate a member for the permanent organization, Connor again nominated Buck, and at the annual meeting of the institute, on January 27, 1938, Buck was formally elected a member of the permanent organization for three years and re-elected a trustee. Buck later informed Connor that "Dr. Tate and Dr. Schellenberg, of the staff of the National Archives are also members of the Institute, having been elected on the nomination of the Society of American Archivists and the American Historical Association respectively."[55] Vernon Tate was also an active member of the American Library Association's Committee on Photographic Reproduction of Library Materials and became editor of the *Journal of Documentary Reproduction* published by that committee between 1938 and 1943.

By summer 1937, many major scientific journals and newsletters carried announcements about the formation of the American Documentation Institute, acknowledging a growing recognition at the highest levels of government, academia, and information institutions that developments in scholarly and scientific methods in multiple disciplines and sectors, as well as developments in new information and reproduction technologies, required the support of new and integrated approaches to information and documentary practices. The first World Congress of Universal Documentation was held in Paris in August of that same year, with Davis representing the ADI. Other attendees included Hilary Jenkinson from the British Public Record Office; Lodewyk Bendikson, head of Photographic Reproduction at the Huntington Library in San Marino, California; Paul

Otlet; Suzanne Briet; Emanuel Goldberg of Zeiss Ikon; and H. G. Wells. Michael Buckland speculates that this constituted a temporary convergence of diverse parties primarily driven by a shared interest in emergent technology (then photographic reproduction, which dominated early twentieth-century technological developments prior to computing) and, possibly, to a much lesser extent, forensic analysis of documents. It was likely much less driven by "conceptual insights into theoretical affinities, let alone amicable professional convergence."[56] He further speculates that this precedent presaged the current reiteration of archives-library convergence around digital technology, but that again this convergence will prove transitory unless technology inhibits professional divergence from recurring.[57]

Among the resolutions of the 1937 World Congress, one called for microfilm copying services to be established by libraries around the world to facilitate scholarly access to their holdings. The new ADI's Auxiliary Publications Program provided services quite similar to those of today's preprint servers and digital repositories. Organized by the participating scientific and professional societies, foundations, and government agencies, the program facilitated the publication and distribution of scholarly papers in the sciences and social sciences that were too long or too complex to publish by traditional means. Instead, a journal could publish an abstract of a paper and include a note that contained an ADI number whereby readers could get the entire paper, figures, tables or images, or the associated research data for a fee.[58] As one academic commentator observed, "In this way the document is perpetually 'in print,' but no extensive, space-consuming stocks need be stored—only the document itself and the microfilm negative from which positives are made for distribution."[59]

While World War II interrupted some of this momentum and coordination, support for the war effort and then coping with its vast and complex documentary aftermath and fears that an atomic strike could result in widespread obliteration of documentation promoted the implementation of state-of-the-art information technologies and the development of new approaches for managing increasing volumes of multimedia documentary materials. The fledgling ADI did not grow until after the war, but its leadership during this period moved between different documentary fields. Watson Davis served as president until 1944 when Keyes Metcalf, librarian of Harvard, succeeded him. Waldo Gifford Leland served as president in 1945. Watson Davis served again in 1946. By 1947, the FID was reconstituting itself after the war and was agitating, as had Otlet between the wars, for Americans to play an active part in the future development of the FID. It requested an American representative for its council.[60] Responding to this request, the American Library Association and the ADI together funded Vernon Tate of the National Archives to attend the 1949 FID meeting in Bern, Switzerland, where the ADI was officially recognized as representing the United States within the FID. Tate went on to serve as president of the ADI in 1949 and also as the first editor in 1951 and 1952 of the ADI journal, *American Documentation*, that would go on to become the *Journal of the American Society for Information Science and Technology*.

Helen L. Chatfield, a records officer with the U.S. Bureau of the Budget, reviewed *American Documentation*'s first issue for *The American Archivist* and was obviously quite familiar with the documentalists and the work of Otlet and Lafontaine. She remarks that their definition of "documentation" as referring to "the creation, transmission, collection, classification and use of documents," the latter being defined as "recorded knowledge in any format," was "novel" in the American context. She also references a talk given in 1946 at the U.S. National Archives by F. Donker-Duyvuis, secretary of the Dutch Institute of Documentation.[61] More significantly, Chatfield discusses the concerns among documentalists, especially American documentalists, about the efficacy and applicability of the Universal Decimal Classification and FID's sponsorship of it, remarking that

> It is not surprising that the American Chapter turned rather to the development of improved methods than to the idea of a standard classification as a means of accomplishing its aims, since the interest of its founders in the broad field of documentation had sprung from an earlier preoccupation with the techniques of reproduction.[62]

Her review ends, nevertheless, with an endorsement of the documentalist approach and a strong exhortation for archivists and librarians to work together more closely:

> . . . At this point the thoughtful archivist will give pause to consider his relation to the new development. Are record documents included in the material to be worked on?—and who are the "documentalists?". . . Surely record documents are included, as well as library material, and both the archivist and the librarian are "documentalists."

With the growing need for a job to be done in the social science field comparable to what had already been achieved for the physical sciences, it is important that documentalists work together. Although the librarian and the archivist have many interests in common, each has lived too long in a world apart with too little understanding of the work of the other. Perhaps in this common activity of documentation a way will be found to bring them together.[63]

In spite of their early support, however, Americans did not continue as active participants in FID, possibly because the ADI was more interested in methods, and in particular in microfilm, then it was in the bibliographic and classification preoccupations of FID. The need to respond to World War II and its aftermath, as well as to tackle the prior uncontrolled accumulation of records from World War I and depression-era projects led the National Archives to delve into records management approaches, to articulate appraisal criteria, and to delineate internal descriptive practices. On a side note, the National Archives also began to grapple with the archival implications of other media—sound and film recordings—during this period. In 1949, the General Services Administration subsumed the National Archives, in large part due to its emphasis on records management and efficiency in record-keeping. At that point, the National Archives' engagement in the documentation movement largely ceased, and since then it has never played a leadership role in the field of information science. Similarly, while the Society of American Archivists developed close ties with related professional organizations such as the Association for Records Managers and Administrators (ARMA) and the American Library Association (ALA), it has never developed the same strength of relationship with what is now known as the Association for Information Science and Technology (ASIS&T).

What then became of the ADI? In the early 1950s, it became a membership-based organization and moved away from being an organization of delegates appointed from among affiliated scientific and professional societies, foundations, and government agencies.[64] As noted, the emerging field of information science took over much of the legacy of the documentation movement. Reacting to the difficulties American scholars had in accessing foreign research materials during and after World War II, as well as the destruction of many of those materials, American research libraries put together the Farmington Plan. A major cooperative microfilm acquisitions initiative between 1942 and 1972 initially sponsored by the Carnegie Corporation and subsequently led by Harvard Library, the Farmington Plan sought to ensure access to research materials and publications by region and subject regardless of war or other events around the world. Among those involved in the plan was, not surprisingly, Waldo Gifford Leland. Ralph Wagner points out several logistical, market, and institutional competition issues that impeded the plan's overall success. One of his conclusions, however, suggests some of the key differences between library and archival fortes and perspectives about the centrality and future value of unpublished primary sources, as opposed to contemporarily important published materials. He begs the question of whether the outcome might have been different if the Farmington Plan had been a collaborative initiative of librarians and archivists:

> [T]he Farmington Plan's failure was almost dictated by the nature of its central concern. Marginal library materials are and will remain politically marginal. They are the concern of scholars working in obscure fields, who are unlikely to unite in support of a concept of collecting the marginal. They are today's legacy to tomorrow's scholars, whose assessment of them may be dramatically different, but who have no voice in today's decisions.[65]

One other interesting debate that emerged in the early 1950s concerned the nature of professional education for documentalists. Of what should it consist and could it be contained within library schools? In the end, most library schools became schools of library and information science and developed specialized courses in information science in addition to those in library science. A few library schools also offered a course or two in archival administration, but it wasn't until the 1990s and later that a substantial number of schools began to offer significant archival concentrations. Even more recently, graduate and continuing archival education began to offer extensive education in digital aspects of archival practice.[66] Perhaps the idea of an integrated education to prepare "documentation specialists" able to bridge different types of documentation and different disciplinary fields and their information practices was ahead of its time and is only now being realized in the possibilities afforded by the *i*School movement.[67]

In 1962, when the first social science data archives were being established and large bureaucracies began to implement mainframe-based
administrative data processing systems, and six years before the American
library field was to begin machine-readable cataloging, Watson Davis
addressed the American Documentation Institute. In his presentation,
"Documentation Unfinished," he reviewed several areas of interest that
had informed his work, all of which are central to scholarly information management today. Among them were developing "one big library"
through a cooperative "net" particularly with the use of microfilming;
auxiliary publishing by means of film, as a "medium for keeping the record
of science simultaneously complete, inexpensive, up-to-date, and personalized"; and building on H. G. Wells's idea of the "World Brain."[68] With
regard to this last theme, Davis concluded:

> Organizing the knowledge of the world is still the prime need that could be filled by
> documentation. . . . The great computer and information systems, added to advanced
> microfilm, developed in recent years makes this more technically possible. . . . Shall
> we read the plans of past decades and then proceed to build them with the tools that
> were not then fashioned?[69]

Conclusion

Several intriguing aspects of the early documentation movement are relevant to twenty-first-century archivists' increasingly technologized and
global field. Imbued with modernist and millennialist ideas about standardization and universalism that emanated out of global changes occur-
ring as a result of new technologies, industrialization, and the accelerated
speed of communication and travel, the work of the International Institute
of Bibliography in the first half of the twentieth century marked the first
attempt to develop a universal classification scheme that included archival ideas and principles. Interaction among the various players, including
leading archivists, librarians, and museum professionals across Europe and
the United States, was unprecedented, and the independent research institute, the Carnegie Institution for Science in Washington was instrumental.
This interaction culminated with the establishment after World War II of
UNESCO in 1945–46 and then of the International Council of Museums in

1946 and the International Council on Archives in 1948—perhaps its most concrete and enduring outcome.

After the 1940s, U.S. international archival involvement declined dramatically, in part due to the National Archives' withdrawal from national and international leadership while it was under the General Services Administration, and in part due to the United States' boycott of UNESCO between 1984 and 2002.[70] At the same time, the National Archives withdrew from its involvement in the ADI, and, as a result, the young fields of archival and information science took divergent courses.

Only in recent years have American archivists reconnected with the international archival and documentation communities. They've begun to learn from and contribute to them, in effect picking up the agenda that was dropped in the 1940s. Again, a confluence of technological, ideological, professional, and logistical factors encouraged this reconnection. As described in detail in other chapters, concomitant with the development of the Internet, an upsurge in the development of archival descriptive standards and bibliographic utilities brought consistency to national practices and supported international data exchange. Since the early 1980s, archivists have come together with bibliographic description and other information experts in national and international groups to work on the development and implementation of descriptive formats, frameworks, and data models such as MARC (MAchine-Readable Cataloging) Archival and Manuscripts Control (AMC), Functional Requirements for Bibliographic Records (FRBR), and Resource Description Framework (RDF), and with other archivists and recordkeeping professionals to develop Encoded Archival Description (EAD) and the suite of International Council on Archives standards based around the *General International Standard Archival Description* (*ISAD (G)*), and ISO records management standards. One important additional factor that led to an increase in international and cross-disciplinary cooperation was the availability of funding for international research relating to the management of digital records, resulting in ground-breaking initiatives such as the InterPARES (International Permanent Authentic Records in Electronic Systems) and CAMiLEON (Creative Archiving at Michigan & Leeds) Projects. The imperative to address digital records issues, coupled with growing uptake of a continuum-based approach to recordkeeping, also brings the records management and archival professions much closer together than they have been since they parted company in the 1950s.

Possibly most intriguing for archivists to contemplate is the birthing of an archival descriptive standardization movement with roots in European government administrative practices and national history making and yet closely associated with a universal classification movement strongly vested in the ideals of social democracy and pacifism. The widespread legacy of the *Dutch Manual* can be seen today in the principles that continue to be central to the archival paradigm around the world and to the *ISAD (G)* suite. The goal of integrating the world's information resources, however, has become largely the province of those engaged in digital library and cyberinfrastructure development. They are inspired less by the work of the IIB and more by Vannevar Bush's iconic, although in many ways considerably less innovative, vision in 1945 of the Memex machine, a mechanized, annotatable hypertext storage and retrieval system for the world's knowledge.[71] Nevertheless, the work of Otlet and Lafontaine and the unprecedented dialogue between European and American archivists and other information and heritage professionals presaged the development since the 1990s of the ever-growing, constantly evolving universe of metadata standards, as well as of multicontent and transdisciplinary digital libraries and archives.

The global potential of this development is only really now starting to become a reality, made both possible and necessary by developments in information technologies and fueled by a renewed desire in light of those technologies to integrate the world's knowledge. However, the archival field can learn some valuable lessons from the experiences of the first half of the twentieth century. The first is never to lose sight of the importance of identifying and pursuing a grand vision. It is very easy to become bogged down in technological and implementation details, processing backlogs and policy wrangling, but, at the end of the day, archivists should seek to contribute more to the world than simply trying to stay afloat in a sea of change. The second is to acknowledge the power of individual initiative and leadership in catalyzing change and, as individuals, to be prepared to exercise both when and where necessary. At the same time, however, archivists should always be cognizant of the sociopolitical context that shapes their approach to initiative and leadership. The third is to be sure that support for a vision or initiative is also nurtured at the ground level and that new ideas are not in danger of being regarded as too top-down or abstracted from application—otherwise they might not survive changes in leadership or in political or economic climate. The fourth is never to underestimate the relevance of international engagement—narrow institutional and national foci limit the innovation and problem-solving capacity of the archival field, as well as its awareness of cultural differences and key issues that traverse institutional, sector, and national boundaries. The fifth, building upon this, is to maintain an awareness that internationalization should not necessarily mean homogenization. It is easy to lose sight of the intellectual lineage of one's own practices, or of the cultural biases within practices that one exports elsewhere, as well as to lose important nuances in local applications through the desire to conform to wider standards. Finally, while conceptual understandings, tools, and practices appropriate to an archivist's professional role and mission are important, too much emphasis on professional differentiation and distinctiveness can make it difficult to work across professional divides to devise the most effective solutions to common problems and to work toward integration of the world's knowledge.

Notes

A version of this paper was presented at the seventy-fifth anniversary conference of the Society of American Archivists, August 2011.

[1] Waldo Gifford Leland (typescript), "Some Fundamental Principles in Relation to Archives," 1 (subsequently published in the American Historical Association's *Annual Report*, 1912, 214–88). Leland, Waldo Gifford, Papers of, 1879–1966, MSS 29900, Library of Congress Manuscript Division.

[2] Leland later went on to an illustrious career that included chairing a committee of the International Congress of Historical Sciences (ICHS) that led to the formation in 1926 of the International Committee of Historical Sciences, for which Leland served first as treasurer and, in 1938, as president. During the same period, he also served as president of the International Union of Academies. He served as president of the Society of American Archivists and was also instrumental in the founding of the National Historical Publications and Records Commission in 1950. After World War II, he worked with the League of Nations and served as a delegate to the 1945 London conference that led to the establishment of the United Nations Educational, Scientific, and Cultural Organization (UNESCO) and to the 1948 UNESCO General Conference in Beirut. From 1946 to 1949, he served as vice chairman (under Milton Eisenhower) of the United States National Commission for UNESCO. See *Register to the Waldo Gifford Leland Papers, 1879–1966*, MSS 29900, Library of Congress; Walter Gifford Leland, "Some Early Recollections of an Itinerant Historian," *Proceedings of the American Antiquarian Society* (October 1951); Rodney A. Ross, "Waldo Gifford Leland: Archivist by Association," *The American Archivist* (Summer 1983): 264–76; "Waldo Gifford Leland and Preservation of Documentary Resources," *Federalist* (Summer 1986); and Peter J. Wosh, ed., Introduction, in *Waldo Gifford Leland and the Origins of the American Archival Profession* (Chicago: Society of American Archivists, 2011).

[3] The Conference of Archivists was instrumental in the founding of the U.S. National Archives in 1934 and the development, promotion, and improvement of other archives in America. It continued to meet annually until the founding of the Society of American Archivists in 1936. Many of the historians involved with the Conference of Archivists became the first staff of the National Archives, as well as early leaders of the SAA. See Frank J. Cook, "The Blessings of Providence on an Association of Archivists," *The American Archivist* 46 (Fall 1983): 374–99.

[4] Jimerson makes the point that neither Leland nor Jameson ever considered themselves to be archivists. See Randall Jimerson, "American Historians and European Archival Theory: The Collaboration of J. F. Jameson and Waldo G. Leland," *Archival Science* 6 (December 2006): 299–312.

[5] These aspects are discussed in much more detail in Jimerson, "American Historians and European Archival Theory." See also Marjorie Rabe Barritt, "Coming to America: Dutch *Archivistiek* and American Archival Practice," *Archival Issues* 18, no. 1 (1993): 43–54.

[6] J. Franklin Jameson, letter to Waldo Leland Gifford, January 15, 1903, Waldo Gifford Leland Papers.

[7] As had Arnold J. F. van Laer, archivist of the New York State Library, *Register to the Waldo Gifford Leland Papers*.

[8] *Register to the Waldo Gifford Leland Papers.*

[9] Wosh, *Waldo Gifford Leland.*

[10] "As public archives present a complete record of public acts it follows that any alienation of portions of the archives make the record incomplete, while the incorporation of extraneous matter makes the record confused. Hence the necessity of maintaining the archives and any collections of historical manuscripts that may have become public property mutually distinct and separate, physically as well as theoretically. This is one of the fundamental principles of what we may call the science or economy of archives. Yet it is a principle that has been violated constantly in America. Even the enlightened policy that directs the Library of Congress has not always observed it. Not long ago the archives of the House of Representatives were offered to the Library. Instead of accepting them as

a whole or rejecting them as a whole, the Library made what it termed a selection, that is it went through a quite inaccurate and misleading list that had been prepared in the House file room and selected a small number of bundles of papers which were supposed to be possessed[?] of unusual value. These bundles were placed with the collections of historical manuscripts in the Library; the remainder of the archives stayed in the attic of the House wing and in the metal file boxes of the file room.

Such an action not only violated the principle already set forth, but it violated another principle of archive economy, equally fundamental—that of the *respect des fonds*: this untranslatable term means simply that the records of any administrative unit have in themselves a unity that is quasi-organic. The whole is necessary for an understanding of any of its parts, and a dispersion of these parts makes each and all of them unintelligible. Thus in the preservation of archives the records of each administrative unit must be preserved together. Furthermore they must be so arranged that they reflect and make clear the processes by which they came into existence." Leland, typescript, "Some Fundamentals Principles in Relation to Archives."

[11] Of course, the position of more mainstream archives in the South was more complicated than this, including that of Mississippi, where Dunbar Rowland, one of the other American archivists/historians who attended the 1910 Brussels congress, was first state archivist. See Patricia Galloway, "Archives, Power, and History: Dunbar Rowland and the Beginning of the State Archives of Mississippi (1902–1936)," *The American Archivist* 69, no. 1 (2006): 79–116.

[12] Wosh, *Waldo Gifford Leland.*

[13] See, for example, the documentary collecting of Carter G. Woodsen, Arturo A. Schomburg, and Charles H. Wesley.

[14] J. Franklin Jameson, letter of introduction to Monsieur Fredericq, October 4, 1909. Waldo Gifford Leland Papers.

[15] The other American attendees were Gaillard Hunt, chief of the Manuscripts Division of the Library of Congress and a proponent of bibliographically based manuscript arrangement and description practices; Arnold J. F. van Laer, who had trained as an archivist in the Netherlands and had introduced the principle of provenance in the Manuscript Division of the New York State Library as early as 1899; and Dunbar Rowland, state archivist of Mississippi. Appendix: Activities of the American Historical Association, 1884–1920, Memorandum for the Committee on Policy, September 1920, *Twenty-Fifth Annual Meeting.* Waldo Leland Gifford Papers; Jimerson, "American Historians and European Archival Theory," 305.

[16] Afterward, Leland wrote home:

> One thing was very interesting—a grand *raout* [reception] given by the city in the Hôtel de Ville for the Congress and for the International Parliamentary Conference being held at the same time. The Hôtel de Ville is a magnificent old gothic building in the Grande Place—which is one of the finest and most perfect mediaeval squares in the world. Full evening dress was required—and I even wore white gloves. One entered by a big stair way—with gorgeous officials at the top who called out your name—and then you shook hands with the Burgermeister (or mayor). Then we passed into the magnificent gothic hall—where an orchestra played—and some of the best opera singers and dancers gave an entertainment. There then were refreshments served in other rooms—ices—cakes—and champagne. One wandered around through a maze of beautiful gothic rooms—with fine carved wood and frescoes.

Waldo Gifford Leland, letter from Switzerland to his wife and child, September 13, 1910. Waldo Gifford Leland Papers.

[17] Draft report to American Historical Association, Waldo Gifford Leland Papers.

[18] "Il faut tacher [sic] d'introduire un peu d'uniformité, un peu d'harmonie, dans les pratiques des traits en administration independents [sic]." ["One must endeavor to introduce a little uniformity, a little harmony, into the practices of independent administrations."] Draft of speech delivered by Leland at 1910 congress, Waldo Gifford Leland Papers.

[19] A report of the AHA from its thirty-fifth annual meeting, discussing the work of the Public Archives Commission, states that "the Commission has been able, through participation in the Congress of Archivists in Brussels and through the annual conferences of archivists which it initiated in 1909 to inculcate and encourage in this country the best methods of archive administration." Appendix: Activities of the American Historical Association, 1884–1920, Memorandum for the Committee on Policy, Waldo Gifford Leland Papers.

[20] Leland, letter to his wife and child, Waldo Gifford Leland Papers.

[21] Dunbar Rowland, "The Importance of the Concentration and Classification of National Archives" (paper presented at the 1910 Congress of Librarians and Archivists), 2, Subject Files of Solon J. Buck Relating to Archival Principles, Practices and Institutions, 1789–1956, Box 1, RG 64 Records of the United States National Archives and Records Administration, National Archives and Records Administration.

[22] Rowland, "The Importance of the Concentration and Classification of National Archives," 3.

[23] Dunbar Rowland, letter to J. Franklin Jameson, May 31, 1910, Papers of J. Franklin Jameson, Library of Congress Manuscript Division.

[24] Jan Van den Broek, "From Brussels to Beijing," in *Proceedings of the 13th International Congress on Archives (Beijing, 2–7 September 1996), Archivum: International Review on Archives* 43 (Munich: K.G. Saur, 1997): 33.

[25] In 1946, Solon Buck noted in a report prepared by the U.S. National Archives that "the first and only international Congress of Archivists and Librarians was held in Brussels in 1910, Dr. Waldo G. Leland, who attended, has stated that the Congress 'permanently influenced archival conceptions and practices in the United States.' It had a comparable influence in many other countries and its papers and discussions, printed in a volume of over 200 pages, are still recommended reading for students of archival administration." *A Proposed Archives Program for the United Nations Educational, Scientific, and Cultural Organization*, September 1946, 1–2. Ernst Posner Papers, Box 4, U.S. National Archives and Records Administration.

[26] John Ridener, *From Polders to Postmodernism: A Concise History of Archival Theory* (Duluth, Minn.: Litwin Books, 2009), 23.

[27] Cook, "What Is Past Is Prologue" (see chapter 2, note 24).

[28] For example, in 1588, Philip II of Spain published the *Instrucción para el gobierno del Archivo de Simancas* (*Instructions for Governing the Archives of the Simancas*) that applied the principle of provenance to the organization of title deeds, or *escrituras*. In 1790, Carlos IV of Spain introduced *Ordinances* governing the handling of the recently created and cosmographically motivated *Archivo General de Indias* (*General Archive of the Indies*) in Seville and proposing that the General Archive be maintained according to its original order. In 1794, shortly after the French Revolution, François Guizot, French minister of public instruction, issued regulations regarding the principle of *respect pour le fonds*. The principle stated that records should be grouped according to the nature of the institution that accumulated them and was to be applied to the records of the *départements* in the Archives Nationales. Heinrich von Sybel's 1881 *Regulative für die Ordnunsarbeiten im Geheimen Staatsarchiv* in Prussia further articulated the principle of provenance, or *Provienzprinzip*.

[29] See Michael Buckland, "The Centenary of 'Madame Documentation': Suzanne Briet, 1894–1989," *Journal of the American Society for Information Science* 46, no. 3 (1995): 235–37; Mary Niles Maack, "The Lady and the Antelope: Suzanne Briet's Contribution to the French Documentation Movement," *Library Trends* 53 (Spring 2004): 719–47; and Ronald E. Day, *The Modern Invention of Information: Discourse, History, and Power* (Carbondale: South Illinois University Press, 2008).

[30] Warden Boyd Rayward, "The International Federation for Information and Documentation," in *Encyclopedia of Library History*, ed. Wayne Wiegand and Don G. Davis (New York: Garland Press, 1994), 290–94.

[31] Historians of science Pyenson and Verbruggen write that "the foundations for the Committee on Intellectual Cooperation (the forerunner of UNESCO) were laid in antebellum Brussels. Otlet and Lafontaine formed what has been called a transnational advocacy network." Lewis Pyenson and Christophe Verbruggen, "Ego and the International: The Modernist Circle of George Sarton," *Isis* 100 (2009): 60.

[32] Rayward, "The International Federation for Information and Documentation." Irene S. Farkas-Conn, *From Documentation to Information Science* (New York: Greenwood Press, 1990).

[33] For example, Gabriel Richou, *Treatise on Archival Theory and Practice* (Paris, 1883); Charles-Victor Langlois, *The Science of Archives* (Paris, 1895); Franz von Löher, *Archivlehre, Principles on the History, Functions and Establishment of Our Archives* (Germany, 1890); and Eduard Heydenreich, *Archival System and Historical Science* (Germany, 1899).

[34] "In 1910 a manual for the use of the classification for the organisation of administrative papers and archival material was issued, a subject which Otlet had become much interested in nine years before." Warden Boyd Rayward, "Paul Otlet, Internationalist and Bibliographer" (PhD diss., University of Chicago, June 1973), 136.

[35] Rayward, "Paul Otlet," 302–3.

[36] Some of the same ideas about administrative documentation as those of the documentalists are evident in the early work of Philip Brooks, who was one of the pioneers of appraisal practices in the early days of the U.S. National Archives. Seemingly unaware of the documentalist ideas, however, or at least not connecting them to his own about appraisal, he writes in 1940 that "continuous attention to the problem of selection from beginning to end of the life history of given bodies has not to my knowledge previously been expounded at length. It has, however, been suggested in a few of the writings dealing with the reduction of records, most of which have been in the field of business." See Philip Brooks, "The Selection of Records for Preservation," *The American Archivist* 3 (October 1940): 221–34. Again in 1943, he wrote: "The whole life history of records is an integrated continuous entity. No period in that history can be ignored." See Philip Brooks, "Current Aspects of Records Administration: The Archivist's Concern in Records Administration," *The American Archivist* 6 (July 1943): 164. The writings of records continuum exponents such as Frank Upward and Sue McKemmish do not reference the work of the documentalists, so it is unclear as to whether they were in any way influenced by them.

[37] Rayward, "Paul Otlet," 302–3. Following up on these resolutions, the IIB published *Le Manuel de l'administration. Receuil de principes, régles et recommandations pour l'organisation des bureaux, des secrétariats et des archives, élaboré en coopération par l'Association Internationale de Comptabilité de Belgique [The Handbook of Administration. A collection of principles, rules and recommendations for the organization of the offices, secretariats and records, elaborated in cooperation with the International Accounting Association of Belgium]*, publication no. 119 (Brussels: IIB, 1911).

[38] Rayward, "Paul Otlet," 326.

[39] Rayward, "Paul Otlet," 326.

[40] Buckland, "The Centenary of 'Madame Documentation.'"

[41] Waldo Gifford Leland, letter to Paul Otley [*sic*], January 30, 1925, Waldo Gifford Leland Papers.

[42] *"Il y a maintenant le plus grand intérêt à voir se dessiner une énergique intervention des américains, les coopérateurs par excellence et les hommes qui aiment à travailler à des grandes choses. Leur esprit est bien necessaire en Europe. Ils peuvent, par leur intervention mettre fin à d'infinies querelles des personne et institutions qu'expliquent sans les excuser un longue passé historique: lutte entre les Associations libres, les Académies, les organisms gouvernementaux, les personnalités tout entiéres engages dans les formes anciennes de l'individualisme intransigeant. Les américains peuvent aussi convaincre ici les esprits qui s'agit de faire oeuvre mondiale il faut travailler non pas à l'échelle de petits organizations européennes trop souvent étriquées, mesquines et pauvres mais à l'échelle des plus grands établissements et des plus grandes oeuvres qu'ont realize notamment les Etats-Unis. Ce sont là deux aspects de l'intervention américaine à mettre en lumière. Ils sont plus importants encore*

que celui des aides matérielles. Europe aussi est riche, riches en nature, riche en hommes, mais elle ne sait pas employer ses grandes richesses. En une certaine manière elle a besoin d'être 'colonisée' mais la colonization ne saurait être qu'internationale (!) et dans cette internationalization-là, toute intellectualle et organisatrice, les Etats-Unis, toute l'Amérique aussi ont une haute mission à remplir." ["There is now the greatest interest in seeing an energetic American intervention taking shape, cooperators par excellence and men who like to work on great things. Their spirit is quite necessary in Europe. They can, by their intervention, put an end to endless quarrels among persons and institutions which are explained, but not excused by, a long historical past: struggle between the independent Associations, the Academies, government agencies, personalities that all together engage in the old forms of intransigent individualism. Americans can also convince the spirits here who seek to create something global, that it is necessary not to work on the scale of small European organizations that too often skimp, are petty and poor, but on the scale of the greatest establishments and works that have notably been realized within the United States. There are two aspects of the American intervention to clarify that are more important still than that of the material aid. Europe also is rich, rich by nature, rich in men, but it cannot employ its great riches. In a certain manner it needs to be 'colonized' but the colonization could be only international (!) and in that internationalization, intellectual and organizational, the United States, all America also have a high mission to fill." Paul Otlet, letter to Waldo Gifford Leland, February 7, 1925, Waldo Gifford Leland Papers.

[43] Appendix: Activities of the American Historical Association, 1884-1920, Memorandum for the Committee on Policy, September 1920, Twenty-Fifth Annual Meeting, Waldo Gifford Leland Papers.

[44] The major U.S. professional associations in the archives, library, and museum fields all include discussions of their twentieth-century development on their websites. The establishment of the American Documentary Institute, which was eventually to become the American Society for Information Science and Technology, is an excellent example of these trends.

[45] *A Proposed Archives Program for the United Nations Educational, Scientific, and Cultural Organization,* 1-2; Records of the National Archives and Records Administration, 1789-ca. 2007.

[46] *A Proposed Archives Program for the United Nations Educational, Scientific, and Cultural Organization,* 1-2.

[47] "Its activities and interests will presumably, in some way, have to be tied into those of the United National Educational, Scientific and Cultural Organization unless it is to continue in competition in many fields of common interest. . . . All of these organizations are an expression of the rising interests and needs of archivists before the last war for close international collaboration. The war itself has given rise to additional needs for common effort, some of them critical indeed, and the movement for closer cultural cooperation in the interests of permanent peace brings forth still other considerations that are pertinent to that goal." *A Proposed Archives Program for the United Nations Educational, Scientific, and Cultural Organization,* 2-4.

[48] Waldo Gifford Leland, report on the Conference to the ACLS, November 27, 1946, Waldo Gifford Leland Papers.

[49] Solon J. Buck, statement to R. D. W. Connors, June 1, 1938, regarding Representation of the National Archives to the ADI, Box 12, Papers of Solon J. Buck.

[50] Historical note, finding aid for Record Unit 7091 Science Service, Records, 1902-1965, Smithsonian Institution Archives, http://siarchives.si.edu/findingaids/faru7091.htm; Claire K. Schultz and Paul L. Garwig, "History of the American Documentation Institute—A Sketch," *American Documentation* 20 (April 1969): 152-60. Peter Hirtle, in his article on Atherton Seidell, also discusses the history of the Bibliofilm Service and states that it was created at the Agriculture Library and then turned over to Science Service a year later. However, it would appear that Davis was also involved in its initial creation. See Peter B. Hirtle, "Atherton Seidell and the Photoduplication of Library Material," *Journal of the American Society for Information Science* 40 (1989): 427.

[51] Edwin Emory Slosson and Watson Davis, "Plan for Film Record Prepared by Science Service," *Science Service Document,* no. 1 (June 5, 1926).

[52] Watson Davis, *Science News Letter* (October 9, 1937), 230.

[53] Watson Davis, *Science Service Document*, no. 45 (Documentation Institute of Science Service, July 11, 1935).

[54] Buck to Connors, June 1, 1938.

[55] Buck to Connors, June 1, 1938.

[56] Michael Buckland, correspondence with the author, August 2012. See also Michael K. Buckland, "Emanuel Goldberg, Electronic Document Retrieval, and Vannevar Bush's Memex," *Journal of the American Society for Information Science* 43 (May 1992): 284–94.

[57] Buckland, correspondence with the author.

[58] American Documentation Institute, *ADI Reports–Technical Reports and Standards*, Library of Congress Science Reference Services, http://www.loc.gov/rr/scitech/trs/trsadi.html.

[59] Steuart Henderson Britt, "The Psychologist and the American Documentation Institute," *American Psychologist* (March 2, 1949): 180.

[60] Henry Dubester, "The Role of the American Documentation Institute in International Documentation," *American Documentation* (January 1962): 115–17.

[61] Helen L. Chatfield, review of *American Documentation*, *The American Archivist* 14, no. 2 (April 1951): 163.

[62] Chatfield, "Review," 165.

[63] Chatfield, "Review," 165.

[64] Farkas-Conn, *From Documentation to Information Science.*

[65] Nicholas Burckel, review essay, *A History of the Farmington Plan*, by Ralph D. Wagner, *The American Archivist* 66 (Spring/Summer 2003), http://www.archivists.org/periodicals/aa_v66/review-burckel-aa66_1.asp.

[66] See, for example, the Digital Archives Specialist (DAS) Curriculum and Certificate Program offered since 2011 by the Society of American Archivists, http://www2.archivists.org/prof-education/das.

[67] See Kelvin White and Anne Gilliland, "Promoting Reflexivity and Inclusivity in Archival Education, Research and Practice," *Library Quarterly* 80 (July 2010): 231–48.

[68] Schultz and Garwig, "History of the American Documentation Institute," 154.

[69] Watson Davis, address delivered during the Annual Meeting of the American Documentation Institute, Hollywood, Florida, December 12, 1962. Quoted in Schultz and Garwig, "History of the American Documentation Institute," 154.

[70] Archival historian Rand Jimerson has argued that American exceptionalism—beliefs that America is in some way qualitatively different from, or even above or beyond the concerns, issues, and needs of, other countries—may also have played a role in the U.S. withdrawal from these forums. Jimerson, "American Historians and European Archival Theory."

[71] Bush felt that men of science, especially physicists, should be deployed in peacetime to make more accessible "our bewildering store of knowledge." He wrote, "A record, if it is to be useful to science, must be continuously extended, it must be stored, and above all it must be consulted. Today we make the record conventionally by writing and photography, followed by printing; but we also record on film, on wax disks, and on magnetic wires. Even if utterly new recording procedures do not appear, these present ones are certainly in the process of modification and extension." In "Mechanization and the Record," Papers of Vannevar Bush, 1901–1974, MSS 14498, Library of Congress Manuscript Division, Box 138. Leland had corresponded with Bush in 1939 (Box 65), http://hdl.loc.gov/loc.mss/eadmss.ms998004.

CHAPTER 4

∞

Standardizing and Automating American Archival Description and Access

This chapter traces the evolution of American archival description in the twentieth century from idiosyncratic, manual, collective, and institutionally defined, to standardized, collective and item-level, automated, and increasingly internationalized practices. As with the progressive development of bibliographic cataloging standards, changes in information and media technologies have both driven and facilitated this evolution. These practices and technologies have also enabled the integration of descriptions of archival resources with those created by other information and heritage fields within digital libraries and digital repositories and across the Web.

The AMC format has the potential both to support successful automation of archival control and to transform the bibliographic utilities as we know them today. Specifically, AMC overthrows the bibliocentrism, the political hegemony, and the existing financial/functional underpinnings of the bibliographic networks. It opens the way to multimedia cultural information systems and new local/national systems architectures. As a consequence, archivists are likely to play a critical role in redesigning library information networks in the decades to come.

—David Bearman, "Archives and Manuscript Control with
Bibliographic Utilities: Challenges and Opportunities," 1989.[1]

Introduction

Many models of the nature and functions of knowledge, information, and recordkeeping have been proposed in the modern era, and from many different perspectives, including cosmographical, scientific, documentary, bibliographic, philosophical, and procedural. Inevitably, however, even though any one of them might have been considered the ideal or most effective model when proposed or adopted, over time, each is challenged, revised, and eventually superseded as information and recordkeeping landscapes and intellectual currents shift. It should not be surprising, therefore, that the history of standardizing and automating professional practices for description and access to information involves a succession of approaches and accelerating turnovers in the models being applied (see Figure 4.1). For the uninitiated, this process can easily congeal into a kind of acronym soup that fails to convey the major ideas and shifts underpinning each development. It can be very confusing for practitioners trying to stay on top of changes in their own field and even for seasoned experts who increasingly are devising ways to bring together or to map between the practices and worldviews of multiple fields.

The Impact of the Public Archives and Historical Manuscripts Traditions on Early American Archival Description

In December 1935, the newly established U.S. National Archives was working to identify the practices, including descriptive practices, that it would implement in the management of its holdings. Waldo Gifford Leland responded to a request from Solon J. Buck for comments on archival descriptive nomenclature. Leland advised that the National Archives should develop its principles in accord with the archival approaches to which he had been introduced in Europe and which he had promoted through the American Historical Association, rather than those that libraries and historical manuscript repositories such as the Library of Congress employed:

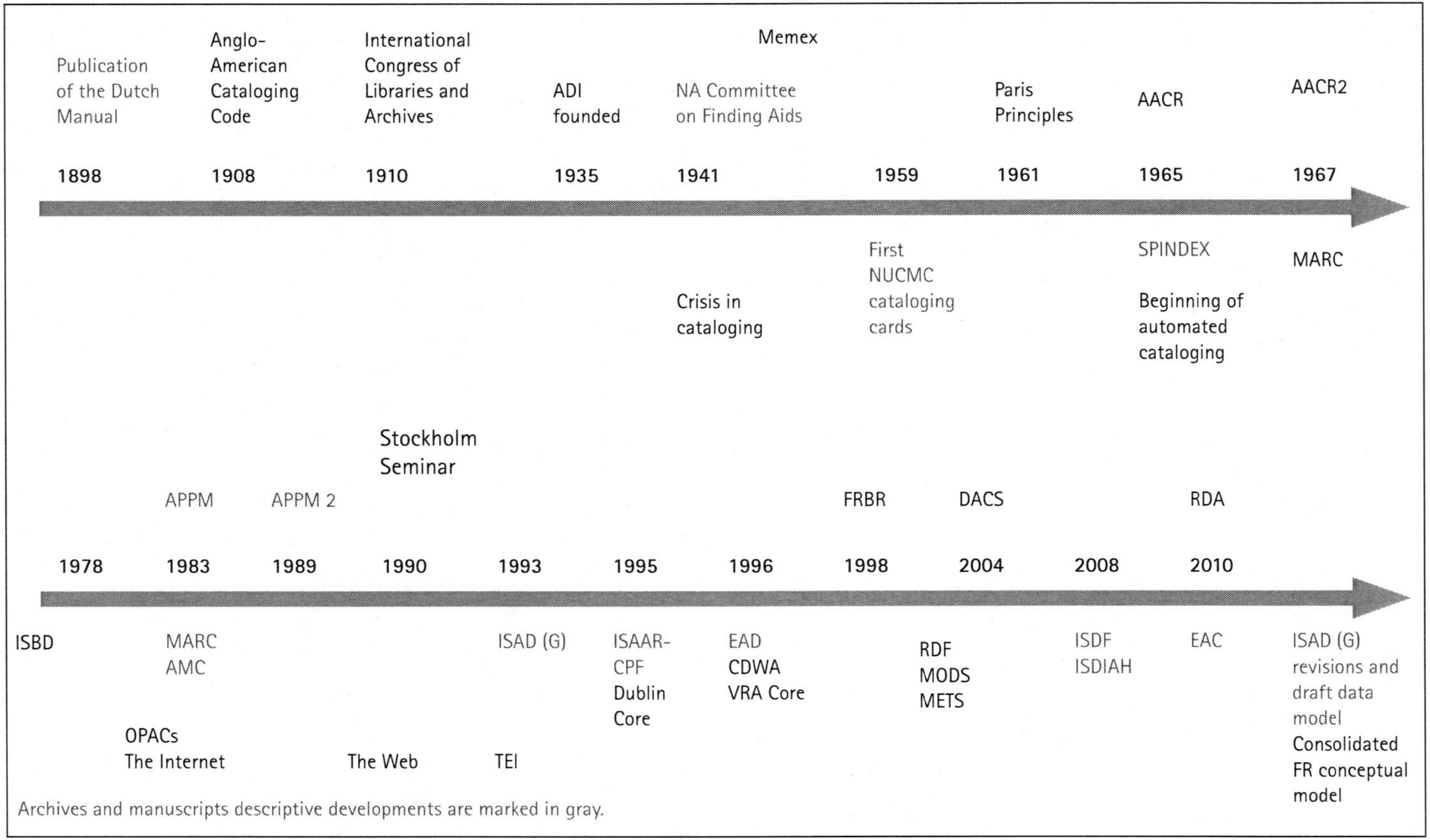

Figure 4.1 — Timeline of developments in American archival and bibliographic description

Upper timeline

1898	1908	1910	1935	1941	1959	1961	1965	1967
Publication of the Dutch Manual	Anglo-American Cataloging Code	International Congress of Libraries and Archives	ADI founded	NA Committee on Finding Aids	First NUCMC cataloging cards	Paris Principles	AACR	AACR2
							SPINDEX; Beginning of automated cataloging	MARC

Memex

Crisis in cataloging

Lower timeline

1978	1983	1989	1990	1993	1995	1996	1998	2004	2008	2010
	APPM	APPM 2	Stockholm Seminar				FRBR	DACS		RDA
ISBD	MARC AMC			ISAD (G)	ISAAR-CPF; Dublin Core	EAD; CDWA; VRA Core	RDF; MODS; METS		ISDF; ISDIAH	EAC; ISAD (G) revisions and draft data model; Consolidated FR conceptual model
OPACs; The Internet			The Web	TEI						

Archives and manuscripts descriptive developments are marked in gray.

Figure 4.1. Timeline of developments in American archival and bibliographic description‡

‡ Adapted with permission from a timeline developed by Luiz Mendes.

At this point, let me urge that it is important to get away from library methods and practice. Archives are entirely different from books, and it would be a real misfortune if the National Archives should endeavor to incorporate library principles, practices, and notions in its procedure.[2]

He continues later in the same letter:

As to a dictionary card catalogue, I confess that I am skeptical. It seems too much like a library device, but simply because I do not quite see how it would work out does not mean that I should be prepared to condemn it. Certainly there must be developed all sorts of devices and contrivances for getting at what is in the archives.[3]

Although European and American archivists participated in discussions with the documentalists about integrating archival materials and descriptions with those of other fields, early twentieth-century European archivists were adamant about the differences between archival and library roles and materials that made bibliographic approaches unacceptable for archival description. These included, from the archival perspective, the prioritization of provenance; collective rather than item-level description; and the importance of capturing, in collection-level description, the context and structure as well as the content of the archival materials. In the succeeding decades, American archives, as well as those around the globe, steadily implemented the approaches to archival arrangement and description delineated in Muller, Feith, and Fruin's *Manual for the Arrangement and Description of Archives*.[4] However, the *Manual*'s relatively heuristic approach remained a long way from the standardization and codification of descriptive "devices and contrivances," which, by the 1980s, had clearly become necessary for the exchange of mutually understandable and detailed descriptive information between repositories. Today these include nationally and internationally adopted descriptive data models, data content rules, authority files, and metadata crosswalks.

For sixty years after Buck and Leland's correspondence, archival description in the United States swung between approaches centered around bibliographic-type catalog records and archival finding aids and finally arrived at a hybrid approach. Differences in emphasis and professional identity between the pre-existing public archives and historical manuscripts traditions that had developed in the vacuum created by the absence of a national archives partly caused this. In addition, the young National Archives, particularly through the work of its Committee on Finding Aids established in 1941, was focused on developing descriptive approaches that would assist it specifically with pressing concerns regarding the management of the federal record rather than promoting a single national approach for all American archives. This work would develop the concept of the record group that the National Archives subsequently employed as a principle organizing concept in place of the European concept of the *fonds*.[5]

At the time, the Library of Congress Manuscript Division was a major proponent of extending bibliographic approaches beyond historical manuscripts to archives. A 1947 report by the American Historical Association Special Committee on Manuscripts recommended that such a register be started. The committee was succeeded in 1949 by the Joint Committee on Manuscripts formed by the Society of American Archivists (SAA) and the American Association for State and Local History (AASLH), which proposed that the register be created as part of the *National Union Catalog* (*NUC*) and would include cataloging manuscripts and selling printed catalog cards. In 1958, the Council on Library Resources gave the Library of Congress a grant to initiate the *National Union Catalog of Manuscript Collections* (*NUCMC*). The Library of Congress printed its first catalog cards in 1959 and the first volume in 1962. From 1964 onward, the U.S. Congress appropriated funding to support *NUCMC*. In the 1980s, the Library of Congress assumed a leadership role in the development and maintenance of the MARC (MAchine-Readable Coding) Archival and Manuscripts Control (AMC) format, and *NUCMC* became an early implementer when it moved from the superseded MARC manuscripts format to the AMC format and began automated cataloging in the Research Libraries Information Network (RLIN).[6] The Library of Congress continued in the role of maintenance agency after Encoded Archival Description was developed in the early 1990s. As a result, the history of the development of standardized archival description in the United States is not directly comparable to the history of archival description elsewhere, and it needs to include a discussion of its interaction with the history of bibliographic description.

The Evolution of Bibliographic Description in the Twentieth Century

Both the American and United Kingdom Library Associations began work on standardized cataloging rules in the last decades of the nineteenth century, and, by 1902, the Library of Congress had published an advance edition of the revised *ALA* (American Library Association) *Rules*. These rules were factored into the (U.K.) *Library Association Cataloging Rules* being revised in the same year. In 1904, at Melvil Dewey's suggestion, the two associations agreed to cooperate on developing a single set of rules, and, by 1908, American and British editions of the first international cataloging code were published. In the 1940s, in the first example of how emerging technologies and media would begin to force ongoing reassessment of descriptive standards, these rules had to be modified to accommodate the cataloging of diverse forms of audiovisual media. This issue was similar to the one appraisal archivists faced at the National Archives as they tried to come up with ways to understand the potential archival nature and value of these media, as discussed in chapter 3. Although American and Anglo traditions diverged following World War II, they were reconciled following the 1961 International Conference on Cataloguing in Paris. The discussions at that conference, attended by European, North American, and Australian cataloging specialists, resulted in a statement of twelve principles known as the Paris Principles. The Paris Principles subsequently formed the basis of *Anglo-American Cataloguing Rules* (*AACR*), published in both the United States and the United Kingdom in 1967.[7] With these rules in place, the library field was well positioned to take advantage of developments in computing and to begin to automate its cataloging processes and to share cataloging data.

Developments in standardizing and automating cataloging from this point on were highly symbiotic. The Library of Congress had been investigating the feasibility of automating its library systems for several years by that time, with the help of a grant awarded by the Council on Library Resources in 1963. Following its own studies and a conference on the topic in 1965, the Library of Congress funded sixteen libraries of various types in an eight-month pilot project to convert card catalog records to machine-readable format. Before the project could commence, the MARC I format needed to be stabilized, but by September 1966, the first test datatape containing machine-readable cataloging records was mailed out to the pilot project participants. By mid-1968, after the addition of four more libraries to the pilot project, the Library of Congress had distributed over fifty thousand MARC format records. By March 1969, MARC was fully operational and weekly datatapes were mailed out to libraries containing approximately a thousand records. In the following three years, the Library of Congress ran projects promoting retrospective conversion of manual cataloging systems. The *Anglo-American Cataloguing Rules, Second Edition* (*AACR2*) was published in 1978, and, in 1981, the Library of Congress, the National Library of Canada, the British Library, and the Australian National Library adopted it. The development of bibliographic cataloging standards continued to respond to changes in media and technology, implementing, for example, a MARC format for computer files that subsequently was revised as a more inclusive format for describing electronic resources. Eventually, in 1997, all the special formats and Canadian and U.S. MARC were harmonized into a single version of MARC—MARC 21.

In 1995, a new, simpler, and less tightly controlled metadata scheme was proposed, in the form of Dublin Core. It was initially conceived as a metadata scheme with only fifteen broad and generic (and initially unstandardized) elements that could be applied to a wide range of resources, including Web resources, although over time these were extended in all sorts of ways. The vision was that Dublin Core could be created not only by catalogers, but also by creators, digitizers, and "lay" metadata creators, thus beginning a movement to distribute more broadly responsibility for metadata creation and to pluralize the kinds of descriptions being created. Presaging more recent arguments about the value of social tagging for enhancing descriptions of information, Dublin Core raised considerable debate in the information professions about the value and utility of nonstandardized metadata not created by information professionals. Today the Dublin Core element set persists, but the Dublin Core impetus has really developed into a framework and a community for metadata innovation on the Web. Other metadata schemes less extensive than MARC emerged that operated at different levels of granularity and specialization and that could be used in conjunction with other schemes, including the Metadata Encoding and Transmission Standards (METS) and the Metadata Object Description Schema (MODS). These kinds of schemes could be used to describe and support retrieval and collation of diverse and distributed Web resources. For archivists, who were accustomed to collective description, they became essential to ensure item-level description of digitized holdings.

From this progression and divergence in the development of metadata schemes, librarians learned to view their cataloging procedures, and the software systems and bibliographic networks they were using, as in a constant state of evolution. Information and communication technologies, metadata standards, and user expectations and practices continuously and symbiotically evolved and diversified. They learned that driving, anticipating, and simply staying on top of so much change requires initiative and flexibility, forward planning, funding for new technology mechanisms and conversion of existing metadata, new forms of education and training for library staff, and, overall, a level of comfort in the knowledge that cataloging practices and library and information technologies will likely always be dynamic. Archivists must now learn to live with the same reality.

Barriers to the Development of Standardized Automated Archival Description in the Twentieth Century

The stories of the development of standardized automated archival description and access differ, sometimes quite considerably, by country. This section will briefly gloss the case of the United States as an exemplar of the kinds of issues that came into play in the course of these developments. The American archival field was slower coming to standardized automated description than was librarianship, which quickly realized the potential benefits to every library of sharing standardized cataloging data in terms of achieving consistent descriptions, making workflow more efficient and less redundant, and reducing the costs of original cataloging of items at individual libraries for which the Library of Congress or another participating library had already prepared a MARC catalog record. The archival field did not have the same kinds of incentives to automate or to standardize description. Because the majority of holdings of most archives are unique, archives could not take advantage of copy cataloging and thereby reduce the costs or workload involved in processing their holdings. Philosophically, not all archivists were convinced it would be possible to devise a descriptive scheme that could accommodate the range of materials found across diverse types of archives and manuscript repositories, or indeed to develop rules that would govern how descriptive information should be formed in the absence of the kind of imprint and other definitive information used in library cataloging. Individual archives still functioned largely as stand-alone repositories, rather than within the systems, consortia, networks, and other collaborative entities that libraries had formed to support interlibrary loan, collection development, public library services, medical information provision, and so forth, and, although it might seem strange and insular today, many archivists were also skeptical about the value of interrepository information sharing of the kind that MARC facilitated in libraries.

Several other factors delayed both the standardization and the automation of archival description. Archives started from a place of less strength than did libraries, lacking any tradition of standardized descriptive practices or even a robust consensus statement such as the Paris Principles around which to build such practices (the *Dutch Manual* being the closest such enunciation). The arrangement and descriptive practices of individual archival and historical manuscript repositories, while they usually adhered to the principle of provenance, were often idiosyncratic and inconsistent in quality and conceptualization. Archivists were still predominantly trained as historians and entered the field with little conceptual knowledge or practical experience in information organization (i.e., the principles and structures underlying the description and retrieval of information). They were working without an overall conceptual framework for recordkeeping, often in small and midsized archives not resourced to support computerized developments and specialized descriptive expertise. The archival field, as discussed in chapter 3, was not as closely involved as was the library field with the information scientists who were beginning to develop online retrieval systems, and in the decades following World War II, the National Archives did not play the same kind of leadership role in the national or international development of descriptive standards as did the Library of Congress for library cataloging.

Early Archival Automation and the Quest for an Archival Descriptive Standard

By the late 1960s and 1970s, several large archival institutions were implementing home-grown mainframe database systems that allowed for the creation and compilation of computerized finding aids. These mainframe systems were developed to speed up manual processing, to facilitate updating and correcting finding aids, and to generate automated indexes of keywords contained in finding aids. For many manuscript repositories that maintained dual descriptive systems—traditional library-style card catalogs, some at the item level, of manuscripts, as well as registers of collections—automation held out the promise of integrating the two systems while maintaining useful elements of both.[8] Most prominently among these mainframe systems were NARS A-1, developed by the National Archives,[9] and SPINDEX,[10] developed in 1964 by the Library of Congress and based on a prior punch-card project. It was used in conjunction with its Master Record of Manuscript Collections (MRMC) for administrative and intellectual control over manuscript holdings. In 1967, the National Archives developed SPINDEX II, more tailored to the descriptive needs of records. In addition to generating finding aids for accumulations of records, SPINDEX II could be used for records management applications. The National Archives also employed SPINDEX II to create the first edition of the National Historical Publications and Records Commission's *Directory of Archives and Manuscript Repositories*. The archives subsequently created a modified version, SPINDEX III, to support the development of a national database of information on archives and manuscripts in the United States.[11] When the National Archives made SPINDEX II available to other repositories, the Smithsonian and several state and university archives as well as corporate records management programs in the United States, Canada, and Australia implemented it.

Noting this growing use of SPINDEX, the Society of American Archivists (SAA) became interested in developing uniform software that could be implemented in different archives to automate descriptions of their holdings and distribute them in electronic form, but as Lewis Bellardo argued in 1981, "At this time the obstacle to interactive archival systems is not SPINDEX, but a lack of standardization in the archival profession, a lack of focused demand among archivists and librarians, and the lack of a cooperative institutional thrust to bring an interactive on-line network into existence."[12] SAA's interest, however, was the impetus for a discussion on standardizing descriptive practices that eventually culminated in the development and adoption, in 1984, of the MARC AMC format as the first American standard for archival description. The SAA Committee on Automated Techniques for Archival Agencies, chaired by Frank Burke from the National Archives, had begun a decade and a half earlier by looking at what kind of information should be entered into uniform software. In 1969, Burke proposed focusing on standardizing institutional codes and descriptive elements. According to Thomas Elton Brown,

> Specifically, he proposed . . . the development of common codes to identify repositories, standards for data notation, consensus on the measurement of records, and accepted definitions on units of description. From this proposal, the committee agreed . . . it would study three areas in detail: establishment of code symbols for repositories, adoption of a glossary of terms to be used in finding aids, and establishment of minimum feasible standards for the format and content of finding aids.[13]

Following this agreement, the committee was renamed Committee on Techniques for the Control and Description of Archives and Manuscripts (COTCADAM), and David C. Maslyn became chair. To carry out this study, the committee reviewed basic elements of description recommended in the professional literature. It then looked at 204 finding aids that had been collected from government, private, and religious archives in the United States and Canada to see how many of these elements were represented within the finding aids. It found that fewer than half of the finding aids contained all of the basic elements, which led the committee in 1971 to recommend that it write standards for each of these elements. Over a two-month period in early 1972, individual committee members worked on different aspects of the proposed standards, which Frank Burke then compiled and edited into *Draft Standards for the Preparation of Registers and Inventories* and submitted to SAA Council for discussion. Council in turn decided that the draft should be refined and submitted to the Editorial Board for possible publication as a handbook of best descriptive practices (published in 1976 under the title *Inventories and Guides: A Handbook of Techniques and Examples*). At the same 1974 meeting, SAA Council approved a proposal to change the name of COTCADAM to the Committee on Finding Aids, an action that was, in Brown's words, "a final note to this evolution from automated retrieval systems to a manual on description."[14] David B. Gracy II took over as chair of the renamed committee and further developed this work into one of SAA's first volumes in its Basic Manual Series, *Archives and Manuscripts: Arrangement and Description.*[15]

Development of the MARC Archival and Manuscripts Control Format

In 1977, SAA formed the National Information Systems Task Force (NISTF), staffed by David Bearman (who became one of the most influential and visionary figures in advancing what came to be termed "archival and museum informatics"), to investigate the development of software that could support the automation of American archival description. By the early 1980s, however, NISTF began to realize that a standardized descriptive format would be more effective in rationalizing idiosyncratic archival practices than would common use of the same software. SAA entered into negotiations with the library community about developing a MARC format tailored to the needs of archivists and based around the *NISTF Data Elements Dictionary*. The *Data Elements Dictionary* was generated from responses to a wide-ranging survey of archival repositories conducted by Elaine Engst about which descriptive data elements they included in their finding aids. Engst found that even though different repositories called them different things, about twenty similar data elements were in common use across the surveyed repositories. This finding demonstrated the existence of sufficient commonality among archival and manuscript practices to make a common standard a possibility.[16] According to SAA,

> NISTF's efforts diverged from those of the earlier Finding Aids Committee, however, in that NISTF did not limit itself to defining the data elements contained in finding aids alone. Instead it sought to identify all elements of information collected or used

by archivists in any aspect of their work. In this sense it was truly grounded in the process of systems analysis and took the earlier concepts of a system of finding aids to its logical extension in an archival information system covering the operations of the entire repository.[17]

The resulting development of the AMC format attempted to reconcile archival and bibliographic description practices and superseded the previous MARC manuscripts format, which was seen to be too bibliographic in approach and which had never been designed to accommodate descriptions of records. Because the rules contained in chapter 4 of *AACR2* did not provide sufficient detail on how MARC AMC fields should be completed by archivists, Steven Hensen, an archival cataloger with the Library of Congress's Manuscripts Division, was commissioned to write *Archives, Personal Papers and Manuscripts* (*APPM*) to provide additional rules, for example, on creating titles for archival collections, describing creators, and forming names.[18]

SAA formally adopted MARC AMC as a descriptive standard in 1983, and the Library of Congress agreed to take on the role of maintenance agency.[19] This adoption led to efforts to develop union databases of archival descriptive records such as the RLIN archival subsystem[20] and MARC-based and MARC-compliant microcomputer-based software (for example, MicroMARC:amc and Minaret) for use by repositories that were not members of RLIN or that lacked the resources to belong to a major bibliographic utility.[21] MARC AMC records could also be integrated into online library catalogs.

In effect, MARC facilitated the development of the first standardized, automated archival information systems. Digital or virtual archives would not begin to become a reality, however, until those automated systems were also capable of providing large volumes of digital archival content.[22]

MARC AMC was not without its detractors and holdouts, however. The detractors felt that the archival worldview had been shoehorned into a library approach, and, thereby, compromised. In particular, they felt that MARC AMC did not always include all of the information contained in a finding aid (and these remained for the most part offline) and that, as a flat data format, the MARC record at the time was unable to represent the structural relationships that exist between different aspects of a collection, especially hierarchical relationships. Added to this were the difficulties of training practicing archivists nationwide, the majority of whom had no background in bibliographic description, to perform what in essence was sophisticated original cataloging and authority work in an unfamiliar data structure and bibliographic paradigm. Institutional holdouts, such as many corporate and government archives, tended to feel that sharing information about their holdings through this format offered little benefit to them, and they simply continued to describe their collections as they had in the past.

Development of an International Archival Descriptive Standard

In the 1990s, several events transpired to change approaches yet again both to automating and standardizing archival description. In 1990, the Canadian archival profession adopted the *Rules for Archival Description (RAD)* (revised in 2003) developed by the Association of Canadian Archivists Planning Committee on Descriptive Standards. *RAD* supported multilevel description and was based on the framework of *AACR2R*,[23] the *International Standard Bibliographic Description (ISBD (G))* that supports international exchange of bibliographic records, and the archival principle of *respect des fonds*. It specifically addressed multiple media *fonds*, textual records, graphic materials, cartographic materials, architectural and technical drawings, moving images, sound recordings, electronic records, and records on microform. International agreement upon a set of guiding principles for archival description was reached in 1993 when a draft developed with United Nations Educational, Scientific and Cultural Organization (UNESCO) support by a subgroup of the ad hoc Commission on Descriptive Standards which had begun work in 1988 was ratified in Stockholm as the International Council on Archives' *General International Standard Archival Description (ISAD (G))*. *RAD* was particularly influential in the development of *ISAD (G)*, which was adopted in 1993, revised in 1999 (*ISAD (G)2*), and is currently undergoing another revision.

The four goals of *ISAD (G)* were to ensure creation of consistent, appropriate, and self-explanatory descriptions; to facilitate the retrieval and exchange of information and archival materials; to enable the sharing of authority data; and to make possible the integration of descriptions from different repositories into a unified information system.[24] Unlike MARC, however, *ISAD (G)*, although it delineated six different components that should be present in archival description (identity statement, context, content and structure, conditions of access and use, allied materials, and notes), did not specify an actual data structure. *ISAD (G)* was always intended to be a general (hence the "*G*") descriptive model that laid out and promoted common archival principles and data elements, and the kinds of detail found in national standards were, therefore, never incorporated. Instead, it promotes the development and implementation of more granular local standards that conform with *ISAD (G)*'s common principles and incorporate its data elements but that also take into account local needs and practices as well as cultural and linguistic contexts.[25]

Development of a "More Archival" Descriptive Standard: Encoded Archival Description

The development of Encoded Archival Description (EAD), a Standard Generalized Markup Language (SGML)–based and *ISAD (G)*–compliant data structure for archival description, grew out of the Berkeley Finding Aids Project (BFAP) led by Daniel Pitti in the mid-1990s. The development team included archivists and catalogers from both the Library of Congress and the National Archives, as well as from other kinds of institutions such as academic archives and libraries. The idea for using SGML came from Pitti, who realized that its recursive structure would provide an excellent mechanism for capturing the hierarchical relationships in finding aids and also in the collections they describe. Furthermore, the hypermedia capabilities of the World Wide Web on which the encoded finding aids were then to be distributed provided additional new opportunities to create links that mirrored other kinds of documentary interrelationships between and within archival collections.

As had been the case in previous efforts to standardize archival description, the alpha version of the data structure was derived from an analysis of exemplary finding aids provided by selected repositories of different types. The philosophy underlying this approach was that rather than trying to identify and then to develop the ideal data structure from the outset, creating a data structure closer to archives' current practices would help them buy in. It could be revised later to further tighten and enhance that description.[26] Another decision made at that time, although some experimentation was done with some examples, was not to design EAD explicitly to incorporate the descriptions of electronic records, which tended to be described using data archiving rather than archival descriptive practices. It was felt that introducing the descriptive needs of electronic records would complicate discussions. Descriptive elements have yet to be included to address some of the particular needs of electronic records, such as description of the technical context of the creation of the records, which electronic records research and practice has identified as so important to understanding the records. In contrast, a few data elements (such as those describing different aspects of physical description) were added to encourage the inclusion of artifactual materials that archives might hold, as well as the possible use of EAD to describe museum collections (as was attempted by the Museums and the Online Archive of California initiative[27]).

Several of the individuals involved in the development of EAD participated in the discussions leading to the ratification of *ISAD (G)*. EAD provided a descriptive data structure for American archivists and enabled full, hierarchical, collection-level description to be disseminated directly over the World Wide Web, thus bypassing library online catalogs and automated archival information systems. SAA adopted it as its new descriptive standard in 1996, and the Library of Congress again agreed to be the maintenance agency.[28] Developed using SGML and based around a set of principles that came to be known as the Ann Arbor Accords, the criteria used in developing EAD were that it had to be both *ISAD (G)* and XML (eXtensible Markup Language) compliant. It also had to be able to present extensive and interrelated descriptive information found in archival finding aids, to preserve the hierarchical relationships existing between levels of description, to represent descriptive information inherited by one hierarchical level from another, to move within a hierarchical informational structure, and to support element-specific indexing and retrieval.[29] The hypermedia capabilities of the Web also facilitated attaching digitized versions of selected archival holdings by linking to a filename or to metadata associated with digital content. With this capacity, automated archival information systems in the United States finally began to develop into digital archives.

EAD, when created in XML, is not only a means of publishing a finding aid online, but also of searching within and manipulating a finding aid online. When encoded in EAD, each individual finding aid resembles a mini-database of hierarchically related elements and subelements. Depending upon the software used, when included in a system that encompasses many finding aids, those encoded in EAD become part of a large database that allows for the virtual federation and cross-collection searching of geographically distributed but thematically or provenancially related collections. EAD also supports the decoupling of arrangement and description in the virtual world in a way that would have involved considerable additional effort in the physical world. A finding aid prepared in EAD, like a traditional finding aid, documents the organization and arrangement of the physical collection. However, because the description is both digital and fielded, it can be presented to the user in any number of ways, as well as abstracted, redacted, or collated with descriptions of similar materials—all without losing its original structure.[30]

Issues Arising out of EAD Implementation

EAD was well received by the American archival community and archivists in the United Kingdom and elsewhere because it automated the finding aid—the tool that they were already creating and that many believed was the one best suited to archival description. Moreover, archives could bypass bibliographic systems and expensive utilities and deliver their descriptive information directly to the public over the Web. EAD precipitated new issues, however. For one thing, XML-based software sufficiently sophisticated to fully exploit the latent power of the EAD data structure was not available, and there was doubt about whether an adequate archival market existed to encourage and sustain commercial development of specialized software. As well, archives that had invested in MARC and oriented their workflow around it were left with a decision to make—to continue creating MARC records, either in addition to or instead of EAD finding aids; to stop creating MARC records and create only EAD finding aids; or to create EAD finding aids but also develop the capability to automatically derive a MARC record out of each EAD instance. In many cases, these considerations arose because archives implementing MARC AMC were units of academic libraries of major research collections, and their MARC records would be integrated into the wider library catalog. In terms of workflow, a double effort might be involved in that either processing archivists developed finding aids and then derived MARC records from the descriptions contained in them, or a specialized archival or library cataloger working separately from the processors executed the latter responsibility. EAD allowed for automated description to be created in a single process, but since all the elements contained in MARC were also integrated into EAD, it was technically possible to generate a MARC record automatically out of an EAD finding aid. This issue gained additional traction when, in 1997, US MARC and CANMARC were harmonized to create MARC 21, the current standard.[31] In the process, some of the data elements that the AMC development group had worked so hard to include were eliminated, but could instead be captured in EAD.

EAD precipitated one other set of key discussions about standardization of description. Although it was a data structure standard, EAD faced the same problem that MARC AMC had encountered in terms of how information was to be entered into its data elements. In other words, it required *APPM*, the data content standard first written in 1983 to accompany MARC AMC, subsequently revised in 1989, and due to be reviewed as an SAA standard in the early 1990s, just as EAD was being developed. It was decided that any revision should extend to finding aids as well as to catalog records; should incorporate *ISAD (G)* and its new companion, the *International Standard Archival Authority Record for Corporate Bodies, Persons, and Families (ISAAR [CPF])*; and also might be created as a joint U.S./Canadian standard.[32] A meeting in Toronto in 1999 resulted in the Toronto Accord on Descriptive Standards, and, in 2001, the Canadian/U.S. Task Force on Archival Description (CUSTARD) began work on a content standard that would replace *APPM* as well as *RAD*. By spring 2003, it was apparent, however, that enough differences existed between U.S. and Canadian descriptive practices that a joint content standard was not, at that point, going to be possible. Instead, CUSTARD's draft document formed the basis for Canadian discussion regarding a revised version of *RAD*. On the U.S. side, the draft evolved into *Describing Archives: A Content Standard (DACS)*, published in 2004. *DACS* is the U.S. implementation of *ISAAR (CPF)* and can be used in conjunction with both EAD and MARC 21, but moves away from the more bibliographic orientation of *APPM* to "reflect a more thoroughly archival approach to description."[33] It also includes crosswalks between EAD and each of MARC, *ISAD (G)* and *ISAAR (CPF)*. Adopted in 1996, *ISAAR (CPF)* was the second descriptive standard developed by the International Council on Archives (ICA). It provides rules for developing authority files for archival descriptions.

The development of *ISAD (G)* and *ISAAR (CPF)* by ICA was followed in 2008 by two additional standards, *International Standard for Describing Functions (ISDF)*[34] and the *International Standard for Describing Institutions with Archival Holdings (ICA-ISDIAH)*.[35] Together, this suite of standards was designed to encompass multiple aspects of archival descriptive needs and essentially make possible an entire archival descriptive system. The rationales for *ISDF*, which distinctively reflects the realities of the world of records and records creation, were that

> Functions are often transferred from one corporate body to another. Therefore, it will be much more difficult for the users to reconstitute the context of records creation, if they are only provided with authority records describing corporate bodies that performed the same function.[36]

Exploiting the hyperlinking capabilities of modern information systems and the Web, the standard notes that

> Separated but linked descriptions of functions can improve the understanding of that context and can be used in conjunction with ICA-ISAD(G) compliant descriptions and ICA-ISAAR(CPF) authority files as a tool for efficient retrieval of archives and creators descriptions in archival descriptive systems.[37]

It should be noted that the Australian series system, which decouples administrative histories from the descriptions of series and then supports linkages between individual series and specific aspects of those administrative histories, is an example of how *ISAAR* and *ISDF* might be implemented. In fact, the proposed data model for the *ISAD (G)* suite owes much of its conceptualization to Australian recordkeeping metadata modeling.

The rationale behind *ICA-ISDIAH,* the fourth component in this suite, is that

> Information about the institution that holds archival materials, as referred to in traditional finding aids, is essential for users to access holdings, especially over the Web, where holdings of multiple repositories may be displayed together, enabling:
>
> - the provision of practical guidance on identifying and contacting institutions with archival holdings, and accessing holdings and available services
> - the generation of directories of institutions with archival holdings and/or authority lists
> - the establishment of connections with authority lists of libraries and museums
> - and/or developing common directories of cultural heritage institutions at a regional, national and international level
> - the production of statistics on institutions with archival holdings, at a regional, national or international level.[38]

Again, this standard addresses a distinctive archival descriptive need evident throughout the history of discussions about standardizing and automating archival description, that is, to break down the isolation of individual archival repositories, indicate thematic relationships and commonalities and regional colocation, and provide users with ready means to identify location and accessibility information.

Supporting More Complexity and More Granular Levels of Description

In 1994, archival visionary David Bearman wrote that "the 'fonds' as a physical construct will completely disappear because the boundaries of recordkeeping systems will be purely logical ones."[39] As with many archival concepts that began with observations and practices relating to managing the physical aspects of records that were subsequently theorized, the notion of the *fonds* is closely related to the eighteenth- and nineteenth-century recordkeeping systems with which the writers of early regulations and manuals for archival practice were familiar. Many of the inherited ideas about description descend from this time, most prominently collective description, the primacy of provenance as an organizational principle, and the emphasis on capturing administrative, procedural, and documentary contexts. Prior to this time, records tended to be cataloged at the item level, for example, in letter books and specialized indexes.[40] Arranging and describing in the aggregate had the very practical advantage of reducing the amount of time the archivist needed to spend on descriptive detail, and the arguments that it kept individual items within their documentary context and that the content of a single document within a record series often did not warrant a detailed description justified this approach. Adherence to provenance supported collective description in that it described records of the same provenance together.

As alluded to already, challenges to the idea of a one-to-one relationship between a single creating entity or provenance and a body of records have been growing since Peter Scott's critique in the 1960s of the record group concept developed by the U.S. National Archives. The Australian Series System consequently separated descriptions of creating entities from those of records, thus enabling archivists to identify and describe a multiplicity of relationships that might exist between specific aspects of a creating entity and of the records at different points in time. This kind of conceptualization, an elucidation of the concepts of provenance and context based upon an analysis of the nature of recordkeeping rather than of the records that were its physical output, presaged Bearman's comment. It is an early example of entity-relationship modeling that occurred long before information systems developed the capacity to exploit such relationships or to provide multiple views or arrangements of the same description (for example, a finding aid). As chapters 5 and 8 discuss in further detail, myriad new descriptive schemas exist, in the archival as well as in other information fields, which uphold the idea of many-to-many relationships that might exist in and over time between an information resource and its creators. These developments have not yet addressed, however, the ethical and power differentials underlying the attribution of records to an "official" provenance (either single or multiple) and the ways in which they might recognize the existence and roles of co-creators of records in the archival multiverse. Duff and Harris raise this issue very compellingly: "Do archivists participate actively in the construction of a record's meanings and significances? . . . Does the archivist have a moral obligation to engage the marginalized and excluded voices in records?"[41]

Granularity refers to the ability to break any kind of system or description into smaller or more fine-grained parts. In the context of archival description, this means describing archival materials at greater and greater levels of detail. Although collective description has been an important part of the modern archival paradigm, the actual principle, which is also fundamental to *ISAD (G)*, is that archival description should be hierarchical (proceeding from the general to the specific) and recursive. Given the volume of modern archival holdings, most archives attempt to strike a balance between a level of description that can support the majority of uses and exhaustiveness. In effect, therefore, item-level description has traditionally been reserved for special cases.

Technological developments have been the primary motivating impetus for the reintroduction of item-level description into the archival practice. David Bearman identified this shift in 1996.[42] It has two major aspects. First, digitization of traditional archival holdings requires item-level description to be created for each item digitized. Without such metadata, it would be impossible to track or retrieve the digitized item, to distinguish it from other digital versions of the same item, or to document the trustworthiness of the digitization process. Often this takes the form of developing a METS, MODS, or Dublin Core metadata record that can then be linked to a collective description such as an archival finding aid. This in turn points to the necessity of metadata mappings that can identify points where different metadata schemes can usefully intersect. Second, as more archival materials are born digital and traditional materials are digitized and made available in searchable form, online searching *within* as well as *across* individual archival materials will increase. While this can occur without additional metadata simply by employing a keyword search, metadata could be generated automatically using methods such as those described in the next chapter, or metadata could be manually created, for example, using document mark-up (for example, using the Text Encoding Initiative [TEI] Guidelines), a metadata scheme such as Dublin Core, or linked data such as that supported by the W3C Resource Description Framework (RDF).

An added wrinkle in this discussion about introducing more complexity and granularity into archival description is the recent widespread adoption of an approach to archival processing (that is, arrangement, description, and preservation activities) developed by American archivists Mark Greene and Dennis Meissner in 2005 and known as More Product, Less Process (MPLP).[43] Asserting that "the perfect should not be the enemy of the good," they argue that backlogs are overwhelming archives and that "'minimal' processing should become the new baseline approach to arranging and describing series and collections."[44] "Minimal" is also described in terms of "accessioning," "extensible," and "basic" description. In 2010, Greene further argued for the extension of the MPLP approach to preservation, reference, digitization, and electronic records activities.[45] Given the obvious resonance of this approach with many American archives and special collections, it would seem that the archival field is faced with competing realities—the push-pull of technological capabilities to exploit and user desire to have available increased descriptive metadata versus the perpetual insufficiency of resources to sustain even traditional archival activities. One source of possible solutions, and an example of where the needs of digital recordkeeping have potential benefits for archival description and access, is ongoing research relating to automated metadata creation and capture. Another is the development of enhanced information retrieval (IR) techniques to support users in searching, retrieving, and compiling data from the actual archival materials rather than relying on the intellectual control provided by subject access points and authority files contained in archival descriptions of those materials. Both approaches are discussed further in later chapters, but it should be noted that they do not change the fact that an archival investment needs to be made in metadata creation and manipulation—it just moves that investment to other points in the recordkeeping process (e.g., to active record creation and maintenance, or to archival reference and access services).[46]

Staying Abreast of Shifts in Descriptive Practices

As this discussion evidences, perhaps the most universal transformative changes in archival workflow and expected archival expertise over the past thirty years have occurred in the area of automated, standardized archival description. Because of these changes, as well as many others identified in this book, archivists have had to become technologically competent, comfortable with the dynamism associated with the evolving standards environment, and skilled in the management, decision-making, and evaluation aspects of automated description. Although software tools for archival description have been developed (some of the more recent being the Archivist's Toolkit, Archon, and the ICA's AtoM), archivists still have to learn how to use them and how to migrate between descriptive software systems and environments. This dynamism in turn has necessitated curricular expansion in graduate archival education as well as in continuing professional education (for example, through the Society of American Archivists Digital Archives Specialist program) and the contemplation of new educational delivery methods for working archivists who need to acquire and update the necessary skills. At the same time, however, they may be facing a new learning curve: developing more sophisticated knowledge of IR techniques and evaluation methods.

If one returns to the agenda laid out by Ham in 1981, archives and archivists today, through their engagement with automated descriptive systems and supported by their professional education, have come a long way in addressing two of the major requirements Ham predicted they would need to meet in the post-custodial era: they are focused on providing easy and centralized access to increasingly complex and dispersed materials, and they are making increasing use not only of national but also of international resources (e.g., networks, federated descriptive databases, descriptive standards, and metadata crosswalks) for archival activity.[47]

Notes

[1] David A. Bearman, "Archives and Manuscript Control with Bibliographic Utilities: Challenges and Opportunities," *The American Archivist* 52 (Winter 989): 26.

[2] Waldo Gifford Leland, letter to Solon J. Buck, December 16, 1935. Buck, Solon J., Papers of, Library of Congress Manuscript Division.

[3] Leland to Buck.

[4] Samuel Muller, Johan Adriaan Feith, and Robert Fruin, *Manual for the Arrangement and Description of Archives*, trans. Arthur Leavitt, Archival Classics Series (Chicago: Society of American Archivists, 2003).

5   Australian archivist Peter Scott provides a number of valid criticisms of the record group concept as a mechanism for the organization of records, especially its inability to represent the multiple interrelationships that develop over time between records and various recordkeeping functions that created them. However, his critique fails to take into account the fact that the record group was a product of a particular time, place, and set of description issues and was not intended to become a universal approach. The context behind the development of the record group is discussed in greater detail in Anne J. Gilliland, "Professional, Institutional and National Identities in Dialog: The Development of Descriptive Practices in the First Decade of the U.S. National Archives," *Information and Culture* (in press). See Peter J. Scott, "The Record Group Concept: A Case for Abandonment," *The American Archivist* 29, no. 4 (1966): 493–504. For more recent reflection on Scott's case, see Kate Cumming, "The Work of Peter Scott: An Overview," *Recordkeeping Roundtable*, November 16, 2011, http://recordkeepingroundtable.org/2011/11/16/the-work-of-peter-scott-an-overview-2/; and Adrian Cunningham, ed., *The Arrangement and Description of Archives amid Administrative and Technological Change: Essays by and about Peter J. Scott* (Brisbane: Australian Society of Archivists, 2012).

6   See Library of Congress, *National Union Catalog of Manuscript Collections*, "NUCMC Timeline," http://www.loc.gov/coll/nucmc/timeline.html.

7   Joint Steering Committee for the Development of RDA, "A Brief History of *AACR*," http://www.rda-jsc.org/history.html. See also Arlene G. Taylor and Barbara B. Tillett, *Authority Control in Organizing and Accessing Information: Definition and International Experience* (New York: Haworth Information Press, 2004); and Michael Gorman, *The Enduring Library: Technology, Tradition, and the Quest for Balance* (Chicago: ALA Editions, 2003).

8   Richard C. Berner, "Manuscript Catalogs and Other Finding Aids: What Are Their Relationships?," *The American Archivist* 34 (October 1971): 367–72.

9   See Alan Calmes, "Practical Realities of Computer-Based Finding Aids: The NARS A-1 Experience," *The American Archivist* 42, no. 2 (1979): 167–77.

10 For further information on SPINDEX, see National Archives and Records Service, *Spindex II: Report and Systems Documentation* (Washington, D.C.: National Archives and Records Service, 1975); H. Thomas Hickerson, *Archives and Manuscripts: An Introduction to Automated Access* (Chicago: Society of American Archivists, 1981); Marie K. Elsen, "SPINDEX in a University Archives," *The American Archivist* 45, no. 2 (1982): 190–92; and Thomas J. Frusciano, "Automation Programs for Archival and Manuscript Repositories," *Library Hi Tech* 1, no. 2 (1983): 72–77.

11 See H. Thomas Hickerson, "Archival Information Exchange and the Role of Bibliographic Networks," *Library Trends* 36 (Winter 1988): 553–71.

12 Lewis J. Bellardo, letter to Readers' Forum, *Midwestern Archivist* 5, no. 2 (1981): 123–24.

13 Thomas Elton Brown, "The Society of American Archivists Confronts the Computer," *The American Archivist* 56 (Summer 1993): 369–70.

14 Brown, "The Society of American Archivists Confronts the Computer," 369–70.

15 Brown, "The Society of American Archivists Confronts the Computer," 370–71.

16 David A. Bearman, *Towards National Information Systems for Archives and Manuscript Repositories: The National Information Systems Task Force (NISTF) Papers, 1981–1984* (Chicago: Society of American Archivists, 1987).

17 Victoria Irons Walch, comp., with contributions from Marion Matters, *Standards for Archival Description: A Handbook* (Chicago: Society of American Archivists, 1994), http://www.archivists.org/catalog/stds99/index.html.

18 Steven L. Hensen, comp., *Archives, Personal Papers, and Manuscripts* (Chicago: Society of American Archivists, 1983). A second edition was published in 1989.

19 See Steven L. Hensen, "Squaring the Circle: The Reformation of Archival Description," *Library Trends* 36 (Winter 1988): 539–52.

20 For further discussion on this subject, see Hickerson, "Archival Information Exchange and the Role of Bibliographic Networks."

21 Frederick L. Honhart, "The Application of Microcomputer-based Local Systems with the MARC AMC Format," *Library Trends* 36 (Winter 1988): 585–92; and "MicroMARC:amc: A Case Study in the Development of an Automated System," *The American Archivist* 52 (Winter 1989): 80–86.

22 See Anne J. Gilliland-Swetland, "Automated Archival Systems," in *Encyclopedia of Library and Information Science*, vol. 48, ed. Allen Kent (New York: Marcel Dekker, 1991), 1–14; and Lyn Martin, "Viewing the Field: A Literature Review and Survey of the Use of U.S. MARC AMC in U.S. Academic Libraries," *The American Archivist* 57 (Summer 1994): 482–97.

23 *Anglo-American Cataloging Rules*, 2nd ed., 2002 revision (Chicago: American Library Association; Ottawa: Canadian Library Association; London: Chartered Institute of Library and Information Professionals, 2002).

24 International Council on Archives, *General International Standard Archival Description*, 2nd ed. (Paris: International Council on Archives, 1999).

25 Society of American Archivists, *Describing Archives in Context: A Content Standard* (Chicago: Society of American Archivists, 2004).

26 Interestingly, this same approach can be seen with the development of the Australian Indigenous Protocols for Libraries and Archives discussed in chapter 8.

27 See Anne J. Gilliland-Swetland, Layna White, and Robin L. Chandler, "We're Building It, Will They Use It? The MOAC II Evaluation Project," in *Proceedings of Museums and the Web 2004, Arlington, Virginia, March 31–April 3, 2004*, http://www.archimuse.com/mw2004/papers/g-swetland/g-swetland.html; Anne J. Gilliland-Swetland, Carina M. MacLeod, M. Kathleen Svetlik, and Layna White, "Evaluating EAD as an Appropriate Metadata Structure for Describing and Delivering Museum Content: MOAC II Evaluation Study," in *Proceedings of the 2004 International Conference of Digital Libraries, February 24–27, 2004, New Delhi, India* (New Delhi, India: The Energy and Resources Institute, 2004), 504–12; and Anne J. Gilliland-Swetland, Robin L. Chandler, and Layna White, "MOAC II User Evaluation: Making Museum Content Useful," in *Proceedings of the 66th Annual Meeting of the American Society for Information and Technology—Humanizing Information Technology: From Ideas to Bits and Back, Long Beach, California, October 20–23, 2003* (Medford, N.J.: Information Today, 2003).

28 See Encoded Archival Description Working Group of the Society of American Archivists and the Network Development and MARC Standards Office of the Library of Congress, *Encoded Archival Description Tag Library, Version 2002* (Chicago: Society of American Archivists, 2002).

29 International Council on Archives, *General International Standard Archival Description*.

30 See Anne J. Gilliland-Swetland, "Popularizing the Finding Aid: Exploiting EAD to Enhance Online Browsing and Retrieval in Archival Information Systems by Diverse User Groups," *Journal of Internet Cataloging* 4, nos. 3–4 (2001): 199–225.

31 See Network Development and MARC Standards Office, Library of Congress, in cooperation with Standards and Support, National Library of Canada, *MARC 21 Format for Bibliographic Data: Including Guidelines for Content Designation* (Washington, D.C.: Library of Congress, Cataloging Distribution Service, 1999).

32 See Network Development and MARC Standards Office, Library of Congress, *MARC 21 Format for Bibliographic Data*.

33 Society of American Archivists, *Describing Archives in Context*, v.

34 Society of American Archivists, *Describing Archives in Context*, vii.

[35] International Council on Archives (ICA), *International Standard for Describing Functions* (Paris: International Council on Archives, 2008).

[36] International Council on Archives, *ICA-ISDIAH, International Standard for Describing Institutions with Archival Holdings*, 1st ed. (Paris: International Council on Archives, 2008).

[37] ICA, *International Standard for Describing Functions*.

[38] ICA, *International Standard for Describing Functions*.

[39] David Bearman, *Electronic Evidence: Strategies for Managing Records in Contemporary Organizations* (Pittsburgh: Archives and Museum Informatics, 1994), 254.

[40] Many early descriptive schemes are described in *Interdisciplinary Essays on European Knowledge Culture, 1400–1900*, ed. Randolph Head, special issue, *Archival Science* 10 (September 2010).

[41] Wendy M. Duff and Verne Harris, "Stories and Names: Archival Description as Narrating Records and Constructing Meanings," in *Archives and Justice: A South African Perspective*, ed. Verne Harris (Chicago: Society of American Archivists, 2007), 133. See also Anne J. Gilliland, "Contemplating Co-creator Rights in Archival Description," *Knowledge Organization* 39 no.5 (September 2012): 340–46.

[42] David A. Bearman, "Item Level Control and Electronic Recordkeeping" (paper presented at the Society of American Archivists 1996 Annual Meeting, San Diego, Calif.)

[43] Mark A. Greene and Dennis Meissner, "More Product, Less Process: Revamping Traditional Archival Processing," *The American Archivist* 68, no. 2 (2005): 208–63.

[44] Mark A. Greene, "MPLP: It's Not Just for Processing Any More," *The American Archivist* 73 (Spring/Summer 2010): 175–203.

[45] Greene, "MPLP: It's Not Just for Processing Any More," 175.

[46] See Shannon Bowen Maier, "MPLP and the Catalog Record as a Finding Aid," *Journal of Archival Organization* 9, no. 1 (2011): 32–44.

[47] Ham, "Archival Strategies for the Post-custodial Era," 207–16 (see chapter 1, n. 16).

CHAPTER 5

∽

Archival Description and Descriptive Metadata in a Networked World

This chapter examines the relationship of archival description to broader notions of descriptive metadata that have emerged from several different areas. These include new developments in the bibliographic world such as Resource Description and Access (RDA), Functional Requirements for Bibliographic Records (FRBR), and Functional Requirements for Authority Data (FRAD); the Semantic Web's Resource Description Framework (RDF); and metadata created by social tagging and crowdsourcing. From there it moves on to discuss and question how archival description might be augmented, enriched, and pluralized by exploiting metadata of multiple types and provenance. Finally, it returns to some of the criticisms that James Rhoads leveled at archival descriptive practices in the opening quote and asks whether digital innovations have the capacity or potential to overcome them.

The inventory format may tend to make moribund a body of living records. Seemingly without recognizing that record holdings grow, are reprocessed, are more deeply analyzed with use, and may be described in a variety of ways by a variety of people, the published inventory effectively freezes the usable quantity of the records to only those that have been included on the day the inventory goes to press; it inhibits reprocessing of records lest the published inventory be made obsolete (and then what does one do with the 200 or so copies still in stock?). The printed inventory does not permit inclusion of new information as such information may emerge from continued use of the records, and it accepts as definitive the description of one archivist, whose own prejudices and historical shortcomings tend to be reflected in the descriptions that he produces. . . . Now, however, the archivist is beginning to appreciate the applicability of some new techniques to his problem. He is beginning to see the computer as a boon, not to the advancement of system and order in archival description but rather to the advancement of specific manipulation of large bodies of data to meet the individual needs of the historian or other researcher. The use of the computer has already begun in archives, and its applications will grow as the initial simple routines to which it is being assigned are mastered.

—James B. Rhoads, Archivist of the United States,
paper presented at the Society of American Archivists' annual luncheon
meeting with the Organization of American Historians, April 17, 1969[1]

Conceptualizing Descriptive Metadata

Even while all of the developments discussed in chapter 4 occurred, another shift was happening—a broadening of the notion of cataloging and archival description as they support access to and collocation of resources, to a concept of metadata that can facilitate not only access and collocation, but also lifelong management, preservation, and manipulability of resources. "Metadata" entered the vocabulary of those engaged in the description of information resources in the mid-1990s. Prior to that, the term was used primarily by communities involved with the management and interoperability of geospatial data and with data management and systems design and maintenance in general. For these communities, "metadata" refers to a suite of industry or disciplinary standards as well as additional internal and external documentation and other data necessary for the identification, representation, interoperability, technical management, performance, and use of data contained in an information system.[2]

Today, *metadata* refers to anything that is said about any information object, at any level of granularity, and at any point in its life. In archival terms, therefore, *metadata* encompasses not only representations of the content, but also descriptions and traces of the various contexts of records and other archival materials. Because it is such an extensive concept, it can provide clarity to subdivide metadata according to type or function (for example, see Table 5.1).

Metadata might be created manually or automatically by an information professional, a domain expert, a resource creator, or an end-user. The presence and utility of a plurality of types and sources of metadata across the life of a resource underlie important tenets of digital recordkeeping and digital preservation, and of digital curation more broadly, and are discussed further in those contexts in subsequent chapters. Professionals

Table 5.1. Different types of metadata and their functions‡

Type	Definition	Examples
Administrative	Metadata used in managing and administering collections and information resources	• Acquisition information • Rights and reproduction tracking • Documentation of legal access requirements • Location information • Selection criteria for digitization
Descriptive	Metadata used to identify and describe collections and related information resources	• Cataloging records • Finding aids • Differentiations between versions • Specialized indexes • Curatorial information • Hyperlinked relationships between resources • Annotations by creators and users
Preservation	Metadata related to the preservation management of collections and information resources	• Documentation of physical condition of resources • Documentation of actions taken to preserve physical and digital versions of resources, e.g., data refreshing and migration • Documentation of any changes occurring during digitization or preservation
Technical	Metadata related to how a system functions or metadata behaves	• Hardware and software documentation • Technical digitization information, e.g., formats, compression ratios, scaling routines • Tracking of system response times • Authentication and security data, e.g., encryption keys, passwords
Use	Metadata related to the level and type of use of collections and information resources	• Circulation records • Physical and digital exhibition records • Use and user tracking • Content reuse and multiversioning information • Search logs • Rights metadata

‡ Reproduced with permission from Anne J. Gilliland, "Setting the Stage," in *Introduction to Metadata Version 3.0*, ed. Murtha Baca (Los Angeles: Getty Research Institute, 2008).

active in the descriptive metadata arena contemplate how metadata might support the various ways information resources might be related to each other; document and track the dynamics of resources that are constantly accumulating and changing; and capture the relationship between creators, the processes of creation, and the resulting work. They also emphasize how multiple ways of describing a resource or of creating an authority form might coexist to support different disciplinary and sector needs (for example, by using semantic networks and metadata crosswalks to map between different metadata schemes and vocabularies) and are increasingly interested in how to ensure that local and global ways of conceptualizing, describing, and understanding resources can be accommodated and that co-creators' perspectives and needs are represented.[3]

Other areas of activity include how to increase automated creation of metadata and how all of this could better support how users might wish to access or use resources on the Web, particularly with the support of linked data.

The Evolving World of Descriptive Metadata

Several themes emerge from these developments. These include the application of entity-relationship modeling to delineate the complex nature of relationships between agents, resources, and functions (as opposed to flat or simple relational models) and by implication, a growing awareness of the many agents involved with a resource throughout its life. They also include a realization that professional metadata creators such as library catalogers or archivists will not have sufficient resources to generate the metadata necessary to integrate all the types of resources now being created; and the desire to draw upon mechanisms such as crowdsourcing and computational analysis to generate an abundance of metadata created from different perspectives. Such automated means of creating metadata have the added benefits of supporting what is being referred to as "machine-actionable data" as well as the pluralization and democratization of description.

Resource Description and Access (RDA)

In the bibliographic world, this movement has influenced the development of the related family of conceptual models: Functional Requirements for Bibliographic Records (FRBR), Functional Requirements for Authority Data (FRAD), and Functional Requirements for Subject Authority Data (FRSAD) as the underlying models for RDA.[4] In 1997, the International Conference on the Principles and Future Development of the *Anglo-American Cataloguing Rules* (*AACR*) convened in Toronto. A decision emerged that rather than undertaking a substantial revision of *AACR*, a new Web-based standard should be developed that would build upon internationally established principles, conceptual models, and standards developed by the International Federation of Library Associations and Institutions (IFLA). It would provide guidelines and instructions for the description of information resources in all media and types held by repositories such as libraries, museums, galleries, and film archives.[5] An international collaborative process led by a joint steering committee subsequently developed RDA.[6] In October 2007, the British Library, Library and Archives Canada, the Library of Congress, and the National Library of Australia, who are all members of the Committee of Principals that is overseeing the development, agreed to support RDA by coordinating training materials and implementation plans.[7] RDA was released in summer 2010, and a U.S. RDA Test was undertaken in the United States within the Library of Congress, the National Library of Medicine, and the National Agricultural Library. The RDA Test concluded that the libraries should adopt RDA, with the earliest possible implementation being March 31, 2013, but only if several changes were made, including possibly developing a standard to replace MARC. RDA and any future metadata developments, however, also need to be compatible with the millions of cataloging records that have already been developed in *AACR*. Moreover, the development of RDA has been controversial among catalogers,[8] many of whom are skeptical about abandoning *AACR* and possibly MARC. The new RDA data elements in both bibliographic and authority data are more granular in that many new fields have been added, and, while there is both a core and many options, it leaves considerable room for the cataloger to exercise judgment.

RDA is so different from *AACR* because, apart from its ability to include descriptive elements commonly used to describe digital resources not included in *AACR*, it is based on the conceptual model, FRBR, which the Standing Committee of the IFLA Section on Cataloguing approved in 1997 and designed to increase terminological and definitional clarity in cataloging, to identify bibliographic relationships, and to support a range of user tasks. In 2009, IFLA adopted a new statement of international cataloging principles, the first such statement since the 1961 Paris Principles. The new principles were designed with Web-based, online catalogs and a diversity of works (i.e., not just those that are textual) and languages, scripts, and cultural variances, as well as FRBR, in mind. Its top three priorities emphasize the needs of local users rather than global consistency:

> *Convenience of the user.* Decisions taken in the making of descriptions and controlled forms of names for access should be made with the user in mind.
>
> *Common usage.* Vocabulary used in descriptions and access should be in accord with that of the majority of users.
>
> *Representation.* Descriptions and controlled forms of names should be based on the way an entity describes itself.[9]

FRBR is based on entity-relationship models that delineate a hierarchy of relationships between information resources, which can be classified as Works, Expressions, Manifestations and Items; and user tasks, categorized as Find, Identify, Select, Obtain, and Navigate. By using FRBR, RDA is able then to display to users' information clustered about the same title, regardless of version, format, translation, and so forth. RDA is also better structured to "fit with emerging database technologies enabling institutions to introduce efficiencies in data capture and storage retrieval," as well as to capture metadata automatically without undertaking extensive editing.[10] FRAD, published in 2009, is a conceptual model that extends FRBR by addressing the attributes of, and relationships between, "various entities that are the centre of focus for authority data (persons, families, corporate bodies, works, expressions, manifestations, items, concepts, objects, events, and places), the name by which these entities are known, and the controlled access points created by cataloguers for them."[11] FRAD is able to include a statement about which cataloging rules are being applied by an institution when choosing forms of names, but not any detail on why those rules were made or chosen.

As with FRBR, these are mapped to a set of user tasks, in this case Find, Identify, Contextualize, and Justify (where users are either authority data creators or library users and patrons).[12] FRSAD, published in 2010, is the third in this set of conceptual models. It addresses the "aboutness" of works and provides a "structured frame of reference for relating the data that are recorded in subject authority records to the needs of the users of those records." Those needs, or tasks, are identified as Find, Identify, Select, and Explore.[13]

The Semantic Web, Linked Data, and Resource Description Framework (RDF)

The Semantic Web is a collaborative movement led by the World Wide Web Consortium (W3C) to enhance the utility and intuitiveness of the Web in line with agendas for the development of Web 3.0. *Linked data*—structured metadata such as Uniform Resource Identifiers (URIs) that come from different sources—that can be automatically connected and queried supports the Semantic Web. The Resource Description Framework (RDF) for embedding structured metadata in Web documents is a central component of developing a common framework whereby data distributed on the Web can be "shared and reused across application, enterprise, and community boundaries" and can be enriched with additional meaning and inferential capabilities,[14] regardless of the underlying metadata schemas employed by exploiting the networking and computational capabilities of machines.

RDF supports the development of simple tripartite statements known as "triples," each providing a single metadata statement about a single property of a single resource, and each capable of being linked to another statement on the basis of some common aspect.[15] Based on descriptive logic related to natural language processing and that employs an entity-relationship approach, each triple has a *subject*, a *predicate* that describes the nature of the statement being made about the subject, and an *object* that provides the value to be applied to the predicate. Because all human statements are potentially ambiguous to a computer, the components of each triple must be identified in an unambiguous manner. RDF, therefore, requires that both the subject and the predicate of a triple be URIs, with the predicate being the most important. An advantage of this approach is that identifiers can then be automatically translated into different languages without needing to be re-created.[16] These predicates might be supplied by existing descriptive standards or schemes, such as RDA, FRBR, ISBD, or the CIDOC CRM (International Committee for Documentation Conceptual Reference Model) for Museums (all of which are being modeled in RDF);

by defined types of resources such as finding aids, manuscripts, or vocabularies; or by defined relationships. The object could also be a URI, or just a simple character string. The object provides the basis for linking between triples. Modeling the Web would require that trillions of these triples be created, and it is envisaged that they will not only be created "top-down" by the authors of various metadata standards and schemes, but also bottom-up in a free and open environment by users of the Web making connections between various entities (i.e., crowdsourced).

RDF is fast becoming embedded in archival work. It is being modeled into the software used in the business applications that generate records, and RDF versions of archival descriptive standards are also under development. One early example of this is the Australian Recordkeeping Metadata Schema (RKMS), which was modeled in RDF when it was originally developed in the late 1990s. Undertaking description in the records continuum, as RKMS was designed to do, requires an approach very different from describing in a life-cycle model because it needs to be incremental throughout the life of the material (hence the reference to recordkeeping metadata rather than to the more narrowly construed archival description[17]), and it also needs to be explicit in how it represents the relationships between different parties or agents essential to the creation and subsequent understanding of the records. RKMS is an entity-relationship model containing four main classes of entities: Business entities; Agent entities involved in creating, controlling, managing, or using records entities; Records entities; and Business-Recordkeeping entities—as well as the types of Relationships between entities and the Mandates that govern the entities and their relationships. Linked descriptions are achieved by aggregating statements about entities, so that every statement includes a characteristic of the entity as well as the value of that characteristic, just as in RDF.[18]

Interestingly, as early as 1994, David Bearman anticipated taking this kind of approach to archival metadata creation because he believed it would ultimately result in being able to automate aspects of electronic records management:

> Implementing responsible solutions to electronic records management can be made easier in the future by adopting architectures that take advantage of some relatively new approaches to computing. Object-oriented systems, when they are implemented,

will allow us to attach object attributes to records that cause them to be filed, retained, and accessed in the ways that a sound records policy would dictate.[19]

As RDF becomes increasingly ubiquitous and bridges between different professional metadata schemes, it may diminish some of the historical tension between recordkeeping and bibliographic approaches and may even lead to greater proximity between the archival community and CIDOC CRM, the sophisticated model developed within the museum community. However, lingering questions mean that archivists may need to wait to understand more fully the potential and impact of linked data on description, access, and use. Is an RDF approach able to represent the contingencies and nuances with which archival description has historically struggled? The answer to that question is as yet unknown. Can, for example, individual triples, concatenations of properties, or relationships that are defined between properties, adequately express fuzzy assertions such as "might be" or "is purported to be" as well as the more definitive "was" or "has," or must users still make their own judgments about the validity of assertions by weighing them against each other? Can RDF be used to capture the continuous processes of records creation and accumulation? The RDF modeling of RKMS, the metadata scheme most inclusive of recordkeeping processes, indicates that it can. Can RDF help to support multiple ways of describing or contemplating objects (for example, as bibliographic, archival, or museum objects) in and over time and from multiple creator and user perspectives? Any individual or entity can create linked data from any perspective at any time, so the hope is that the multiplicity of triples that can be created by institutions and through social tagging and then linked together will afford increased access points to an object over what might currently be available. In this way, crowdsourced linked data might also help to pluralize description. It can also change how archives users employ archival materials and understand history. For example, Web users are using linked data to create mash-ups that overlay historical and contemporary images in ways that can make the past seem more real or that can change their perceptions of history, for example, by providing a better spatial sense of places and events.

New Ways to Create and Exploit Descriptive Metadata

In 1965, with reference to the experience of manuscript repositories contributing to the Library of Congress's *National Union Catalog of Manuscript Collections* (*NUCMC*), T. R. Schellenberg asserted that

> Several observations about the use of automation in controlling documentary source material may be made . . .
>
> 1. *The use of modern gadgetry cannot supplant the use of proper techniques and principles in describing documentary material.*
>
>   Shortcuts to the control of such material can be found in mechanical, photographic, or electronic devices only after the material has been organized and interpreted by conventional methods.
>
> 2. *Documentary material can be controlled on a nationwide basis only after descriptive techniques have been defined and standardized.*
>
>   Repositories must first describe their own material before they can make information in regard to it available for a union catalog, and they must describe it according to standardized procedures.[20]

Many of the developments already discussed materialized in response to the demand for the kind of granular, relational, and constantly accumulating metadata that the Web can potentially support and that might facilitate the kinds of integration of digital descriptions of resources held in archives, libraries, and museums, as well as other digital content on the Web. However, they are also in response to the realization that sufficient resources will never be available in those kinds of repositories to generate and update that volume of metadata without some kind of help. Two kinds of help are pursued in particular—social tagging, now supported by many archives, and automatic metadata creation and extraction, which is still in quite a nascent state of development. Both take descriptive activities beyond the realm of the description expert, thereby provoking reactions from library catalogers and archivists that are remarkably similar to Schellenberg's in 1965 and raising questions about where and when it might be most effective to concentrate the expertise of the description expert, as well as how to keep track of and make evident the provenance of different metadata.

Social Tagging

The previous discussion about developing RDF triples from the bottom up introduced the notion of crowdsourced metadata. *Social tagging*, also known as *collaborative tagging* and *social indexing*, is a process whereby users of the Web can annotate resources they encounter, add descriptors, or, taking the use of social media one step further, contribute their own content. Social bookmarking and recommender systems take this a step further yet by providing paths through and to resources for other users. By so doing, anyone using the Web can contribute expertise different from that of professional describers or catalogers, fill in gaps in missing knowledge about a resource, and contribute alternate perspectives and additional tagged content. If a sufficient amount of social tagging occurs, it may be possible to discern emergent community vocabularies or ontologies, often different from those applied by the archivist or librarian, and even generational shifts in vocabulary and language conventions.[21] The Next Generation Finding Aids Project at the University of Michigan is an example of an effort to combine traditional EAD-based metadata with shared authority and collaboration, as well as collaborative filtering and social navigation mechanisms to re-imagine traditional finding aid structure and functionality.[22] Its Polar Bear Project highlighted some of the implications of such collaboration both for maintaining trust in the archives and for increasing pluralization in description. Your Archives at the U.K. National Archives is another example. Launched in 2007 in a wiki format to encourage the public to contribute their knowledge of archival sources held by the National Archives and other archives throughout the United Kingdom, it closed in February 2012 so that a new, more seamless social tagging and annotation system could be put in place that will also distinguish between catalog descriptions and user-contributed content.[23] Many archives now support Web 2.0 capabilities (a.k.a. Archives 2.0) so that users can contribute both metadata and content, and provide feedback on both, in ways that also make clear which metadata is repository-created and which is generated through social tagging. Concerns that such capabilities might result in the incorporation of spurious or ideologically motivated metadata appear for the most part unfounded, and Web 2.0 is proving to be a particularly potent mechanism for augmenting and broadening the description of community archival holdings.

Automated Tools for Metadata Creation and Exploitation

Almost twenty years ago, my colleague Carol Hughes and I published an article that explored statistically based approaches to the automatic description of computer conferences, a form of online group discussion that was an early forerunner of social media (but organized around topics or threads, rather than by individual or individual contribution as are many of today's social media such as Facebook).[24] The conferences were hosted at the University of Michigan where an electronic records research project funded by the National Historical Publications and Records Commission (NHPRC) at the Bentley Historical Library was investigating the development of appraisal and accessioning mechanisms for computer conferences that might potentially capture documentation of campus activities typically underrepresented in university archives, such as teaching and socializing.[25] We found that a considerable amount of additional and more precise descriptive information could be generated by using structural analysis and statistical techniques, and this, in turn, could be used to appraise and capture the content of the conferences. This approach enabled us, for example, to identify key conference discussion topics in terms of longevity and activity patterns (analogous to looking for "fat files" in archival sampling); the nature of the internal structure and arrangement of the conferences; the breadth and periods of individuals' participation in both the whole conference and in individual items; dominators or key players among item respondents and initiators; and the degree of relationship between item respondents and initiators. We speculated that such an approach might both assist archivists in describing records generated by various electronic communications mechanisms in greater depth and provide the basis for developing automated tools to assist archival users in analyzing those records (an approach that today might be viewed as closer to some of the work in the digital humanities). We were doing proof-of-concept work—in the absence of automated tools, we examined the conferences and compiled the statistics manually. It seemed to us, however, that much of this work could be automated if more robust technology and consistent data structures were available and applied.

At the time, automating aspects of description seemed to be quite radical and very far removed from both archival theory and reality. Archivists were concerned that the "art" of archival practice, and the value-added aspects of manual description that included the hindsight of the archivist on events associated with the records, as well as the connections that might be made to other records and descriptive information held by the archives (i.e., integrating the records being described into the archival bond), necessitated manual description. Archivists were not yet dealing upstream with such massive volumes of electronic records that might nudge them toward automating certain aspects of appraisal, accessioning, or description. This has since occurred, most notably in the United States with the National Archives' imperative to deal immediately, when the administration in Washington changes, with the accessioning and processing of tens of millions of emails—a highly influential circumstance in the decision to develop the Electronic Records Archive at the National Archives and the automatic ingestion and preservation technologies discussed in chapters 7 and 9. Looking at the same approaches today as a means to assess and describe high volumes of digital materials, such as electronic mail or Twitter feeds, automatic pattern and semantic analyses might assist in making visible aspects of records not easily perceived by manual means. This approach might also control for electronic records' integrity by using statistical analysis to identify and flag outlying attribute values or significantly different data structures, which could then be examined for possible processing errors that might have occurred during accessioning or ongoing preservation activities such as migration. These approaches could also identify materials that, in their differences from the surrounding documentation, are potentially significant and deserving of additional descriptive attention.

In the early 2000s, several experimental and applied research projects began to identify some of the potential of automatic processing of electronic records. Researchers at the San Diego Supercomputer Center (SDSC) developed the Persistent Archives Technology for the U.S. National Archives, a collaborative approach to the preservation and reconstitution of electronic records informed by the theoretical conceptualizations and practices of recordkeeping being developed through other electronic records projects at the time (discussed further in chapter 7). Derived and inferred metadata such as document structures and activity patterns played a key role in that work. Between 2000 and 2003, two of those researchers, Amarnath Gupta and Richard Marciano, directed an NHPRC-funded project to conduct research on the long-term preservation of and access to software-dependent data objects and to develop prototype tools for archivists to use in carrying out these functions. The underlying premise of the Archivists' Workbench Project is that it is possible to scale down and at the same time extend the knowledge-based Persistent Archives Technology for application in smaller institutional environments where computing and financial resources and archival programs and priorities might be quite different. The approach applied by the Archivists' Workbench involved creating "imperfect" software-neutral digital proxies that, while they likely did not address all the complexities and subtleties of the records, could render and layer a range of types of copies or views of the records, thus providing new visualization as well as querying and access capabilities. The Archivists' Workbench, however, was predicated upon a custodial model for electronic records, while today many repositories are investigating collaborative preservation repositories or completely noncustodial models, thus raising a question about whether the workbench approach could work if electronic records were never physically removed from the recordkeeping environment in which they were created. The researchers continued to build on this work through the National Science Foundation–funded project, Constraint-based Knowledge Systems for Grids, Digital Libraries, and Persistent Archives, which started in 2004 and which in turn led to the current *i*Rule Oriented Data Systems (*i*RODS) adaptive middleware being developed by the DICE Group at the University of North Carolina at Chapel Hill in support of next-generation cyberinfrastructure for distributed data management.[26] In both cases, metadata and metadata management played a central role.

In 2008, International Project of Permanent Archival Records in Electronic Systems (InterPARES) 2 researchers found that metadata embedded both explicitly and implicitly in recordkeeping systems related to aspects such as "identity, linkages, documentation of documentary forms, juridical requirements, business rules and technical procedures, access privileges, establishment of the authoritative record when multiple copies exist and transfer of relevant documentation."[27] The research also demonstrated that much of the relevant juridical-administrative, provenancial, procedural, documentary, and technological context resides within a diversity of metadata and metadata processes created through the workflows and activities with which the record is associated in its life before the archivist describes it. It pointed to the potential for automated tools to create, capture, infer, or inherit metadata that could then be incorporated into the description of that record.[28] Experimental work currently underway at the Texas Advanced Computing Center (TACC) at the University of Texas at Austin looking at automated methods for analysis and description of archives addresses some of these ideas about context and exploits the kinds of intra- and interdocumentary relationships inherent in the archival bond to identify latent "stories" that might emerge out of a collection of documents. To do this, TACC has been using density-based clustering to compute and data visualization to represent similarities between paragraphs contained in collections of electronic mail messages.[29]

These kinds of developments lead us to a set of questions about which aspects of archival description might reasonably be automated and which should continue to be done manually, which should not be automated, and what additional description and user services automation might support. Context is a key aspect here. Without deep context, automatic analysis of records could end up at such a surface level as to be practically useless. Traditionally, through appraisal reports and extensive descriptive notes, archivists do a lot of value-added work identifying and documenting context. Some of this context building is unlikely ever to be successfully achieved automatically. Moreover, as research by InterPARES found, many of the elements present in traditional records are not explicit in digital records and recordkeeping systems. Instead, they are inferred, implied, or inherited, and archivists need to make them explicit. Moreover, the authenticity of an electronic record tends to be assured primarily by procedural means, rather than by explicit elements of identity, and so automatic processing supporting that aspect of description must exploit recordkeeping procedures and workflow, and not just record content or documentary structure.

However, as some of the other examples described here indicate, other characteristics of digital materials can be transparent to the human eye or are simply submerged within the vast quantities of materials now being generated digitally, but can be identified through automatic analysis of their structural, semantic, and temporal characteristics or documentary interrelationships. What other sorts of tools and services might be desirable? One interesting capability would be to identify and exploit indicators that could help archivists to identify when change occurs in the functionality, forms, implementation, and even crowdsourced description of records. This would enable them to flag descriptions of those records for updating, or even to augment those descriptions automatically. Could the user be provided with more detail about how the records looked and felt when they were being used by their original creator? For example, could system and audit metadata be used to help reconstruct temporal views of database or social media materials? In the digital world, is it also possible to exploit recordkeeping metadata inherent or latent within the originating system and the digital records to automate some functions currently carried out manually in most archives, for example, supporting automated user clearances for access to sensitive information or redaction of restricted content? Finally, closer specification of metadata, and metadata that exists at a very granular level, can potentially support a range of end-user visualization, statistical, and data-mining and extraction tools that could be used to manipulate retrieved electronic records and create customized output.

Ongoing Considerations

Archival description has clearly undergone tremendous changes in the past forty or so years, not just in terms of standardization and automation, but also in terms of the conceptual thinking that necessarily underpins both activities. At the same time, archives, largely as a result of technological and metadata developments, have moved out of their isolation as individual entities with idiosyncratic practices to establish deeper, innovative relationships with other information professions, with technological research and development, and with their publics.

In the opening quote, James Rhoads voices several criticisms of traditional archival description: how, through its structure and the fact that it is only done at one particular moment, it can "freeze" living, organic collections and be impervious to all the changes in the records and interpretations of them that accrue over time; and how the published nature of the finding aid inhibits archivists from going back and reprocessing or redescribing the collection. What, if anything, has changed since 1968 in the conceptualization and practice of archival description? Teasing out his concerns reveals four different points to consider.

First, unless the originating activity has ended, records, organic entities generated through that activity, will continue to accumulate, as will the web of documentary inter- and intrarelationships that exist inside a given *fonds* or collection. At the same time, the provenance and function under auspices of which they are created may undergo various changes and mergers. Archivists now have several tools to help them to address these dynamics, including the ability to identify and update metadata automatically for records that are born digital and metadata standards that help them to track evolving recordkeeping functions.

Second, notwithstanding that descriptive metadata models such as RKMS allow for dynamic description as well as description of dynamic entities across the records continuum, archival description tends to be done only once for a given aggregation of records. The exception is the appending of descriptions of new accumulations received in an open accession, which is thus an "in time" activity. Meanwhile, both the records and the archives are entities that exist and evolve "over time." In the future, however, automated metadata tools that monitor changes in the records could either update current descriptions or flag the need for a manual update; while social tagging already allows the public to add to and comment on the descriptions on an ongoing basis, thus keeping the description not only alive, but also layering in new perspectives, vocabularies, and connections between records over time. If RDF lives up to the vision of its founders, archivists can expect that many more pathways between their holdings will be constructed that will help users to navigate them in meaningful ways. Potentially, these pathways will more extensively surface or expose to users the various kinds of contexts within which records are embedded (i.e., juridical-administrative, provenancial, procedural, documentary, technological, historical, and cultural) than was previously possible with traditional archival description. In so doing, they will also vastly exceed the amount of unexpressed or tacit knowledge about holdings and their contexts that individual archivists carry in their heads.

Third, the finding aid is largely a static document too cumbersome or expensive to keep changing. In this case, technology and descriptive standards working in concert have very clearly made a big difference. Descriptive information of all kinds is easily updated without laborious retyping or expensive republishing. It is also possible to keep an audit trail of what was changed, when, and by whom. EAD has been particularly instrumental in this respect. However, too often the conversion of manual to EAD finding aids is treated as a matter of filling in the blanks on a template, rather than significantly redescribing when needed, and the ease of updating in EAD may further encourage this. Moreover, the "good enough" approach to archival description encouraged by the More Product, Less Process movement has significantly diminished the potential power and richness of description based in EAD for supporting online browsing and retrieval. Archives online require not just good, but better, description if they are merely to support users in the same level of access that they might have in a mediated physical reference environment. Enabling users to take advantage of all the new ways in which they might find, refind, compile, manipulate, and re-use online resources will require significantly better description yet, as well as the provision of Web-based tools beyond online finding aids. Social tagging and crowdsourcing may provide additional avenues for enhancing or even correcting less than optimal archival description, as well as contributing additional perspectives to that description.

Finally, for closed *fonds* or collections, such as those from colonial eras, that might seem the most "frozen" of archival holdings, there may be new opportunities today to bring them back to life, especially if they have been digitized. Would some of them be prime candidates for redescription, or perhaps for additional description that might draw out counter-narratives and other voices and experiences, or that might support reading against the grain? Could scholars and other communities be drawn into that endeavor?

Notes

[1] James B. Rhoads, "The Historian and the New Technology," *The American Archivist* 32 (July 1969): 211.

[2] Anne J. Gilliland, "Setting the Stage," in *Introduction to Metadata: Pathways to Digital Information, Version 3.0,* ed. Murtha Baca (Los Angeles: J. Paul Getty Trust, 2008), http://www.getty.edu/research/publications/electronic_publications/intrometadata/setting.html.

[3] See, for example, Gilliland, "Contemplating Co-creator Rights in Archival Description"; Constantia Kakali et al.,"Integrating Dublin Core Metadata for Cultural Heritage Collections Using Ontologies," *2007 Proceedings of the International Conference on Dublin Core and Metadata Applications, Singapore 27–31 August, 2007,* 129–39, http://dcpapers.dublincore.org/pubs/article/view/871/867; Ramesh Srinivasan, Alberto Pepe, and Marko A. Rodriguez, "Eliciting Cultural Ontologies: A Comparison between Hierarchical Clustering Methods and Participatory Design Processes," *Journal of the American Society of Information Science and Technology* 60, no. 2 (2009).

[4] See Shawne D. Miksa, "Resource Description and Access and New Research Potentials," *ASIS&T Bulletin* (June 2009), http://www.asis.org/Bulletin/Jun-09/JunJul09_Miksa.pdf.

[5] "Resource Description and Access," brochure, http://www.rda-jsc.org/docs/rdabrochureJanuary2010.pdf.

[6] See Joint Steering Committee for the Development of RDA, *Resource Description and Access,* http://www.rda-jsc.org/rda.html.

[7] "Resource Description and Access."

[8] For example, Michael Gorman, one of the editors of *AARC2,* argues that "there are a number of reasons why this calamity is looming. One is the drive to resolve the problem of cataloguing and giving access to electronic records through the use of 'metadata' applied by non-cataloguers. The simplistic idea is that vast numbers of electronic documents can be catalogued effectively by having their creators apply uncontrolled terms in a few simple categories. In other words, that the results achieved by cataloguing using controlled vocabularies and the bibliographic structures of catalogues—complex, labor-intensive, skilled activities—can be achieved on the cheap and without the use of those essential structures." Michael Gorman, "RDA: The Coming Cataloguing Debacle," n.d., http://www.slc.bc.ca/rda1007.pdf.

[9] International Federation of Library Associations (IFLA), *Statement of International Cataloguing Principles,* http://www.ifla.org/files/cataloguing/icp/icp_2009-en.pdf.

[10] Barbara Tillett, *What Is FRBR? A Conceptual Model for the Bibliographic Universe* (Washington, D.C.: Library of Congress Cataloging Distribution Service, 2003), http://www.loc.gov/cds/downloads/FRBR.PDF.

[11] Glenn E. Patton, ed., "Functional Requirements for Authority Data—A Conceptual Model" (Munich: K. G. Saur, 2009), IFLA, http://www.ifla.org/publications/ifla-series-on-bibliographic-control-34.

[12] Glenn E. Patton, "From FRBR to FRAD: Extending the Model" (report of the IFLA Working Group on Functional Requirements and Numbering of Authority Records, December 8, 2009), http://conference.ifla.org/past/ifla75/215-patton-en.pdf.

[13] IFLA Working Group on Functional Requirements for Subject Authority Records (FRSAR), *Functional Requirements for Subject Authority Data (FRSAD) A Conceptual Model* (draft report, June 10, 2009), http://nkos.slis.kent.edu/FRSAR/report090623.pdf.

[14] W3C, "W3C Semantic Web Activity," http://www.w3.org/2001/sw/.

[15] Diane Hillman, Karen Coyle, Jon Phipps, and Gordon Dunsire, "RDA Vocabularies: Process, Outcome, Use," *D-Lib Magazine* 16 (January/February 2010), http://dlib.org/dlib/january10/hillmann/01hillmann.html. See also W3C: Semantic Web, "RDF Web Applications Working Group," http://www.w3.org/2010/02/rdfa/.

[16] Hillman et al., "RDA Vocabularies."

[17] "Recordkeeping metadata is defined broadly to include all standardised information that identifies, authenticates, describes, manages and makes accessible documents created in the context of social and organisational activity. The RKMS provides a standardised set of recordkeeping metadata that enables the identification and description of records that document social and organisational activity, as well as significant features of the business contexts in which records are created, managed and used." Monash University, "Recordkeeping Metadata Schema (RKMS)," http://www.infotech.monash.edu.au/research/groups/rcrg/projects/spirt/deliverables/austrkms-intro.html.

[18] See Sue McKemmish, Glenda Acland, and Barbara Reed, "Towards a Framework for Standardising Recordkeeping Metadata: The Australian Recordkeeping Metadata Schema," *Records Management Journal* 9 (December 1999); Sue McKemmish, Glenda Acland, Nigel Ward, and Barbara Reed, "Describing Records in Context in the Continuum: The Australian Recordkeeping Metadata Schema," *Archivaria* 48 (Fall 1999); and Sue McKemmish and Dagmar Parer, "Towards Frameworks for Standardising Recordkeeping Metadata," *Archives and Manuscripts* 26 no. 1 (1998). See also Monash University, "Recordkeeping Metadata Schema (RKMS)."

[19] David A. Bearman, "Electronic Mail," in *Electronic Evidence: Strategies for Managing Records in Contemporary Organizations* (Pittsburgh: Archives and Museum Informatics, 1994), 201.

[20] Theodore R. Schellenberg, "A Nationwide System of Controlling Historical Manuscripts in the United States," *The American Archivist* 28 (July 1965): 409–10.

[21] See, for example, Emma Tonkin et al., "Collaborative and Social Tagging Networks," *Ariadne* 54 (January 2008), http://www.ariadne.ac.uk/issue54/tonkin-et-al/; Valentin Robu, Harry Halpin, and Hana Shepherd, "Emergence of Consensus and Shared Vocabularies in Collaborative Tagging Systems," *ACM Transactions on the Web (TWEB)* 3, no. 4 (2009); and Ramesh Srinivasan, Robin Boast, Katherine Becvar, and Jonathan Furner, "Blobgects: Digital Museums and Diverse Cultural Knowledges,"*Journal of the American Society of Information Science and Technology* 60, no. 4 (2009).

[22] Elizabeth Yakel, Seth Shaw, and Polly Reynolds, "Creating the Next Generation of Archival Finding Aids," *D-Lib Magazine* 13 (May/June 2007), http://www.dlib.org/dlib/may07/yakel/05yakel.html.

[23] Your Archives, "Home Page," http://yourarchives.nationalarchives.gov.uk/index.php?title=Home_page.

[24] Anne J. Gilliland-Swetland and Carol Hughes, "Enhancing Archival Description for Public Computer Conferences of Historical Value: An Exploratory Study," *The American Archivist* 55 (Spring 1992): 316–30.

[25] See Anne J.Gilliland-Swetland and Gregory T. Kinney, "Uses of Electronic Communications to Document an Academic Community: A Research Report," *Archivaria* 38 (Fall 1994): 79–96.

[26] See Data Intensive Cyberinfrastructure Foundation, "Introduction to iRODS and Data Management," https://www.irods.org/index.php/Introduction_to_iRODS.

[27] Luciana Duranti and Randy Preston, eds., *International Research on Permanent Authentic Records in Electronic Systems (InterPARES) 2: Experiential, Interactive, and Dynamic Records* (Padova, Italy: Associazione Nazionale Archivistica Italiana, 2008), 13, http://www.interpares.org/ip2/book.cfm.

[28] Anne Gilliland et al., "Investigating the Roles and Requirements, Manifestations and Management of Metadata in the Creation of Reliable and Preservation of Authentic Electronic Entities Created by Dynamic, Interactive and Experiential Systems: Report on the Work and Findings of the InterPARES

2 Description Cross Domain Group," part 6, in *International Research on Permanent Authentic Records in Electronic Systems (InterPARES) 2*, 261–307, http://www.interpares.org/ip2/book.cfm.

[29] Aaron Dubrow, "Behind the Scenes: A Glimpse to the Archives of the Future," March 24, 2011, Live Science, http://www.livescience.com/13406-glimpse-archives-future-bts-110325.html.

❦

CHAPTER 6

Early Analog Computing, Machine-Readable Records, and the Transition to Digital Recordkeeping

Throughout the twentieth century, archivists struggled with how to accommodate visual and audio materials such as films, home videos, and cassette recordings that only started to come into existence during the latter half of the nineteenth century. By the mid-twentieth century, archivists also began to be faced with "machine-readable" data and records generated by automated data processing. This chapter discusses the development of electronic records management and the attitudes, affiliations, and priorities of so-called first- and second-generation electronic records archivists and the emergence of the current generation of archivists who are increasingly skilled in working in a thoroughly digital world.

The first proposal for scheduling the disposition of records on electronic media was serendipitous. In 1962, as a member of the Office of Records Appraisal . . . of the [U.S.] National Archives, one of my projects was to draft a plan for the retention of specific classes of records created by the Bureau of the Census. After completing a draft plan, I conducted a survey of the bureau in late 1963 to determine whether the plan was feasible and would ensure the preservation of records of enduring value. A room with a glass front and extensive shelving caught my attention. It was the "tape library," which contained magnetic wire and magnetic tape with the data from a variety of censuses and surveys from the 1950s. With changes in the processing system, the bureau used UNIVAC to tabulate source data from 1960 census schedules.

I conducted many interviews to learn major elements of the computer system. To my question about eventual disposition of the tapes, the managerial staff told me that the tapes would be erased and reused to save money. When I told the records manager of the bureau that the disposition of the records on this new media must be scheduled for erasure or retention, he pointed out, mistakenly, that the National Archives had declared punch cards and machine-readable media to be "non-records." After much discussion, the Census Bureau agreed to temporarily discontinue erasing their magnetic tapes.

—Meyer Fishbein, "Recollections of an Electronic Records Pioneer," 2003[1]

Early Applications of Computing

When Charles Samaran was writing in 1938 (quoted at the beginning of chapter 2), ferment in world politics and technological advances were provoking professional concerns about the nature and preservation of, as well as access to, the world's archives. Rapidly developing records creation and reprographic and audiovisual technologies were dramatically altering the nature, volume, and administration of records and archives. As in the case of others before them, these new technologies made the creation, duplication, and dissemination of records and documents easier and faster. However, they also made them more difficult to locate, appraise, and preserve. These new media challenged the physically oriented archival paradigm of the time because their archival value was unclear and their usability depended upon frequently unstandardized playback technology in a constant state of obsolescence. As a result, in many cases, specialized archives developed staffed by specially trained archivists who handled only these kinds of materials. In other cases, audiovisual and machine-readable materials languished in traditional archives where the expertise, equipment, preservation facilities, and other resources for their proper care were lacking.

With the storm clouds of World War II gathering and the experiences of World War I still in very recent memory, a keen awareness existed of the risk to archives of war and social unrest. Shortly after Samaran made his statement, France, Europe, and eventually most of the world was plunged into the Second World War. Like most conflicts, that war left an enduring legacy of records issues. And, also like most conflicts, warring nations exploited existing technologies and pushed the development of new ones to gain strategic advantage. Aerial reconnaissance generated extensive image materials, and national governments employed analog computing to process data, keep records, and break codes. The evolution of automated tabulating machines developed by Herman Hollerith, a mathematician and employee of the U.S. Census Bureau in the late 1870s, is a premier example of this. Hollerith moved to the Massachusetts Institute of Technology (MIT) in 1882 and filed a patent for his machine in 1884. This machine allowed the Census Bureau to meet its deadline for the 1890 census and marked the beginning of the era of modern administrative data processing. It took nine years and $5.8 million to tabulate the 1880 census and less than one year and $11.5 million to complete the 1890 census. In 1896, Hollerith formed the Tabulating Machine Company, and other countries, such as Australia, soon employed his technology for tabulating census data. In 1924, after various mergers, the Tabulating Machine Company evolved into the International Business Machine (IBM) Corporation, and, by 1928, its punch-card technology had become an industry standard. Investigative journalist Edwin Black claims, however, amid some controversy, that IBM's automated counting machines not only tabulated Hitler's 1933 and 1939 censuses in Germany, they also subsequently created analyses of censuses in occupied countries that facilitated the identification of those of Jewish ancestry and of Gypsies and other groups deemed undesirable by the Third Reich. Black also believes that IBM equipment was installed in each concentration camp and used to keep records of the inmates. Documentation more widely substantiates the adaptation by governments in the 1920s of encryption technology—originally designed to support commercial applications such as banking—for intelligence applications. Many governments also realized that punch-card technology could be used to try to break enemy codebooks, which led to a build up, especially by the United States and England, of IBM and other technology deployed for decryption purposes. By 1935, the United States had a large installation in Hawaii, and the United Kingdom soon began developing similar installations. The United States, which was also developing computing technology to assist with military calculations such as those needed to create firing tables for big guns, used the IBM Automatic Sequence Controlled Calculator (ASCC)[2] in computations for the U.S. Navy Bureau of Ships in 1944, although the machine was already obsolete by 1945.

After the war, these technologies were applied to peacetime ends—
for research (especially in emerging social science fields in the 1950s),
communication, commerce, entertainment, and the arts. But, at the same
time, computing became even more integral to military activity and
thereby generated whole new categories of records in electronic form. For
example, the Vietnam War was the first the United States fought with a
fully automated strategic command, resulting in the creation of important datafiles. These datafiles were transferred in the early 1980s to the
Machine-Readable Archives Division of the U.S. National Archives and
Records Administration (NARA). Since then, the largest number of user
requests of NARA's electronic records, particularly from the general public,
has been for information relating to individual casualties during the Korean
and Vietnam Wars, much of which is to be found in these datafiles.[3]

All this is to say that computing and records creation and analysis
have been tightly coupled from the outset. Some of the earliest machine-
generated materials with which archivists worked in the United States were
a few datasets created using punch cards as part of World War II data-
processing applications such as firing tables, cryptology, aerodynamics,
and meteorology. Even though the creation of records using computing
technology was in its infancy, archivists as well as information scientists
were challenged by the vision of Vannevar Bush, director of the Office of
Scientific Research and Development (OSRD) in the 1940s. Bush anticipated research developments, such as the work today of scientists at the
San Diego Supercomputer Center, and demonstrated in his 1945 *Atlantic
Monthly* article, "As We May Think," a keen awareness of the interrelationships between record creation technologies and processes and the accumulation and exploitation of vast stores of knowledge:

> A record, if it is to be useful to science, must be continuously extended, it must be
> stored, and above all it must be consulted. Today we make the record conventionally
> by writing and photography, followed by printing; but we also record on film, on wax
> disks, and on magnetic wires. Even if utterly new recording procedures do not appear,
> these present ones are certainly in the process of modification and extension.[4]

Nevertheless, archival regimes for managing and disseminating the
records created by computing technologies tend to lag considerably behind
the development and implementation of those technologies. In 1939, only

five years after the founding of the U.S. National Archives, the U.S. Records Disposition Act, the first piece of legislation to permit the destruction of U.S. federal records, included punch cards in its definition of the types of materials that could be records. A committee at the U.S. National Archives determined, however, that federal agencies, and not government archivists, should decide whether records stored in punch cards had historical value and should be preserved. As a result, few agencies retained punch cards for historical purposes, seeing them as interim processing data rather than as records with permanent value.[5]

The First Generation of Electronic Records Archivists

The development of electronic records management closely parallels developments in the record-keeping technology itself, but almost always with some degree of lag time while archivists identify how to address new technological capabilities and implementations. After World War II, the archival field took its lead from developments in the field of social science research, applying little traditional archival theory and practice in its work with machine-readable records. Terry Cook has named these the *first generation* of electronic records archivists.[6] In 1946, the Elmo Roper Organization created one of the first social science data archives (SSDAs), the Roper Public Opinion Research Center based at Williams College, to house machine-readable data from Roper surveys. For the next several decades, especially in the 1960s and 1970s, the SSDA community was at the center of a revolution in using quantitative methods in social science research. Unlike the social science data archives movement, however, in which universities played a leading role as repositories of research data, machine-readable records programs developed almost entirely in state and federal government settings. With no existing archival models to follow, archivists looked to those working with social science data, such as statistical and survey files, and applied their techniques to the mainframe-based, batch-processed materials generated for or by automated administrative functions such as accounts receivable and payroll.[7] Although many of these materials had little evidential value because official or record copies were generally produced in paper form, they were retained for their

value as statistically manipulable datasets. In one of the first archival articles on the subject, Morris Rieger of the National Historical Publications
Commission noted the gradual shift in government to reliance upon the
electronic versions of records:

> There has been a considerable growth in the special types of documentation (such as
> punch cards and magnetic tapes) associated with ADP [Automated Data Processing]
> procedures. Such documentation, when produced by governmental agencies, is
> necessarily of interest and concern to public archival institutions. For a long period,
> however, it was regarded by them as lacking in record character, as merely transitory
> work material linking the input and output records at the beginning and end of the
> ADP process. As it has become increasingly clear that creating agencies rely on parts
> of their ADP documentation for record purposes—preserving them for long periods or
> indefinitely and referring to them frequently in connection with official operations—
> archival attitudes are now changing, certainly on the national level.[8]

In 1960, Mary Givens Bryan, sitting president of the Society of American
Archivists, noted that records managers are more future oriented than are
archivists: "We are a common profession but we serve different interests
in the records field . . . how many people in the archives profession are
interested to the full extent in information theory—new communications
and computing devices—in charting or planning for the future?"[9] Archival
awareness relating to machine-readable records began to grow along with
the machine-readable holdings of government repositories from the 1960s
onward.

In 1963, Myron Lefcowitz and Robert O'Shea published a proposal in
the *American Behavioral Scientist* calling for a National Archive of survey
data,[10] and, in 1964, at its Fifth Congress, the International Council on
Archives (ICA) began considering the implications of machine-readable
records and the possibility of accessioning them. The United Nations
Educational, Scientific, and Cultural Organization (UNESCO) and the
newly formed United States Council on Social Science Data Archives
(USCSSDA) encouraged an international effort to establish social science
data archives. In 1972, ICA instituted its ad hoc Working Party on the
implications of ADP in archives. Also in 1972, the national archival repositories in Canada, Sweden, the United Kingdom, and the United States
all launched machine-readable records programs. The following year,

the International Association for Social Science Information Service and Technology (IASSIST) was established and became an important cross-domain forum for those interested in machine-readable records (MRRs), including archivists. IASSIST had three categories of membership: creators and disseminators of MRR, social science data archivists and librarians, and data users, especially social scientists.

Awareness of machine-readable records issues increased considerably in the 1980s with the rapid development of personal computing and computer networking. This decade saw the beginnings of several key state government machine-readable records programs, some of the most notable being those of Wisconsin, Kentucky, and New York, as well as increased activity on the subject by professional archival associations, the most influential of which were the Society of American Archivists' Committee on Automated Records and Techniques (CART)[11] and the National Association of Government Archivists and Records Administrators' Information Technology (IT) Committee.[12] Out of these conjunctions emerged a nascent research infrastructure in the form of programmatic bases, strategic collaborations, and intellectual forums through which to address the inevitable challenges that acquiring and preserving such records presented for archivists. In 1985, the State Archives of New York, which took an early lead in electronic records research, initiated the Special Media Records Project, in cooperation with the Governor's Office of Management and Productivity and nineteen state agencies. The project was to assess the adequacy of state government policies and procedures for the management of computer-generated, machine-readable records and to develop a program for the long-term preservation of selected machine-readable records at the state archives.

In 1987, the United States National Archives and Records Administration (NARA) contracted with the National Bureau of Standards (NBS) to investigate the role of standards in the creation, processing, storage, access, and preservation of electronic records. The resulting report led to NARA's strategy, adopted in 1990, for the development and implementation of standards for the creation, transfer, access, and long-term storage of electronic records created by the federal government.[13] The strategies of most government archives during this period were still primarily data centric in that they focused on rendering the records into software-independent form, maintaining accompanying documentation such as codebooks and creating specialized indexes of selected materials to facilitate use. From a research perspective, these archives focused on determining the life expectancies of magnetic media used in recording the digital data, a topic also of interest to other communities at the time, such as electrical and sound engineers, but that would gradually become less relevant as preservation depended less on media.[14]

The Second Generation of Electronic Records Archivists

Cook argues that the machine-readable records programs that first-generation electronic records archivists oversaw had diminished significantly by the early 1990s. Several new publications[15] heralded the birth of a *second generation* of electronic records archivists, who responded to the increasingly complex nature of computer-generated materials and focused on concerns such as determining the recordness and evidentiality of these materials.[16] Because of their charge to preserve the noncurrent, but still useful, records of their organizations, second-generation electronic records archivists found themselves unprecedentedly engaged, in some cases together with government and scientific agencies, in assessing the preservation implications of the new technologies and media on which those records would be created;[17] identifying specifications for future record-keeping software and systems, sometimes in collaboration with commercial software developers;[18] and recommending strategies for active record-keeping, including analyzing and making recommendations about organizational workflow.[19]

During the late 1980s and early 1990s, following much concern and early work by United Nations (UN) agencies such as the World Bank, the Advisory Committee for the Co-ordination of Information Systems (ACCIS) established a Technical Panel on Electronic Records Management (TP/ REM). The charge to the Technical Panel was to develop guidelines for the implementation of electronic archives and records management programs for use in United Nations organizations, taking into account traditional archives and records management practices; to identify and describe standards that could facilitate effective utilization of the broad range of new technologies in UN organizations; and to facilitate coherent and integrated development of electronic archives and records management and electronic records transmission, so that the implementation and goals of these efforts could be jointly optimized wherever feasible.[20] Significant about this initiative, as well as about a study published by UNESCO and an article by Catherine Bailey, is that it began to frame electronic records issues within the context of traditional archival theory, marking the beginning of theory building around the electronic record.[21]

Another critical component in developing electronic records awareness and seeding electronic records research initiatives was a series of Institutes on Advanced Archival Administration sponsored by NAGARA and held at the University of Pittsburgh from 1989 to 1996. These institutes not only educated government archivists, but also drew attention to the need for strengthened government management of information resources, especially those records required to be preserved for long-term access.[22] In particular, government archivists recommended seeking a National Historical Publications and Records Commission program of challenge grants to develop electronic records programs; identify strategic issues such programs might encounter; implement a mechanism to establish a dialog between records administrators and information resource managers; and study applicable state laws.[23]

The 1990s, therefore, was a critical decade for electronic records management. It saw a transition from a data-centric to a record-centric approach to electronic records management and a new emphasis on building an educational infrastructure to support the development of necessary archival expertise in the area. Recognizing that education is a key component in creating this second generation of electronic records archivists, a CART curriculum, SAA workshops, and the first graduate school courses in electronic records management were all developed in the early 1990s.[24] Most important for the focus of this chapter, the nineties saw the beginnings of a robust research base, largely as a result of the funding agenda adopted by the NHPRC, which allowed archives other than very large governmental repositories to develop electronic record programs and research test beds (notably, Indiana University, the City of Philadelphia, and states such as Michigan, Minnesota, and Mississippi). The support also allowed academic researchers to develop large-scale projects that would begin to generate a theoretical base for electronic records management and to experiment with technological requirements and tools.

Transitioning to Digital

The implementation in the 1990s of prominent agendas for electronic records research and development by national funding agencies, such as the U.S. National Historical Publications and Records Commission (NHPRC),[25] and by government archival institutions in North America, Europe, Australia, and elsewhere—as well as the fallout from high-profile litigation—provided the impetus for the development of a strong evidence-based approach to the nature and management of electronic records,[26] even while researchers and practicing archivists increasingly grappled with the status of those records as technological and social constructs. Chapter 7 discusses the research and conceptual development that emerged from this impetus in more detail.

Now, more than fifty years after Bryan's question, and more than seventy years after the U.S. government recognized the potential record status of computer punch cards, the American archival field still grapples with a professional paradigm and life-cycle model that struggles to move beyond the paper-based era. (The notable exceptions would be institutions whose recordkeeping regimes are based in records continuum thinking and continuum-based practice, which transcend such media and custody-centric ideas). Archivists also wrestle with severely limiting notions of what constitutes a record and an archives in the context of the twenty-first-century media applications, cultural pluralism, and community authorship that are hallmarks of the digital world.

The transition from analog to digital computing is not simply a linear or temporal one. Chapters 1 and 2 delineate many of the changes that have occurred as society passes into and functions within a digital world. The generation of archivists taking over from the second generation of electronic records archivists represents a much broader section of the archival profession. Indeed, they are becoming the norm rather than the isolated specialists. Their areas of responsibility have similarly broadened as digital creation, organization, preservation, and use become the primary modes for such activities. In short, members of the third generation are no longer electronic records archivists. They are simply archivists.

While appraisal, acquisition, authentication, and preservation were the central preoccupations of the earlier generations, some of the most pressing challenges facing archivists today relate to the generation, mining, and compilation of vast accumulations of digital materials and the implications of ensuring accountability, protecting citizen privacy, and encouraging and enhancing the widest possible access to and use of the digital record. Chapter 7 discusses some of the areas of research that have emerged in relation to these challenges. The following are but three examples of areas of increasing concern and focus in archival practice.

1. **Protecting or providing access to sensitive records.** Digital technologies provide a means to manipulate, mine, reinterpret, and match or map records created by both analog and digital computing. This has important implications for managing and making available often highly sensitive records created during one of the most turbulent centuries, as well as the stores of big data, social media, and digital records accumulating in the twenty-first century. Around the world, problematic histories relating to the two world wars; redrawing national borders and the creation of new states; the rise and fall of monarchies, fascism, communism, apartheid, and dictatorships; the demise of colonial empires; and genocides of a scale and regularity not previously documented live very close to the surface in local communities and in the memories of survivors, perpetrators, and their descendants. Archivists face questions of enormous sensitivity regarding the opening of records of these events, as well as how to document recent wars and atrocities that have an unprecedented immediacy and an instant global audience because of the Web and social media. The decisions they make and the stands they take face scrutiny in the popular media as well as high-level political attention and, potentially, pressure. For example, records declassified and made available online in one country may result in public pressure on another country to

open its records relating to the same matter earlier than originally scheduled. National archives, often wrong footed, have been forced to respond when active government records created by digital systems for components for which they will ultimately be responsible are legally requested under Freedom of Information legislation or illegally purged, hacked, or stolen and instantaneously disseminated on the Web. Prime examples of this are the succession of White House email scandals[27] and WikiLeaks.[28] Such instances often illustrate a frustration on the part of the press and many other parties with the apparent lack of proactivity by government archives in promoting public access to such materials as transparently and expeditiously as is possible under the law. However, they also demonstrate how difficult it is to protect confidentiality or the privacy of those mentioned in records when they are digitally created, maintained, disseminated, and mined.[29] A different kind of example is the painstaking digital reconstruction of partially destroyed records, such as was undertaken using state-of-the art technology with shredded Stasi informant files, which raises interesting questions about reliability, authenticity, and digital restoration practices.[30] And yet a third example are new initiatives by intelligence agencies to develop temporal and visualization algorithms that can mine large accumulations of electronic information, such as economic forecasts, Twitter feeds, news reports, and blogs in an attempt to discern patterns and predict potential hot spots, protests, and economic instability before they occur.[31]

2. **Promoting accountability in conflict and postconflict situations.** Over the past three decades, several countries have engaged in wars with considerably more technological direction than the Vietnam War, including digital strategic command, digitally directed remote missile strikes, and drone deployment. Over the same period, the International Criminal Tribunal for the former Yugoslavia (ICTY) in The Hague, and a growing number of criminal prosecutions and restorative or reparative justice bodies worldwide such as truth and reconciliation commissions, have extensively employed and generated records and recordkeeping in their investigations.

Ever since the successful deployment of *Sputnik* in 1957, satellites have been used for government and commercial purposes to collect data about the earth from orbit. The recent work of the Satellite Sentinel Project at Harvard uses publicly available satellite images to track the compliance of government, military, and other parties in conflicts with conventions and agreements relating to human rights. All of these developments raise questions about how accountability is designed into the systems being used; about who are the stewards of the resulting records; about what constitutes authenticity and reliability; about the nature of and reliance upon deliberate, incidental, and accidental human and material witnessing; and about the kinds of forensic and evidentiary expertise necessary to cross-examine such digital evidence.

Are archivists sufficiently involved in the design of such systems to guarantee that reliable digital records are created, preserved, safeguarded, and accessible to support government and military transparency and accountability, to provide evidence of how and why conflicts were waged and by whom, and to ensure that responsibilities relating to veterans, refugees, and dislocated people, victims, prisoners, and detainees are documented and met? Can archives provide the descriptive and analytical tools to support sophisticated cross-examination of those records?

3. **Digital annotation of the record.** Technology also allows the public to be involved more broadly and actively in records production, description, and preservation, as well as use. While the contributions to archival description of social tagging receive wide attention, other forms of digital contributions to archives by the public have also developed. Examples include "citizen archivists," who work directly with archival organizations or on their own using social media to contribute new content, digital transcriptions of nondigital records, and commentary on items found in the archives; citizen digitizers who voluntarily assist with mass digitization efforts in archives; and initiatives such as StoryCorps that recruit members of the public to digitally record, share, and preserve the stories of their lives.[32]

Notes

This chapter includes, with permission, some updated and revised sections of the following previously published article: Anne J. Gilliland-Swetland, "Management of Electronic Records," *Annual Review of Information Science and Technology (ARIST)* 39 (2005): 219–53.

[1] Meyer Fishbein, "Recollections of an Electronic Records Pioneer," in *Thirty Years of Electronic Records*, ed. Bruce Ambacher (Lanham, Md.: Scarecrow, 2003), xiv–xv.

[2] Subsequently called the Mark I by Harvard University.

[3] See Margaret O'Neill Adams, "Three Decades of Description and Reference Services for Electronic Records," in *Thirty Years of Electronic Records*, 63–90.

[4] Vannevar Bush, "As We May Think," *Atlantic Monthly* 176 (1945): 104.

[5] Ironically, over fifty years later, the National Archives was to find itself embroiled in a series of high-profile lawsuits relating to the lack of archival oversight of White House electronic mail hosted on the IBM PROFS system that was not viewed as containing records. See David A. Bearman, "The Implications of *Armstrong v. Executive Office of the President* for the Archival Management of Electronic Records," *The American Archivist* 56 (1993): 674–89.

[6] Terry Cook, "Easier to Byte, Harder to Chew: The Second Generation of Electronic Records Archives," *Archivaria* 33 (1992): 202–16.

[7] Terry Cook and Eldon Frost, "The Electronic Records Archival Programme at the National Archives of Canada: Evolution and Critical Factors of Success," in *Electronic Records Management Program Strategies: Archives and Museum Informatics Technical Report No. 18*, ed. Margaret Hedstrom (Pittsburgh: Archives and Museum Informatics, 1993), 38–47.

[8] Morris Rieger, "Archives and Automation," *The American Archivist* 29 no. 1 (1966): 109.

[9] Mary Givens Bryan, "Changing Times," *The American Archivist* 24 (January 1961): 6.

[10] M. J. Lefcowitz and R. M. O'Shea, "A Proposal to Establish a National Archives for Social Science Survey Data," *American Behavioral Scientist* 6 (1963): 27.

[11] Nancy McGovern, email to the author, August 2011.

[12] Author's note: In summer 2011, while I was working on this book, I contacted Nancy McGovern, as one of the founders of the Society of American Archivists' Committee on Automated Records and Techniques, to ask her about some of the history of the group and its legacy. She reflected on the energy that went into the pioneering group's electronic records work, which I share here. CART was unusual in that it was a working group as well as a committee. It was also where so many pioneers in archival activities relating to technology convened, and where I first encountered many of them. Nancy remembers it as

> A fun, interesting group—a group like CART (pretty much anyone interested in computer-related issues) would be huge now. . . . Each word of CART was significant in its history—Committee, which led to it being rationalized in the early 90s into a section—Automated: reflected ongoing (endless) discussion of what to call things—it included automation techniques and records.

She continues:

> The history of CART represents innovation, early adopters, ability, dedication—in the forming, storming, norming sense. The 90s represented storming. . . . We started the roundtable to reach out to SAA members—CART was like a walking bibliography: Margaret Hedstrom, Tom Brown, David Bearman, Lisa Weber; Canadians: John McDonald, Sue Gavrel, Harold Naugler . . . a long and illustrious list. . . . CART was productive: [it] organized electronic records workshops that were well-attended, wrote reports (on request and *ad hoc*), tracked standards, developed the CART Curriculum.

About the electronic records issues that were the early focus of CART discussion:

> Are electronic records really records? [hard to imagine the need for that now]. Terminology—machine-readable, electronic, digital. . . . Lots of focus on appraising electronic records. The Pittsburgh functional requirements, the beginnings of InterPARES. . . . We wanted to make ERS [the Electronic Records Section] a virtual section—we thought electronic records issues should be (would be) integrated throughout SAA so an online forum would be helpful.

And finally, regarding the outcomes and legacy of CART:

> Measure of success then: Tom [Ruller] and I worried about achieving a critical mass of people for the [new SAA] section and that we would have to keep at it to keep it going—my final meeting on the steering committee, the incoming chair didn't recognize me, but luckily, someone vouched for me. . . . Measures of success now: ERS is still running—the section grapples regularly with current issues . . . such as how to deal with digital preservation that cuts across ERS and Preservation? Through collaboration to address range of topics.

Nancy McGovern, email to the author, 6 September 2011.

13 National Institute of Standards and Technology, *Framework and Policy Recommendations for the Exchange and Preservation of Electronic Records, Prepared for the National Archives and Records Administration* (Washington, D.C.: National Institute of Standards and Technology, 1989).

14 Elisabeth F. Cuddihy, "Aging of Magnetic Recording Tape," *IEEE Transactions on Magnetics* 16 (July 1980): 558–68; Fynnette Eaton, "Electronic Media and Preservation," *IASSIST Quarterly* 181 (1994): 14–17; Sidney B. Geller, *Care and Handling of Computer Magnetic Storage Media*, NBS Special Publication 500–101 (Washington, D.C.: Institute for Computer Sciences and Technology, National Bureau of Standards, 1983); Committee on Preservation of Historical Records, *Preservation of Historic Records: Magnetic Recording Media* (Washington, D.C.: National Academy Press, 1986).

15 For example, David A. Bearman, ed., *Archival Management of Electronic Records*, Technical Report 13 (Pittsburgh: Archives and Museum Informatics, 1991); Katharine Gavrel, *Conceptual Problems Posed by Electronic Records: A RAMP Study* (Paris: UNESCO, International Council on Archives, 1990); National Academy of Public Administration, *The Archives of the Future: Archival Strategies for the Treatment of Electronic Databases. Report to the National Archives and Records Administration* (Washington, D.C.: National Academy of Public Administration, 1991); National Archives and Records Administration, *Managing Electronic Records* (Washington, D.C.: National Archives and Records Administration, 1990); National Historical Publications and Records Commission, *Research Issues in Electronic Records: Report of the Working Meeting* (St. Paul: Published for the National Historical Publications and Records Commission by the Minnesota Historical Society, 1991); Barbara Reed and David Roberts, eds., *Keeping Data: Papers from a Workshop on Appraising Computer-based Records* (Sydney: Australian Council of Archives and the Australian Society of Archivists Incorporated, 1991); United Nations Advisory Committee for the Co-ordination of Information Systems, *Management of Electronic Records: Issues and Guidelines* (New York: United Nations, 1990); and the United States House of Representatives Committee on Government Operations, *Taking a Byte Out of History: The Archival Preservation of Federal Computer Records*, House Report 101-978 (Washington, D.C.: Committee on Government Operations, U.S. House of Representatives, 1990).

16 Cook, "Easier to Byte."

17 National Academy of Public Administration, *The Effects of Electronic Recordkeeping on the Historical Record of the U.S. Government: A Report for the National Archives and Records Administration* (Washington, D.C.: National Academy of Public Administration, 1989); National Institute of Standards and Technology, *Framework and Policy Recommendations*; United States House of Representatives Committee on Government Operations, *Taking a Byte Out of History*; United Nations Advisory Committee for the Co-ordination of Information Systems, *Management of Electronic Records*; National Association of Government Archives and Records Administrators, *A New Age: Electronic Information Systems, State Governments, and the Preservation of the Archival*

Record (Lexington, Ky.: NASIRE/The Council of State Governments, 1991); National Research Council, *Preserving Scientific Data on Our Physical Universe: A New Strategy for Archiving the Nation's Scientific Information Resources* (Washington, D.C.: National Academy Press, 1995); National Research Council, *Study on the Long-term Retention of Selected Scientific and Technical Records of the Federal Government: Working Papers* (Washington, D.C.: National Academy Press, 1995).

[18] Justine Heazlewood et al., "Electronic Records: Problem Solved? A Report on the Public Record Office Victoria's Electronic Records Strategy," *Archives and Manuscripts* 27, no. 1 (1999): 96–113; National Archives and Records Administration, *A National Archives Strategy for the Development and Implementation of Standards for the Creation, Transfer, Access, and Long-term Storage of Electronic Records of the Federal Government*, National Archives Technical Information Paper 8 (Washington, D.C.: National Archives and Records Administration, 1990); National Archives of Canada, *Managing Information in Office Automation Systems: Final Report on the FOREMOST Project* (Ottawa: National Archives of Canada, 1990); United Nations Advisory Committee for the Co-ordination of Information Systems, *Strategic Issues for Electronic Records Management: Towards Open Systems Interconnection* (New York: United Nations, 1992); New York State Department of Education, *Building Partnerships: Developing New Approaches to Electronic Records Management and Preservation: Final Report* (Albany: New York State Department of Education, 1994); New York State Department of Education, *Building Partnerships for Electronic Recordkeeping: The New York State Information Management Policies and Practices Survey: Summary of Findings* (Albany: New York State Department of Education, 1994); National Archives of Canada and the Canadian Workplace Automation Research Centre, *IMOSA Project: Functional Requirements: Corporate Information Management Application (CIMA)* (Ottawa: National Archives of Canada and the Canadian Workplace Automation Research Centre, 1991); National Archives of Canada and Department of Communication, *The IMOSA Project: An Initial Analysis of Document Management and Retrieval Systems* (Ottawa: National Archives of Canada, Department of Communications, 1993); John McDonald, "Managing Information in an Office Systems Environment: The IMOSA Project," *The American Archivist* 58 (1995): 142–53; Kenneth Thibodeau and Darryl Prescott, "Reengineering Records Management: The U.S. Department of Defense, Records Management Task Force," *Archivi and Computer* 6, no. 1 (1996): 71–78.

[19] Philip C. Bantin and Gerald Bernbom, "The Indiana University Electronic Records Project: Analyzing Functions, Identifying Transactions, and Evaluating Recordkeeping Systems: A Report on Methodology," *Archives and Museum Informatics: Cultural Informatics Quarterly* 10 (1996): 246–66.

[20] United Nations Advisory Committee for the Co-ordination of Information Systems, *Management of Electronic Records: Issues and Guidelines.*

[21] Catherine Bailey, "Archival Theory and Electronic Records," *Archivaria* 29 (1990): 180–96; Gavrel, *Conceptual Problems Posed by Electronic Records*; United Nations Advisory Committee for the Co-ordination of Information Systems, *Management of Electronic Records: Issues and Guidelines.*

[22] National Association of Government Archives and Records Administrators, *A New Age.*

[23] David Olson, "'Camp Pitt' and the Continuing Education of Government Archivists, 1989–1996," *The American Archivist* 60, no. 2 (1997): 202–14.

[24] Victoria Irons Walch, "Automated Records and Techniques Curriculum Development Project, Committee on Automated Records and Techniques," *The American Archivist* 56 (1993): 468–505 and "Innovation Diffusion: Implications for the CART Curriculum," *The American Archivist* 56 (1993): 506–12.

[25] See, for example, National Historical Publications and Records Commission, *Research Issues in Electronic Records*; and Minnesota Historical Society, State Archives Department, *Electronic Records Agenda Project Final Report* (June 2003), http://www.mnhs.org/preserve/records/docs_pdfs/eragenda_main_june03.pdf.

[26] Bearman, "The Implications of *Armstrong v. Executive Office of the President* for the Archival Management of Electronic Records"; and Bearman, *Electronic Evidence: Strategies for Managing Records in Contemporary Organizations* (Pittsburgh: Archives and Museum Informatics, 1994).

[27] For a chronology of events surrounding the so-called PROFS email scandal, see the National Security Archive, "White House Email," http://www.gwu.edu/~nsarchiv/white_house_email/index.html.

[28] For an excellent discussion of Wikileaks, see Frank Upward, Sue McKemmish, and Barbara Reed, "Archivists and Changing Social and Information Spaces: A Continuum Approach to Recordkeeping and Archiving in Online Cultures," *Archivaria* 72 (Fall 2011): 197–238.

[29] For a report on citizen behavior and attitude on this issue, see, for example, TNS Opinion and Social, "Attitudes on Data Protection and Electronic Identity in the European Union," *Special Eurobarometer 359* (Brussels: European Commission, June 2011).

[30] Andrew Curry, "Piecing Together the Dark Legacy of East Germany's Secret Police," *Wired Magazine* 16 (January 2008), http://www.wired.com/politics/security/magazine/16-02/ff_stasi?currentPage=all.

[31] For example, see Dina Temple-Raston, "Predicting the Future: Fantasy or a Good Algorithm?," National Public Radio, October 8, 2012, http://m.npr.org/news/U.S./162397787.

[32] "Since 2003, StoryCorps has collected and archived more than 40,000 interviews from nearly 80,000 participants. Each conversation is recorded on a free CD to share, and is preserved at the American Folklife Center at the Library of Congress." See StoryCorps: Every Voice Matters, http://storycorps .org/.

CHAPTER 7

∞

Research in Electronic Records Management

This chapter reviews the development of research relating to electronic records management from the 1990s onward. It highlights interdisciplinary and trans-sector collaborative research initiated both from within the field and externally. Key areas of focus include the nature of the record in increasingly distributed, dynamic, and multimedia digital contexts and the development of functional requirements and technological and procedural specifications for creating, managing, and preserving reliable and authentic records.

It seems to me that you lay too much stress on the term "legal" in connection with the evidential character of archival material. Fundamentally there is no difference between legal evidence and historical evidence or any other kind of evidence, or rather evidence used for any other purpose. Even though records are to be preserved solely for non-legal historical use—that is, there is no possibility of their being used for legal evidence in courts—nevertheless they should be preserved as bodies of records, that is, as archives, because their evidential value for historical or other research purposes is dependent on their provenance.

—Carbon copy of letter from Solon J. Buck to Margaret Cross Norton, January 24, 1944, regarding her presentation "Archives and Historical Evidence" to the Princeton meeting of the Society of American Archivists and published in the December 1943 issue of *Illinois Libraries*[1]

American archivists have operated, far too long, as if their mission was only a cultural mission, when in fact the real mission should be to ensure that the essential evidence of organizations will be maintained, in whatever form is necessary— including electronic. . . . The preservation of the evidence will provide more than is necessary for historians and others to conduct their research, and this focus on evidence—which the recordkeeping functional requirements return to us—is much more manageable and crucial to the archival mission.

—Richard J. Cox, "Re-discovering the Archival Mission . . . ," 1994[2]

A Restated Emphasis on Evidence

A solid, knowledge-based understanding of the nature of legal, historical, and cultural digital evidence, as well as how best to select and eliminate,[3] describe, preserve, and present it, is essential to the sound management of records created and maintained in digital form. Being able to play a leading role in that management is essential to the future of the archival field. For these reasons, electronic records management and digital recordkeeping more broadly are the loci of the most intensive concentration of empirical and conceptual research and attention from government and business of any aspect of the archival endeavor to date. Among the information professions, archival science focuses most centrally around the ways certain kinds of information are capable of bearing witness to (*dispositive* capabilities) or serving as evidence of (*probative* capabilities) facts, acts, processes, responsibilities, rights, and consequences. The nature of that evidence and the extent of the archivist's enduring responsibility to preserve and elucidate it, however, have been the subjects of ongoing debate throughout the history of the American archival profession, as well as among scholars, and have become evermore difficult to pinpoint as documentary forms shift and boundaries between the official and the personal blur.[4]

By the late 1980s, while archivists were concerned about systems obsolescence, deteriorating media, and the effect these would have on the integrity of records, they had come to realize the fundamental importance of identifying what constitutes a record in the sense understood by the law.[5] Australian archivist David Roberts characterizes these definitional issues as especially related to drawing distinctions between data management and administration, and the management of electronic records based upon their transactional and evidential nature.[6] Fellow Australian Glenda Acland argues that

> The pivot of archival science is evidence not information. Archivists do not deal with isolated and free-floating bits of information, but with their documentary expression, with what has been recently referred to in Australia as the archival document.[7]

The shift in emphasis from information to evidence by second-generation electronic records archivists, as discussed in chapter 6, led to

an increased research focus on the nature of the record, its legal requirements, and its appraisal for legal and other values, and on preserving its
evidence.[8] However, it is important to note that the notion of evidence
as applied in electronic records research was tightly coupled with legal
and business requirements, and with the exception of some of the records
continuum work did not centrally address the ways in which requirements
for historical, cultural, and research evidence might overlap with those of
the law and of business.

The impact of high-profile, long-running litigation relating to the
National Archives' management of presidential electronic mail spurred
on American archivists in this focus on evidence. The seminal case was
Armstrong v. the Executive Office of the President (a.k.a. the PROFS case),
which revolved around the evidential status of electronic mail generated
by the PROFS system in place in the Reagan-Bush White House and how
the National Archives approached scheduling it for retention and disposition. In his initial judgment, Federal District Court Judge Charles R. Richey
stated that electronic mail in its native state within the PROFS system is
the official record because its electronic metadata made it a more complete
record than a print version. The metadata, mostly the routing and header
information, made it possible to identify who knew what, and when. The
judge also found that the National Archives had acted arbitrarily and capri-
ciously by not promulgating adequate guidelines for the management of
electronic mail.[9] The funding agenda published by the National Historical
Publications and Records Commission (NHPRC) in 1991 also reflected this
focus on evidence. It is hardly surprising, therefore, that American electronic records researchers became primarily concerned with identifying
functional requirements for creating reliable and preserving authentic
electronic records and the metadata and automated tools and techniques
to support those requirements.

In 1991, prominent American electronic records archivist Margaret
Hedstrom published a framework for research in electronic records that
remains today probably the most durable articulation of research needs
relating to electronic records. In the same year, the NHPRC report, *Research
Issues in Electronic Records*, identified several applied research questions and called upon the archival community to undertake research and

development activities to identify strategies and solutions to those questions (see Figure 7.1).[10] The NHPRC report was likely the single most important factor in developing an electronic records research front in North America, not only because it articulated research needs, but also because it set the research agenda for an NHPRC funding initiative devoted entirely to electronic records research and development, the first of its kind. Another research stimulus was initiated in 1996 in the United Kingdom when the Joint Information Systems Committee (JISC) of the U.K. higher education funding councils and the National Preservation Office (NPO), concerned

Hedstrom's framework on electronic records research, 1991	NHPRC's *Research Issues in Electronic Records* research agenda, 1991
1. What is the relationship between activities, organizational structures, information technology, information flows, decision making, and documentation?	1. What functions and data are required to manage electronic records in accord with archival requirements? Do data requirements and functions vary for different types of automated applications?
2. What new forms of material do users create with information technology?	2. What are the technological, conceptual, and economic implications of capturing and retaining data, descriptive information, and contextual information in electronic form from a variety of applications?
3. Can archivists intervene at critical points in the development and introduction of new technologies?	3. How can software-dependent data objects be retained for future use?
4. How will changes in the supply of, demand for, and costs of storing and disseminating information change archival practice?	4. How can data dictionaries, information resource directory systems, and other metadata systems be used to support electronic records management and archival requirements?
5. How should the requirements for management and preservation of electronic records change archives as institutions and the archival profession?	5. What archival requirements have been addressed in major systems development projects and why?
	6. What policies best address archival concerns for the identification, retention, preservation, and research use of electronic records?
	7. What functions and activities should be present in electronic records programs and how should they be evaluated?
	8. What incentives can contribute to creator and user support for electronic records management concerns?
	9. What barriers have prevented archivists from developing and implementing archival electronic records programs?
	10. What do archivists need to know about electronic records?

Figure 7.1. Hedstrom's framework for research on electronic records and NHPRC's research agenda questions (1991)

about the preservation of electronic materials, agreed to fund a program of studies in several relevant areas to be administered by the British Library Research and Innovation Centre (BLRIC):

- An analysis of the U.S. Task Force on the Archiving of Digital Information report.
- A framework of data types and formats.
- Who should be responsible for preservation and access?
- The post hoc rescue (data archaeology) of high-value digital material.
- The preservation requirements of universities and research funding bodies.
- Comparison of methods of digital preservation.
- Strategies for creating and preserving digital collections.[11]

The allocation of research funding by NHPRC, the Social Sciences and Humanities Research Council of Canada (which has been the major funder of a series of InterPARES Projects undertaken since 1998), the United Kingdom's JISC, the Australian Research Council, the European Framework Programs for Research and Technological Development, and the U.S. National Science Foundation also happily coincided with the moment when schools around North America and internationally began to hire career archival faculty and became heavily involved in electronic records and digital preservation research. Those faculty led many of the major electronic records and digital preservation research projects of the 1990s and 2000s in groundbreaking, cross-disciplinary, cross-sector, and often international collaborations (see Table 7.1).[12] Indeed, among the unforeseen consequences of these initiatives, the opportunities to undertake this funded research helped several academics not only to solidify their own careers but also to strengthen the precarious toehold of archival science within the academy and to modernize and expand its curriculum to include what had been learned through this research. These initiatives also nurtured close working relationships between archival academics, both nationally and internationally, that blossomed into fruitful research and educational collaborations that addressed other aspects of digital record-keeping, metadata schema development, digital preservation, and digital and data curation.

Table 7.1. Key research projects in electronic records management and related areas, 1993 to the present

Name	Date	Major Funding	Key Personnel	
Variables in the Satisfaction of Archival Requirements for Electronic Records Management (*The Pittsburgh Project*)	1993–1996	National Historical Publications and Records Commission (NHPRC) (U.S.)	Richard Cox, James Williams, Wendy Duff and David Wallace (University of Pittsburgh), David Bearman (consultant)	To identify: <ul><li>Record-keeping functional requirements for electronic information systems;</li><li>Variables in organizations that affect the way in which both software and hardware are utilized and which may affect the degree to which archival functional requirements can be adopted;</li><li>Technical capabilities of organizational software products to satisfy archival requirements;</li><li>Other means, such as policy and standards, to satisfy archival functional requirements;</li><li>Effectiveness of technology and policy strategies to ensure that archival interests can be met.</li></ul>

Deliverables/Outcomes:
Standards for Business Acceptable Communications consisting of four main products: functional requirements, production rules, metadata specifications, and literary warrant

See http://www.sis.pitt.edu/~bcallery/pgh/index.htm.

Name	Date	Major Funding	Key Personnel	
Preservation of the Integrity of Electronic Records Project (*The UBC Project*)	1994–1997	Social Sciences and Humanities Research Council (SSHRC) (Canada)	Luciana Duranti, Terry Eastwood, Heather MacNeil (University of British Columbia)	<ul><li>Establish what a record is in principle and how it can be recognized in an electronic environment;</li><li>Determine what kind of electronic systems generate records;</li><li>Formulate criteria that allow for the appropriate segregation of records from all other types of information in electronic systems generating and/or storing a variety of data aggregations;</li><li>Define the conceptual requirements for guaranteeing the reliability and authenticity of records in electronic systems; to assess those methods against different administrative, juridical, cultural, and disciplinary points of view.</li></ul>

Deliverables/Outcomes:

The findings of the research project fall into two categories:
(a) specific methods for ensuring the reliability and authenticity of electronic records; and

(cont.)

(b) management issues concerning the maintenance and preservation of reliable and authentic records.

Under (a), the findings are that

1. the reliability and authenticity of electronic records are best ensured by embedding procedural rules in the overall records system and by integrating business and documentary procedures;
2. the reliability and authenticity of electronic records are best guaranteed by emphasizing their documentary context; and
3. the reliability and authenticity of electronic records can only be preserved if they are managed together with all the other records belonging in the same fonds.

Under (b), the findings are that

1. the life cycle of the managerial activity directed to the preservation of the integrity of electronic records can be neatly divided into two phases: one phase directed to the control of the creation and maintenance of reliable and authentic active and semiactive records, and the other phase directed to the preservation of authentic inactive records; and
2. the integrity of electronic records is best preserved by entrusting the creating body with responsibility for their reliability and the preserving body with responsibility for their authenticity.

See http://www.interpares.org/UBCProject/intro.htm.

| Indiana University Electronic Records Project | 1995–1997 | NHPRC (U.S.) | Philip Bantin (Indiana University) | An implementation project designed to develop a strategy and methodology for incorporating recordkeeping requirements into Indiana University's transaction processing and information systems.

Stage 1: Functional analysis of business units, identification of business transactions, and identification of basic information categories necessary for establishing evidence of specific business transactions;
Stage 2: Identify and describe existing information systems that store the data on the previously identified business transactions;
Stage 3: Evaluate the existing systems in terms of the Functional Requirements for Evidence in Recordkeeping and the "Metadata Specifications Derived from the Functional Requirements" developed at the University of Pittsburgh;
Stage 4: Analyze results and report on findings. |
| --- | --- | --- | --- | --- |

Deliverables/Outcomes:

1. Evaluation of results derived from the field tests of the methodology
2. An evaluation of the attempt to create recordkeeping systems from information systems
3. An analysis of costs associated with implementing the methodology
4. Rationales for selecting a subset of the Pittsburgh "Functional and Metadata Requirements"

(cont.)

5. A methodology for evaluating recordkeeping systems based on several field tests

See Philip Bantin, "Strategies for Managing Electronic Records: Lessons Learned from the Indiana University Electronic Records Project," *The Information Management Journal*, 35 (January 2001): 16–24, http://www.indiana.edu/~libarch/ER/marticle2.pdf.

| Victorian Electronic Records Strategy (VERS) | 1996–ongoing | Public Record Office Victoria (PROV) | PROV, CSIRO, Ernst and Young | Develop a test bed system to prototype a "future state" electronic document processing and record capture system, using the Department of Infrastructure as the source of records and record capture processes. |

Deliverables/Outcomes:

In 1998 the VERS Demonstrator System authenticated that it was possible and practical to capture, manage, and access digital records using a VERS Encapsulated Object (VEO) format. See http://prov.vic.gov.au/wp-content/uploads/2012/02/VERS-Final-Report.pdf.

The VERS Standard, PROS 99/007 was developed in 2000, and the most current version was released in July 2002. During this time at the Department of Infrastructure (DOI), the VERS@ DOI Pilot Implementation Project was demonstrating the capture of records at the point of creation and the management and export of VEOs in a live environment.

The VERS Centre of Excellence was established in May 2002. Located at PROV, the Centre of Excellence was responsible for overseeing the development of a strategy for the initial rollout of VERS across the Victorian government. The Centre provided resources, advice, and guidance to Victorian government agencies as well as conducting further research into the long-term preservation of electronic records and overseeing the construction of an electronic records repository at PROV (Digital Archive).

See http://prov.vic.gov.au/government/vers.

| Recordkeeping Metadata Standards for Managing and Accessing Information Resources in Networked Environments Over Time for Government, Commerce, Social and Cultural (cont.) | 1998–1999 | The Australian Research Council (ARC) and the industry partners: a National Archives of Australia–led Records and Archives Coalition, involving State Records NSW, Queensland State Archives, Records Archives (cont.) | Sue McKemmish (Monash University), Glenda Acland (research consultant), Kate Cumming (State Records NSW), Barbara Reed (Record-keeping Systems Pty Ltd), Nigel Ward (DSTC Monash University) | Working within the context of a range of metadata-related initiatives in Australia and elsewhere, the Recordkeeping Metadata Project aims to comprehensively specify and codify recordkeeping metadata in ways that enable it to be fully understood and deployed both within and beyond the records and archives profession. The main objectives of the Project were to • codify, i.e., specify and standardize, the full range of recordkeeping metadata needed to manage records in electronic networked environments to meet current and future requirements for access to essential evidence; • classify metadata elements according to their role in managing records to support decision making about what metadata to capture, and to assist in managing related risks (i.e., to enable people to make business cases about what level of functionality to build into their recordkeeping systems (cont.) |

Purposes (SPIRT Recordkeeping Metadata Research Project)			Management Association of Australia, and the Australian Council of Archives.	based on considerations like – how robust does this record need to be? – does it have to persist over long periods of time? – how sensitive are related terms and conditions re access and use? – how important is it to track and document its use?); • support interoperability with generic metadata standards, e.g., the Dublin Core and other sector-specific sets; • support initiatives in relation to information locator systems, e.g., the Australian Government Locator Service (AGLS).

Deliverables/Outcomes:
- The main deliverable of the project was the Australian Recordkeeping Metadata Schema (RKMS) which provides a
  - standardized set of structured recordkeeping metadata elements;
  - framework for developing and specifying recordkeeping metadata standards;
  - framework for reading or mapping metadata sets in ways that can enable their semantic interoperability by establishing equivalences and correspondences that can provide the basis for semi-automated translation between metadata schemas;
- input to Australian National Standard;
- conceptual and relationship models: records in business and sociolegal contexts;
- classification of recordkeeping metadata by purpose;
- metadata concept maps.

See http://www.infotech.monash.edu.au/research/groups/rcrg/projects/spirt/index.html.

CURL Exemplars in Digital ARchiveS Project (CEDARS)	1998–2001	Joint Information Systems Committee (JISC) (U.K.)	Consortium of University Research Libraries (CURL). Lead sites: the universities of Cambridge, Leeds, and Oxford. Other collaborators: UKOLN, the Arts and Humanities Data Service (cont.)	• Promote awareness about the importance of digital preservation, both among research libraries and their users and among the data-creating and data-supplying communities upon which they depend. • Identify, document, and disseminate strategic frameworks within which individual libraries can develop collection management policies that are appropriate to their needs and that can guide the necessary decision making to safeguard the long-term viability of any digital resources that are included in their collections. • Investigate, document, and promote methods appropriate to the long-term preservation of different classes of digital resources typically included in library collections and to develop costed and scalable models.

		(AHDS), the British Library, the Data Archive, the British Library National Preservation Office (NPO), and the Research Libraries Group (RLG).	

Deliverables/Outcomes:
- Guidelines for developing collection management policies that will ensure the long-term viability of any digital resources included in the collection
- Demonstrator projects to test and promote the technical and organizational feasibility of a chosen strategy for digital preservation
- Methodological guidelines developed by the demonstrator projects providing guidance about how to preserve different classes of digital resources
- Clearly articulated preferences about data formats, content models, and compression techniques that are most readily and cost effectively preserved
- A study of digital preservation metadata.

See http://www.rluk.ac.uk/node/80 and Michael Day, "CEDARS: Digital Preservation and Metadata," http://www.ukoln.ac.uk/metadata/presentations/delos6/cedars.html.

International Research on Permanent Authentic Records in Electronic Systems Project (InterPARES 1)	1998–2002	SSHRC and the National Archives of Canada (Canada), NHPRC and the National Archives and Records Administration (U.S.), the National Research Council and Central State Archives (Italy)	Luciana Duranti, Terry Eastwood, Heather MacNeil, Bruce Walton (Canada), Philip Eppard, Anne Gilliland, Ken Thibodeau (U.S. National Archives and Records Administration); Chen Wei and Wai-kwok Wan (Asia); Peter Horsman, Seamus Ross, Ken Hannigan, (cont.)	The goal of the InterPARES 1 Project was to develop the theoretical and methodological knowledge necessary for the permanent preservation of authentic records generated and/or maintained electronically. On the basis of this knowledge, the project aimed to formulate model policies, strategies, and standards capable of ensuring that preservation.

To accomplish its goal, the research was divided into four domains of inquiry, each with its own goal and methodological approaches:

Authenticity domain: to identify conceptual requirements for assessing and maintaining the authenticity of electronic records

Appraisal domain: to determine whether the selection of electronic records should be based on the same or different criteria as those for traditional records and how digital technologies affect appraisal methodology

Preservation domain: to develop preservation methods for authentic electronic records

(cont.) |

Hans Hofman, Torbjorn Hornfeldt, Ian Macfarlane, Christine Petillat (Europe); Maria Guercio, Paola Carucci (Italy); Rich Lysakowski, Bill Rhind (global industry research team)	*Strategy domain*: to develop an intellectual framework for the articulation of international, national, and organizational policies, strategies, and standards for the long-term preservation of authentic electronic records

Deliverables/Outcomes:

The Authenticity Task Force developed a Template for Analysis of electronic records, on which it based its questionnaire (Case Study Interview Protocol) for the case studies, and two sets of authenticity requirements:

- Benchmark Requirements, which support the presumption of the authenticity of electronic records before they are transferred to the preserver's custody and
- Baseline Requirements, which support the production of authentic copies of electronic records after they have been transferred to the preserver's custody.

In addition, main findings of the Authenticity Task Force include the following:

- Electronic records are deeply embedded within the specific juridical-administrative, provenancial, procedural, documentary, and technological contexts in which they are created.
- Most contemporary records systems are a hybrid of electronic and paper records.
- Few explicit measures are employed to ensure the authenticity of electronic records.
- Measures that ensure authenticity are generally procedural.
- The only way of preserving authentic electronic records over the long term is to make authentic copies of them.
- Archival description is the best method of collective authentication of an archival aggregation of electronic records.

The major products of the work of the Appraisal Task Force were a literature review, procedures and methods in relation to the conceptual requirements for assessing authenticity developed by the Authenticity Task Force, and a model for the selection of electronic records. The major activities represented in the model are

- managing the selection function,
- appraising electronic records,
- monitoring appraised electronic records, and
- carrying out disposition of electronic records.

(cont.)

In addition, main findings of the Appraisal Task Force include
- The assessment of authenticity of electronic records is critical to the appraisal of electronic records.
- The determination of the feasibility of preservation is critical to the selection of electronic records.
- It is important that electronic records be appraised early in their life cycle.
- Monitoring the appraisal decision is a necessary activity in the process of selection of electronic records.

The main products resulting from the work of the Preservation Task Force are a survey of current preservation practices in the area of electronic records, a white paper on storage media for digital information storage, and a model of the activities involved in the preservation of authentic electronic records. The major activities represented in the preservation model are
- managing the preservation process;
- bringing in electronic records;
- maintaining electronic records; and
- outputting electronic records.

In addition, main findings of the Preservation Task Force include the following:
- Electronic records cannot be preserved as such, only the ability to reproduce them can be preserved.
- Considering that the processes of storage and retrieval imply transformations both physical and of presentation, the traditional concept of unbroken chain of custody must be extended to include the processes necessary to ensure the unaltered transmission of the record through time.
- Technology cannot determine the solution to the long-term preservation of electronic records.
- Archival needs define the problem and archival principles must establish the correctness and adequacy of each technical solution.
- Solutions to the preservation problem are inherently dynamic.

The Strategy Task Force developed an Intellectual Framework for the formulation of policies, strategies, and standards regarding the long-term preservation of electronic records.

See http://www.interpares.org/ip1/ip1_index.cfm.

| Creative Archiving at Michigan and Leeds Emulating the Old on the New (CAMiLEON) Project | 1999–2003 | JISC (U.K.) and the NSF (U.S.) | Margaret Hedstrom (University of Michigan), Chris Rusbridge and Paul Wheatley (University of Leeds) | • To explore the options for long-term retention of the original functionality and "look and feel" of digital objects
• To investigate technology emulation as a long-term strategy for long-term preservation and access to digital objects
• To consider where and how emulation fits into a suite of digital preservation strategies |

Deliverables/Outcomes:
- Cost comparisons of different levels of emulation as it may be used as a strategy for long-term preservation
- A set of preservation tools that will be available for use and further testing in libraries
- Preliminary guidelines for the use of different technical strategies (migration and emulation) for preserving digital collections
- Definitions of attributes of different types of digital objects (e.g.. multimedia products, images with textual description, simulation and vector graphics) that must be preserved to satisfy user needs and requirements
- Strategies for preserving digital objects for which there is no known method of long-term preservation and access

See http://www2.si.umich.edu/CAMILEON/about/aboutcam.html.

Indiana University Electronic Records Project, Phase II	2000–2007	NHPRC	Philip Bantin (Indiana University)	To implement and test the methodology for evaluating electronic recordkeeping systems developed under Phase I, including reviewing and refining functional requirements and metadata specifications

Deliverables/Outcomes:
See *Final Report*, https://scholarworks.iu.edu/dspace/bitstream/handle/2022/2347/nhprcfinalreport.pdf?sequence=1.

InterPARES 2	2002–2007	SSHRC, NHPRC, NSF (U.S.)	Luciana Duranti, Terry Eastwood, Philip Eppard, Anne Gilliland, Kevin Glick, Elaine Goh, Yvette Hackett, Babak Hamidzadeh, Ken Hannigan, Hans Hofman, Sally Hubbard, Brent Lee, Richard Marciano, Sue McKemmish, Isabella Orefice, Andrew Rodger, John Roeder, Jim Suderman, Fraser Taylor, Malcolm Todd, William Underwood	• To develop an understanding of experiential, interactive, and dynamic information systems, of the records produced and maintained within them, and of their present and potential use in artistic, scientific, and governmental sectors • To formulate methods for ensuring that these records are generated and maintained by the creator in a way that guarantees their accuracy, reliability, and authenticity • To formulate methods for selecting these records for long-term preservation in a way that guarantees that the authentic records are identified, monitored, and maintained with their identity and integrity intact until they are transferred to the responsibility of the preserver • To develop methods and strategies for the long-term preservation of the authenticity of the selected records • To identify and/or develop specifications for policy, metadata, and tools appropriate for the design of electronic infrastructures ensuring that these records are created accurate and reliable, and maintained and preserved authentic • To develop criteria for evaluating advanced technologies appropriate for implementing the above objectives, in ways that respect cultural diversity and pluralism

Deliverables/Outcomes:
For full set of outcomes, including body of concepts, authenticity requirements, frameworks, models, guidelines, and case studies, see http://www.interpares.org/ip2/ip2_products.cfm

| Create Once, Use Many Times: The Clever Record-keeping Metadata Project (*CRKM Project*) | ARC (Australia) | 2003–2006 | Joint research project involving the Records Continuum Research Group at Monash University, the National Archives of Australia (NAA), the State Records Authority of New South Wales (SR NSW), and the Australian Society of Archivist's Committee on Descriptive Standards (ASA CDS); investigators: Sue McKemmish (Monash University), Anne Gilliland (UCLA), Adrian Cunningham (National Archives of Australia) | To bring together researchers and practitioners to investigate how standards-compliant metadata could be created once in particular application environments, then used many times to meet a range of business and recordkeeping purposes. The project wished to explore how to move away from the current resource intensive process of manual metadata attribution and stand-alone systems, toward an integrated suite of business systems and processes supporting recordkeeping functions. |

Deliverables/Outcomes:
Broad research findings:
• There is currently a limited capacity to support recordkeeping metadata re-use because recordkeeping processes, practices, standards, and infrastructure still largely operate in paper-based paradigms.

(cont.)

- Current recordkeeping metadata standards lack semantic precision and canonical machine processable encodings, both of which inhibit their uptake.
- Deployment of a metadata broker modeled on the CRKM Metadata Broker I will provide immediate practical use in environments where recordkeeping metadata is to be passed from one known environment to another, for example between a specific business system and a records system.
- However, the CRKM Metadata Broker I model is of limited flexibility, scalability, and robustness, as it relies on hand-crafted metadata crosswalks.
- The notion of Metadata Registries as currently in use in the literature is a compound concept that needs to be broken down into more granular statements of functionality, which include different uses of the term "metadata registry" to include authoritative schema registries, and multiple functionality required to support specific services.
- The emergence of services-oriented architectures and the re-articulation of metadata broker components as services in these kinds of environments, as per the CRKM Metadata Broker II model, has the potential to provide greater return on investment and cost effectiveness.
- The services-oriented environment is much hyped and represents a significant shift in the technological environment, but the reality of sustainable implementation is likely to take many years.
- The recordkeeping profession has an opportunity with this anticipated lead time to both re-envision recordkeeping functions and processes in service-oriented terms and to address and influence the broader technology community on the role of recordkeeping in the service-oriented environment.

Outcome Areas:
- Impact of different information paradigms on metadata interoperability
- Recordkeeping metadata standards
- Paper paradigms prevail
- Reconceptualizing the delivery of recordkeeping services
- Service orientation for recordkeeping
- Metadata registry functionality and general robustness of technology infrastructure

See http://www.infotech.monash.edu.au/research/groups/rcrg/crkm/index.html.

InterPARES 3	2008–2012	SSHRC (Canada)	Luciana Duranti, and academic and professional participants from Africa, Brazil, Canada, Catalonia, China, Colombia, Italy, Korea, Malaysia, Mexico, Norway, Turkey	The overall goal is to enable small and medium-sized public and private archival organizations and programs, which are responsible for the digital records resulting from government, business, research, art and entertainment, and social and/or community activities, to preserve over the long term authentic records that satisfy the requirements of their stakeholders and society's needs for an adequate record of its past. Objectives: • promote an environment supportive of the research goal by demonstrating to regulatory and auditing bodies and to policy makers that it is essential to (cont.)

integrate digital records preservation requirements in any activity that they regulate, audit, or control;

- collaborate with small and medium-sized archival organizations and programs in the development of scalable policies, strategies, procedures, and/or action plans that they can implement to preserve the digital materials that they expect to acquire or have already acquired, using the recommendations and products of leading-edge research projects;
- assess the applicability of the recommendations of InterPARES and other projects about trusted recordmaking and recordkeeping to the situations of the small and medium-sized archival organizations or programs selected as testbeds, and in particular the validity of statements about the relationship between preservers and records creators;
- assess the applicability of these projects' preservation solutions to the concrete cases identified by the test-bed partners as needing immediate attention, both when the records in question are already in their custody and when they still reside with their creator;
- refine and further elaborate the theory and methods, concepts and principles developed by these research projects on the basis of the results of the above activities;
- establish when such theory and methods, concepts and principles apply across jurisdictions, regardless of legal/administrative, social, and cultural environment; and, in the situation where they do not apply, to identify why and determine the measures that are required to ensure the preservation of digital records;
- assist small and medium-sized archival organizations or programs in addressing the legal issues that have been identified by the relevant research projects as providing obstacles to long-term digital preservation and those that could be specific to their situation;
- formulate models that, for each choice of preservation methods and of digital objects to be preserved, identify the ethical consequences for individuals and society;
- create evaluation models capable of measuring the success of the preservation solutions that have been proposed and implemented;

(cont.)

- develop models of preservation costs for various types of records and archives;
- develop awareness and educational materials that can (a) enable the staff of small archival organizations and programs to plan for and carry out digital preservation, (b) assist professional associations in promoting career development of their members, and (c) provide university programs with content and structure for university courses on digital preservation and identify effective delivery methods;
- ensure transfer of the knowledge generated by this research—including actual examples and success stories—to appropriate local, national, and international stakeholders; and
- establish a strong network of research and education on digital preservation that is deeply rooted in the various communities served by each of its partners and that integrates academic work with social and community action.

Deliverables/Outcomes:
For full set of products, see http://www.interpares.org/ip3/ip3_products.cfm?item=1.

BitCurator	2011–	Andrew W. Mellon Foundation	Christopher (Cal) Lee, Kam Woods (University of North Carolina, Chapel Hill), Matthew Kirschenbaum (University of Maryland)	Addresses two fundamental needs for collecting institutions that are not addressed by software designed for the digital forensics industry: incorporation into the workflow of archives/library ingest and collection management environments, and provision of public access to the data. Working with a Professional Expert Panel (PEP) of individuals who are at various levels of implementing digital forensics tools and methods in their collecting institution contexts and a Development Advisory Group (DAG) of individuals who have significant experience with development of software, BitCurator is defining and testing support for a digital curation workflow. The workflow begins at the point of encountering holdings that reside on removable media—either new acquisitions or materials that are within a repository's existing holdings—and extends to the point of interaction with an end user. BitCurator is addressing both client-side tools required at the point of initial data extraction and back-end tools for batch processing of disk images, which are likely to reside on a remote server.

Deliverables/Outcomes:
For findings and publications to date, see http://www.bitcurator.net/.

In the United States, the NHPRC report marked the end of the domi-
nance of social science, data-driven approaches that had developed in
many government archives. It resulted in the development of record- and
evidence-driven approaches to electronic records management informed
by empirical study and deductive and inductive reasoning. A similar
shift to a contextual, provenance-centered, evidential orientation was
also noted at the National Archives of Canada.[13] Both American archival
scholar Richard Cox and Canadian archival scholar Terry Cook argue that
this shift from the first generation of machine-readable records archivists
to second-generation electronic records archivists indicated a new integration of electronic records management with the theoretical and practical
concerns of traditional archivists.[14] Cox's study of whether the archival
profession was prepared in the early 1990s to carry out its mission in
the modern electronic information technology environment, however,
concluded that the archival profession in the United States had not done
well in structuring itself to manage electronic records, particularly in
respect to educating electronic records practitioners and researchers.[15]
Cox, who also criticized the field for being reactive rather than proactive, noted the lack of consensus regarding the nature of the impact of
electronic records upon archival theory and practice. His research found
that state government archivist job descriptions did not reflect the skills
and knowledge required to work with electronic records; that almost no
positions for electronic records specialists were advertised between 1976
and 1990; that a very limited base of electronic records curriculum existed
in graduate archival education programs; and that the archival profession
still relied on continuing education, such as the Archival Administration
in the Electronic Information Age: Advanced Institutes for Government
Archivists offered by the University of Pittsburgh between 1989 and 1993,
to develop the practice base of electronic records management.

Overarching Questions in Electronic Records Research

What is an electronic record, how should it best be preserved and made
available, and to what extent do traditional paradigmatic archival precepts
such as provenance, original order, and archival custody hold when

managing it? Over more than five decades of work in the area of electronic records, practitioners, systems designers, and scholars have offered answers to these questions—or at least have devised approaches for trying to answer them. However, a set of fundamental questions about the nature of the record and the applicability of traditional archival theory still confronts archivists and researchers seeking to advance knowledge and development in this increasingly active, but contested, area. For example, in the world of bureaucratic records, where institutional policy often dictates that its own archives is responsible solely or primarily for organizational records, which characteristics differentiate a record from other types of information objects (such as publications or raw research data)?[16] Are these characteristics consistently present regardless of the medium of the record? Must the record always have a tangible form? How does the record manifest itself within different technological and procedural contexts, and, in particular, how do archivists determine the parameters of electronic records created in relational, distributed, or dynamic environments that bear little resemblance on the surface to traditional paper-based environments?

As already noted, at the heart of electronic records and digital record-keeping research, as in practice, is a dual concern with the nature of the record as a specific type of information object and the nature of legal and historical evidence in a digital world. However, such research is relevant to the agendas of many communities besides archivists. Its emphasis on accountability and on establishing trust in records, for example, addresses concerns central to digital government, e-commerce, and digital scholarship. While digital recordkeeping is a more recent and broader concept that opens up many avenues for research into social, cultural, and human rights considerations, research relating to electronic records has been relatively homogeneous in terms of scope. Most major research initiatives addressed some combination of the following: theory-building in terms of identifying the nature of the electronic record, developing alternative conceptual models, establishing the determinants of reliability and authenticity in active and preserved electronic records, identifying functional and metadata requirements for recordkeeping, developing and testing preservation strategies for archival records, and prototyping automated tools and techniques.

Definitions and Definitional Issues

Determining the nature of the record and reconceptualizing the role of archives have been dominant foci of archival theory building since the 1990s, in large part driven by the challenges faced in electronic records research but also as a result of changes in the nature of scholarship.[17] Definitional concerns go far deeper than noting common differences or apparent similarities in terminology used by archivists, other information professionals, and other disciplines. These are gradually being addressed through the adoption of the cross-domain terminologies promulgated by metadata standards and high-level models such as the Open Archival Information System Reference Model (OAIS).[18] Rather, they exemplify significant differences in archival and recordkeeping traditions, approaches, and assumptions that underpin key research initiatives and make it difficult to communicate a unified, succinct, and yet nuanced set of definitions of archival concepts and needs beyond the immediate field.

Defining Electronic Records Management as an Area of Research

Any discussion of the problems with defining first a record and then an electronic record as an intellectual construct, a physical information object, and a unit of analysis for the purposes of research must also reflect on the utility of the term "electronic records management" as applied to this research in the 1990s. The evolution of "machine-readable records" into "electronic records management" signaled a movement away from a data archives approach to one driven by the principles of managing records, both those that are archival and those created and actively used within their bureaucratic contexts. "Electronic records management" became a blanket term that refers both to the practical management of electronic records, from birth to final disposition, and to theoretical and applied research relating to the nature, management, and use of those records. It is also distinct from "archival informatics," a less prevalent term that tends to include the design, development, and use of information systems containing description and digitized versions of archival holdings.[19] By contrast, "digital recordkeeping" is a more inclusive term that refers to all of the documentary, technological, and sociocultural aspects of records and recordkeeping in the continuum in the digital age.

The use of the term "electronic records management" indicated a rapprochement between the practice areas of records management and archival administration as archivists became, of necessity, more involved in the design of record-keeping systems and the management of the active record to ensure it would be technologically possible to segregate and preserve the future archival record. The term also, however, indicates a bifurcation that historically existed within the archival community between traditional archival management and the management of electronic records. Fifty years of developments in Australia, where recordkeeping professionals addressed these issues by fundamentally reconceptualizing the entire area of records and archival management and research under the rubrics of "recordkeeping" and "recordkeeping research," offer one solution to the problems of conceptualization, imprecision, and siloing engendered by these terminological issues and professional divides. (Although even Australians recognize that the recordkeeping and archiving community is not "contiguous" with the records and archives community.)[20] This reconceptualization is premised upon several notions, including "understandings of the nature of records and archives as evidence, the record-keeping and workflow processes associated with registry systems, and the concepts of multiple provenance and the rich and dynamic contexts of records."[21] The Australian approach, however, although influential (particularly as it is reflected in the ISO 15489 Records Management Standard, which was based on the 1996 Australian standard AS4390), has not yet been widely adopted within the United States.

Methodological Considerations

Methodological points of contention also exist between electronic records research approaches. For example, should research be deductive or inductive in its approaches? A theoretical deductive (top-down) approach begins with a theory and uses logical reasoning to move through hypothesis and observation of actual instances and situations with a view to confirming that theory. The International Research on Permanent Authentic Records (InterPARES) Projects have employed the most prominent example of such an approach, primarily utilizing a framework and techniques derived from diplomatics. *Diplomatics* is a body of techniques developed over several centuries to assess the authenticity of individual archival documents. It assumes that records can take a finite and knowable number of documentary forms, which, while they might change their physical manifestation, do not radically vary in nature or function over time. An ideal version or template of each documentary form can, therefore, be constructed, and then actual examples of records can be compared against that template to understand the extent to which they might fall short of the ideal, or be in some way deficient. This approach can also be used to delineate requirements for designing recordkeeping systems and procedures to ensure that they result in the creation of reliable electronic records. The benefits of the approach are that it is firmly rooted in archival principles and it underscores the continuities in role, characteristics, and use among records of all types, across time and space, regardless of media. A limitation is its restricted ability, as a consequence of being rooted only in the recognition of known characteristics of records and established principles of archival science, to discern if and when some truly new phenomenon occurs in the electronic environment.[22]

Inductive, or bottom-up, approaches such as those employed in the Pittsburgh Project use direct observation of specific phenomena or examples to determine patterns and then to develop tentative hypotheses and eventually infer general principles or theories. Historically, much of archival theory was developed in this way, and, in 1991 when proposing her agenda for electronic records research, Margaret Hedstrom argued that the inductive approach could "contribute answers to broader questions, if a series of more manageable research projects are designed with fundamental issues in mind."[23] She continued, "Small, practical research projects can build on each other's results if they are coordinated and carefully controlled to account for the setting in which the project occurs."[24] In electronic records research, case studies, grounded theory development, and ethnography have all been used inductively. The strength of the bottom-up approach is that requirements are generated by analyzing actual electronic records and record-keeping applications. This approach also has a limitation, however, because almost all electronic records studied were, by definition, created on systems that do not adhere to archival requirements and often, therefore, serve as poor examples of good records. This provides a weak basis for making recommendations about requirements.

To counter these limitations and maximize the benefits, research projects are increasingly combining top-down and bottom-up approaches and employing multiple research methods.[25] Reflecting upon the work that has been done in this field, several archival scholars concur that the two approaches are complementary, not competing, and also that undertaking this research calls for applying multiple methods (for example, diplomatics used in combination with genre theory), where each method is capable of illuminating different aspects of the problems or questions being examined.[26]

Another methodological question arises over the unit of analysis for electronic records research. Archival science as a discipline is still heavily material centric, despite Australian work with continuum theory and recordkeeping metadata that examines business, agents, business recordkeeping entities, and associated relationships, and mandates as well as records.[27] While diplomatics looks at individual, document-like objects and thus requires a close delineation of the physical and intellectual parameters of those objects, archival science examines records in their aggregates and draws heavily upon different kinds of contexts to define both the scope of the record aggregate and its "recordness." However, in the process of electronic records research, the delineation of context as a concept has also been expanded to include technological context as well as the more customary juridical-administrative, procedural, and documentary contexts, thus making context a possible unit of analysis as well.

Problematizing the Record

The record, both as an information construct and as an object and subject of research and development, has particular administrative, juridical, cultural, and historical dimensions and management needs that tend to set it apart from research underway in information science and technology. Arguably, this separation, which emphasizes how the record is different from, rather than similar to, other types of information objects, is attributable to several factors within the archival and recordkeeping community more broadly that are most closely identified with record-related research and development. This community focuses its attention on the record rather than on other types of information (i.e., nonrecord materials). This is both a theoretical and a pragmatic consideration because legislation and organizational policy often mandate that distinctions be made between record and nonrecord for the purposes of implementing effective legal control over records created and maintained in bureaucratic contexts.[28] Historically, the needs and concerns of archivists and records managers were poorly articulated to other communities that might be able to provide additional expertise, such as information technology and policy research. In part, this was due to a lack of empirical and technological research skills and experience, but archivists and records managers were also concerned that their research issues might be submerged or compromised if they became part of larger information research agendas. Added to this, as described in chapter 2, was the increasing siloing of the information professions from the 1950s until the end of the twentieth century, in large part due to the evolution of distinct professional practices and identities. This resulted not only in increased separation of the archival field from others involved with documentation, but also in its isolation from other communities engaged in information management research.

Today, much about this situation has changed, and a hallmark of ongoing digital recordkeeping research is its interdisciplinary nature. Nevertheless, the record remains a contested concept inside the archival community. How the record as a construct might be operationalized in complex digital environments—for example, in distributed and multiprovenancial databases where often no readily discernible physical information object corresponds to paper notions of a record—is also an ongoing subject of research and debate.[29] As both David Bearman and Sue McKemmish point out, definitions of common concepts, such as *the record* or even *archives* themselves, tend to be nationally and jurisdictionally contingent.[30] This fact is not always recognized at the outset of transnational archival research collaborations, but it inevitably needs to be addressed as those projects attempt to develop consistency or standards in areas such as terminology and metadata.

The 1992 Society of American Archivists (SAA) *Glossary* defined a record as a "document created or received and maintained by an agency, organization, or individual in pursuance of legal obligations or in the transaction of business,"[31] but since that time it is possible to chart the growing complexity even of canonical understandings of the term. Other definitions augment this statement with the notions that a record comprises content, context, and structure "sufficient to provide evidence of the activity regardless of the form or medium";[32] that a record may comprise one or more documents; and that a record cannot be changed (that is, it must have fixity).[33] Records also embody record-keeping processes and transactions. Bearman argued that "records are at one and the same time the carriers, products, and evidence of business transactions. . . . Business transactions must create records which logically are metadata encapsulated objects."[34] In many organizational environments, however, the definition can be much simpler—a record is anything that an agency or legislation treats as a record.[35] The most recent SAA *Glossary* provides multiple definitions that encompass much of the above and explicitly relate the notion of the record to evidence, accountability, and memory. However, it also indicates ways in which "record" is a term of art in some other communities also (and, by implication, can be a source of possible confusion, especially in cross-disciplinary or cross-field collaborations).[36]

Traditional archival theory holds that a record is created in the course of practical activity and is used as a record, it encompasses more than content, it can be a collective information object, and it requires fixity. While it might be fairly straightforward, therefore, to determine what is and is not a record in the paper environment, these principles do not provide the archivist, systems designer, or archival researcher with much assistance in identifying how this construct manifests itself in a digital world of dynamic and interactive, distributed databases; Web pages; electronic mail; virtual reality environments; social networking sites; and experiential systems. Certainly, not all information systems are record-keeping systems. As David Bearman noted, "Recordkeeping systems are a special kind of information system . . . [they] are distinguished from information systems within organizations by the role they play in providing organizations with evidence of business transactions (by which is meant actions taken in the course of conducting their business, rather than 'commercial' transactions)."[37] For example, when Charles McClure and Timothy Sprehe investigated the practices of state and federal governments with regard to records management and preservation for digital materials on agency websites, they found a fundamental problem with the absence of a clear definition of what constitutes a record in the Web environment.[38] These definitions also provide few if any criteria for assessing the quality of an active or preserved record. For example, an organization may treat an information object as a record even if it does not conform to all or even most of the characteristics identified here. Such an information object might indeed still be a record, by some definitions, but it is likely not a very good one.[39] It has been a theoretical and a practical challenge, therefore, to operationalize such definitions for electronic records research and development purposes. As Bearman pointed out:

> The essential difference between electronic and paper records is that the former are only logical things while paper records are usually thought of as only physical things. Physical things can be stored in only one place and in one observable order, logical things can be physically housed in many places but seen together. They can appear to have different arrangements depending upon the views accorded to their users. In other words, the properties of logical things are associated with them through formal, defined, logical relations while the properties of physical things are associated with them as material objects with concrete locations, attachments and marking.[40]

Electronic records research defined electronic records variously—a brief review of these definitions illustrates not only the debate over the nature of records, but illuminates the conceptual bases of some of the research approaches that have been taken. For example, according to American government archivist Charles Dollar, electronic records are "recorded information that is communicated and maintained by means of electronic equipment in the course of conducting a transaction."[41] In this definition, the salient aspects are that a record is a type of information that is recorded and communicated, and is a result of a transaction. The communication must be between at least two agents, the creator and the receiver, and these agents may be human or computer. One benefit of working with such a definition using a systems design approach is that it can assist with identifying, and potentially capturing, a record through its association either with a computing event, such as a transaction, or when it passes across some communication boundary. It can also be used as the basis for research approaches, such as those employed by the Pittsburgh and Victorian Electronic Records Strategy VERS projects, which emphasized the embeddedness of records within their business and other procedural contexts.[42]

Early research by the InterPARES projects identified the following as necessary characteristics of an electronic record:

> (1) a fixed form, meaning that the entity's content must be stored so that it remains complete and unaltered, and its message can be rendered with the same documentary form it had when first set aside; (2) an unchangeable content; (3) explicit linkages to other records within or outside of the digital system, through a classification code or other unique identifier; (4) an identifiable administrative context; (5) an author, an addressee, and a writer; and (6) an action, in which the record participates or which the record supports either procedurally or as part of the decision making process.[43]

This definition harkened back to the diplomatic conception of the record as a document that has inherent documentary characteristics and is either a probative or a dispositive instrument (that is, it either serves as proof of, or it effects an action). InterPARES director Luciana Duranti expanded this conception to include the notion of supporting and narrative documents.[44] Key to this definition is that, to be a record, the document must somehow be "set aside."[45] As that research progressed, its findings indicated that medium is incidental to the status of recordness for electronic records.[46] The *fixity* that in the traditional archival paradigm is so integral to the status of both *record* and *reliable record*, in electronic records today comes not from their affixedness to a medium, but rather, in light of their inherent manipulability and transportability, from the ability to document the original record and to re-create an authentic copy of it. Subsequent findings of InterPARES research have contributed to the evolving conceptualization of electronic records. For example, while the physical medium is an essential aspect of physical records, it is not a significant consideration for electronic records. However, the ways in which those records are organized and stored in one or more bit streams correspond to the role of the physical medium in relation to the record. Those ways could be considered, together with other embedded components of a record such as attached images, spreadsheets, or animated gifs, to be "digital components" of the record and thus might require specific measures to preserve the integrity of the entire record over time. Closely associated with this are the findings that how an electronic record is manifested to a person differs from how it is stored digitally, and, furthermore, that it is not possible to produce the original record from a preserved digital recordkeeping system, only to create an authentic copy of that record. Finally,

> Given the essential memorial function of a record, the digital components might them-selves constitute a record or a set of records, depending on how they are instanti-ated in the system. The digital components and the document reproduced from these components may constitute, that is, related but distinct records: the digitally stored record(s), and the "manifested record," which can be defined as the visualization or materialization of the record in a form suitable for presentation to a person or another system. The primary purpose of keeping the stored record is to be able to reproduce the manifest record, while the manifest record is preserved to communicate information to persons or other systems.[47]

Anne Gilliland and Philip Eppard offer a definition that speaks to the technological, procedural, and temporal complexity of electronic records:

> Records are heterogeneous distributed objects comprising selected data elements that are pulled together by activity-related metadata such as audit trails, reports, and views through a process prescribed by the business function for a purpose that is juridically required. . . . Records are temporally contingent—they take on different values and are subject to different uses at different points in time. Records are also time-bound in the sense that they are created for a specific purpose in relation to a specific time-bound action.[48]

One more definition, that makes some comparisons between digital and paper records, comes from the Dutch Digital Testbed Project:

> Digital records are not simply the 21st century equivalent of traditional paper records. They have other properties, characteristics and applications. However, both digital and paper records must meet the same legal requirements. In practice, this requires a different approach. Digital records are not tangible objects like a book or a maga-zine, but a combination of hardware, software and computer files. This combination is necessary to be able to use the documents or examine them. . . . An important differ-ence compared to paper records is the greater loss of information that can occur even

while the records are being used, or afterwards when the records are being maintained. After all, hard discs and computers are replaced regularly and there are few barriers to destroying computer files. A single click on the "delete" button and a record disappears without leaving a trace.[49]

Consensus about the nature of the record, whether electronic or not, among the varying definitions used in both archival research and practice can be summarized as follows: a record is always associated with some action, transaction, or event; a record can be a product, a by-product of, or even an agent or actor in an action, transaction, or event; and a record includes, at a minimum, a definable set of metadata that serves to provide contextual and other forms of evidence about that action, transaction, or event.

Moving Away from a Custodial Approach

Several other concepts integral to research in electronic records management also emerged or were redefined. The term "archives" (in the plural), as used by the archival field, traditionally refers not only to records generated in the course of organizational activities that are no longer current but are still useful, but also to the repository that takes custody of those archival records and the program that ensures their preservation and access. Research in electronic records, in recordkeeping in general, and also within information science and informatics challenges the standard archival definition in two significant ways. First, as the worlds of recordkeeping, data management, and information systems design increasingly converged, electronic records researchers worked to differentiate between "archive" and "archiving" as they are used with reference to backing up and storing data and the selective and distinct processes of appraisal and transfer of inactive records of continuing value into archival control. The adoption of the OAIS Reference Model[50] as the underlying information and process model in several research projects investigating aspects of the preservation of and access to electronic records as well as other digital materials further blurred this distinction, however.[51]

The second challenge to the traditional concept of archives has to do with its traditional custodial conceptualization. As introduced in chapter

1, the role of archives in many settings is traditionally a custodial one in which the archives takes physical custody of noncurrent but still valuable institutional records and thenceforth is responsible for preserving the physical and intellectual integrity of those records and making them available for secondary use. One of the most significant aspects of this approach is that the archivist takes on a unique role in providing for the "physical and moral defense" of the record, as advocated in 1944 by English archivist Hilary Jenkinson:

> . . . the Archivist has so to govern his own and other people's conduct in relation to the Archives in his charge as to preclude to the greatest possible extent, short of locking them up and refusing all access to them, any . . . modification.[52]

This approach reasons that records creators have a compelling interest in maintaining reliable records for as long as those records are actively used in daily business. Once the records become inactive, however, records creators may have a less compelling interest in maintaining their reliability and may even have reason to alter inactive records to reflect organizational activities in a more positive light. When the records become inactive, therefore, the archivist must step in and ensure they are transferred into the physical and intellectual control of the archives, otherwise the continued reliability and authenticity of those records cannot be guaranteed. Likewise, the archivist should be the long-term steward of records transferred into his or her custody and should avoid actions that might affect the shaping of the future record when it is first created and used. Of course, this ignores the fact that records management, appraisal, and documentary activities are all processes whereby twentieth-century archivists determine the scope and extent of the historical record that will eventually come under their purview.

In the United States, this custodial approach is described within a life-cycle model first developed over fifty years ago by the National Archives and Records Administration. The life cycle is a simple, custodial model that addresses how records are created and used. It assumes that records move through predictable phases from creation through eventual destruction or archival custody. Usage of records by their creators drops rapidly soon after they are created and continues to diminish until the records are either inactive and destroyed or are judged to have continuing value and are transferred to the archives and made available to secondary users such as historical scholars, journalists, and genealogists.[53] Although some major research projects, notably the UBC (University of British Columbia) and InterPARES Projects,[54] the Persistent Archives Projects developed by the San Diego Supercomputer Center in association with the U.S. National Archives and Records Administration,[55] and the subsequent Electronic Records Archive at the U.S. National Archives,[56] were constructed according to this life-cycle approach, post-custodial ideas challenge this model, especially as articulated in the records continuum model developed in Australia and embedded in related Australian developments such as the *DIRKS Manual*[57] distributed by the Australian National Archives and the Recordkeeping Metadata Schema (RKMS). The continuum model has also been influential elsewhere, most notably in countries such as the Netherlands, and in smaller, nongovernmental archives in the United States. More fundamentally, the technical pragmatics and costs involved in identifying the future historical record and taking on long-term responsibility for the complex, often distributed digital recordkeeping systems out of which records may be generated also challenge the life-cycle approach. Archivists find they have no choice but to become involved with recordkeeping systems at the design stage if they are to ensure that those systems generate good (i.e., reliable, complete, accurate) records and that those records can be identified and managed according to archival requirements over the long term. Deep epistemological differences between the life-cycle and continuum models, therefore, lie at the center of ongoing discourse within different archival traditions about optimal approaches to electronic records management and research, and about how to conceptualize records and archives as physical and intellectual entities. While they are discussed in more detail in chapter 9, at this point it is important to understand the influence of these models on ideas about the custodial and postcustodial roles of archivists expressed by those centrally engaged with electronic records. In the early 1990s, Charles Dollar promoted the need to transform

> the role of archival institutions from a custodian to a regulatory and access facilitative role. . . . Archivists should define a centralized archives as an "archives of last resort" and take physical custody of electronic records only when their maintenance and

migration across technologies can not be assured. Archivists should facilitate access to electronic records over time by helping to develop, promote, and implement international standards that minimize hardware and software dependence. . . . Archivists should identify the functional requirements for the life cycle management of recorded information.[58]

Likewise, Terry Cook argues against the role of archivists as merely records custodians, calling for them to "shift [their] professional attention from archives to archiving."[59] The postcustodial approach encourages the archivist to move beyond the function of custodian of records and to assume a role of records and recordkeeping consultants and access brokers within their organizations. The related noncustodial approach reflects a growing reality for many archivists that technological, fiscal, or human resources will always be insufficient to take physical custody of archival electronic records and that those records instead should remain within the record-keeping system and environment where they were created, but be subject to archival requirements and supervision. The approaches come together in advocating that archivists exercise an important intellectual role with relation to records rather than necessarily taking all or any records into physical custody. Instead, archivists should be involved from the inception of the recordkeeping system, articulating functional and metadata requirements, monitoring compliance with these requirements by records creators, and brokering secondary user access to archival records within the system.[60]

These approaches also incorporate the idea that the record is a conceptual entity and thus more than the physical manifestation of paper in folders and boxes or even a logical (i.e., digital) manifestation. It views the archive as a conceptual as well as a physical space, thus beginning to build an important bridge toward broader recordkeeping discourse and postmodern and postcolonial notions of "the archive" (in the singular) as both a place and a reflection of social and institutional authority and power.[61] Upward presaged the considerable recent writing on this topic in archival as well as other fields when he remarked on the "overdependence upon the significance of archives as a physical space within which we hold society's most important legal, administrative and historical record."[62]

As already noted, postcustodial and noncustodial approaches have practical appeal, given the growing realization that many records, especially those contained in databases, have the best chance of being preserved with their evidential value intact if they remain within the active record-keeping system maintained by the creating unit, providing that both the system and the unit abide by technological and procedural requirements established by the archives. Moreover, archivists are more likely to raise their status within the organization, as well as to preserve archival records, if they come out of the archives and interact with and provide advice to those designing record-keeping systems and creating records. The New York State Department of Education's Building Partnerships Project tested the immediate viability of this approach.[63] There is, however, a need for future research to conduct a systematic evaluation of the effectiveness of noncustodial approaches on records preservation over longer periods of time, as bureaucratic regimes change.

In international research and standards development, the life-cycle and records continuum models often come into direct conflict. However, as Philip Bantin points out, "It is simply not a choice between one extreme or another, but a much more complicated and rich process or dialectic of combining and joining old and new into a modified theoretical construct."[64]

Such ferment has resulted in considerably expanded notions of both the role and expected activities of the archivist and an increasing level of discussion about the role and nature of the archives as a conceptual as well as a physical space.

Developing Requirements for Electronic Records Management

To conceive of archives in functional rather than physical terms, it is important to delineate clearly and unambiguously the conceptual bases, juridical warrant,[65] and procedural and functional requirements for managing records created and maintained digitally *as records*. Several major research projects have identified and/or modeled functional requirements for electronic recordkeeping (although the resulting requirements are not always in accord with each other, in part because of the differing perspectives from which they are developed). These projects include the Pittsburgh Project,[66] which was the first, and probably the most influential major project funded by NHPRC; VERS in Australia;[67] and the Indiana University Electronic Records Project.[68] The latter two based their work on the outcomes of the Pittsburgh Project, refining the Pittsburgh functional requirements in the process.

The National Archives of Canada's Information Management and Office Systems Advancement (IMOSA) Project[69] and the United Kingdom Public Record Office's Electronic Records in Office Systems (EROS) Programme[70] are both examples of embedding functional requirements within electronic office systems. The IMOSA Project, which ran from 1989 to 1992, is notable as an early collaboration between several Canadian government agencies and the private sector and as an early example of integrating functional requirements into office automation systems.[71] The resulting software, FOREMOST (Formal Records Management for Office Systems Technologies), has been successfully applied by government agencies, and its utility in creating and maintaining reliable records was evaluated through case studies conducted by InterPARES.[72]

Between 1993 and 1996, the Pittsburgh Project generated what proved to be the most influential set of functional requirements for good record-keeping or "business acceptable communications." These requirements, which addressed the needs of several different kinds of organizations, had the added benefit of articulating for archivists necessary or desirable properties of organizational records that in the paper world might have been implicit or assumed. According to the Pittsburgh Functional Requirements, records should be accurate, assigned, auditable, authorized, available, coherent, compliant, comprehensive, consistent, documented, evidential, exportable, identifiable, implemented, inviolate, meaningful, redactable, removable, renderable, and understandable.

The requirements were largely derived from an examination of literary warrant as well as case studies of record-keeping implementations in a range of settings. The use of literary warrant—essentially an analysis of laws, regulations, standards, guidelines, and best practices within those communities—was perhaps the most innovative aspect of this research and also resulted in the development of a methodology for identifying warrant in different settings.[73] Based upon this analysis, the project identified three groups of attributes of evidentiality. The first of these groups addresses how a conscientious organization complies with meeting its legal and administrative accountability requirements; the second group specifies requirements for accountable record-keeping systems; and the third group specifies how the record itself should be created or captured, maintained, and made available and usable. A third product of the Pittsburgh Project was a set of production rules that formally expressed each functional requirement as logical statements of simple, observable attributes that systems designers and metadata creators could use.[74]

VERS, conducted by the Public Record Office Victoria (PROV) in Australia working with the Department of Infrastructure, identified essential archiving requirements across the life of the record. It developed a test bed to prototype a potential system for document processing and record capture and then to test different techniques. The project concluded that it is possible to capture electronic records in a format suitable for long-term retention, with a large proportion of the contextual information automatically captured. The project delineated records capture requirements, archival system requirements, and records retrieval requirements, and also included process maps, metadata requirements, and technology cost analysis, thus laying the groundwork for future research in developing additional automated tools and techniques.[75]

Wendy Duff's research with the Pittsburgh Project suggests that if archivists and other recordkeepers couple functional requirements with literary warrant drawn from professional fields that deal with risk management, such as law and auditing, organizations are more likely to seriously consider the requirements.[76] While it could be argued that risk and enterprise management were always at least implicitly present in records management, they explicitly entered the archival lexicon and toolkit through work undertaken in electronic records management and in particular through the writings of David Bearman. The underlying notion is that risk is present in all settings, but organizations are more likely to manage their records according to the kinds of requirements laid out by archivists and records managers if they perceive that so doing will help them to avoid high levels of risk or will support them in taking advantage of particular opportunities. The auditor general of Victoria in Australia lays out six categories of relevant risks that different kinds of agencies might wish to avoid:

1. Strategic risks (risks to the agency's direction, external environment and to the achievement of its plans)
2. Commercial risks (risks to core business activities, such as inadequate human resources, physical damage to assets, or threats to physical safety)
3. Technical risks (risks of managing assets, such as equipment failure)
4. Financial and systems risks (risks with financial controls and systems, such as fraud)
5. Compliance risks (risks to meeting regulatory obligations).
6. There are also important strategic balances to be struck between managed risk avoidance and flexibility to pursue enterprise or opportunity.[77]

Enterprise management, on the other hand, is associated with promoting organizational agility and innovation to capitalize on emergent opportunities. A related area is digital asset management, which promotes consciousness of the organizational value of diverse types of digital knowledge, information, or media assets, and structures local or enterprise-wide asset management and workflow in support of, for example, new product or concept development; or for optimization, collaboration, sharing, and integration.

The Protection of the Integrity and Reliability of Electronic Records (UBC) Project resulted in a set of requirements subsequently built into the U.S. Department of Defense Design Criteria Standard for Electronic Records Management Software Applications (DOD 5015.2-STD)[78] and were also inputs into the European Commission's *Requirements for the Management of Electronic Records (MoReq Specification)* (updated in 2010 as *MoReq2*)[79] and InterPARES.[80] InterPARES, funded by government and private sector agencies in several countries, has further developed this work by identifying conceptual requirements for reliability and authenticity not only in government, but also in science and the arts.

Although, as the above discussion reflects, many sets of functional requirements have been generated from different theoretical stances and in different organization types and national jurisdictions since the mid-1990s, there is considerable agreement among them. Most, for example, require that an organization comply with existing legal, audit, technological, or other warrant and ensure responsibility for recordkeeping. Records in the system should be able to be identified, fixed, segregated, and migrated to new software and hardware configurations. They should include an audit trail. It should also be possible to ensure that they are complete and that their physical and intellectual integrity has not been compromised in any way. The main criticism of functional requirements generated through this kind of research, especially from institutional information technology and systems staff and software vendors, is that they remain too narrative and conceptual. The Pittsburgh Project tried to obviate this criticism by generating production rules, as did the UBC and InterPARES Projects by developing complex IDEF0 (Integration Definition for Function Modeling) models of activities and metadata associated with records appraisal and preservation processes (see chapter 9 for more detail on modeling and recordkeeping).

There remain some key concerns with functional requirements research relating to electronic/digital records management. First, it struggles with fundamental definitional and conceptual issues and, without consensus on these issues, it generates competing sets of functional requirements. Second, a lack of real-life bureaucratic or archival test beds means that few of the requirements sets have been implemented and tested iteratively in a range of record-keeping domains. Third, some institutions believe that the requirement sets are too complex and costly to implement and might not reflect how people actually use software.[81]

Preserving Authentic Electronic Records

Many communities consider the obsolescence of record-creating technologies to be more problematic than that of the media on which the records are recorded.[82] Obsolescence concerns are increasingly coupled with concerns over the ease with which the reliability and authenticity of an information object can be undermined due to the actions of its creators or preservers. Peter Graham addressed this when he introduced the concept of "intellectual preservation," which is concerned with the "integrity and authenticity of the information as originally recorded."[83] He observed that "the ease with which an identical copy can quickly and flawlessly be made is paralleled by the ease with which a change may undetectably be made." Gilliland and Eppard proposed that identifying the boundaries of such intellectually complex objects as records and then moving those objects forward through time and through migrations without compromising their authentic status is a significant research issue.[84] In 2000, the Council on Library and Information Resources (CLIR) convened a group to ask, "What is an authentic digital object?" and to "create a common understanding of key concepts surrounding authenticity and of the terms various communities used to articulate them." As the authors of the report of that meeting note:

> "Authenticity" in recorded information connotes precise, yet disparate, things in different contexts and communities. It can mean being original but also being faithful to the original; it can mean uncorrupted but also of clear and known provenance, "corrupt" or not. . . . In each context, however, the concept of authenticity has profound implications for the task of cataloguing and describing an item. It has equally profound ramifications for preservation by setting the parameters of what is preserved and, consequently, by what technique or series of techniques.[85]

Among the questions the CLIR report asked were "Does the concept of an original have meaning in the digital environment?" and "What implications for authenticity, if any, are there in the fact that digital objects are contingent on software, hardware, network, and other dependencies?"[86] David Levy responded that

> One challenge comes from the fact that the digital realm produces copies on an unprecedented scale. It is a realm in which . . . there are no originals (only copies—lots and lots of them) and no enduring objects (at least not yet). This makes assessing authenticity a challenge.[87]

Traditionally, in the life-cycle model, the need for creators to rely upon their own active records, the fixity of those records, a documented unbroken chain of custody from the creators to the archivists, and the description of the archival record within a finding aid are the perquisites of assuring authenticity of preserved records.[88] The UBC Project sought to identify and define the requirements for creating, handling, and preserving reliable and authentic electronic records.[89] The InterPARES Project, building on this work with an examination of the conceptual requirements for ensuring the continued authenticity of preserved records, found that the degree to which a record can be considered reliable depends upon the completeness of its form and the level of procedural and technical control exercised during its creation and management in its active life. Thus, reliability is the responsibility of the record creator. Authenticity, by contrast, is the responsibility of the preserver (which most commonly takes the form of archival management of inactive records) and is an absolute concept.[90] Yet again, the notion of what is reliable and authentic is heavily vested in ideas about evidence derived from legal, regulatory, and administrative warrant and how that evidence is manifested in the records themselves and in record-keeping processes. The objective of the authenticity requirements generated by InterPARES, together with the appraisal and preservation activity models demonstrating the application of those requirements, was to provide a risk management framework within which records preservers could assess the most appropriate preservation strategy or technique to use for a particular aggregation of records and to provide a blueprint for systems developers.

Little research has examined whether the constructs of reliability and authenticity promulgated by the kinds of archival requirements sets discussed above map onto the understandings of records creators and users,[91] although case studies undertaken during the second phase of InterPARES (InterPARES 2) examined conceptualizations of the constructs in scientific and artistic domains. InterPARES 3, which has focused on implementing the requirements and models developed in the previous InterPARES projects in real-life settings, may provide additional insight into these understandings.

Metadata for Electronic Recordkeeping

David Wallace made one of the first references to recordkeeping metadata in the archival literature in 1993.[92] Wallace's article raised the expectations of many in the archival community that metadata might provide the "magic bullet" to bring the problematic area of electronic records under control. Since then, metadata has become a very specific area of research in electronic records management that has strong connections to metadata research agendas outside archival science.[93] David Bearman was one of the first people in the field to recognize why the need for archivists and recordkeepers to address metadata was so pressing:

> Because the way that the records are organized on any storage device will not give evidence of their use or the business processes that employed them we must rely for such evidence on metadata (information about information systems and business processes) created contemporaneously with the record and its interaction over time with software functionality and user profiles.[94]

In other words, as Table 5.1 in chapter 5 indicates, recordkeeping includes not only descriptive metadata about the record as an information object (for example, indexes, archival finding aids, Web resource metadata), but also event- and process-based metadata to document all the dimensions involved in the processes and technologies of recordkeeping. According to Wendy Duff and Sue McKemmish, writing about compliance with ISO 9000 requirements for quality control in recordkeeping, "a quality system requires three different types of documentation: records of business processes; business rules that control the business processes; and systems documentation."[95] Recordkeeping metadata facilitates the management, continued use, and reuse of the records as they move forward through time, across space, and among users; and the responsibility for creating that metadata, through both automatic and manual means, is distributed across many different agents and domains of use.[96] Through metadata, reliability and authenticity are documented, functional requirements are embedded in system design, and archived records and their components are described and made accessible to end users in accordance with their needs.

Many research projects such as the Pittsburgh Project have made recommendations about metadata, but two in particular deserve attention. The Australian Recordkeeping Metadata Project identified eight goals or purposes that metadata may serve: unique identification; authentication of records; persistence of records content, structure, and context so that they can be re-presented with their meaning preserved for subsequent use; administration of terms and conditions of access and disposal; tracking and documenting use history, including record-keeping and archiving processes; enabling discovery, retrieval, and delivery for authorized users; restricting unauthorized use; and assuring interoperability in networked environments.[97] These goals are embodied in the Recordkeeping Metadata

Schema (RKMS), an entity-relationship-based metadata scheme that employs a taxonomy of interrelationships between entity types—business, agent, records, and business recordkeeping processes.[98]

Arguing that "preservation metadata is the information infrastructure that supports the processes associated with digital preservation [and] more specifically . . . is the information necessary to maintain the *viability, renderability* and *understandability* of digital resources over the long-term," the Online Computer Library Center (OCLC) and the Research Libraries Group (RLG) established the multinational, multisector PREMIS (Preservation Metadata: Implementation Strategies) working group to "support the preservation of digital objects and ensure their long-term usability."[99] PREMIS was "charged to define a set of semantic units that are implementation independent, practically oriented, and likely to be needed by most preservation repositories." The working group developed an expanded conceptual structure for the OAIS Information Model, and metadata elements were mapped to this conceptual structure to reflect the information concepts and requirements articulated in the OAIS Reference Model.[100] The *PREMIS Data Element Dictionary* includes semantic units for three types of object entities (file, bit stream, and representation) as well as for event, agent, and rights entities.

In 2001, Michael Day commented on the still-experimental and conceptual state of the development of metadata specifications in the field of digital preservation that "more time and effort has been expended on developing conceptual metadata specifications than in testing them in meaningful applications. This is not intended as a criticism, but is just a reflection of how experimental the digital preservation area remains."[101] While PREMIS has contributed to addressing Day's comment, a similar statement could still be made about the state of electronic recordkeeping metadata. Although this area has seen tremendous development over the past decade and will continue at a constant level of proliferation and evolution, wider implementation and evaluation of current schemas is still needed. Several emergent areas of research also need to be tackled. These include identifying how different types of metadata—process, event, and object based—are going to interact in future record-keeping systems; identifying the requirements for metadata management, including more automatic ways in which metadata can be created, for example, through event triggers, inheritance, inference, or derivation, and managed by the various responsible agents;[102] and identifying techniques for long-term metadata management to ensure that metadata essential to identifying and authenticating records is preserved and that links between preserved records and associated metadata retain their referential integrity over time in the face of systems obsolescence, data migration, and evolution of metadata schema.[103]

Yet another area relates to the development of metadata-based tools and techniques that will help users working in a digital archives environment such as those conforming to the OAIS Reference Model to retrieve and manipulate electronic records and their components. In the past, electronic records researchers who focused on identifying, acquiring, and preserving electronic records have paid scant attention to access and use. However, as Peter Hirtle states,

> We need self-conscious documentation by the creators and preservers of digital representations that details the methods employed in making and maintaining the representations. We also need to know what researchers need to know about the transformations from analog to digital format, as well as about any transformations that may occur as digital data are preserved.[104]

One of the most promising series of developments addressing these potential areas for research emanates out of the Persistent Archives Technology first developed by the San Diego Supercomputer Center in collaboration with the U.S. National Archives and Records Administration and subsequently through the University of North Carolina's DICE Center and Sustainable Archives and Leveraging Technologies (SALT) group. This work, based around the OAIS Reference Model, used computational power to ingest high volumes of records; to identify commonalities in their structure, behaviors, and metadata attributes and create from these an XML (Extensible Markup Language) DTD (Document Type Definition) on the fly; and to store the records as collections in infrastructure-independent form. At any later point, collections could be virtually re-created through the application of the DTD to the stored records. Moreover, researchers could use the DTD as a tool for querying and manipulating the records.[105] This work was subsequently scaled down for test-bed application in real-life archival settings smaller than NARA via the Archivists' Workbench initiative. The Archivists' Workbench took advantage of data grid technology and its distributed service model to automate appraisal, accession, description, preservation, and access processes. Part of this approach included the ability to transform metadata and to add rule-based metadata.[106]

Although archival researchers will continue to work on questions such as, "How much metadata is part of the record and how much resides outside but provides necessary context?" and "In what ways might functional requirements for recordkeeping be implemented in record-keeping systems through the use of metadata?" (which itself begs the question of which kinds of metadata might be associated with each requirement), a whole new set of metadata questions has emerged. For example, if metadata are essential to creating, managing, and preserving a reliable and authentic record, how do those metadata need to be managed? How do we ensure that a preserved record that contains a link to a metadata scheme continues over time to refer to the appropriate version of that scheme? If metadata continues to accrue around a preserved record as documentation of ongoing preservation and use processes, how do we ensure that only necessary metadata are preserved over time? Should we be building record-keeping systems for metadata? Another evolving area of research relates to use. For example, how do we support increased demand for interoperability of systems containing preserved archival records with other information systems? How can we provide users of an OAIS-based archives with dissemination information packages according to users' own custom specifications? In both cases, metadata will play an essential role. What might we learn from electronic records research that might help us with customizing output according to different cultural sensibilities? Could we design archival systems able to manage and automatically handle a range of rights management and user clearance activities? How could we build into archival systems provisions for users to provide annotations, suggest corrections, and submit feedback on the records they have used (for example, giving the users the ability to "set the record straight")?[107]

The first of these questions, that is, how to manage the burgeoning volume of records in ways that ensure their reliability and authenticity, was a driver in the development of the Metadata and Archival

Description Registry and Analysis System (MADRAS) developed through InterPARES 2.[108] MADRAS was designed to address the recordkeeping needs relating to recordkeeping metadata by supporting the unambiguous registration of relevant metadata schemas, sets, and application profiles. It also supported the analysis of registered items against requirements derived from the InterPARES1 Benchmark and Baseline Requirements as well as the ISO 23081 Recordkeeping Metadata Standard, archival description rules, sets, related practices (e.g., *ISAD (G)/ISAAR*, EAD/EAC/DACS, RAD, and the Australian Series System), and relevant discipline-based metadata sets and schemes such as those relating to geographic information. It could make recommendations about how metadata schemes might be extended or otherwise revised to address the reliability, authenticity, and preservation needs of records created within the domain, community, or sector to which they pertain. Finally, it provided a standardized framework with which to assess any existing or draft metadata schema or set for its ability to address the above-mentioned requirements. Such a framework could be adopted by standards-setting bodies in different areas of practice, and was used to generate analytical data to provide to the ISO TC46/SC11-WG1, which oversees the development of the Recordkeeping Metadata Standard (ISO 23081).

Conclusion

Electronic records research remains a pressing area of need for archivists confronted with managing the born-digital bureaucratic record. It was the single biggest area of recordkeeping research concentration for almost two decades from the 1990s onward and has made significant contributions to the conceptualization of the field and to recordkeeping more broadly, as well as to the development of national, international, and industry-accepted standards and requirements for records management, electronic document management systems (EDMSs), and electronic information systems.[109] Electronic and now digital records research has also moved archivists away from a paper and custodial mindset and positioned them to, in Wendy Duff's words, "take their rightful place as regulators of an organization's documentary requirements."[110] With its empirical approach, emphasis on theory building, and growing convergence with the research interests of the digital preservation and metadata development communities; and its more recent relationships with the data/digital curation, cyberinfrastructure development, digital forensics, and digital humanities communities, electronic records research has arguably outgrown its initial applied and distinctively records focus. Funding for digital records initiatives today is more closely directed at translating the outcomes of prior research into practice through such activities as building model programs and education and training curricula for archivists than it is on conceptual research. Although this has led to a less close research and development connection between archival faculty and archival institutions, it has promoted the integration of the archival perspective and preoccupations within other fields and vice versa. In the long run, this should result in more nuanced approaches to the long-term appraisal, retention, and use of digital resources in nonarchival environments, as well as a heightened awareness of the continuing role of and need for rigorous recordkeeping regimes and repositories, whether physical or virtual.

Notes

This chapter includes, with permission, some updated and revised sections of the following previously published article: Anne J. Gilliland-Swetland, "Management of Electronic Records," *Annual Review of Information Science and Technology (ARIST)* 39 (2005): 219–53.

1   Record Group 64, Records of the National Archives and Records Administration, Subject Files of Solon J. Buck Relating to Archival Principles, Practices, and Institutions, 1789–1956.

2   Richard J. Cox, "Re-discovering the Archival Mission: The Recordkeeping Functional Requirements Project at the University of Pittsburgh, A Progress Report, *Archives and Museum Informatics* 8 (1994): 294.

3   Ironically, one of the challenges archivists may increasingly face is the persistence of digital materials that they or the creators wish to destroy, which have been widely or serendipitously distributed or caught in random or systematic ways by computer backup systems and thus are beyond the reach of most records retention scheduling and disposition controls.

4   For example, in 1944, early in the history of the American archival profession, Buck wrote to Margaret Cross Norton in the Archives Division of the Illinois State Library. He took issue with statements she had recently made regarding the difference between archives and historical manuscripts, statements that have a lot of similarity in tone to those that more recently drove electronic records management:

It seems to me that you lay too much stress on the term "legal" in connection with the evidential character of archival material. Fundamentally there is no difference between legal evidence and historical evidence or any other kind of evidence, or rather evidence used for any other purpose. Even though records are to be preserved solely for non-legal historical use—that is, there is no possibility of their being used for legal evidence in courts—nevertheless they should be preserved as bodies of records, that is, as archives, because their evidential value for historical or other research purposes is dependent on their provenance. The objective in all use of records is to ascertain the facts, and the purpose of the rules of legal evidence is to promote the attainment of that objective. There are of course recognized rules of historical evidence, which are about as strict as the rules of legal evidence, but there is no way of requiring histories to observe them. Of course historical manuscripts that are not included in bodies of archives may also be preserved for their evidential value, in fact most of them are, with the exception perhaps of those that are treated as curios, museum pieces, collectors' items and the like, but there is always more doubt about their authenticity than there is with documents that have been preserved as parts of bodies of archives in responsible custody.

Solon J. Buck, carbon copy of letter to Margaret Cross Norton, January 24, 1944, regarding her presentation "Archives and Historical Evidence" to the Princeton meeting of the Society of American Archivists and published in the December 1943 issue of *Illinois Libraries*, Papers of Solon J. Buck, Library of Congress Manuscript Division.

⁵ S. C. Newton, "The Nature and Problems of Computer-generated Records," in *Computer Generated Records: Proceedings of a Seminar*, ed. Michael Cook (Liverpool, U.K. University of Liverpool, 1987), 1–4.

⁶ David Roberts, "Defining Electronic Records, Documents and Data," *Archives and Manuscripts* 22, no. 1 (1994): 14–26.

⁷ Glenda Acland, "Managing the Record Rather than the Relic," *Archives and Manuscripts* 20, no. 1 (1992): 58–59.

⁸ Terry Cook, "It's 10 O'Clock—Do You Know Where Your Data Are?," *Technology Review* 98 (1995): 48–53.

⁹ Armstrong v. Executive Office of the President, 303 U.S. App. D.C. 107 (1993); Bearman, "The Implications of *Armstrong v. Executive Office of the President* for the Archival Management of Electronic Records"; David A. Wallace, "Preserving the U.S. Government's White House Electronic Mail: Archival Challenges and Policy Implications" (paper presented at the Sixth DELOS Workshop, "Preserving Digital Information," Lisbon, Portugal, June 17–19, 1998), http://www.ercim.eu/publication/ws-proceedings/DELOS6/wallace.pdf; Thomas S. Blanton, *White House E-Mail: The Top-Secret Messages the Reagan/Bush White House Tried to Destroy*, book and disk (New York: The New Press, 1995).

¹⁰ National Historical Publications and Records Commission, *Research Issues in Electronic Records*.

¹¹ Michael Day, "CEDARS: Digital Preservation and Metadata" (paper presented at "Preserving Digital Information"), http://www.ukoln.ac.uk/metadata/presentations/delos6/cedars.html.

¹² For example, the Pittsburgh Project, InterPARES 1, 2, and 3 Projects, CAMiLEON, ERPANET, and the Clever Recordkeeping Project. See also Margaret Hedstrom, "Understanding Electronic Incunabula: A Framework for Research on Electronic Records," *The American Archivist* 54 (Summer 1991): 334–54.

¹³ Terry Cook and Eldon Frost, "The Electronic Records Archival Programme at the National Archives of Canada: Evolution and Critical Factors of Success," in *Electronic Records Management Program Strategies: Archives and Museum Informatics Technical Report 18*, ed. Margaret Hedstrom (Pittsburgh: Archives and Museum Informatics, 1993), 38–47.

¹⁴ Cook, "Easier to Byte"; and Richard J. Cox, *The First Generation of Electronic Records Archivists in the United States: A Study of Professionalization* (New York: Haworth Press, 1994).

[15] Cox, *The First Generation of Electronic Records Archivists in the United States.*

[16] This question might be differently framed in repositories that have a broader conception of a record.

[17] Catherine Bailey, "Archival Theory and Electronic Records," *Archivaria* 29 (1990): 180–96; Katharine Gavrel, *Conceptual Problems Posed by Electronic Records: A RAMP Study* (Paris: UNESCO, International Council on Archives, 1990); Acland, "Managing the Record Rather than the Relic"; Richard J. Cox, "The Record: Is It Evolving?," *Records and Retrieval Report* 10 (1994): 1–16; Cook, "What Is Past Is Prologue" (see chapter 2, note 24); Philip C. Bantin, "Strategies for Managing Electronic Records: A New Archival Paradigm? An Affirmation of Our Archival Traditions?," *Archival Issues* 23, no. 1 (1998): 17–34; Sue McKemmish, "'Constantly Evolving, Ever Mutating': An Australian Contribution to the Archival Metatext (PhD diss., Monash University, Melbourne, 2001).

[18] Consultative Committee for Space Data Systems/International Organization for Standardization, *Space Data and Information Transfer System: Open Archival Information System: Reference Model* (Geneva: International Organization for Standardization, 1999); Brian F. Lavoie, *The Open Archival Information System Reference Model: Introductory Guide,* Digital Preservation Coalition Technology Watch Series 04-01, (January 2004).

[19] Although, with a developing focus on retrieval and use of archival electronic records, for example, through some of the work undertaken by computer scientists at the San Diego Supercomputer Center relating to persistent archives, and the Data Intensive Cyber Environments (DICE) Center and Sustainable Archives and Leveraging Technologies group (SALT) at the University of North Carolina, Chapel Hill, these two areas could merge.

[20] Sue McKemmish, "Placing Records Continuum Theory and Practice," *Archival Science* 1 (2001): 333–59.

[21] Sue McKemmish, "Understanding Electronic Recordkeeping Systems: Understanding Ourselves," *Archives and Manuscripts* 22 (1994): 150–62. See also Barbara Reed, "Electronic Records Management in Transition," *Archives and Manuscripts* 22, no. 1 (1994): 164–71; and McKemmish, "Placing Records Continuum Theory and Practice."

[22] Anne J. Gilliland-Swetland, "Testing Our Truths: Delineating the Parameters of the Authentic Archival Electronic Record," *The American Archivist* 65, no. 2 (2002): 196–215.

[23] Hedstrom, "Understanding Electronic Incunabula," 351–52.

[24] Hedstrom, "Understanding Electronic Incunabula," 352. This comment points to an ongoing deficiency in archival research, which is the failure to develop a substantial track record of evaluating and building upon prior research.

[25] Sue McKemmish, Glenda Acland, Nigel Ward, and Barbara Reed, "Describing Records in Context in the Continuum: The Australian Recordkeeping Metadata Schema," *Archivaria* 48 (1999): 3–42; and Gilliland-Swetland, "Testing our Truths."

[26] See, for example, Heather MacNeil, "Contemporary Archival Diplomatics as a Method of Inquiry: Lessons Learned from Two Research Projects," *Archival Science* 4, nos. 3–4 (2004): 199–232; Gillian Oliver, "Investigating Information Culture: Comparative Case Study Research Design and Methods," *Archival Science* 4, nos. 3–4 (2004): 287–314; and Fiorella Foscarini, "Diplomatics and Genre Theory as Complementary Approaches," *Archival Science* (preprint).

[27] McKemmish et al., "Towards a Framework for Standardising Recordkeeping Metadata," 177–202 (see chapter 5, n. 18).

[28] David A. Bearman, *Electronic Records Guidelines: A Manual for Policy Development and Implementation* (Pittsburgh: Archives and Museum Informatics, 1990); Charles R. McClure and J. Timothy Sprehe, *Analysis and Development of Model Quality Guidelines for Electronic Records Management on State and Federal Websites: Final Report* (Washington, D.C.: National Historical

Publications and Records Commission, 1998), http://www.mybestdocs.com/mcclure-sprehe-nagara5. html.

29 Anne J. Gilliland-Swetland and Philip B. Eppard, "Preserving the Authenticity of Contingent Digital Objects: The InterPARES Project," *D-Lib Magazine* 6 (2002), http://www.dlib.org/dlib/july00/ eppard/07eppard.html; Roberts, "Defining Electronic Records, Documents and Data"; Cox, "The Record: Is It Evolving?"; Cox, "The Record in the Information Age: A Progress Report on Reflection and Research," *Records and Retrieval Report* 12 (1996): 1–16.

30 David A. Bearman, "Diplomatics, Weberian Bureaucracy, and the Management of Electronic Records in Europe and America," *The American Archivist* 55 (1992): 168–81; McKemmish, "'Constantly Evolving, Ever Mutating.'"

31 Lewis J. Bellardo and Lynn Lady Bellardo, *Glossary for Archivists, Manuscript Curators, and Records Managers* (Chicago: Society of American Archivists, 1992).

32 International Council on Archives Committee on Electronic Records, *Guide for Managing Electronic Records from an Archival Perspective* (Paris: International Council on Archives, 1997), 9.

33 European Commission. *Requirements for the Management of Electronic Records (MoReq Specification)* (Brussels and Luxembourg: Cornwell Affiliates, 2001).

34 David A. Bearman, "Item Level Control and Electronic Recordkeeping" (paper presented at the Society of American Archivists 1996 Annual Meeting, San Diego, Calif.), 6.

35 United Nations Advisory Committee for the Co-ordination of Information Systems, *Strategic Issues for Electronic Records Management: Towards Open Systems Interconnection* (New York: United Nations, 1992).

36 "n.–1. A written or printed work of a legal or official nature that may be used as evidence or proof; a document.–2. Data or information that has been fixed on some medium; that has content, context, and structure; and that is used as an extension of human memory or to demonstrate accountability. –3. Data or information in a fixed form that is created or received in the course of individual or institutional activity and set aside (preserved) as evidence of that activity for future reference.–4. An instrument filed for public notice (constructive notice); see recordation.–5. Audio A phonograph record.–6. Computing A collection of related data elements treated as a unit, such as the fields in a row in a database table.–7. Description An entry describing a work in a catalog; a catalog record." See Richard Pearce-Moses, *A Glossary of Archival and Records Terminology* (Chicago: Society of American Archivists, 2005), http://www.archivists.org/glossary/index.asp. SAA's 1992 and 2005 definitions of "electronic records" have not provided much guidance to either practitioners or researchers, nor do they reflect the amount of knowledge that has been developed in recent years on the subject:

"records on electronic storage media" (1992) and "also digital record; automated record, largely obsolete), n.–Data or information that has been captured and fixed for storage and manipulation in an automated system and that requires the use of the system to render it intelligible by a person" (2005). See also Bellardo and Bellardo, *Glossary for Archivists, Manuscript Curators, and Records Managers.*

37 David A. Bearman, *Electronic Evidence: Strategies for Managing Records in Contemporary Organizations* (Pittsburgh: Archives and Museum Informatics, 1994).

38 McClure and Sprehe, *Analysis and Development of Model Quality Guidelines.*

39 Case studies undertaken by InterPARES 1 provided several examples of digital systems failing to support the requirements necessary to create and maintain good records. In the absence of record-keeping requirements being built into off-the-shelf software for common recordkeeping and infor-mation management practices, these examples, even more than a decade later, are more likely to be the norm than the exception. These findings, when taken in conjunction with the fact that decontex-tualized pieces of evidence are now routinely excavated by digital forensics and admitted into legal

proceedings, as well as the paucity of situations where organizations suffer negative consequences from not creating and maintaining adequate electronic records, has to leave the archivist to wonder whether the gold standard for assessing the nature and reliability of a record in terms of diplomatic and archival theory will need to be loosened. InterPARES Project, *The Long-term Preservation of Authentic Electronic Records: Findings of the InterPARES Project*, ed. Luciana Duranti and Randy Preston (2002), http://www.interpares.org/book/index.htm.

[40] Bearman, "Item Level Control," 1.

[41] Charles M. Dollar, *The Impact of Information Technologies on Archival Principles and Method* (Macerata, Italy: University of Macerata Press, 1992); Roberts, "Defining Electronic Records, Documents and Data."

[42] Cox, "Re-discovering the Archival Mission," 279–300; Justine Heazlewood et al., "Electronic Records: Problem Solved? A Report on the Public Record Office Victoria's Electronic Records Strategy," *Archives and Manuscripts* 27, no. 1 (1999).

[43] Luciana Duranti and Kenneth L. Thibodeau, "The Concept of Record in Interactive, Experiential and Dynamic Environments: The View of InterPARES, *Archival Science* 6, no. 1 (2008): 15–16.

[44] Luciana Duranti, *Diplomatics: New Uses for an Old Science* (Lanham, Md.: Society of American Archivists, Association of Canadian Archivists, and Scarecrow Press, 1998).

[45] Heather MacNeil, "Providing Grounds for Trust: Developing Conceptual Requirements for the Long-term Preservation of Authentic Electronic Records," *Archivaria* 50 (2000): 52–78; *Trusting Records: Legal, Historical and Diplomatic Perspectives* (Dordrecht, Neth.: Kluwer Academic, 2000); and "Providing Grounds for Trust II: The Findings of the Authenticity Task Force of InterPARES," *Archivaria* 54 (2002): 24–58.

[46] "Diplomatic examination shows that an electronic record, just like every traditional record, is comprised of medium (the physical carrier of the message), form (the rules of representation that allow for the communication of the message), persons (the entities acting by means of the record), action (the exercise of will that originates the record as a means of creating, maintaining, changing, or extinguishing situations), context (the juridical-administrative framework in which the action takes place), archival bond (the relationship that links each record to the previous and subsequent one and to all those which participate in the same activity), and content (the message that the record is intended to convey). However, with electronic records, those components are not inextricably joined one to the other, as in traditional records: they, and their parts, exist separately, and can be managed separately, unless they are consciously tied together for the purpose of ensuring the creation of reliable records and the preservation of authentic records." Luciana Duranti and Heather MacNeil, "The Protection of the Integrity of Electronic Records: An Overview of the UBC-MAS Research Project," *Archivaria* 42 (1996): 49. See also Gilliland-Swetland, "Testing Our Truths."

[47] Duranti and Thibodeau, "The Concept of Record in Interactive, Experiential and Dynamic Environments," 13–68.

[48] Gilliland-Swetland and Eppard, "Preserving the Authenticity of Contingent Digital Objects," 2.

[49] *Preserving Email* (Digital Preservation Testbed, The Hague, 2003), part of the series From Digital Volatility to Digital Permanence, http://en.nationaalarchief.nl/sites/default/files/docs/kennisbank/volatility-permanence-email-en.pdf.

[50] Consultative Committee for Space Data Systems, *OAIS Reference Model*.

[51] InterPARES Project, *The Long-term Preservation of Authentic Electronic Records*; *International Research on Permanent Authentic Records in Electronic Systems (InterPARES) 2: Experiential, Interactive and Dynamic Records* (Padova, Italy: Associazione Nazionale Archivistica Italiana, 2008), http://www.interpares.org/ip2/book.cfm; OCLC/RLG Working Group on Preservation Metadata, *Preservation Metadata and the OAIS Information Model: A Metadata Framework to Support the Preservation of Digital Objects, A Report* (June 2002), http://www.oclc.org/research/

pmwg/pm_framework.pdf; Kenneth Thibodeau, "Building the Archives of the Future: Advances in Preserving Electronic Records at the National Archives and Records Administration," *D-Lib Magazine* 7 (2001), http://www.dlib.org/dlib/february01/thibodeau/02thibodeau.html.

52 Maygene F. Daniels and Timothy Walch, *A Modern Archives Reader: Basic Readings on Archival Theory and Practice* (Washington, D.C.: National Archives and Records Service, 1984), 20.

53 Jay Atherton, "From Life Cycle to Continuum: Some Thoughts on the Records Management-Archives Relationship," in *Canadian Archival Studies and the Rediscovery of Provenance*, ed. Tom Nesmith (Metuchen, N.J.: Scarecrow, 1993), 391–402. See also Elizabeth Shepherd and Geoffrey Yeo, *Managing Records: A Handbook of Principles and Practice* (London: Facet Publishing, 2003).

54 Duranti and MacNeil, "The Protection of the Integrity of Electronic Records," 46–67; Luciana Duranti and Heather MacNeil, "Protecting Electronic Evidence: A Third Progress Report on a Research Study and Its Methodology," *Archivi and Computer* 6, no. 5 (1996): 343–404; Luciana Duranti, Terry Eastwood, and Heather MacNeil, *Preservation of the Integrity of Electronic Records* (Dordrecht, Neth.: Kluwer Academic, 2002); InterPARES Project, *The Long-term Preservation of Authentic Electronic Records*; Duranti and Preston, eds., *InterPARES 2* (see chapter 5, n. 27).

55 Reagan Moore et al., "Collection-based Persistent Digital Archives—Part 1," *D-Lib Magazine* 6 (2000), http://www.dlib.org/dlib/march00/moore/03moore-pt1.html; Reagan Moore et al., "Collection-based Persistent Digital Archives—Part 2, *D-Lib Magazine* 6 (2000), http://www.dlib.org/dlib/april00/moore/04moore-pt2.html.

56 National Research Council, "Building an Electronic Records Archive at the National Archives and Records Administration" (Washington, D.C.: National Academy Press, 2003).

57 National Archives of Australia, *The DIRKS Manual: A Strategic Approach to Managing Business Information* (2007).

58 Dollar, *The Impact of Information*, 75–76.

59 Terry Cook, "Electronic Records, Paper Minds: The Revolution in Information Management and Archives in the Post-custodial and Post-modern Era," *Archives and Manuscripts* 22 (1994): 309.

60 David A. Bearman, "An Indefensible Bastion: Archives as a Repository in the Electronic Age," in *Archival Management of Electronic Records*, ed. David Bearman (Pittsburgh: Archives and Museum Informatics, 1991), 14–24; Sue McKemmish and Frank Upward, "Somewhere Beyond Custody," *Archives and Manuscripts* 22, no. 1 (1994): 138–49; Adrian Cunningham, "Commentary: Journey to the End of the Night: Custody and the Dawning of a New Era on the Archival Threshold," *Archives and Manuscripts* 24, no. 2 (1996): 312–21; Greg O'Shea and David Roberts, "Living in a Digital World: Recognizing the Electronic and Post-custodial Realities," *Archives and Manuscripts* 24, no. 2 (1996): 286–311.

61 Verne Harris, "Law, Evidence and Electronic Records: A Strategic Perspective from the Global Periphery," *Comma, International Journal on Archives* 1–2 (2001): 29–44; Joan M. Schwartz and Terry Cook, "Archives, Records and Power: The Making of Modern Memory," *Archival Science* 2 (2002): 1–19; Eric Ketelaar, "Archival Temples, Archival Prisons: Modes of Power and Protection," *Archival Science* 2, nos. 3–4 (2002).

62 Frank Upward, "Structuring the Records Continuum Part One: Post-custodial Principles and Properties," *Archives and Manuscripts* 24 (1996): 272.

63 New York State Department of Education, *Building Partnerships: Developing New Approaches to Electronic Records Management and Preservation: Final Report* (Albany: New York State Department of Education, 1994); New York State Department of Education, *Building Partnerships for Electronic Recordkeeping: The New York State Information Management Policies and Practices Survey: Summary of Findings* (Albany: New York State Department of Education, 1994).

64 Philip C. Bantin, "Strategies for Managing Electronic Records: A New Archival Paradigm? An Affirmation of Our Archival Traditions?," *Archival Issues* 23, no. 1 (1998b): 18.

[65] The first major piece of research investigating warrant was conducted by Wendy Duff as part of the Pittsburgh Project. See Wendy Duff, "Harnessing the Power of Warrant," *The American Archivist* 61 (1998): 88–105; Richard J. Cox and Wendy Duff, "Warrant and the Definitions of Electronic Records: Questions Arising from the Pittsburgh Project, *Archives and Museum Informatics* 11 (1997): 223–31.

[66] Cox, "Re-discovering the Archival Mission."

[67] Public Record Office Victoria, *Victorian Electronic Records Strategy Final Report* (Melbourne: Public Records Office Victoria, 1998).

[68] Philip C. Bantin, "Developing a Strategy for Managing Electronic Records: The Findings of the Indiana University Electronic Records Project," *The American Archivist* 61 (1998): 328–64; Bantin, "The Indiana University Electronic Records Project Revisited," *The American Archivist* 62 (1999): 153–63; Philip C. Bantin and Gerald Bernbom, "The Indiana University Electronic Records Project: Analyzing Functions, Identifying Transactions, and Evaluating Recordkeeping Systems: A Report on Methodology," *Archives and Museum Informatics: Cultural Informatics Quarterly* 10 (1996): 246–66.

[69] John McDonald, "Information Management and Office Systems Advancement," in *Information Handling in Offices and Archives*, ed. Angelika Menne-Haritz (New York: K. G. Saur, 1993),138–51; McDonald, "Managing Records in the Modern Office: Taming the Wild Frontier," *Archivaria* 39 (1995): 70–79; McDonald, "Managing Information in an Office Systems Environment: The IMOSA Project," *The American Archivist* 58 (1995): 142–53.

[70] Richard Blake, "Overview of the Electronic Records in Office Systems (EROS) Programme," in *Electronic Access: Archives in the New Millennium* (London: Public Record Office, 1998), 52–58; The National Archives Public Record Office, *ERM Systems Evaluation Scheme Functional Requirements and Testing of Electronic Records in Management Systems* (December 21, 2000), http://www.21cfrpart11.com/files/library/government/uk_erecsystemsevaluationscheme.pdf.

[71] McDonald, "Information Management and Office Systems Advancement"; McDonald, "Managing Records in the Modern Office"; McDonald, "Managing Information in an Office Systems Environment."

[72] InterPARES Project, *The Long-term Preservation of Authentic Electronic Records*.

[73] Cox and Duff, "Warrant and the Definitions of Electronic Records"; Duff, "Harnessing the Power of Warrant."

[74] Cox, "Re-discovering the Archival Mission"; Peter Hirtle, "Archival Authenticity in a Digital Age," in *Authenticity in a Digital Environment* (Washington, D.C.: Council on Library and Information Resources, 2000), Council on Library and Information Resources, http://www.clir.org/pubs/abstract/pub92abst.html.

[75] Public Record Office Victoria, *Victorian Electronic Records Strategy Final Report*.

[76] Duff, "Harnessing the Power of Warrant."

[77] Auditor General of Victoria, *Managing Risk: Good Practice Guide* (State of Victoria: 2004), 2, http://download.audit.vic.gov.au/files/20040630-Public-Sector-Managing-Risk.pdf.

[78] Duranti et al., *Preservation of the Integrity of Electronic Records*; United States Assistant Secretary of Defense for Networks and Information Integration/Department of Defense Chief Information Officer, *DOD 5015.2-STD, Design Criteria Standard for Electronic Records Management Software Applications* (rev. April 2007), http://www.dtic.mil/whs/directives/corres/pdf/501502std.pdf.

[79] European Commission, *Requirements for the Management of Electronic Records*.

[80] International Research on Permanent Authentic Records in Electronic Systems (InterPARES Project), www.interpares.org.

[81] Hirtle, "Archival Authenticity in a Digital Age."

82 Peter S. Graham, *Intellectual Preservation: Electronic Preservation of the Third Kind* (Washington, D.C.: Commission on Preservation and Access, 1994), Council on Library and Information Resources, http://www.clir.org/pubs/reports/graham/intpres.html; Michael Lesk, *Preservation of New Technology: A Report of the Technology Assessment Advisory Committee to the Commission on Preservation and Access* (Washington, D.C.: Commission on Preservation and Access, 1992), Council on Library and Information Resources, http://www.clir.org/pubs/reports/lesk/lesk2.html.

83 Graham, *Intellectual Preservation*, 1.

84 Gilliland-Swetland and Eppard, "Preserving the Authenticity of Contingent Digital Objects."

85 Charles T. Cullen, Peter B. Hirtle, David Levy, Clifford A. Lynch, and Jeff Rothenberg, *Authenticity in a Digital Environment*, (Washington, D.C.: Council on Library and Information Resources, 2000), 4, http://www.clir.org/pubs/abstract/pub92abst.html.

86 Cullen et al., *Authenticity in a Digital Environment*, vii.

87 David Levy, "Where's Waldo? Reflections on Copies and Authenticity in a Digital Environment," in *Authenticity in a Digital Environment*, 1.

88 Anne J. Gilliland-Swetland, *Enduring Paradigm, New Opportunities: The Value of the Archival Perspective in the Digital Environment* (Washington, D.C.: Council on Library and Information Resources, 2000); Hirtle, "Archival Authenticity in a Digital Age."

89 Luciana Duranti, "Reliability and Authenticity: The Concepts and Their Implications," *Archivaria* 39 (1995): 5–10; Duranti and MacNeil, "The Protection of the Integrity of Electronic Records"; Duranti and MacNeil, "Protecting Electronic Evidence"; Duranti et al., *Preservation of the Integrity of Electronic Records*.

90 Duranti et al., *Preservation of the Integrity of Electronic Records*; Duranti et al., InterPARES Project, *The Long-term Preservation of Authentic Electronic Records*.

91 Eun Gyung Park, "Understanding 'Authenticity' in Records and Information Management: Analyzing Practitioner Constructs," *The American Archivist* 64 (2001): 270–91.

92 David A. Wallace, "Metadata and the Archival Management of Electronic Records," *Archivaria* 36 (1993): 87–110.

93 Margaret L. Hedstrom, "Recordkeeping Metadata: Presenting the Results of a Working Meeting," *Archival Science* 1 (2001): 243–51; Anne J. Gilliland, Nadav Rouche, Joanne Evans, and Lori Lindberg, "Towards a Twenty-First Century Metadata Infrastructure Supporting the Creation, Preservation and Use of Trustworthy Records: Developing the InterPARES2 Metadata Schema Registry," *Archival Science* 5, no. 1 (2005): 43–78; Anne Gilliland et al., "Investigating the Roles and Requirements, Manifestations and Management of Metadata in the Creation of Reliable and Preservation of Authentic Electronic Entities Created by Dynamic, Interactive and Experiential Systems: Report on the Work and Findings of the InterPARES 2 Description Cross Domain Group," part 6, in *International Research on Permanent Authentic Records in Electronic Systems (InterPARES) 2*; Anne J. Gilliland, "Setting the Stage," in *Introduction to Metadata: Pathways to Digital Information*, 2nd ed., ed. Murtha Baca (Los Angeles: Getty Information Institute, June 2008): 1–19, the Getty Research Institute, "Electronic Publications," http://www.getty.edu/research/conducting_research/standards/intrometadata/; Devan Ray Donaldson and Paul Conway, "Implementing PREMIS: A Case Study of the Florida Digital Archive," *Library Hi-Tech* 28, no. 2 (2010): 273–89; Anne Gilliland, "Reflections on the Value of Metadata Archaeology for Recordkeeping in a Global, Digital World," *Journal of the Society of Archivists* 32 (April 2011): 97–112.

94 Bearman, "Item Level Control," 1.

95 Wendy Duff and Sue McKemmish, "Metadata and ISO 9000 Compliance," *Information Management Journal* 34 (2000), Monash University, http://infotech.monash.edu/research/groups/rcrg/publications/smckduff.html.

96 Gilliland et al., "Towards a Twenty-First Century Metadata Infrastructure."

[97] Duff and McKemmish, "Metadata and ISO 9000 Compliance."

[98] Sue McKemmish and Dagmar Parer, "Towards Frameworks for Standardising Recordkeeping Metadata," *Archives and Manuscripts* 26 (1998): 24–45; McKemmish and Parer, "Towards a Framework for Standardising Recordkeeping Metadata" (see chapter 5, n. 18); McKemmish et al., "Describing Records in Context in the Continuum."

[99] PREMIS: Preservation Metadata Maintenance Activity, "Premis 2.2," http://www.loc.gov/standards/premis/. See also Priscilla Caplan and Rebecca Guenther, "Practical Preservation: The PREMIS Experience," *Library Trends* 54, no. 1 (2005): 111–24.

[100] OCLC/RLG Working Group on Preservation Metadata, *Preservation Metadata and the OAIS Information Model: A Metadata Framework to Support the Preservation of Digital Objects, A Report* (June 2002), 4, http://www.oclc.org/research/pmwg/pm_framework.pdf.

[101] Michael Day, "Metadata for Digital Preservation: A Review of Recent Developments," in *Proceedings of the European Conference on Digital Libraries, ECDL 2001, Darmstadt* (Berlin: Springer, 2001): 161–72.

[102] Jason R. Baron, "Recordkeeping in the 21st Century," *Information Management Journal* 33 (1999): 8–16; Gilliland et al., "Investigating the Roles and Requirements, Manifestations and Management of Metadata."

[103] Gilliland et al., "Towards a Twenty-First Century Metadata Infrastructure."

[104] Hirtle, "Archival Authenticity in a Digital Age," 13.

[105] Bertram Ludaescher, Richard Marciano, and Reagan Moore, "Towards Self-validating Knowledge-based Archives," in *11th Workshop on Research Issues in Data Engineering (Ride)* (Heidelberg, Ger.: IEEE Computer Society, 2001), http://www.sdsc.edu/~ludaesch/Paper/ride01.html; Moore et al., "Collection-based Persistent Digital Archives: Part 1"; Moore et al., "Collection-based Persistent Digital Archives: Part 2."

[106] Richard Marciano, "Archivists' Workbench: A Framework for Testing Preservation Infrastructure" (2004), http://www.interpares.org/display_file.cfm?doc=ip2_dissemination_cs_marciano_us-interpares_symposium_2004.pdf.

[107] See, for example, the Final Report of the Trust and Technology Project, *Koorie Archiving: Trust and Technology Project, Final Report*, Monash University, http://infotech.monash.edu/research/centres/cosi/projects/trust/final-report/; and the ongoing research being undertaken by Alexandra Eveleigh at University College London in association with the National Archives, http://www.ucl.ac.uk/infostudies/research/icarus/projects/user-participation/.

[108] Gilliland et al., "Towards a Twenty-First Century Metadata Infrastructure," 43–78.

[109] Xiaomi An, "Research in Electronic Records Management," in *Managing Electronic Records*, ed. Julie Mcleod and Catherine Hare (London: Facet Publishing, October, 2005), 63–80.

[110] Duff, "Harnessing the Power of Warrant," 105.

CHAPTER 8

Emergent and Related Areas of Research

While chapters 9 and 10 address some of the major areas of research over the past decade that relate to archival activities in a digital environment and developments in digital preservation and archiving, this chapter addresses some of the promising but more nascent areas of research that complement, augment, or build upon electronic records research: personal digital archives and social media; digital archaeology, digital forensics, and digital recovery; and cloud and mobile computing.

Archivists can analyse what is happening in personal recordkeeping in much the same way as they analyse corporate recordkeeping. Just as they can identify significant business functions and activities and specify what records are captured as evidence of those activities, so they can analyse socially assigned roles and related activities and draw conclusions about what records individuals in their personal capacity capture as evidence of these roles and activities—"evidence of me."

—Sue McKemmish, "Evidence of Me," 2001[1]

Personal Digital Archives and Social Media

Do approaches developed in bureaucratic environments translate to more idiosyncratic and less controlled areas of digital records creation such as personal digital archives and materials created or disseminated through social media?[2] Indeed, is it valid to think of materials such as blogs, personal electronic mail, Facebook pages, tweets, or mash-ups as records (bearing in mind that many organizations are using social media for business purposes, and prominent officials, including the president of the United States, tweet)? This convergence of interests in social media brings the two lineages of the American archival profession—the historical manuscripts and the public archives traditions—again into proximity with each other in their concern for how to manage different facets of these increasingly multicharacterized digital traces. This line of questioning again raises perennial definitional concerns about what a record is and why it might have long-term value, not only in digital recordkeeping, but also in terms of human experience. Examining records that are the products of other human activities besides bureaucratic ones perhaps offers archivists a way to move beyond prior juridically and technologically framed perspectives of electronic records toward a more inclusive and culturally based conceptualization of the human record as it is digitally inscribed. It also builds upon a promising area of archival investigation notably delineated by Sue McKemmish in 1996 in her groundbreaking article, "Evidence of Me," by opening up new avenues for exploring how individuals think about themselves as creators of records and managers of their own memories and documentary traces. This has recently come to the forefront of public consciousness with the Facebook timeline feature and the demise of several early social networking sites. In addition to several archival scholars who are pursuing these lines of research,[3] major organizations that are notably not archival repositories in the traditional sense have stepped in to capture and provide access to these kinds of materials, among them the Internet Archive and the Library of Congress.

The Internet Archive began to archives the World Wide Web in 1996 and now hosts a number of other archives projects such as the Prelinger Archive, the NASA Images Archive, the Open Library, and the Web crawler Archive-It. It has also sponsored a Personal Digital Archiving Conference annually for several years. The conference addresses such digital materials as family archives of photographs and home movies, personal health and financial data, scrapbooking, social network posts, genealogy, blogs, and email and other correspondence. As illustrated by the 2013 Conference Call for Proposals, the kinds of topics treated in the conference reflect a desire for creator communities to become more engaged in maintaining the content they generate and a hunger for practical strategies for managing the digital documentation and detritus accumulating around every individual today:

- What new social norms are emerging around preservation, access, and disclosure?
- How should libraries, museums, and archives help collect personal digital materials? What are some practical strategies for helping libraries, museums, and archives conduct personal archiving outreach to their communities?
- What are effective outreach strategies for encouraging individuals to undertake personal digital archiving?
- How can we cope with the intersection between personal data and collective or social data that is personal?
- What tools and services are needed to better enable self-archiving?
- What models for user interfaces are most appropriate?
- What viable existing economic models can support personal archives?
- What new economic models should we evaluate?
- What are the key issues associated with digital estate planning and "the digital afterlife"?[4]

The Library of Congress entered into a partnership with social data provider Gnip to archive Twitter, which is currently generating several hundred million tweets a day, from its 2006 founding on. This initiative, however, raises several questions with significant archival dimensions. For example, do tweets as historical or cultural documentation warrant the considerable amount of public money being expended to preserve them? Given that Gnip's data mining is already required to protect deleted tweets from public disclosure, might other, sensitive tweets be similarly protected? What are the implications of such public-commercial partnerships for archives and libraries? Does it provide a new source of financial support for these resource-intensive undertakings, and, if so, is this always in the best interest of social media users or the general public? The Twitter Archive is being made available for commercial parties such as financial services providers, marketing companies, and social monitoring and analytics firms to mine, to use for predictive modeling, and to build additional services and capabilities. If Twitter were to be subject to an appraisal regime that weeded out the proportion of tweets without sufficient historical, cultural, or informational value to be retained or those too sensitive for public disclosure (a very difficult analytical process due to the brevity and interrelatedness of individual tweets), then the value to the commercial sector could be significantly curtailed. Aware that someone can always find a use for any kind of document or information and understanding that preservation resources are limited and retaining too much information can present both retrieval and privacy challenges, archivists have spent a considerable amount of time and effort over the past sixty years devising and implementing appraisal frameworks. Given the strong focus of first-generation archivists on the appraisal of machine-readable records and that of the second generation of electronic records archivists on what constitutes a record in the digital world, it is interesting to contemplate, in the context of social media archiving, the minimization if not rejection of the practice of appraisal and of constricting definitions of *record*. Are these harbingers of a more universal demise of appraisal in the digital world and of strict delineations between archival and other forms of digital data management?

Digital Archaeology, Digital Forensics, and Digital Recovery

Digital archaeology, digital forensics, and digital recovery are a cluster of technologically interconnected but conceptually distinct areas of related research. Digital archaeology addresses the reconstruction or recovery of electronic records that have become unavailable as a result of damaged media or systems obsolescence. Records and other digital content (for example, computer games) can be recovered and/or reconstructed through techniques such as baking, chemical treatments, searching the binary structures to identify recurring patterns,[5] reverse engineering of the content, and inferencing based upon knowledge about workflow processes and surviving recordkeeping metadata. This area has until recently been a focus of digital humanists and historians, notable for the extent to which creator communities such as the gaming community have been involved.[6] Its techniques can be applied to legacy electronic records that have no true paper counterparts, but where archival requirements were not factored into their design, as well as to damaged records.

Digital forensics is the branch of forensic science that relates to the recovery and investigation of evidence located on digital media of all kinds. Fundamentally, data files are palimpsests that retain all sorts of trace data, such as drafts, geo-references, and time stamps, that can be extracted using the appropriate software tools. It is even possible to analyze the physical bit encoding where it exists on digital media. Digital forensics was applied early to criminal investigations. Copies of electronic materials such as dump and backup tapes and digital storage media are subjected to a barrage by various software tools to retrieve anything that might be relevant to a particular information need or, more likely, criminal investigation or litigation.[7] Ironically, case law indicates that electronic evidence thus retrieved has a strong likelihood of being admitted in court,[8] even though it does not meet the rigorous requirements for electronic records being established by the archival community.

Digital forensics has much wider application, however, including helping archivists to identify, describe, and preserve aspects of digital materials that might not be immediately apparent, but that could be salient to the evidentiality of preserved records and also to the kinds of scholarship that might be performed on them, such as the digital components and their bit stream considerations identified by InterPARES 2 research.[9] Cal Lee, director of the BitCurator Project, argues that digital forensics will not only assist with these archival practices, but also that it will make possible new forms of scholarship working with digital materials, scholarship that potentially can probe very intimate details about the creator and the ways in which those materials were created:

> Those who are interested in the underlying data that is hidden by the filesystem can instead generate and interact with disk images, which are low-level, sector-by-sector copies of all the data that resides on the storage medium. Inspection of the disk image can reveal a significant amount of information that users of the drive did not consciously or intentionally leave there, but can serve as traces of valuable contextual information.[10]

Recognizing that while several pieces of Linux-based software provide digital forensic functionality, but that none adequately supports archives or library applications and workflow, the archival and digital humanities researchers working on the BitCurator Project are developing an open source system that will do so.[11] The BitCurator Project addresses both the incorporation of digital forensics into the workflow involved in ingesting digital materials into collection management environments and the provision of public access to the digital materials ingested.[12] Such a system could potentially extract traces of activity, such as date and time stamps, file and personal data transfers, sites visited, email addresses contacted, and pointers to where to find data from a transferred forensic disk image, and correlate these to archival concepts such as provenance and original order. It could also infer that certain materials might be missing from among those transferred into archival control.

This work has several implications for archives and archival ideas, but perhaps the most compelling are those relating to archival ethics. Being able to recover digital traces at this level of granularity makes it practically impossible to eliminate traces of the private or the personal from digital materials, whether official or personal. Would alerting the creators and donors of archival materials to the various ways those materials might potentially be probed change their record-creating behaviors or their willingness to donate the materials? With forensic developments happening so rapidly, is it possible for creators and donors to understand how their materials might possibly be probed and to give prior, full, and informed consent when they hand their materials over to archival control? If the forensic disk copy of the materials has the most evidential value but makes possible investigations into records that might compromise personal privacy, should it be retained once a use copy has been created? Finally, should archives develop and provide digital forensic tools for use by their patrons? Lee specifies three changes wrought by digital forensics in the archival field. The first is the introduction of new vocabulary such as *disk image, hex[adecimal] viewer, cryptographic hash,* and *filesystem.* The second is the increased interaction with new professional communities and sources of guidance about how to create, read, and mount disk images of old storage media. The third, which overlaps with developments in metadata research, is the application of tools that work on archival materials at a very granular level—in this case at the level of raw bit streams—rather than at the file level. Finally, he argues, the introduction of digital forensics into archives has the potential to shift the "center of gravity" about electronic records in the archival literature from the design of institutional recordkeeping systems toward the acquisition and management of records from a much more diverse and unpredictable set of sources.[13]

Digital recovery relates to the use of digital technology to recover, rediscover, or re-create lost knowledge, memory, and practices. It is closely associated, but not coterminous, with digital repatriation, whereby materials that belong to, originated in, or were created by recordings of particular communities but that were subsequently held elsewhere, are digitized and the digital copies returned to those communities. Digital recovery is about more than making copies of the materials on another medium because of the capabilities that digitization affords. For example, sound and video recordings of songs, dances, and rituals now lost within their creating communities can not only be replayed and reviewed, they can be incorporated into "living archives" and digital keeping places, and used to create other digital artifacts such as documentaries, mash-ups, remixes, and animated sequences (for example, the Monash Country Lines Archive[14]). Similar to digital forensics with born-digital materials, digitized materials can be subjected to new kinds of close scrutiny and analysis, for example, of the kinds of media used in a text, the ways in which language was enunciated or music performed, and comparisons between different images or recordings.

Cloud and Mobile Computing

Recordkeeping professionals and archival researchers are converging around an increasingly vexing set of concerns related to pinning down "what, where, and when" is a record in a digital world. These concerns are invoked by cloud computing and data sharing, by storage and retrieval services that are often offshore and managed by commercial vendors, by mobile computing and texting using handheld devices such as cellular phones and personal digital assistants, and by SSDs (solid state drives) such as highly portable flash drives that do not use any mechanical components and whose flash memory can store data without a power source. Each of these developments can challenge the implementation of the kinds of

controls and requirements that archivists and electronic records researchers are trying to put in place to ensure the creation and preservation of
trustworthy digital records. They further blur the boundaries between the
official and the personal, and record and nonrecord by creating or storing all data together in an undifferentiated way (for example, replacing
university email services with Gmail, or sending and receiving business
communications on a personal cell phone); and they raise new policy
considerations relating to transborder dataflow, the extensibility of individual pieces of national legislation to the management and discoverabil-
ity of digital data and records being stored in other national jurisdictions,
and the legality of storing national or state government records within
other legal jurisdictions.

Jean-François Blanchette reminds us that the cloud is actually very
material—a physical infrastructure with massive data centers whose energy
consumption and geographic location are issues of growing environmental
and economic concern,[15] and Cal Lee suggests that "the Cloud is simply a
hard disk that is not in front of you." But the lack of transparency regarding
the cloud's operation and reliability is the most troubling to the electronic
records community. Noting that people use the cloud for various reasons
that will likely not go away, including to save money on local information
technology installations, for "centralized storage," and to provide scalable solutions to data sharing, storage, processing, and networking needs,
InterPARES 3 has identified several digital recordkeeping concerns:

- The chain of custody is not demonstrable and therefore is not
  transparent. This means that the reliability and authenticity of
  digital materials stored in the cloud can be challenged.
- Records are not auditable.
- Backups of data in the cloud can be made without authorization,
  raising questions about which is the record copy.
- Because multiple parties' data can be stored on one server, if a
  server is seized to obtain one set of data, the security of everyone
  else's data can be compromised.
- Records might or might not be encrypted at some point in the storage process.[16]

Frank Upward asks, "How can we get a recordkeeping mind into cloud computing?" What would an archival architecture for the development, delivery, operation, and servicing of modular, tailorable, and archivally approved applications using trusted third parties look like?[17] If records are always in a process of becoming, what is the documentary web that accumulates around the cloud? In a similar vein, Cal Lee speculates on what digital forensics might look like in the cloud and what kind of conditions should be incorporated into donor agreements if archives themselves plan to store their digital holdings in the cloud.

Any recordkeeping endeavor encompassing both the cloud and addressing glocalism factors would be massive and would need to go

---

1. Know your local legal environment and what might happen legally/jurisdictionally when you transcend that by using the cloud.

2. Do you know enough about when, how, where, and by whom services are performed to enter knowledgeably into a service agreement with a cloud vendor? Will your contracts prevail in the eventuality of a dispute or to ensure adequate recordkeeping controls are implemented? In what ways could you introduce a recordkeeping consciousness at this level to promote transparency in what is often primarily a commercial or customer/client relationship? (e.g., How do you know you are dealing with trusted third parties? What requirements have those parties had to meet to establish that trust? Are they the same requirements that recordkeepers would set?) Make decisions about local vs. offshore cloud services accordingly.

3. Institute a negotiating team to develop recordkeeping agreements with cloud providers. Members of that team should include lawyers (including intellectual property experts and those knowledgeable about recordkeeping requirements such as scheduling and disposition and metadata creation).

4. Identify how recordkeeping requirements for different types of records will be established and implemented (e.g., FOIA and accountability requirements for records created using public monies; records that are subject to specific institutional review or ethics board requirements for storage and eventual retention or destruction; records that were co-created with an additional dissimilar party, e.g., academic-industry or academic-private community partnerships; student or patient records).

5. Identify how records that should not or cannot be stored or processed in the cloud will be segregated and maintained in an appropriate, cost-effective, and scalable manner (i.e., what gets kept close to home and what goes to the cloud/inside or outside a firewall?).

6. Applying a records rather than an information or knowledge management sensibility, identify the appropriate balance between risk management and enterprise or opportunity agility in specific contexts and the extent to which using the cloud might facilitate either or both. Indicators might include customizability, privacy/sensitivity, data mining, standards requirements, laws and regulations, conventions, and prior agreements.

7. Educate records creators, managers, and consumers in recordkeeping considerations.

Figure 8.1. Some actions involved in devising a recordkeeping regime for storing records in the cloud

well beyond archivists and other recordkeepers. It must acknowledge and take into account a convergence between bits that can simultaneously be regarded as data, information, or records, depending upon the viewer's perspective. It must be capable of dealing with opacity on the side of the cloud vendors and likely transnational jurisdictional considerations not well fleshed out in legal actions. It must be overt in its trust infrastructure, for example, by defining what is considered to be a trusted third party in terms of data storage and preservation and by implementing rating systems for different aspects of recordkeeping such as metadata registries. It must be secure, segregable, and modular enough to prevent leaks or incidental seizure while agile enough to scale with increasing data size and to evolve with new data storage technologies and services. It must engage with big ideas and multiple policy and human infrastructure concerns that need to be implemented and addressed through a systematic series of small actions before the technology components can be completely specified (see Figure 8.1).

Conclusion

The previous chapter on electronic records research describes the movement in electronic records research away from concentration on the physical record to a conceptualization of the record as an intellectual object embedded in a strong procedural and juridical-administrative context. This movement has also been characterized as a change in emphasis from content—a data-centric perspective inherited from the data archives community—to context, with an ensuing expansion of the notion of context and evidence in archival theory. Certain contexts were privileged in electronic records research, especially government and corporate settings, and the social dimensions of electronic records were largely excluded (despite Margaret Hedstrom's prescient urging that for the archival field to get the most out of this research, "questions must be ambitious, think far ahead, and account for the social and cultural environment in which new information technology is applied"[18]). As the discussion in this chapter indicates, however, the social and cultural construction and import of the digital record are subjects of increasing discussion and investigation in more recent research relating to digital recordkeeping, especially as it relates to personal digital archives and social media. With the development of some of the research areas discussed in this chapter that focus on very granular aspects of digital inscription, personal privacy, evidence, and data-centricity increasingly interact with each other and at the same time, expand notions of context.

Although, as this chapter and chapter 7 demonstrate, there is a tremendous amount of extant and ongoing research in electronic records management and digital recordkeeping more broadly, several areas of important, under- or unaddressed research remain. Briefly, among these is digital recordkeeping policy, as well as associated areas such as privacy and digital rights management.[19] Gail Hodge observed in a 2000 study of digital archiving that "because of the speed of technological advances, the time frame in which we must consider archiving becomes much shorter. The time between manufacture and preservation is shrinking."[20] The study identifies intellectual property as a key concern relating to the acquisition of materials for archives. It points out that approaches vary from country to country because of variant national information policies or legal deposit laws. Hodge also identifies several digital archiving access issues that relate to rights management: "What rights does the archive have? What rights do various user groups have? What rights has the owner retained? How will the access mechanism interact with the metadata created by archives to ensure that these rights are managed properly?"[21] The more recent research discussed above raises additional questions relating to fully alerting creators and donors openly and transparently about the ways in which their digital materials might be analyzed and what could be uncovered, and about working in consultation with Indigenous communities or groups historically regarded as vulnerable or underrepresented within archives and that might have their own protocols and practices regarding community knowledge and archival management. A further issue relates to the implications of acquiring and attempting to preserve electronic records encoded in software legally protected not only by copyright but also by patent restrictions (and often physically protected by anticircumvention technologies). Resolving this issue will require considerable heightening of public and industry awareness of the problems caused by the proprietary control over, as well as the rapid obsolescence trajectories of software.

Identifying and addressing variances in the information policy infra-structure that affect electronic records management concerns has been an ongoing research focus within the InterPARES Projects. A 2012 report of the Digital Preservation Coalition examines legal issues such as the process of obtaining copyright clearance for preservation and access of archived materials, which can contribute significantly to the cost and complexity of digital preservation. Nevertheless, a broad and dynamic set of concerns remains that need to be addressed and revisited on an ongoing basis.[22]

A second closely related area is the need for economic metrics for assessing the costs of creating, preserving, making available, and using reliable and authentic electronic records over periods of time that may be longer than the lives of the creators, their families, and their institutions. These metrics also need to include a component for predicting future rates of creation and accrual of digital materials, or, if this proves to be impossible due to the speed at which new technological capabilities and user trends emerge, to address how to develop metrics in the absence of such ability to predict. This need for metrics to plan around has emerged as an important area for research within many communities that maintain repositories of digital content. Potentially, these communities can come together to design standardized data-collection strategies and benchmarks from which metrics may be derived.

Notes

[1] Sue McKemmish, "Evidence of Me . . ." *Archives and Manuscripts* 29, no. 1 (2001), http://www.mybestdocs.com/mckemmish-s-evidofme-ch10.htm.

[2] One of the first archivists to point out this possibility was Adrian Cunningham at the National Archives of Australia. See Adrian Cunningham, "The Archival Management of Personal Records in Electronic Form: Some Suggestions," *Archives and Manuscripts* 22, no. 1 (1994): 94–105.

[3] See, for example, Christopher A. Lee, ed., *I, Digital: Personal Collections in the Digital Era* (Chicago: Society of American Archivists, 2011); Donghee Sinn, S. Syn, and S. Kim, "Personal Records on the Web: Who's in Charge of Archiving, Hotmail or Archivists?," *Library and Information Science Research* 33, no. 4 (2011): 320–30; Joseph "Jofish" Kaye et al., "To Have and to Hold: Exploring the Personal Archive," *CHI 2006* (April 22–28, 2006), http://alumni.media.mit.edu/~jofish/writing/tohaveandtohold.pdf.

[4] Personal Digital Archiving 2013, University of Maryland, http://mith.umd.edu/pda2013/.

5   However, Ross and Gow warn that recovering binary patterns may not be sufficient for users to understand what those patterns represent, thus raising interesting questions about data intelligibility. Seamus Ross and Ann Gow, *Digital Archaeology? Rescuing Neglected or Damaged Data Resources* (London: British Library and Joint Information Systems Committee, 1999), http://www.ukoln.ac.uk/ services/elib/papers/supporting/pdf/p2.pdf. See also Christopher Mims, "Digital Archaeologists Excavate Chips, Not Dirt," *MIT Technology Review*, July 19, 2011, http://www.technologyreview .com/blog/mimssbits/27013/.

6   See, for example, Matthew G. Kirschenbaum, *Mechanisms: New Media and the Forensic Imagination* (Cambridge, Mass.: MIT Press, 2008); "Extreme Inscription: The Grammatology of the Hard Drive," *Text Technology* 13, no. 2 (2004): 91–125; Megan A. Winget and William Aspray, eds., *Digital Media: Technological and Social Challenges of the Interactive World* (Lanham, Md.: Scarecrow Press, 2011).

7   These issues have been discussed for several years by legal experts at the annual Sedona Conference, http://www.thesedonaconference.org/ and have been a new focus of the third phase of the InterPARES Project (InterPARES 3). See Luciana Duranti, "From Digital Diplomatics to Digital Records Forensics," *Archivaria* 68 (Fall 2009): 39–66.

8   See, for example, Mark Reith, Clint Carr, and Gregg Gunsch, "An Examination of Digital Forensic Models," *International Journal of Digital Evidence* (2002); Paul R. Rice, *Electronic Evidence Law and Practice* (Chicago: American Bar Association, 2005); Shira E. Scheindlin and Daniel J. Capra, *Electronic Discovery and Digital Evidence: In a Nutshell* (Sedona Conference: West Nutshell Series, 2009).

9   Luciana Duranti and Kenneth L. Thibodeau, "The Concept of Record in Interactive, Experiential and Dynamic Environments: The View of InterPARES," *Archival Science* 6, no. 1 (2008): 20.

10 Christopher A. Lee, "Archival Application of Digital Forensics Methods for Authenticity, Description and Access Provision" (paper presented at the International Council on Archives Congress, Brisbane, Australia, August 20–24, 2012, http://www.ica2012.com/files/data/Full%20papers%20upload/ ica12Final00290.pdf.

11 BitCurator: Tools for Digital Forensics Methods and Workflows in Real-world Collecting Institutions, http://www.bitcurator.net/.

12 See Christopher A. Lee, Matthew Kirschenbaum, Alexandra Chassanoff, Porter Olsen, and Kam Woods, "BitCurator: Tools and Techniques for Digital Forensics in Collecting Institutions," *D-Lib Magazine* 18 (May/June 2012), http://www.dlib.org/dlib/may12/lee/05lee.html; Kam Woods and Christopher A. Lee, "Acquisition and Processing of Disk Images to Further Archival Goals," in *Proceedings of Archiving 2012* (Springfield, Va.: Society for Imaging Science and Technology, 2012), 147–52.

13 Lee, "Archival Application of Digital Forensics Methods," 7.

14 Monash Country Lines Archive, http://www.infotech.monash.edu.au/research/projects/independent/ countrylines-archive/.

15 Jean-François Blanchette, "Infrastructural Thinking: A Pedagogical Approach to Information Technology and Archives" (plenary address, AERI 2012, Los Angeles, July 2012). See also Jean-François Blanchette, *Burdens of Proof: Cryptographic Culture and Evidence Law in the Age of Electronic Documents* (Cambridge, Mass.: MIT Press, 2012).

16 Luciana Duranti, "Archival Legislation for Engendering Trust in an Increasingly Networked Digital Environment" (paper presented at the International Congress on Archives, Brisbane, August 2012).

17 Frank Upward, "Cloud Computing and the Post-custodial Archive" (workshop presented at AERI 2012, Los Angeles, July 2012). See also Frank Upward, Sue McKemmish, and Barbara Reed, "Archivists and Changing Social and Information Spaces: A Continuum Approach to Recordkeeping and Archiving in Online Cultures," *Archivaria* 72 (Fall 2011): 197–237.

18 Hedstrom, "Understanding Electronic Incunabula," 339 (see chapter 7, n. 13).

[19] Gary M. Peterson, "New Technology and Copyright: The Impact on the Archives," *Comma: International Journal on Archives* 1–2 (2001): 69–76.

[20] Gail M. Hodge, "Best Practices for Digital Archiving: An Information Life Cycle Approach," *D-Lib Magazine* 6 (2000), http://www.dlib.org/dlib/january00/01hodge.html.

[21] Hodge, "Best Practices for Digital Archiving."

[22] Andrew Charlesworth, *Digital Preservation Coalition Report on Intellectual Property Rights for Digital Preservation* (2012), http://dx.doi.org/10.7207/twr12-02.

CHAPTER 9

∞

Recordkeeping Models

This chapter reviews the utility, nature, and limitations of different kinds of models and then discusses, with illustrations, some of the major models that recordkeepers might encounter.

Lacking an approved statement of underlying principle, international descriptive standards have been cobbled together so they can be read in different ways— instead of providing an integration of descriptive thought. This, it may be argued, is welcome flexibility. They allow implementation according to different methods. But implementation of what? The purpose and basis of description remains unclear. There is no unifying elaboration of purpose upon which different implementation strategies can be based because that was lost in Stockholm in 1993 when debate over a disputed statement of principles was discontinued by the Ad Hoc Commission on Descriptive Standards. The standards subsequently developed do not support a shared view of the archival enterprise in the achievement of which different methods may be employed. To that kind of flexibility there can be no objection. What we have, however, does not represent coherent disagreement (much less a unified view) about what we do, but deep confusion and lack of leadership.

—Chris Hurley, "Parallel Provenance (If These Are Your Records,
Where Are Your Stories?)," 2005[1]

Modeling and Recordkeeping

The networked digital world challenges archivists and other information professionals to rethink and move beyond conceptualizations and practices that have arisen from the physical, the eye-readable, the directly observable, and the hands-on materials and processes around which archives developed. The desire to exploit the power of the networked digital world to federate and traverse information, record, and cultural heritage collections or data repositories presents additional challenges regarding how best to integrate or map between descriptive metadata schemes developed by different information and disciplinary communities or that operate at different levels of granularity or from different ontological perspectives. Modeling has become an important descriptive, explanatory, and evaluation tool for archivists in addressing these challenges. It has been used in theory building, in explaining and communicating archival and record-keeping ideas, for depicting the nature of the record and identifying where and when it should be created, for delineating ideal and actual record-keeping processes and workflow, and for structuring and mapping across diverse metadata schemes. Such models have become important points where archival practices relating to both traditional and digital materials converge (for example, in description or in preservation), where the entire recordkeeping enterprise can be contemplated holistically (for example, in continuum informatics), where the archival field can interface with other information professions (for example, in metadata crosswalks or in digital archiving), and where creators, consumers, and information management professionals can all contemplate their various and interacting roles with respect to digital materials (for example, in digital curation). The reliance on models to some extent parallels how the world of data management dealt with a similar increase in complexity by moving away from structuring data in tables that do not scale or represent complex relationships well, to building systems that manage data based on graphs, nodes, and links.

Models seek to unambiguously represent real-life entities, processes, relationships, constraints, and inputs and outputs in ways that will visually or textually elucidate them for another party (for example, they might be used by an archivist to explain to a system analyst how functional requirements for recordkeeping might be designed into a recordkeeping system). A model may depict either an idealized or an actual situation or set of relationships and would be employed in different ways accordingly.

For the most part, the models used in archival and recordkeeping as well as in other information fields are models of concepts (for example, recordkeeping), conceptual models (for example, metadata schemes), or models of systems, processes, or workflows (for example, the Open Archival Information System Reference Model or InterPARES's activity models). As Figure 9.1 indicates, a considerable number of recordkeeping and metadata models and schemes have been devised over the past two decades, and many of these have been revised and updated several times since they were first published. This multiplicity indicates a fundamental characteristic of models, to which Hurley alludes in the above quote, which is that a model can only be developed from one perspective and must be built upon rigorous definitions of any concepts, terms, or processes used. A model too vague or ambiguous is useless. However, a very specific model is also limited in its applicability if the targeted constituency does not agree with its stance or if it is too high level or too granular. As a result, different creators (for example, the geospatial research and media communities) and information and heritage management communities (for example, library, W3C, and museum communities) have devised their own metadata models and schemes, convinced that other models and schemes cannot adequately address their specific worldviews or requirements. These models and schemes often become the basis for professional, industry, or technical standards that may be promulgated nationally or internationally and may be more or less open or proprietary.

Sometimes it is possible to reconcile or link such models and schemes using mappings or crosswalks, but only if the conceptual understandings and semantics upon which each model is predicated can be aligned. Unfortunately, this has rarely been the case in the archival field, where worldviews and descriptive practices have been considerably bifurcated. As indicated in chapter 7, regarding how adherence to the records continuum and life-cycle models led to very different electronic records management and research approaches in different national settings, a fundamental epistemological disjuncture exists between the two worldviews. It is not necessarily the case that the worldviews could not be reconciled—indeed, it is possible to identify ways in which the records life cycle might be represented within certain aspects of the broader records continuum model. Research in China relating to metasynthetic approaches to electronic records management is attempting to layer the continuum model on top of the life-cycle model and then to add another layer—an ecosystem model, on top of that.[2] Rather, entire archival traditions, terminologies, and professional and legal infrastructures have been constructed around one model or the other, making flexibility, dynamism, and consensus development more difficult.

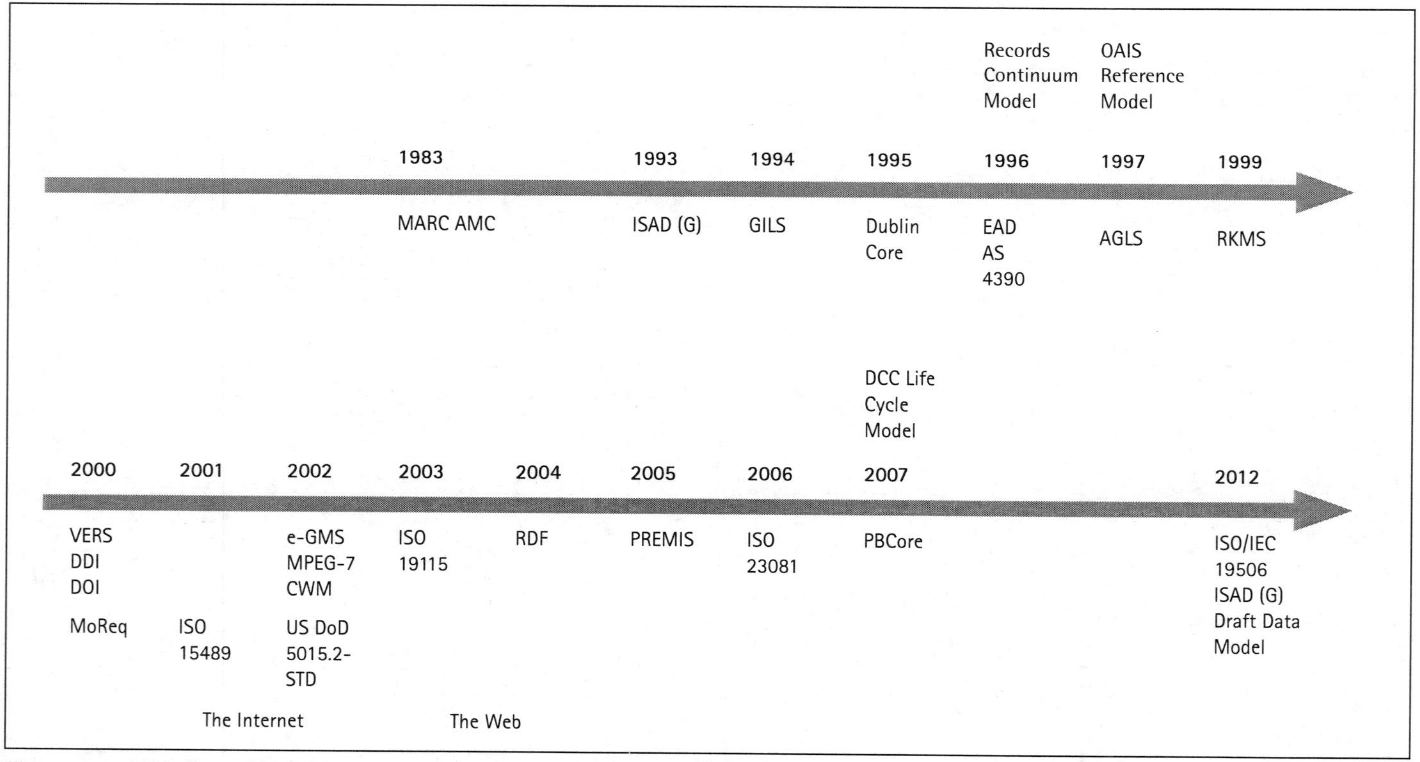

Figure 9.1. Timeline of key developments in recordkeeping, preservation, and locator models and metadata schemes*

* Only the dates of first releases of models and metadata schemes are indicated.

Additional bifurcations that contribute to difficulties in modeling, and ultimately in reconciling, integrating, or even pluralizing archival ideas and practices, can be perceived from the discussion in previous chapters regarding the development of archival description and its tensions between record-centric and bibliographic approaches, and in the development of descriptive standards separate from the development of metadata standards for electronic recordkeeping (i.e., the International Council on Archives [ICA] suite of standards and the International Standards Organization [ISO] Records Management Standards, such as ISO 23081).[3] These represent strands that, in the United States, remain separated by a sometimes implicit, sometimes explicit focus on either traditional or digital materials or on the type of repository involved. Again, the bifurcations are by-products of the history and evolution of the American archival field, but will not be overcome in ways that can exploit the full potential of the digital environment without what Hurley refers to as a "shared view of the archival enterprise." To address the dimensions of glocalism and support the pluralization necessary to empower the archival multiverse, however, that shared view must take into account the global multiplicity of archival and recordkeeping traditions, worldviews, and practices. It must also identify ways to include additional cultural and community ontologies such as those expressed in recent Indigenous protocols for archives and library materials.[4]

The following sections introduce prominent models in the fields of digital recordkeeping, digital data management, and metadata scheme and framework development.

The Records Continuum Model

In the life-cycle approach that dominated twentieth-century archival practices in Europe and North America, the management of records progresses through several distinct phases. These phases are conceptualized in different ways in different archival traditions, but they typically correspond to the creation, capture, storage, use, and disposal of records.[5] In 1985, Canadian archivist Jay Atherton, referencing a 1984 report by the U.S. National Archives and Records Service that described that agency's interpretation of the life cycle as a series of related but separate functions and responsibilities, laid out a detailed description of how the life cycle was conceptualized in Ottawa. It began with the creation or receipt of records, followed by the classification of those records in some kind of logical organization system, the maintenance and use of those records, and their disposition, which might take the form of destruction or transfer to an archives. All of these phases were viewed as the purview of a records management program. Another set of phases followed for which the archives was responsible: the appraisal or selection and accessioning of records of long-term value, the description of those records, the preservation of the records, and their access and use by the original creators as well as by secondary users, for example, scholars, lawyers, genealogists, journalists, and schoolchildren.[6]

Building on ideas first enunciated in Australia by archivists such as Peter Scott and applying structuration theory and Anthony Giddens's proposition that all actions can influence the development of other actions and inform and change structures in society, Frank Upward developed the Records Continuum Model in 1995. The Records Continuum Model is a descriptive model that provides a complex and holistic way to think about the nature, role, use, and life of records, regardless of their media, as they exist and constantly interact across four dimensions: create, capture, organize, and pluralize; and four axes: identity, evidentiality, transactionality, and recordkeeping entity (see Figure 9.2).[7] In this model, no parties are specifically designated as responsible for or limited to certain aspects of recordkeeping. Instead, recordkeeping consciousness and responsibilities are integrated across all four dimensions and ultimately include both personal and societal agency as well as that of particular institutions. Upward explains that

> a records continuum is continuous and is a time/space construct not a life model . . . no separate parts of a continuum are readily discernible, and its elements pass into each other. . . . The axes encapsulate major themes in archival science, and each axis presents four coordinates which can be linked dimensionally.[8]

Subsequent to its publication, this model's continuum thinking became the basis for the development of Australian Standard 4390 that in turn was the model for the ISO 15489 Records Management Standard, the Victorian Electronic Records Strategy (VERS), the Recordkeeping Metadata Schema

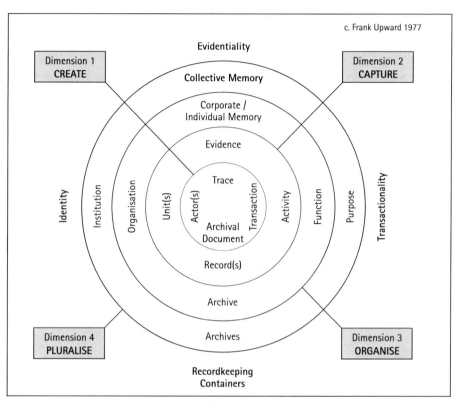

Figure 9.2. The Records Continuum Model (Upward)

Reproduced with permission from Frank Upward. "Modelling the Continuum as Paradigm Shift in Record-keeping and Archiving Processes, and Beyond—A Personal Reflection," *Records Management Journal* 10, no. 3 (2000): 115–39.

(RKMS), and the ISO 23081 Records Management Metadata Standard. Its worldview is, therefore, embedded both nationally and internationally and is particularly influential in the heavily regulated and compliance-oriented industry sector, even as major archival traditions and institutions around the globe continue to espouse a life-cycle approach.

This embeddedness in different approaches raises an important question as to whether it is possible to devise functional requirements and metadata schemes that can be used regardless of the model being applied. In the years since its first publication as archivists become more aware of the complexities and dynamics of the digital world, more turn to continuum approaches. At the same time, research and practical implementations have identified some areas where the records continuum model is lacking.

This is an inevitable outcome of model development, particularly with a model that attempts to be universal and to address the many variables and the fluidity associated with time, space, agency, and entities, while physically limited in the number of dimensions that can be represented simultaneously. As stated above, all models must be developed from a particular stance, and that stance is going to omit, discount, or undervalue certain aspects that someone coming from another stance might prioritize. For example, several psychological and phenomenological aspects not overtly expressed in the model but whose importance recent research highlights include intentionality, spirituality, and affect or emotion. As Upward himself notes, "Part of the continuing significance of the modelling will be how to develop archival control within the knot of creation in digital recordkeeping (which will require creation based models from different perspectives)."[9] Interestingly, while Giddens's work addresses the presence of power,[10] it was not explicitly represented in this 1995 model. With the increased focus on the presence and effects of power in postmodern and postcolonial critiques of archives and recordkeeping, one might anticipate that these might be made more explicit in future continuum-based modeling.

Upward and colleagues Barbara Reed and Don Schauder also pursued the relevance of continuum approaches to adjacent areas of information and heritage management. Naming this line of research "continuum informatics," Upward states that it "covers the convergence of recordkeeping, information management, information systems, publishing, digital forensics, cultural heritage, etc., all of which require different metadata sets, but as archivists we are stewards for recordkeeping metadata in particular. What strategies, tactics and structures will help in handling convergence without giving up on specializations?"[11] The Information Continuum Model developed by Reed, Schauder, and Upward illustrates how continuum thinking that developed in the archives and recordkeeping fields might be extended into information management (see Figure 9.3).

The Digital Curation Center Curation Lifecycle Model

A more complex iteration of the life-cycle model is the Curation Lifecycle Model promulgated by the Digital Curation Center (DCC) "as a training tool for data creators, data curators and data users; to organise and plan their resources; and to help organisations identify risks to their digital assets and plan management strategies for their successful curation."[12] Sarah Higgins, when introducing the model, argued for the necessity of a lifecycle approach to ensure the continuity of digital material:

> Digital material, by its very nature, is susceptible to technological change from the moment of creation. The curation and preservation activities undertaken, or neglected, in different stages of their management, can influence the ability to look after them successfully at subsequent stages. A lifecycle approach ensures that all the required stages are identified and planned, and necessary actions implemented, in the correct sequence. This can ensure the maintenance of authenticity, reliability, integrity and usability of digital material, which in turn ensures maximisation of the investment in their creation.[13]

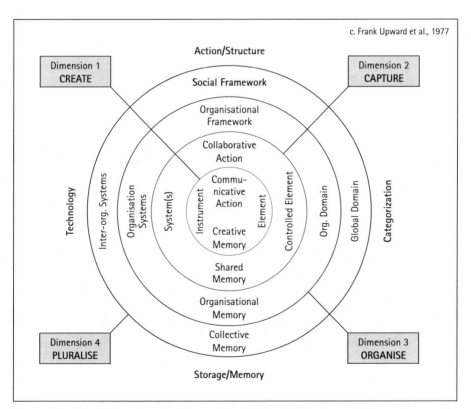

Figure 9.3. The Information Continuum Model (Reed, Schauder, and Upward)

Reproduced with permission from Frank Upward. "Modelling the Continuum as Paradigm Shift in Record-keeping and Archiving Processes, and Beyond—A Personal Reflection," *Records Management Journal* 10, no. 3 (2000): 115–39.

The model is directed at those working with digital data of all types, rather than with records or some other specific form of digital information. Rather than representing a sequence of processes, it seeks to provide a sense of which actions are occasional, which sequential, and which occur throughout the life cycle of the digital data in question. It also overtly acknowledges that digital data can and should be re-used and transformed in various ways and that these re-uses and transformations result in the creation of new content that in turn enters into the life cycle. One other interesting facet of this model is its inclusion of "community watch and participation" within the same band of activity as preservation planning, thus acknowledging not only the social contexts of digital data, but also the ways in which not just professional institutions and fields, but individuals,

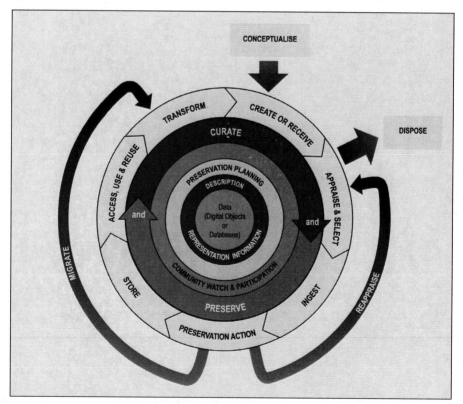

Figure 9.4. The DCC Digital Curation Model

© The University of Edinburgh. S. Higgins. "The DCC Curation Lifecycle Model," *The International Journal of Digital Curation* 3, no. 1: 134–40, http://www.ijdc.net/index.php/ijdc/article/viewFile/.

specific communities, and society at large all bear responsibility for the preservation of their digital legacy (see Figure 9.4).

The Open Archival Information Systems (OAIS) Reference Model

The space science community developed the Open Archival Information Systems (OAIS) Reference Model to manage and process massively high volumes of digital data in multiple media and formats collected, for example, through remote sensing, and to ensure that it could, if necessary, be preserved for indeterminably long periods of time and across all necessary migrations. First published in 1997 by the Consultative Committee for Space Data Systems (CCSDS), in 2003 it was adopted as an ISO standard, ISO 14721: 2003. This is an example of a high-level model designed to describe and define, for nonarchival organizations, the basic processes involved in the long-term preservation of and access to digital data. In this intent, it is quite similar to the DCC Curation Lifecycle Model. Its title refers more to scientific notions of data archiving (see chapter 10) than to the management of records by archives (as evidenced by terminology such as "ingest" and "dissemination information packages"). However, the

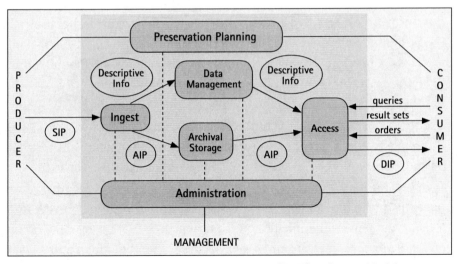

Figure 9.5. The Open Archival Information Systems (OAIS) Reference Model

workflow that it lays out should seem very familiar, even to traditional archivists (see Figure 9.5). By establishing a standard terminology and exposition of concepts and processes, it aspires to provide an extensible framework that can be used to build or compare actual architectures, data models, applications, and preservation strategies and techniques, and to promote vendor development of preservation and access systems. As discussed in prior chapters, the OAIS Reference Model has been used as the basis for several electronic recordkeeping endeavors, including the U.S. National Archives' Electronic Records Archive (ERA) and the activity models developed by InterPARES 2.

The InterPARES Activity Models

In addition to OAIS, archivists, recordkeeping professionals, and researchers have developed multiple models that delineate various aspects of the functions, activities, and processes involved in recordkeeping. Chapters 4 and 5 discuss the data models being developed for the Functional Requirements for Bibliographic Records (FRBR) and for the International Council on Archives (ICA) suite of descriptive standards; and chapter 7 discusses the entity-relationship model that underlies the RKMS and how the Preservation Metadata: Implementation Strategies (PREMIS) metadata set has been designed to expand upon and specify the kinds of preservation information required in the OAIS Model. Both macro-appraisal and the Designing and Implementing Recordkeeping Systems (DIRKS) methodology also apply the technique of functional decomposition that underpins many recordkeeping modeling endeavors.[14]

　Probably the most prominent research application of activity modeling in the archival and recordkeeping field is that of the InterPARES Projects and the forerunner University of British Columbia (UBC) Project on the Preservation of the Integrity of Electronic Records. Those projects used Integration Definition for Function Modeling (IDEF0), one particular modeling technique, to depict and name the actions ideally involved, from a life-cycle perspective, in the creation and preservation of reliable and authentic records in electronic systems. These models build on and expand the framework provided by the OAIS Reference Model. They take the form

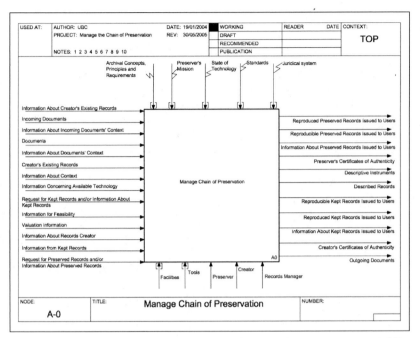

Figure 9.6. Manage Chain of Preservation (InterPARES 2 Activity Model)[15]

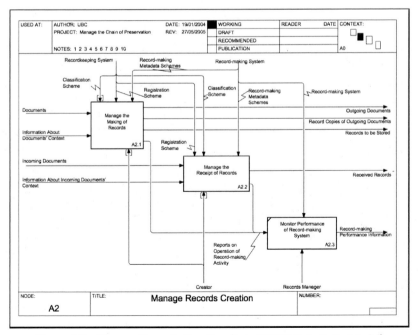

Figure 9.7. Manage Records Creation (InterPARES 2 Activity Model)

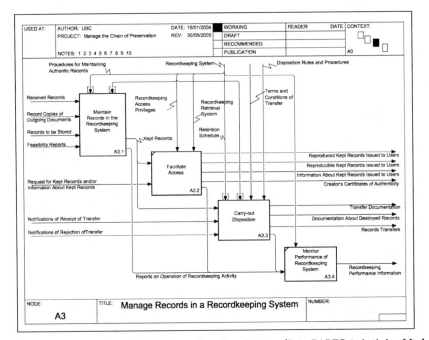

Figure 9.8. Manage Records in a Recordkeeping System (InterPARES 2 Activity Model)

of a series of very detailed models that successively decompose one aspect depicted on a higher-level model. Figure 9.6 depicts the highest-level model of activities that would be undertaken in preserving records. Arrows that enter from the left-hand side indicate inputs and those that exit from the right-hand side indicate outputs. Arrows coming in from the top represent constraints, and those coming in from below represent resources required.

Figures 9.7. and 9.8., by contrast, show the decomposition of just one aspect of the preceding model into its constituent activities.

Notes

[1] Chris Hurley, "Parallel Provenance (If These Are Your Records, Where Are Your Stories?)," 6, http://www .infotech.monash.edu.au/research/groups/rcrg/publications/parallel-provenance-combined.pdf.

[2] See Xiaomi An, *Towards a Best Practice Framework for Managing Urban Development Archives: Case Studies from the U.K. and China* (PhD diss., University of Liverpool, 2001); Xiaomi An,

Shuyang Sun, and Wei Zhang, "Managing Electronic Records in E-Government: Current Trends and Future Directions Internationally," *Proceedings of the 2011 International Conference on Management and Service Science, 12-14 August 2011,* IEEE Xplore Digital Library, http://ieeexplore.ieee.org/stamp/stamp.jsp?tp=&arnumber=5999074; Xiaomi An, "Meta-synthetic Strategies to Digital Recordkeeping: International Trends and Future Directions" (paper presented at the International Council on Archives Congress, Brisbane, August 2012), http://www.ica2012.com/files/data/Full%20 papers%20upload/ica12final00020.pdf.

3   See Jennifer J. Bunn, *Multiple Narratives, Multiple Views: Observing Archival Description* (PhD diss., University College London, 2011), 32, http://discovery.ucl.ac.uk/1322455/1/1322455.pdf.

4   For example, The Aboriginal and Torres Strait Islander Library and Information Resources Network, "ATSILIRN Protocols," http://www.aiatsis.gov.au/atsilirn/protocols.php; the Aboriginal and Torres Strait Islander Data Archive, "ATSIDA Protocols," http://www.atsida.edu.au/protocols/atsida; First Archivist Circle, "Protocols for Native American Archival Materials" (2007), http://www2.nau.edu/libnap-p/.

5   Elizabeth Shepherd and Geoffrey Yeo, *Managing Records: A Handbook of Principles and Practice* (London: Facet Publishing, 2003).

6   Jay Atherton, "From Life Cycle to Continuum: Some Thoughts on the Records Management-Archives Relationship," in *Canadian Archival Studies and the Rediscovery of Provenance,* ed. Tom Nesmith (Metuchen, N.J.: Scarecrow, 1993), 391-402. Reprinted in *Archivaria* 21 (1985): 43-51.

7   Frank Upward, "Structuring the Records Continuum Part One: Postcustodial Principles and Properties," *Archives and Manuscripts* 24 (1996): 268-85; Upward, "Structuring the Records Continuum Part Two: Structuration Theory and Recordkeeping," *Archives and Manuscripts* 25 (1997): 10-35.

8   Upward, "Structuring the Records Continuum Part One," 281.

9   Frank Upward and author, email correspondence, October 7, 2012.

10 Anthony Giddens, *The Constitution of Society: Outline of the Theory of Structuration* (Berkeley: University of California Press, 1984).

11 Upward, "Cloud Computing and the Post-custodial Archive" (see chapter 8, n. 17).

12 Sarah Higgins, "The DCC Curation Lifecycle Model," *International Journal of Digital Curation* 1, no. 3 (2008): 134.

13 Higgins, "The DCC Curation Lifecycle Model," 135.

14 Macro-appraisal is an approach pioneered by Terry Cook and his colleagues at the National Archives of Canada in the 1990s that analyzes institutional functions, asks which functions are to be documented, and then looks for records that meet those documentary objectives. See Terry Cook, "Macroappraisal in Theory and Practice: Origins, Characteristics, and Implementation in Canada, 1950-2000," *Archival Science* 5, nos. 2-4 (2005): 101-61. The National Archives of Australia promulgated the Designing and Implementing Recordkeeping Systems (DIRKS) approach until 2007, when new recordkeeping guidelines superseded it.

15 All models are reproduced with permission from Terry Eastwood, Hans Hofman, and Randy Preston, "Part Five—Modeling Digital Records Creation, Maintenance and Preservation: Modeling Cross-domain Task Force Report," in *International Research on Permanent Authentic Records in Electronic Systems (InterPARES) 2: Experiential, Interactive and Dynamic Records,* ed. Luciana Duranti and Randy Preston (Padova, Italy: Associazione Nazionale Archivistica Italiana, 2008), http://www .interpares.org/ip2/display_file.cfm?doc=ip2_book_part_5_modeling_task_force.pdf.

CHAPTER 10

∞

From Custody to Stewardship: Digital Repositories, Preservation, and Curation

This chapter reviews the factors behind the rise of data archiving and the shift in focus from the custody of computer-generated data to that of multiprofessional, community, and individual stewardship over diverse types of born-digital materials. It delineates preoccupations of digital preservation research and the relationship of this work to data and digital curation. Throughout, it contemplates the current and potential engagement of archivists and the contributions that archival ideas might make to these developing fields.

Posterity will view us largely through the records we preserve, and it may not be wholly satisfied with our selection of those records. We may not ourselves be satisfied with it a few years from now, but practical considerations force us to make the selections. That is a difficult responsibility to exercise. . . . The ivory tower is rapidly losing caste as the supposed residence of archivists. The exigencies of historical records are leading the keeper of historical records out of that sanctum and into more extensive associations with the users and with the makers of archives. Of these associations, that with the users is the better understood. That with the makers of archives needs elucidation. And in the latter relationship the salient problem is the selection of the records that are to be preserved.

−Philip C. Brooks, U.S. National Archives Records
Appraisal Officer, 1940, "What Records Shall We Preserve?"[1]

Introduction

"This is big."[2] David Green's opening assertion in his 2007 article, "Cyberinfrastructure for Us All," is simple, yet it powerfully characterizes ambitious contemporary national and international agendas to use networked computing to transform how academic, scientific, government, and, indeed, most knowledge production and data management processes and collaborations are effected. Green, formerly executive director of the National Initiative for a Networked Cultural Heritage (NINCH), commented on a series of reports calling for the development of a human-centered and multilayered, publicly and privately supported digital infrastructure, or "cyberinfrastructure," that will "harness the power of distributed, computer-assisted collaborative production."[3] These reports, Green noted, "forcefully and formally call attention to the shift in economic and social production from a classic industrial base to a networked information base." One important aspect of this shift to networked production is "cyberscholarship," that is, research, teaching, and learning facilitated by high-performance collaborative computing, digital data management and analysis tools, digital information resources, and electronic publishing capabilities.[4]

Academic and scientific archives increasingly encounter the transformative effects of cyberscholarship on the nature and dissemination of the resulting record of knowledge production. In the past, the products of such scholarship included monographs and journal articles purchased and made available through academic libraries. In some cases, manuscript drafts of those items and scholarly correspondence might be retained as part of a collection of personal papers in the archives of the researcher's institution, or collected as part of a thematic special collection, for example, in the history of science. Filing cabinets filled with research data and related technical documentation and instrumentation, if not governed by institutional review board requirements, would probably not be acquired by an institutional archives and would remain with the researcher until eventually being discarded or destroyed. Today, not only these products, but also underlying data and documentation of the processes by which they were developed (for example, electronic mail correspondence, wikis, blogs, and mash-ups used by individual and collaborating researchers) are all likely to be created digitally and may well be candidates not only for inclusion in institutional archives, but also integrated into more broadly based digital repositories.

Digital repositories, and especially institutional repositories (IRs) maintained by academic and other scholarly institutions, are among the key components in the development of cyberinfrastructure and the kinds of scholarship it supports. They can potentially encompass a range of digital content relating to a single disciplinary or thematic area or to multiple areas, where that content might be variously, and sometimes simultaneously, viewed as data, information, records, evidence, artifacts, or aesthetic objects. The content, especially when it takes the form of research data, can vary considerably in terms of complexity and rate of acquisition, and these two variables can be harder to cope with than issues presented simply by very high-volume materials. Traditionally, the responsibility for different kinds of content (primary/secondary, textual/nontextual, and so forth) has fallen to specialized repositories and professionals. In such a model, primary emphases are placed on the selection and preservation of and access to *extant* nondigital and digital content according to the best practices of the professional approach (for example, bibliographic, archival, data archiving, or museum) employed by that repository. In the world of digital repositories, however, the emphasis has shifted away from such siloed and custodially oriented professional approaches to one that integrates diverse professional expertise and invests in proactive partnerships with systems developers, content creators, and end users to support *lifelong* stewardship and curation of digital content (i.e., from conception on). Moreover, since digital repository content might be the product of collaborations that traverse institutions, sectors, and national boundaries as well as the public and private sectors, a repository might not be associated exclusively with one institution but rather with a shared entity, where stewardship responsibilities are potentially distributed across multiple parties.

In such a curatorial model, the active participation of both systems designers and the creators of digital resources, for example, scientists or digital artists, are needed so that the resources are initially created and described in ways that will ensure they are able to be identified, acquired, preserved, and made available by a digital repository and re-used by others over the long term. This approach should sound familiar to archivists, since it is similar to that being applied in electronic records management. Different in the digital repository context, however, is that all the output of scholarly or artistic production might not be, or might not be viewed as, records in a legal or regulatory sense, and even when they are, mandates for their management might be less clear or not strictly implemented or followed. For digital repository developers, this situation has three important implications. The first is to find ways to become involved at the design and creation stages of environments and tools that support cyberscholarship, even in the absence of any legal, funder, or other mandate to do so. The second is to ensure when designing the capabilities to identify, capture, preserve, and disseminate relevant digital materials that those materials that must meet electronic recordkeeping or archival requirements can do so (and currently most digital repositories are unable to meet the evidentiary bar set by electronic recordkeeping requirements). The third is to promote the notion of community responsibility, something incorporated into the Digital Curation Center (DCC) Lifecycle Model as "Community Watch and Participation." However, given that creators tend to be most concerned with the immediate creation and use of their data and digital output according to their own disciplinary or sector practices, research modes, and personal aesthetics, there is also a need to develop automated tools to embed digital repository and electronic recordkeeping requirements into the systems they are using as transparently and easily as possible. In cases where this does not occur, and likely such cases will exist for the foreseeable future, a need will remain for professionals capable of addressing the capture or recovery, appraisal, preservation, and long-term management of digital materials not created with a view toward their archival future.

Other aspects to contemplate are the workflow and long-term functionality of digital repositories. By integrating a life-cycle approach, repository developers will need not only to contemplate the creation of digital content, but also how that content and its salient characteristics will travel through time and through variations in uses and users that cannot be anticipated in the present. The design, metadata practices, services, and staffing of digital repositories will all need to be sufficiently flexible to accommodate the differing needs, methods, aesthetics, and modalities of secondary users who wish to use digital content and re-analyze it in new contexts, not just today, but also in the future.[5] This last point gives many involved in the preservation and access of digital content pause. They wish to have available digital tools as yet undeveloped, and they wonder what kind of workflow, what metrics, and what bases for decisions should be employed to preserve and make available digital content for future uses that cannot be anticipated. These developments and needs suggest that archivists have an important role to play in the creation of digital content, the building and managing of digital repositories, anticipating future uses, and developing policy to address sensitive and proprietary data management, and more broadly in the discourse around cyberinfrastructure development.[6] In 2007, Markey et al. published the results of a *Census of Institutional Repositories in the United States*, one of several activities of the MIRACLE (Making Institutional Repositories a Collaborative Learning Environment) Project.[7] The census found that "archivists generally play a quiet but persistent role in institutional repositories, and archival and special collections materials are a major source of content in institutional repositories." That role includes involvement in planning and committee membership relating to institutional repository development and implementation, but not leadership. The authors concluded that "a potential, albeit currently unfilled, role for the archivist exists in providing digital preservation expertise for the IR."[8] While preservation expertise is certainly part of an archivist's professional portfolio, he or she might also contribute other areas of expertise, such as managing digital materials as evidence rather than as data or information, maintaining the trustworthiness of materials over time, and appraising and describing high volumes of organically related materials with a view to possible future uses.

At the same time, these developments raise several questions that tend to bother archivists. Just as electronic records management found itself needing to address a central definitional concern about what constitutes a record in the digital environment, definitional clarity is needed around the construct of "data," which is so central to much of the rhetoric of cyberscholarship. If, in the sciences and social sciences, data equate to evidence of research processes and decisions, as well as to the information upon which findings or conclusions are based, that would seem to have at least some of the hallmarks associated with the traces of acts and facts of organizational and human activity that archives consider to be records in other spheres. But then there is the niggling question of whether the creators themselves view their data as records. Many scientists take the view that the report or article disseminated with their findings is the actual record, the primary source. Increasingly in the digital world, that report or article will include links to the underlying compiled data, and both will be preserved and made available from a digital repository. The raw data, however, as well as the associated procedural documentation, is often treated as being too raw and too early in the research process to be of note.

This question about what the record of science is, of course, is not a new issue for archivists involved in the appraisal of such materials, but it has only recently begun to attract the attention of those in the digital curation world, which focuses largely on preservation and access concerns. Science, of course, is not the only domain to generate data and to have ongoing storage, use, and re-use needs. In the social sciences, and also in the humanities and the arts, less research has been done to understand the work practices and the kinds of digital materials practitioners might generate.[9] Do humanists and artists create data in the same way as do the scientists and social scientists? If data in certain respects might be equated to evidence (in the scientific, not the legal sense), around what evidence and forms of reasoning do scholars in these fields base their scholarship? How much of that evidence is already or might in the future be held in archives? What characteristics of this evidence would it be important for repositories to maintain and elucidate? What methodological approaches should their search, retrieval, and display capabilities support? Terry Cook criticizes the digital curation field for not undertaking appraisal and for viewing appraisal as "un-archival," thus harkening back to the days when an archives was viewed as a natural accumulation, "a kind of Darwinian construction."[10] The subject also raises old questions and debates about the need for appraisal and the role of archivists in shaping the historical record. It also leads to queries about when a record becomes a record—when it is completed? Should drafts and interim documentation be kept? If the record, in Sue McKemmish's words and in the continuum view, is "always in the process of becoming,"[11] what kind of repository can support that organic evolution and how?

The Evolution of Data Archives and Cyberinfrastructure

The conceptual, technical, and disciplinary developments of cyberinfrastructure (and the cyberscholarship it is in part designed to facilitate) are logical outgrowths of the deployment of technology in military, scientific, and social scientific applications from the 1940s onward, as discussed in chapter 2, and the documentation movements of (primarily) the first half of the twentieth century in Europe and America discussed in chapter 3. Although the impetus of the American Documentation Institute and scholarly microfilming efforts dissipated somewhat after the 1950s, the second half of the twentieth century saw very rapid developments in the application of computing and information technology in research in the emerging social sciences as well as in libraries that together continued to lay the groundwork for today's cyberinfrastructure.

Social science fields were early adopters of computing technology to collect, analyze, and manipulate very large and often longitudinal datasets in ways that would not previously have been possible. Such datasets, however, were expensive and difficult to collect, thus incentivizing sharing and re-use. Repositories were needed that could collect and manage datasets compiled through such research (for example, by validating, describing, and anonymizing them, as well as rendering them software independent) and make them available to other researchers, since government and institutional archives, at least in the United States, were not mandated or funded to address that need.[12] In 1946, the Elmo Roper Organization created the Roper Public Opinion Research Center based at Williams College to house machine-readable data from Roper surveys, thus becoming one of the first social science data archives (SSDAs). In the same year, Murray Lawson presented a paper, subsequently published in *The American Archivist*, on the potential of automation for historical research. According to electronic records archivist Thomas Elton Brown, "Lawson's paper prophetically outlined the capability of the emerging technology to facilitate both intellectual control over resource material and research using statistical techniques."[13] In 1962, the Inter-University Consortium for Political and Social Research (ICPSR) was founded at the University of Michigan, Ann Arbor, as the first academic social science data archives, and, in the following year, Myron Lefcowitz and Robert Shea published their proposal in *American Behavioral Scientist* calling for a National Archive of survey data. In 1964, an international effort was begun, with encouragement from United Nations Educational, Scientific, and Cultural Organization (UNESCO) and the newly formed United States Council on Social Science Data Archives (USCSSDA), to found social science data archives, and, in 1973, the International Association for Social Science Information Services and Technology (IASSIST) was established. IASSIST was a notable organization in that it brought together all the parties involved with social science data: those creating and disseminating the data, data users (especially social scientists), and social science data archivists and librarians.[14] Today, IASSIST still draws from these communities, although they are somewhat more closely specified: "Social science researchers and scientists who are producers and users of micro and macro-level social data; Information specialists, who preserve social data, manage facilities and provide services that promote the secondary use of social data; Methodologists and computing specialists who advance technical methods to manipulate and analyze social data."[15] Little interchange remains, however, between the IASSIST community and traditional archivists.

In the late 1960s, libraries also began to take advantage of computing capabilities, sharing machine-readable cataloging data first on magnetic tape and later over computer networks (as discussed in chapter 4), automating library management systems, and providing access to fee-based online databases containing scientific and other technical information. Instrumental in the development of these databases, created by corporations such as Lockheed and DIALOG and research organizations such as the American Chemical Society and the National Agricultural Library,[16] were information scientists who became important figures in the American Society for Information Science.[17] Again, however, while archivists began to collaborate with librarians in the 1980s regarding the development and exchange of standardized descriptive information, little interaction occurred at this time between traditional archivists and the information scientists developing much of the broader technology infrastructure.

In the 1970s and 1980s, sibylline predictions of the *paperless office* presaged today's integrated digital record-keeping and asset management systems,[18] but the actualization of the promise of digital technology really came with the rapid succession of Internet and then World Wide Web (WWW) developments in the 1990s. In 1991, the Wide Area Information Server (WAIS) protocol was introduced, allowing collections of indexed data to be retrieved by searches. In the same year, an initial draft of the HyperText Transfer Protocol (HTTP) and an early WWW system were released, the latter being distributed by CERN to the high-energy physics community to support its scholarly communication by networking computers. In 1993, the graphical browser Mosaic was released. This was followed by open commercialization of the Web in 1995 and the release of Windows 98 with a built-in Internet browser. Taken together, these developments made possible a digital infrastructure capable of supporting global collaborative and multimedia knowledge production, dissemination, and re-use. By the late 1990s, many areas of human endeavor sought to transform themselves into this Web world: *e*government, *e*science, *e*commerce, and *e*learning; *digital* medicine, *digital* humanities, *digital* libraries, and *digital* archives; and *virtual* museums and *virtual* communities. With the rise of mobile computing and social media in the twenty-first century, for example, using personal digital assistants (PDAs) and cell phones, networked digital technology has become diversified, democratized, personalized, and culturally embedded to the point where, although certain populations, regions, and sectors are still irrefutably more advantaged than others, Nicholas Negroponte's iconic 1995 vision of a pervasive global digitality, in the shape of cyberinfrastructure, has become a reality.[19]

Mandates for the Management of Digital Research Data

In the United States, the two biggest federal funding agencies—the National Science Foundation (NSF) and the National Institutes for Health (NIH)—both underscore the need for funded researchers to develop data management plans that include mechanisms for preserving and providing open access to their research data.[20] An important motivation underlying this requirement, as was the case with the development of social science data archives in the second half of the twentieth century, is the potential for re-use of that data (although studies examining the extent to which such data are either easily re-used, or indeed, would be re-used if they were maintained in a digital repository, are insufficient to date). Scientific data are expensive to produce and can be both technically and fiscally difficult for producing researchers and research collaborations to maintain on their own. However, beyond the importance of data remaining available for use by those who wish to replicate or to challenge a particular research activity, the cyberinfrastructure vision is that the data may also be usable in other ways—as inputs for other research projects in the same and different fields, and as source materials for academic instruction, particularly in science education. For example, in the United States, a 2009 National Institutes of Health funding opportunity announcement (FOA) called for proposals that would "develop, enhance, or extend infrastructure for connecting people and resources to facilitate national discovery of individuals and of scientific resources by scientists and students to encourage interdisciplinary collaboration and scientific exchange."[21, 22] This call recognized the difficulties that individuals in very different settings and fields experience in communicating and working across very different kinds of information resources (as examples of information resources the call gives data, animal models, reagents, assays, cores, literature, materials, and tools, although interestingly it does not mention records or other archival materials). The call also acknowledges the sentiment that "the biomedical community has barely tapped the power of web-based tools, currently exploited for social networking, for professional connection and collaboration to serve biomedical research."[23] This latter point recognizes the innovative ways in which social networking capabilities allow specific communities to design less institutionalized, or even noninstitutionalized, digital environments closely patterned on, or emanating directly out of, the behaviors and priorities of those communities.

While much impetus for the building (and funding) of cyberinfrastructure has come from the sciences, health sciences, and engineering, the management and exploitation of digital materials generated by research activities are not only concerns of the more scientific and technical fields. In the United States, where the social sciences include fields such as economics, political science, sociology, public policy, anthropology, and history, considerable innovation has occurred in recent years in research methods along with a broadening of the kinds of digital data collected and how they are collated. The resulting data are no longer primarily quantitative, and many are not suitable for anonymization or rendering into software-independent forms to support sharing and re-use. Ethnographic field recordings, oral and video histories, geo-referenced datasets, and dynamic visualizations are only some of the complex data types resulting from new modes of inquiry that are technologically facilitated, stored, and shared. The social sciences, therefore, while not as heavily funded as the natural, physical, and health sciences, also have complex digital data management and data sharing needs.[24] A recent study conducted by Jolene Beiser in association with the UCLA Institute for Social Research Social Science Data Archive examines how UCLA researchers in the social sciences think about and manage their data.[25] In the social sciences, despite a culture of re-using others' data and a strong awareness of privacy and security concerns associated with improperly prepared or distributed data, researchers may be subject to less stringent data management requirements than those imposed by funding agencies in the health, natural, and physical sciences. They also often have less infrastructure in the form of research funding, labs, specialized technology, and student research assistants to help them in managing their data. Beiser found that the academic researchers she interviewed for this study have widely differing notions about what "data," "data gathering, "data management," "data preservation," and "data sharing" mean. She also found that most of the researchers are unaware of the services available on campus to help them with these kinds of activities and that they are attempting to manage data on their own. Her study concluded by recommending that both faculty and student researchers be trained in curating data (i.e., how to create and manage data in ways that support ongoing preservation, sharing, and accessibility), in budgeting and finding funding for data preservation activities, and in employing best practices for choosing preservation-friendly file formats, database construction, digitization, and portable storage device selection and use.[26] These findings are very similar to those of electronic records archivists over the past twenty years or so in emphasizing that the creators of digital materials must also be involved at the front end in creating "archivable" materials if those materials are eventually to be preserved and accessed through a digital repository.

But what of the fields that are traditionally less "data centric" and historically less technological? The humanities are also invested in cyberinfrastructure development. David Green draws our attention to the importance of incorporating and supporting humanistic perspectives in the cyberinfrastructure (and to these we should also add the arts). In reviewing *Our Cultural Commonwealth*, the 2006 report of the American Council of Learned Societies (ACLS) Commission on Cyberinfrastructure for the Humanities and Social Sciences, he notes that the report "underscores the values of designing an environment that cultivates the richness and diversity of human experience, cultures and languages, using the strengths of this community: 'clarity of expression, the ability to uncover meaning, the experience of organizing knowledge and above all a consciousness of values'."[27] Green's comments may well resonate with archivists since humanistic metaphors, epistemologies, values, preoccupations, and processes strongly and conceptually influence the archive, as a physical as well as an intellectual entity. This is most apparent in the archival focus on identifying and preserving evidence present, latent, or, often just as importantly, absent, through value determination (e.g., appraisal, selection for digitization), contextualization (e.g., arrangement and description, presentation), and meaning making (e.g. proving, accounting for, storytelling). While these activities certainly also occur in the more overtly data-centric sciences and social sciences, humanistic approaches, with their focus on storytelling and narrative, intuition, personal context, and meaningful silences or white spaces, have the potential for texturizing, analyzing, and culturally embedding the management, aesthetics, discovery, and use of information as cultural as well as scientific evidence.

Moving from Digital Preservation to Digital Curation

Government extensively funds academia to play a central role in building cyberinfrastructure: developing technologies; hosting networks; generating and consuming digital data; collaborating virtually across space, time, and discipline; publishing scholarly output; identifying policy requirements; and training future generations of scholars and information professionals. Librarians and, to a lesser extent, archivists, are involved together with academics in shaping future research as well as research-funding agendas, especially in the areas of digital preservation and curation, spearheading changes in library and other information practices, establishing electronic journals, operating preprint servers, and now, building and curating digital repositories as an essential part of the cyberinfrastructure that needs to sustain all of these endeavors.

Many flavors of digital repositories containing different kinds of published and unpublished content are variously hosted within and across institutions today. The historical model of each institution providing the content it owns or holds via its own university library and/or archives, and indeed the prestige that accrues to the institution by virtue of the extent and nature of its library and archival holdings, are rapidly breaking down. In a 2002 opinion piece, Richard Johnson of SPARC (the Scholarly Publishing and Academic Resources Coalition) differentiated between institutional digital repositories that "centralize, preserve, and make accessible an institution's intellectual capital, at the same time [as they] form part of a global system of distributed, interoperable repositories that provides the foundation for a new disaggregated model of scholarly publishing" and discipline-specific repositories and subject-oriented or thematic digital libraries.[28] He goes on to lay out what he sees, from a library perspective, as the characteristics of the academic institutional repository:

> . . . a digital archive of the intellectual product created by the faculty, research staff, and students of an institution and accessible to end users both within and outside of the institution, with few if any barriers to access. In other words, the content of an institutional repository is:
> - Institutionally defined;
> - Scholarly;
> - Cumulative and perpetual; and
> - Open and interoperable.[29]

However, this definition lacks what an archival (rather than a library) perspective would contribute: the incorporation of the documentation of the scholarly process as well as its products, and a focus on the evidential as well as on information management and the uses of the digital content. The preservation of cultural materials has been a broadly and essentially transdisciplinary activity throughout its history, drawing upon the arts, humanities, social sciences, and sciences. This transdisciplinarity, therefore, is not a phenomenon that emerged since electronic records and digital preservation imperatives brought computer and information scientists into the mix. Nevertheless, an analysis of the participants, goals, and activities of major funded projects in digital preservation indicates that while a broad range of materials is being addressed (including government records, scientific data, sound, still and moving images, and other creative materials), the digital preservation and traditional preservation/conservation communities are largely separately constituted (with digital preservationists coming predominantly from computer and information science backgrounds and traditional preservationists having library science, archival science, conservation science, and arts curatorial backgrounds). With the exception of library preservation and electronic records management, the two communities have not strategized closely over how to address and prioritize holistically societal preservation needs across digital and nondigital materials.

One way to understand the current scope of digital preservation within this context is to review aspects that recent prominent projects address.[30] It is a long list and includes some topics already surfaced in previous chapters. They can be loosely and nonexclusively grouped as shown in Figure 10.1.

Research relating to digital preservation has identified several areas for further investigation. Many of these involve developing a better understanding of user behaviors; preferences and expectations regarding preservation, preserved materials, and preserved virtual environments; the properties of different kinds of digital objects and environments and which aspects are most important or salient to preserve; how to harness public knowledge and expertise (e.g., of video gamers) in support of preserving and re-creating digital materials; and how to support small organizations and individual creators (e.g., artists) in preserving their digital products/ assets. It has also identified a need to delineate more closely the parameters of digital objects and aggregate objects; test metadata specifications

Data aspects: Characterizing and identifying digital object types; preserving the look, feel, and behavior of digital objects; data mining; digital forensics; preservation of software-dependent data; accuracy, completeness, reliability and authenticity of digital content; evaluation and appraisal; how to populate digital repositories; the nature of the life cycle for digital information

Metadata aspects: Capturing complete or adequate context for data; creation and demonstration of trustworthy metadata; metadata management; creator incentives for generating adequate metadata; metadata extraction; semantic interoperability

Shared infrastructure: Collaborative/shared repositories; clarification of roles and responsibilities; identifying management needs for digital evidence; user profiling services; digital rights management regimes; data and metadata registries

Technical concerns with digital media: Managing high-volume data/scalability of technical solutions; automated tool development for activities and services across the life cycle; security and privacy protection mechanisms; emulator development; migration management.

Access and accessibility: Continued access to trustworthy digital assets; generating dissemination information packages out of preservation systems; evaluation of delivery options; development of discovery, retrieval and data manipulation tools.

Knowledge transfer: Turning prototype systems and software into production versions; helping creators manage their own digital outputs.

Policy: Intellectual property concerns; data security and privacy concerns.

Metrics: Long-term economics; usage; growth in volume of data and metadata over time.

Promoting public awareness: Boosting public awareness of preservation issues; identifying creator incentives for creating preservable data.

Digital preservation education: Professional education; technology training; end-user education; educational needs assessment; curriculum development.

Figure 10.1. Aspects addressed by recent research in digital preservation

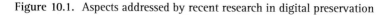

in meaningful applications and identify how different types of metadata (e.g., process, event, and object based) are going to interact in future systems; identify more specific requirements for metadata management, including more automatic ways in which metadata can be created (e.g., through event triggers, inheritance, inference, or derivation) and managed by responsible agents.

Some additional areas that might be examined more directly include collaboration parameters and dynamics; how preserved digital content can be structured to support different methodological approaches applied in research; globalization and international dimensions of preservation, including "digital preservation divide" issues; temporal aspects of digital preservation, especially the semantic, aesthetic, or behavioral drift that might occur as objects and environments are preserved and migrated; support for and assessment of the effectiveness of personal digital preservation capabilities; digital preservation in community archives/heritage institutions; integration of institutional preservation regimes across all media types, whether analog or digital; and cultural sensitivities and community collaboration in regard to preservation decisions, techniques, and regimes. Emergent areas for research include digital reconstruction or reconstitution, digital repatriation, and co-creator rights in data and data management.

The term "digital curation" has emerged in recent years as a transprofessional umbrella covering digital preservation and other activities involved in creating, managing, disseminating, and using digital content.[31] As with digital preservation, digital curation focuses exclusively on the digital, but the exact scope of the concept is still being defined. The familiar problem of definition occurs again with digital curation. Different definitions offer some clues to the professional communities of practice influential in their development. According to a 2006 report of the United Kingdom's Joint Information Systems Committee (JISC), digital curation involves

> Maintaining and adding value to a trusted body of digital information for future and current use; specifically, the active management and appraisal of data over the entire life cycle. Digital curation builds upon the underlying concepts of digital preservation whilst emphasizing opportunities for added value and knowledge through annotation and continuing resource management. Preservation is a curation activity, although both are concerned with managing digital resources with no significant (or only controlled) changes over time.[32]

The DCC provides a similar description, but with more emphasis on both archival practices and scientific data production:

> Digital curation, broadly interpreted, is about maintaining and adding value to a trusted body of digital information for current and future use. The digital archiving and preservation community now looks beyond the preservation, cataloguing and cross referencing of static digital objects such as documents. The scientific community has data characterised by structure, volatility and scale. These require us to extend our notions of curation. We must also investigate the principles that underlie appraisal, and lessons learnt about the economics of preservation.[33]

ICPSR offers a definition that includes more delineation of the "curatorial" activities involved, which also clearly demonstrates the bridge between this approach and past data archive practices:

> Digital curation, which encompasses both data curation and digital preservation activities, is the active management and enhancement of trusted digital resources across the life cycle.

Sound curation practices assure that

- Digital content is captured for long-term use and its integrity assured.
- Researchers can find and use digital content for secondary analysis.
- Digital content is available in an appropriate form for the designated community.
- Privacy is protected for research subjects represented in data.
- Digital content is secured in online, near-line, and offline storage.
- Digital content is stored in preservable formats for current and future use.[34]

DRAMBORA (the Digital Repository Audit Method Based on Risk Assessment) offers a rather different description that draws on approaches also used in electronic records management and was developed jointly by the DCC and DigitalPreservationEurope (DPE):

> . . . digital curation is characterised as a risk-management activity; the job of digital curator is to rationalise the uncertainties and threats that inhibit efforts to maintain digital object authenticity and understandability, transforming them into manageable risks. Six stages are implicit within the process. Initial stages require auditors to develop an organisational profile, describing and documenting the repository's mandate, objectives, activities and assets. Latterly, risks are derived from each of these, and assessed in terms of their likelihood and potential impact. Finally, auditors are encouraged to conceive of appropriate risk management responses to the identified risk. The process enables effective resource allocation, enabling repository administrators to identify and categorise the areas where shortcomings are most evident or have the greatest potential for disruption. The process itself is an iterative one and therefore subsequent recursions will evaluate the effectiveness of prior risk management implementations.[35]

The term "digital curation," however, has not been implemented without some misgivings in the archival community, notably expressed by Australian archivist Adrian Cunningham, who argues:

> Instinctively I find the phrase inappropriate for a lot of what recordkeeping professionals do because it suggests antiquarian scholarship rather than modern information

management. The phrase *data stewardship*, which is sometimes used as an alternative, is in many ways more attractive, though it too has some drawbacks. Nevertheless, the value of the phrase digital curation is that it attempts to unite into a coherent whole various threads of related professional endeavors spanning the entire life of digital information. Included within the definition of digital curation are the noble endeavors of digital preservation, digital librarianship, digital archiving, and data management.[36]

Archivists, Digital Repositories, and Digital Curation

It should be evident from the preceding overview that many interests are converging around cyberinfrastructure development and the associated development of various types of digital repositories, and that common imperatives support certain synergies. At the same time, the need to bring together skill sets distinctive to different professional or disciplinary fields necessitates a certain mutual dependence, or at the very least, dialogue. Most archivists today are only too aware of the shift in economic and social production engendered by digital network capabilities that Green claims has profoundly altered the ways in which the bureaucratic, scholarly, and personal record is created, maintained, and used. They struggle with how to work with creators, systems designers, systems administrators, and policy makers to influence the generation of identifiable, segregable, preservable, trustworthy electronic records, as well as to build or locate digital storage capacity that meets archival specifications for preserving and making available authentic copies of those records. Incorporating these activities into digital repositories may provide archivists with a broader, higher-profile platform for ensuring that evidentiary requirements are met. It may also give them access to a deeper knowledge base about different kinds of users and their needs and modalities, information retrieval techniques, user interface design, customized user services, automated protocols and metadata structures for secure user registration or rights clearances, and end-user data manipulation tools that could enhance discovery and use of digital archival materials.

Archival practices and experiences together provide a body of knowledge that can be applied to help address such challenges by contributing to the functionality of a digital repository. They can also provide a frame for understanding the nature, values, and future potential uses of evidence (as opposed to information or data) and the paradigms and processes that might help to identify, preserve, and explicate it.[37] However, as noted, while archivists understand these issues with traditional media, they need to become more engaged in the presentation and retrieval of digital evidence in ways that draw upon not only advanced technological capabilities, but also upon humanistic ideas about the role and design of the archive and the values and use of evidence. A major educational initiative focused on the educational preparation required for archivists and other information and content specialists to engage in digital curation activities is the DigCCurr I and II Projects (2006–2012) based at the University of North Carolina at Chapel Hill.[38]

Enduring Paradigms argued in 2000 that "the archival science perspective can make a major contribution to a new paradigm for the design, management, preservation, and use of digital resources because it is fundamentally concerned with the organizational and personal processes and contexts through which records and knowledge are created as well as the ways in which records individually and collectively reflect those processes."[39] It does this through

- life-cycle or continuum control of both born-digital and digitized materials;
- establishment and preservation of the integrity of digital materials;
- identification and preservation of the evidential value of digital materials through design, description, preservation, and evaluation of information systems;
- exploitation of context, hierarchy, and other documentary relationships in the design and use of digital materials;
- elucidation of the nature, genesis, and use of those materials by their creators and managers; and
- identification and exploitation of the interdependencies among digital and related nondigital materials, as well as their various associated metadata.[40]

Almost a decade later, these practices are still essential to the management of evidence in digital settings, and they are still too frequently lacking in digital repositories and other resources developed by area specialists, technologists, or even librarians. Discipline or subject specialists may have different and highly relevant notions about evidence as construed within their disciplines that also should be incorporated. There have certainly been significant areas of development since 2000. Archivists are getting better at justifying and explicating the processes they have historically undertaken and demonstrating how these might transfer into the digital environment. The work of the InterPARES Projects over the past decade and a half, which includes the development of detailed sets of activity models and conceptual definitions, is an excellent example of this; as is the work of the Practical E-Records Method at the University of Illinois at Urbana-Champaign.[41]

Three outstanding areas remain where archivists, and especially academic archivists, need to ponder further the nature and scope of the archival endeavor if they are to participate more fully in the development of cyberscholarship and the cyberinfrastructure more broadly. First, like librarians, who are adjusting to the notion of digital libraries and licensed access to digital journals and other digital content, archivists need to contemplate more systematically what an archives with limited or even no physicality might look like, especially if it were not specifically tied to one institution or even to one national or legal jurisdiction. Could that archives be centered around capturing the evolving record of a particular function or research or development activity that multiple actors in multiple locations might carry out (for example, sequencing the human genome or tracking global climate change), rather than around the bureaucratic, scholarly, educational, and social activities of a single institution? As Helen Samuels points out, archivists have not been particularly good at documenting the full range of academic activities, even in the nondigital environment.[42] What unique roles of archives remain valuable in a digital world and must be engineered into the design of digital repositories? What values and bureaucratic, disciplinary, and cultural imperatives for evidence need to be met? And, finally, while the benefits to archives of digital technology and the Internet, including heightened visibility, enhanced searchability, and remote access, are evident, is there anything in the physicality of the archives itself—its use of space and order, its atmosphere, its sense of stability—that should not be lost in a transition to a digital archives or when archival materials are incorporated into a shared digital repository?

Second, the imperative for archivists to contemplate their current and future roles in a digital world is not simply because of the need to respond to technological developments. Strong intellectual rationales for doing so also exist. It is true that new technologies are generating types of digital materials that have no direct traditional counterparts. They also blur the boundaries between the personal and the institutional, the singly and the collaboratively authored, the interim draft and the final copy, the unpublished and the published, and the two-dimensional and the multidimensional object. However, as discussed in chapters 1 and 2, postmodern, postcolonial, ethnic, Indigenous, Critical Race, and many other theoretical frameworks that have evolved out of the arts, humanities, and social sciences also challenge archivists to broaden their conceptualizations of what they consider to be a record and thus might or should fall under their professional purview. If digital repositories are to be spaces where objects can be thought of or approached as sociocultural evidence as well as data or information, then archivists need to spend more time contemplating the qualities of recordness that might exist within a broader range of objects. They also need to contemplate how these qualities might be maintained within the digital repository and how users might wish to approach them culturally and methodologically.

Third and finally, archivists, like librarians, need to give some thought to the distinctions or overlaps that might exist between their efforts to make content available digitally and those of digital humanities scholars. For four decades or so, scholars who previously might have been users of traditional archives have found that archives, through the limitations of their holdings, services, and technologies, do not or cannot support their needs. Instead, these scholars amass and present their own primary data, for example, oral and video histories. Digital humanities researchers, however, in fields such as history, art, music, dance, archaeology, classics, and literature are building computational tools and overlays to facilitate the visualization, mining, analysis, mash-up, even virtual re-enactment of their own, or pre-existing historical, numeric, spatial, cultural, or performance data. The differences in perspectives here between the digital humanist and the archivist may well be immediate expertise in the subject of the content as opposed to expertise in the long-term evidentiary management of that content, and they definitely have different audience orientations. However, does the development of digital archives in the digital humanities mean that traditional archives have failed these humanities scholars in terms of providing deep, useful content and sophisticated tools for carrying out research on digital resources, or are digital humanities archives filling a niche in their own fields that traditional archives have never sought to address and should not now attempt? Are there still ways in which the two might reconcile or at least fruitfully collaborate? Recognizing that the digital data, tools, and environments that they create pose a host of long-term reliability and sustainability issues, digital humanities programs in some universities now incorporate aspects of archival, preservation, and informatics education as part of student preparation. It remains to be seen whether this will result in increased collaboration between archivists and digital humanists, or in increased ability by digital humanists to go it alone, or indeed in a new kind of hybrid digital humanities archival or curatorial specialist.

Notes

Portions of this chapter were presented in papers at the ICA Section on University and Research Institutions Conference and the Fourth Conference on Scientific Archives as well as at "At the Nexus of Analog and Digital: A Symposium for Preservation Educators," University of Michigan, Ann Arbor, June 2011. See Anne J. Gilliland, "Synergy and Symbiosis: Archival Practice and Academic Digital Repositories," *Proceedings of the International Council on Archives Section on University and Research Institution Archives (SUV) Conference and the Fourth Conference on Scientific Archives: A Natureza dos Arquivos Universitários e de Instituições de Pesquisa, Perspectiva Internacional, 8–11 September, 2009, Rio de Janeiro, Brazil* (Rio de Janeiro: ANAIS, 2009), 164–72.

[1] Philip C. Brooks, typescript subsequently published as U.S. National Archives Staff Information Circular 9 (1940), in Record Group 64, Subject Files of Solon J. Buck.

[2] David Green, "Cyberinfrastructure for All of Us: An Introduction to Cyberinfrastructure and the Liberal Arts," *Academic Commons*, December 16, 2007, http://www.academiccommons.org/commons/essay/cyberinfrastructure-introduction.

[3] Green, "Cyberinfrastructure for All of Us."

[4] William Y. Arms and Ronald L. Larsen, cochairs, "The Future of Scholarly Communication: Building the Infrastructure for Cyberscholarship" (report, NSF/JISC workshop, Phoenix, Arizona, April 17–19,

2007), http://www.sis.pitt.edu/~repwkshop/NSF-JISC-report.pdf; Christine L. Borgman, *Scholarship in the Digital Age: Information, Infrastructure, and the Internet* (Cambridge, Mass.: MIT Press, 2008).

[5] See, for example, Esther Conway, David Giaretta, Simon Lambert, and Brian Matthews, "Curating Scientific Research Data: A Preservation Analysis Method in Context," *International Journal of Digital Curation* 2, no. 6 (2011): 38–52; Ixchel M. Faniel and Ann Zimmerman, "Beyond the Data Deluge: A Research Agenda for Large-scale Data Sharing and Re-Use," *International Journal on Digital Curation* 1, no. 6 (2011): 58–69.

[6] The findings of several studies by archival researchers also support this. See for example, Kalpana Shankar, "Recordkeeping in the Production of Scientific Knowledge: An Ethnographic Study," *Archival Science* 4 (2006): 367–82; and Dharma Akmon, Ann Zimmerman, Daniels, Morgan, and Margaret Hedstrom, "The Application of Archival Concepts to a Data-intensive Environment: Working with Scientists to Understand Data Management and Preservation Needs," *Archival Science* 3–4 (2011): 329–48.

[7] Karen Markey et al., *Census of Institutional Repositories in the United States MIRACLE Project Research Findings* (Washington, D.C.: Council on Library and Information Resources, February 2007).

[8] Elizabeth Yakel, Soo Young Rieh, Beth St. Jean, Karen Markey, and Jihyun Kim, "Institutional Repositories and the Institutional Repository: College and University Archives and Special Collections in an Era of Change," *The American Archivist* 71 (Fall/Winter 2008): 324.

[9] The largest archival study to date was conducted as part of InterPARES 2, where multiple case studies were undertaken of the work and attitudes of individual artists, musicians, composers, and photographers, as well as general studies of academic practices and conceptualizations in the arts and humanities. See InterPARES 2, "Case Studies," http://www.interpares.org/ip2/ip2_case_studies .cfm and "General Studies," http://www.interpares.org/ip2/ip2_general_studies.cfm.

[10] Terry Cook, "'We Are What We Keep: We Keep What We Are': Archival Appraisal Past, Present and Future," *Journal of the Society of Archivists* 32, no. 2 (2011): 176.

[11] Sue McKemmish, "Traces: Document, Record, Archive, Archives," in *Archives: Recordkeeping in Society*, ed. Sue McKemmish, Michael Piggott, Barbara Reed, and Frank Upward (Wagga Wagga, Aus.: Centre for Information Studies, Charles Sturt University, 2005), 5.

[12] It should be noted, however, that the ways in which these datasets were managed in data archives were designed to facilitate research re-use and not to maintain legal evidential value, as later became the focus of archival electronic records endeavors.

[13] Thomas Elton Brown, "The Society of American Archivists Confronts the Computer," *The American Archivist* 47, no. 4 (1984): 367.

[14] Margaret O'Neill Adams, "The Origins and Early Years of IASSIST," *IASSIST Quarterly* (Fall 2006): 5–12.

[15] International Association for Social Science Information Services and Technology, "About IASSIST," http://www.iassistdata.org/about/index.html.

[16] See Charles P. Bourne, "On-line Systems: History, Technology, and Economics," *Journal of the American Society for Information Science* 31, no. 3 (May 1980): 155–60; Charles P. Bourne and Trudi Bellardo Hahn, *A History of Online Information Services, 1963–1976* (Cambridge, Mass.: MIT Press, 2003), 1.

[17] See Susanne Bjorner and Stephanie C. Ardito, "Online Before the Internet: Early Pioneers Tell Their Stories," *Searcher*, 9-part series, Information Today, http://www.infotoday.com/searcher/jun03/ ardito_bjorner.shtml.

[18] For an excellent study of the impact of F. W. Lancaster's predictions of a paperless society, see Arthur P. Young, "Aftermath of a Prediction: F. W. Lancaster and the Paperless Society," *Library Trends* 56, no. 4 (2008): 843–58.

[19] See Nicholas Negroponte, *Being Digital* (London: Vintage Books, 1995).

[20] See, for example, National Science Board and National Science Foundation, *Long-lived Digital Data Collections: Enabling Research and Education in the 21ˢᵗ Century* (Washington, D.C.: National Science Foundation, 2005); Interagency Working Group on Digital Data, *Harnessing the Power of Digital Data for Science and Society* (Washington, D.C.: National Science and Technology Council, 2009).

[21] National Center for Research Resources, *Recovery Act 2009 Limited Competition: Enabling National Networking of Scientists and Resource Discovery (U24)*, http://grants.nih.gov/grants/guide/rfa-files/RFA-RR-09-009.html.

[22] In the United Kingdom, similar priorities have been expressed in reports commissioned by JISC (formerly the Joint Information Systems Committee). See Philip Lord and Alison Macdonald, *e-Science Data Curation* (briefing paper, Joint Information Systems Committee, 2004), http://www.jisc.ac.uk/publications/documents/pub_escience.aspx; Neil Beagrie, Julia Chruszcz, and Brian Lavoie, *Keeping Research Data Safe*, JISC, May 12, 2008, http://www.jisc.ac.uk/publications/documents/keepingresearchdatasafe.aspx; and Raivo Ruusalepp, *Infrastructure Planning and Data Curation: A Comparative Study of International Approaches to Enabling the Sharing of Research Data*, Version 1.6 (London, U.K.: JISC, 2008).

[23] National Center for Research Resources, *Recovery Act 2009.*

[24] See Ellen Collins, "Use and Impact of U.K. Research Data Centres," *International Journal of Digital Curation* 1, no. 6 (2011): 20–31.

[25] Jolene Martin Beiser, "Data Management in the Social Sciences: An Environmental Scan" (master's thesis, University of California, Los Angeles, 2009). See also Kathleen Fear, "'You Made It, You Take Care of It': Data Management as Personal Information Management," *International Journal of Digital Curation* 2, no. 6 (2011): 53–77.

[26] Beiser, "Data Management in the Social Sciences," 6–7.

[27] Green, "Cyberinfrastructure for All of Us.

[28] Richard K. Johnson, "Partnering with Faculty to Enhance Scholarly Communication," *D-Lib Magazine* 8, no. 11 (2002), http://www.dlib.org/dlib/november02/johnson/11johnson.html.

[29] Johnson, "Institutional Repositories."

[30] Projects examined include NDIIPP Projects, DIGARCH Projects, CAMiLEON, InterPARES, NIST/NIH/NLM/NARA/VA collaborations, e-Depot, Dioscuri, NDHA, PLANETS, CASPAR, DPE, and DigCCurr.

[31] According to DigCCurr I, "A decade of work in digital preservation and access . . . resulted in an emerging and complex life-cycle constellation of strategies, technological approaches, and activities now termed 'digital curation.'" See DigCCurr: Preserving Access to Our Digital Future: Building an International Digital Curation Curriculum, "About Our Projects," http://ils.unc.edu/digccurr/. See also Sarah Higgins, "Digital Curation: The Emergence of a New Discipline," *International Journal of Digital Curation* 2, no. 6 (2011): 78–88.

[32] JISC, *Digital Preservation Briefing Paper*, http://www.jisc.ac.uk/publications/briefingpapers/2006/pub_digipreservationbp.aspx.

[33] The Digital Curation Centre (DCC) in the United Kingdom defines *digital curation* as follows: "Digital curation, broadly interpreted, is about maintaining and adding value to a trusted body of digital information for current and future use. The digital archiving and preservation community now looks beyond the preservation, cataloguing and cross referencing of static digital objects such as documents. The scientific community has data characterised by structure, volatility and scale. These require us to extend our notions of curation. We must also investigate the principles that underlie appraisal, and lessons learnt about the economics of preservation," DCC, "About the DCC," http://www.dcc.ac.uk/about/what/.

[34] Inter-University Consortium for Social and Political Research (ICPSR), "Digital Curation," http://www.icpsr.umich.edu/icpsrweb/datamanagement/support/glossary#D.

[35] Digital Repository Audit Method Based on Risk Assessment (DRAMBORA), "Drambora: About," http://www.repositoryaudit.eu/about/.

[36] Adrian Cunningham, "Digital Curation/Digital Archiving: A View from the National Archives of Australia," *The American Archivist* 71 (Fall/Winter 2008): 531.

[37] See Gilliland-Swetland, *Enduring Paradigms*, (see Introduction, n. 5).

[38] See Christopher A. Lee and Helen Tibbo, "Where's the Archivist in Digital Curation? Exploring the Possibilities through a Matrix of Knowledge and Skills," *Archivaria* 72 (2011): 123–68; Helen R. Tibbo and Christopher A. Lee, "Closing the Digital Curation Gap: A Grounded Framework for Providing Guidance and Education in Digital Curation," in *Proceedings of Archiving 2012* (Springfield, Va.: Society for Imaging Science and Technology, 2012), 57–62.

[39] Gilliland-Swetland, *Enduring Paradigms*.

[40] Gilliland-Swetland, *Enduring Paradigms*.

[41] See www.interpares.org; Christopher Prom, "Making Digital Curation a Systematic Institutional Function," *International Journal of Digital Curation* 1, no. 6 (2011): 139–52.

[42] Helen Samuels, *Varsity Letters: Documenting Modern Colleges and Universities* (Metuchen, N.J.: Scarecrow Press, 1992).

CHAPTER 11

Conclusion:
The Archival Paradigm
in the Postphysical World

Although this book addresses archives and archival ideas in a digital age, technology per se is not its central preoccupation. Rather, the book is concerned with the shifts and divergences in archival discourse that technological developments necessitate, facilitate, or inspire: from documentalists to documentation strategists, from stand-alone to networked repositories and initiatives, from archival practices established by regulations to those negotiated through cultural protocols, and from situatedness in the local and the national to the global and the international. In so doing, it also alludes to the multiple "-tions" that tug increasingly at different corners of archival consciousness and practices—including globalization, pluralization, integration, collaboration, participation, democratization, liberation, reconciliation, co-creation, repatriation, and replication.

Technology is like air. It is everywhere and it is always moving. It has also become essential to how much of the world operates in official and personal capacities, and it has significantly merged the official and personal lives of individuals, making it hard to draw clean distinctions between the two, especially as evidenced in the documentary traces of those lives. Records in the paradigmatic archival sense have become secondary to doing business and are no longer integral to many business processes. Technology won't stop evolving and influencing the production, description, preservation, dissemination, and utilization of the human record. It has evolved since the earliest recordkeeping, and it always will. Nor will scholarly trends and political currents stop shaping the centers of interest in those traces. In concert with these dynamics, archival ideas, vocabularies, best practices, standards, and even the curricula and pedagogies with which we prepare new generations of archivists and archival studies academics, of necessity and out of proactivity, will and must be considered dynamic in concept and in practice. At the same time, however, regardless of how integrated the fields engaged in data, information, and heritage management might become, these aspects of the archival endeavor must be formulated with a strong sense of what the particular contribution of the archives and recordkeeping field and its paradigm is to the creation, management, preservation, use, and re-use of trusted evidence that remains essential to individuals and communities, bureaucracies, and societies across time and space.

It is important to note in all this—and I mention this fully cognizant of the risks of reviving old debates about the value of archival theory to practice—that the ability to conceptualize archival ideas and practices, especially independent of the considerations and constraints associated with the physicality of the traditional record, and to express them lucidly to others is an essential part of twenty-first-century archival work. Clearly, without sound postphysical and nuanced understandings of such central constructs as *records, archives, creator, custody,* and *metadata,* as well as of the processes and activities in which they are implicated, it will be exceptionally difficult to work with electronic records, scientific data, digital repositories, virtual archives, participatory and community archival activities, digital policy development, and many other areas integral to the contemporary archival landscape. It is certainly possible, and, as this book illustrates, often essential, to express archival constructs, functions, processes, and metadata in the form of unambiguous definitions, entity-relationship or activity models, functional analyses, or crosswalks. But such approaches, by definition, almost always need to come from specific perspectives and assumptions, and this constraint regularly takes us back to a central conundrum for archivists working in a digital, global world. Pragmatism and empiricism are mainstays of professional and social scientific approaches. They help to break down assertions, practical problems, and technological implementations into more objective, identifiable, and actionable components and best practices. But, on their own, these approaches cannot address many of the cultural, affective, and phenomenological aspects that lie at the heart of the complexity archivists face today and that need to be identified and expressed. As it is, these approaches have not yet managed even to integrate or reconcile the diversity of technical, community, professional, and intellectual understandings of basic archival constructs that exist across different fields and archival traditions.

Archivists, therefore, in addition to approaching their work conceptually, also need a broader knowledge of this diversity and must be able to think flexibly and innovatively about how to move their practices beyond single fixed perspectives. They must also think more strategically and systematically about why, when, and how they should share professional or intellectual territory with other communities through collaboration, cooperation, or layering of expertise and other resources. In a digital and glocal world, with all its variables and constituencies, many forms of expertise are needed, and the increasing convergence of archives, libraries, and museums (ALM) as well as the rise of digital curation as a professional concentration are but two examples of how different forms of expertise are, of necessity, coming together to address complex questions relating to integrating and preserving data, knowledge, and culture.

Some forms of expertise, however, especially those of creator and user communities, have not been fully acknowledged or integrated in the past but certainly will be in the future, whether archivists welcome it or not. In a recent presentation, Chris Hurley deftly put his finger on two important changes that have already taken place in the relationship between users and archives. He noted that Web-based tools are able to shape the results of the search and retrieval process based on "signals" from both the user's profile and by characteristics of the target resource. Even more profoundly, he observes that "the Internet moves the power to shape the narrative from the provider to the user."[1] Social media capabilities allow users to annotate the record, to emend the archivist's description of holdings, to insert a different narrative, to contribute a story, and to take digital content, turn it into something new, and contribute it back to the archives. As techniques for mining large repositories of scientific and social data (and their metadata) and for rendering customized output in response to user specifications become more sophisticated, users are likely to ask that archives retain more digital materials (i.e., resisting large-scale appraisal) so that they can take advantage of pattern recognition, network analysis, and inferencing techniques to draw out latent characteristics of massive accumulations of materials that are difficult or impossible to discern using manual techniques. This trend, taken to its logical conclusion, will ultimately mean that the citizen of the global village will have no more privacy than the citizen of the local one. In other words, archivists can no longer exercise the same degree of control, and by implication, power, over what their archives contain, what they say, when and how users can obtain access, and how they might be used or what they might be able to reveal. All of these issues, of course, raise important considerations for the nature and scope of professional education and training as well as for professional practice and research.

If the field were to start afresh, knowing what is known now, and deal with all the technology, media, social, and political dimensions that have emerged in the twenty-first century, how would it do what it does? Would it inductively end up with the same fundamental principles laid out in Table 1.1, or would it come up with completely different approaches—or has it already lost its place to the metafield of digital curation? Does the emergence of new ways of looking at traditional concepts such as provenance or the emergence of new constructs such as the archival multiverse pose a fundamental challenge to the archival paradigm or simply bear witness to the kinds of shifts noted by Terry Cook and others? Are these concepts and principles indeed ineluctable, enduring, and robust, or is the archival and recordkeeping field guilty of shoehorning today's realities into a paradigm predicated on those of the past?

These questions underlie many of the subjects of the chapters in this book. The constant throughout is that this is the profession of the record, and regardless of where one draws a boundary around that record bureaucratically or humanly, the record is in its essence about evidence. The archival paradigm has demonstrably evolved, and continues to evolve, in response to evermore expansive conceptualizations of the nature and role of evidence in different contexts and how that evidence should be managed and might be used. Its focus on evidential approaches provides a fundamental continuity in the digital world and allows archival activities and concerns to traverse formal and less formal, but no less important contexts; to permeate distinctions between conscious and less conscious creation of evidence; and to engage genuinely and respectfully with communities and expertise of all types and at all points in the lifespan of that evidence.

Note

1 Chris Hurley, "Strength Below and Grace Above: The Structuration of Records" (presented at "Hacking the Archives: Archival Description in an Online World," Recordkeeping Roundtable, September 2011), http://recordkeepingroundtable.files.wordpress.com/2011/08/hurley-description-in-an-online-world.pdf.

Bibliography

Archival Sources

Buck, Solon J., Papers. Library of Congress Manuscript Division.

Bush, Vannevar, Papers, 1901–1974. MSS 14498, Library of Congress Manuscript Division. http://hdl.loc.gov/loc.mss/eadmss.ms998004.

Jameson, J. Franklin, Papers. Library of Congress Manuscript Division.

Leland, Waldo Gifford, Papers, 1879–1966. MSS 29900, Library of Congress Manuscript Division.

Posner, Ernst, Papers. National Archives and Records Administration, 1789–ca. 2007 [U.S.].

Records of the United States National Archives and Records Administration. Record Group 64, National Archives and Records Administration [U.S.].

Science Service, Records, 1902–1965. Record Unit 7091, Smithsonian Institution Archives. http://siarchives.si.edu/findingaids/faru7091.htm.

Published and Web Sources

The Aboriginal and Torres Strait Islander Data Archive. "ATSIDA Protocols." http://www.atsida.edu.au/protocols/atsida.

The Aboriginal and Torres Strait Islander Library and Information Resources Network. "ATSILIRN Protocols." http://www.aiatsis.gov.au/atsilirn/protocols.php.

Accurate Information Systems. "International Data Protection Legislation Matrix." http://www.accinfosys.com/docs/International_Data_Protection_Laws.pdf.

Acland, Glenda. "Managing the Record Rather than the Relic." *Archives and Manuscripts*, 20, no. 1 (1992): 57–63.

Adams, Margaret O'Neill. "The Origins and Early Years of IASSIST." *IASSIST Quarterly* (Fall 2006): 5–12.

———. "Three Decades of Description and Reference Services for Electronic Records." In *Thirty Years of Electronic Records*, edited by Bruce I. Ambacher, 63–90. Lanham, Md.: Scarecrow Press, 2003.

Akmon, Dharma, Ann Zimmerman, Morgan Daniels, and Margaret Hedstrom. "The Application of Archival Concepts to a Data-intensive Environment: Working with Scientists to Understand Data Management and Preservation Needs." *Archival Science* 3–4 (2011): 329–48.

Ambacher, Bruce I., ed. *Thirty Years of Electronic Records*. Lanham, Md.: Scarecrow, 2003.

American Documentation Institute. "ADI Reports–Technical Reports and Standards." Library of Congress Science Reference Services. http://www.loc/rr/scitech/trs/trsadi.html.

American Society for Information Science and Technology. "History of ASIST&T." http://www.asis.org/history.html.

An, Xiaomi. "Meta-synthetic Strategies to Digital Recordkeeping: International Trends and Future Directions." Paper presented at the International Council on Archives Congress, Brisbane, August 2012. http://www.ica2012.com/files/data/Full%20papers%20upload/ica12final00020.pdf.

———. "Research in Electronic Records Management." In *Managing Electronic Records,* edited by Julie Mcleod and Catherine Hare, 63–80. London: Facet Publishing, October, 2005.

———, Shuyang Sun, and Wei Zhang. "Managing Electronic Records in E-Government: Current Trends and Future Directions Internationally." In *Proceedings of the 2011 International Conference on Management and Service Science, 12–14 August 2011.* http://ieeexplore.ieee.org/stamp/stamp.jsp?tp=&arnumber=5999074.

———, and Wang Wang. "Towards Comprehensive Integration Management of Business Continuity, Records and Knowledge." In *Proceedings of the 6th International Conference on Networked Computing and Advanced Information Management, Seoul, South Korea, August 16–18, 2010,* 5–9.

Anderson, Scott R., and Robert B. Allen. "Envisioning the Archival Commons." *The American Archivist* 72 (Fall/Winter 2009): 383–400.

Anglo-American Cataloging Rules. 2nd ed., 2002 revision. Chicago: American Library Association; Ottawa: Canadian Library Association; London: Chartered Institute of Library and Information Professionals, 2002.

Appel, John J. *Immigrant Historical Societies in the United States, 1880–1950.* New York: Arno Press, 1980.

Archival Education and Research Institute (AERI) Pluralizing the Archival Curriculum Group (PACG). "Educating for the Archival Multiverse." *The American Archivist* (Spring/Summer 2011): 68–102.

Arms, William Y., and Ronald L. Larsen, cochairs. *The Future of Scholarly Communication: Building the Infrastructure for Cyberscholarship.* NSF/ JISC workshop, Phoenix, Arizona, April 17–19, 2007. http://www.sis.pitt .edu/~repwkshop/NSF-JISC-report.pdf.

Armstrong v. Executive Office of the President, 303 U.S. App. D.C. 107 (1993).

Association for Computing Machinery. "ACM at a Glance." http://www.acm.org/ membership/acm-at-a-glance.

Atherton, Jay. "From Life Cycle to Continuum: Some Thoughts on the Records Management-Archives Relationship." In *Canadian Archival Studies and the Rediscovery of Provenance*, edited by Tom Nesmith, 391–402. Metuchen, N.J.: Scarecrow, 1993.

Auditor General of Victoria. *Managing Risk: Good Practice Guide.* State of Victoria, 2004, 2. http://download.audit.vic.gov.au/files/20040630-Public-Sector-Managing-Risk.pdf.

Bailey, Catherine. "Archival Theory and Electronic Records." *Archivaria* 29 (1990): 180–96.

Bannon, Liam J. "Forgetting as a Feature, Not a Bug: The Duality of Memory and Implications for Ubiquitous Computing." *CoDesign* 2, no. 1 (2006): 3–15.

Bantin, Philip C. "Developing a Strategy for Managing Electronic Records: The Findings of the Indiana University Electronic Records Project." *The American Archivist* 61 (1998): 328–64.

——. "The Indiana University Electronic Records Project Revisited. *The American Archivist* 62 (1999): 153–63.

——. "Strategies for Managing Electronic Records: A New Archival Paradigm? An Affirmation of Our Archival Traditions?" *Archival Issues* 23, no. 1 (1998): 17–34.

——, and Gerald Bernbom. "The Indiana University Electronic Records Project: Analyzing Functions, Identifying Transactions, and Evaluating Recordkeeping Systems: A Report on Methodology." *Archives and Museum Informatics: Cultural Informatics Quarterly* 10 (1996): 246–66.

Baron, Jason R. "Recordkeeping in the 21st Century." *Information Management Journal* 33 (1999): 8–16.

Barritt, Marjorie Rabe. "Coming to America: Dutch *Archivistiek* and American Archival Practice." *Archival Issues* 18, no. 1 (1993): 43–54.

Bastian, Jeannette. *Owning Memory: How a Caribbean Community Lost Its Archives and Found Its History.* Westport, Conn.: Libraries Unlimited, 2003.

——. "Taking Custody, Giving Access: A Postcustodial Role for a New Century." *Archivaria* 53 (2002): 76–93.

——, and Ben Alexander, eds. *Community Archives: The Shaping of Memory.* London: Facet Publishing, 2009.

Bayhylle, Ruth. "Tribal Archives: A Study in Records, Memory and Power." PhD diss., University of California, Los Angeles, 2011.

Beagrie, Neil, Julia Chruszcz, and Brian Lavoie. "Keeping Research Data Safe." JISC. May 12, 2008. http://www.jisc.ac.uk/publications/documents/keepingresearchdatasafe.aspx.

Bearman, David A., ed. *Archival Management of Electronic Records.* Pittsburgh: Archives and Museum Informatics Technical Report no. 13, 1991.

——. "Archives and Manuscript Control with Bibliographic Utilities: Challenges and Opportunities." *The American Archivist* 52 (Winter 1989): 26–39.

——. "Diplomatics, Weberian Bureaucracy, and the Management of Electronic Records in Europe and America." *The American Archivist* 55 (1992): 168–81.

——. *Electronic Evidence: Strategies for Managing Records in Contemporary Organizations.* Pittsburgh: Archives and Museum Informatics, 1994.

——. *Electronic Records Guidelines: A Manual for Policy Development and Implementation.* Pittsburgh: Archives and Museum Informatics, 1990.

——. "The Implications of *Armstrong v. Executive Office of the President* for the Archival Management of Electronic Records." *The American Archivist* 56 (1993): 674–89.

——. "An Indefensible Bastion: Archives as a Repository in the Electronic Age." In *Archival Management of Electronic Records*, edited by David Bearman, 14–24. Pittsburgh: Archives and Museum Informatics, 1991.

——. "Item Level Control and Electronic Recordkeeping." Paper presented at the Society of American Archivists Annual Meeting, San Diego, Calif., 1996.

——. "Record-keeping Systems." *Archivaria* 36 (1993): 16–37.

——. *Towards National Information Systems for Archives and Manuscript Repositories: The National Information Systems Task Force (NISTF) Papers, 1981–1984.* Chicago: Society of American Archivists, 1987.

Beiser, Jolene Martin. *Data Management in the Social Sciences: An Environmental Scan.* Master's thesis, University of California, Los Angeles, 2009.

Bellardo, Lewis J. Letter to Readers Forum. *Midwestern Archivist* 5, no. 2 (1981): 123–24.

——, and Lynn Lady Bellardo. *Glossary for Archivists, Manuscript Curators, and Records Managers.* Chicago: Society of American Archivists, 1992.

Berner, Richard C. "Manuscript Catalogs and Other Finding Aids: What Are Their Relationships?" *The American Archivist* 34, no. 4 (1971): 367–72.

BitCurator: Tools for DigitalForensics Methods and Workflows in Real-world Collecting Institutions. http://www.bitcurator.net/.

Bjorner, Susanne, and Stephanie C. Ardito. "Online before the Internet: Early Pioneers Tell Their Stories." *Searcher,* 9-part series. Information Today. http://www.infotoday.com/searcher/jun03/ardito_bjorner.shtml.

Blake, Ben. "The New Archives for American Labor: From Attic to Digital Shop Floor." *The American Archivist* 70 (Spring/Summer 2007): 130–50.

Blake, Richard. "Overview of the Electronic Records in Office Systems (EROS) Programme." In *Electronic Access: Archives in the New Millennium,* 52–58. London: Public Record Office, 1998.

Blanchette, Jean-François. *Burdens of Proof: Cryptographic Culture and Evidence Law in the Age of Electronic Documents.* Cambridge, Mass.: MIT Press, 2012.

——. "Infrastructural Thinking: A Pedagogical Approach to Information Technology and Archives." Plenary address, AERI 2012, Los Angeles, July 2012.

Blanton, Thomas S. *White House E-Mail: The Top-Secret Messages the Reagan/ Bush White House Tried to Destroy.* Book and disk. New York: The New Press, 1995.

Booth, W. James. "Communities of Memory: On Identity, Memory, and Debt." *American Political Science Review* 93 (1999): 249–63.

Borgman, Christine L. *Scholarship in the Digital Age: Information, Infrastructure, and the Internet.* Cambridge, Mass.: MIT Press, 2008.

Bourdieu, Pierre. *Distinction: A Social Critique of the Judgment of Taste.* Translated by Richard Nice. Cambridge, Mass.: Harvard University Press, 2000.

Bourne, Charles P. "On-line Systems: History, Technology, and Economics." *Journal of the American Society for Information Science* 31 (May 1980): 155–60.

——, and Trudi Bellardo Hahn. *A History of Online Information Services, 1963– 1976.* Cambridge, Mass.: MIT Press, 2003.

Britt, Steuart Henderson. "The Psychologist and the American Documentation Institute." *American Psychologist,* March 2, 1949, 180–81.

Brockmeier, Jens. "After the Archive: Remapping Memory." *Culture and Psychology* 16 (March 2010): 5–35.

Brooks, Philip. "Current Aspects of Records Administration: The Archivist's Concern in Records Administration." *The American Archivist* 6 (July 1943): 158–64.

——. "The Selection of Records for Preservation." *The American Archivist* 3 (October 1940): 221–34.

Brown, Thomas Elton. "A Decade of Development: Educational Programs for Automated Records and Techniques within the Society of American Archivists." *The American Archivist* 56 (Summer 1993): 410–23.

——. "The Society of American Archivists Confronts the Computer." *The American Archivist* 47, no. 4 (1984): 366–82.

Bryan, Mary Givens. "Changing Times." *The American Archivist* 24 (January 1961): 3–10.

Buck, Solon J. "The Archivist's One World." *The American Archivist* 10 (January 1947): 9–24.

Buckland, Michael K. "The Centenary of 'Madame Documentation': Suzanne Briet, 1894–1989." *Journal of the American Society for Information Science* 46, no. 3 (1995): 235–37.

——. "Emanuel Goldberg, Electronic Document Retrieval, and Vannevar Bush's Memex." *Journal of the American Society for Information Science* 43 (May 1992): 284–94.

Bunn, Jennifer J. "Multiple Narratives, Multiple Views: Observing Archival Description," 32. PhD diss., University College London, 2011. http://discovery.ucl.ac.uk/1322455/1/1322455.pdf.

Burckel, Nicholas. Review of *A History of the Farmington Plan*, by Ralph D. Wagner. *The American Archivist* 66 (Spring/Summer 2003). http://www.archivists.org/periodicals/aa_v66/review-burckel-aa66_1.asp.

Bush, Vannevar. "As We May Think." *Atlantic Monthly* 176 (1945): 101–8.

Calmes, Alan. "Practical Realities of Computer-Based Finding Aids: The NARS A-1 Experience." *The American Archivist* 42, no. 2 (1979): 167–77.

Calvino, Italo. *Grand Bazaar* (Milan, Sept.–Oct. 1980. Essay collected in *The Literature Machine.* London: Vintage, 1997, 339.

Caplan, Priscilla and Rebecca Guenther. "Practical Preservation: The PREMIS Experience." *Library Trends* 54, no. 1 (2005): 111–24.

Caswell, Michelle. "Khmer Rouge Archives: Accountability, Truth, and Memory in Cambodia. *Archival Science* 11 (2011): 25–44.

Charlesworth, Andrew. *Digital Preservation Coalition Report on Intellectual Property Rights for Digital Preservation* (2012). http://dx.doi.org/10.7207/twr12-02.

Chatfield, Helen L. Review of *American Documentation. The American Archivist* 14 (April 1951): 163–65.

Clay, Diskin. "Epicurus in the Archives of Athens." In *Studies in Attic Epigraphy, History and Topography.* Hesperia Supplement 9. Princeton, N.J.: American School of Classical Studies at Athens, 1982, 17–26.

Collins, Ellen. "Use and Impact of U.K. Research Data Centres." *International Journal of Digital Curation* 1, no. 6 (2011): 20–31.

Committee on Preservation of Historical Records. *Preservation of Historic Records: Magnetic Recording Media.* Washington, D.C.: National Academy Press, 1986.

Connerton, Paul. *How Societies Remember.* Cambridge: Cambridge University Press, 1989.

Consultative Committee for Space Data Systems/International Organization for Standardization. *Space Data and Information Transfer System: Open Archival Information System: Reference Model.* Geneva, Switzerland: International Organization for Standardization, 1999.

Conway, Esther, David Giaretta, Simon Lambert, and Brian Matthews. "Curating Scientific Research Data: A Preservation Analysis Method in Context." *International Journal of Digital Curation* 2, no. 6 (2011): 38–52.

Cook, J. Frank. "The Blessings of Providence on an Association of Archivists." *The American Archivist* 46, no. 4 (1983): 374–99.

Cook, Terry. "Easier to Byte, Harder to Chew: The Second Generation of Electronic Records Archives." *Archivaria* 33 (1992): 202–16.

——. "Electronic Records, Paper Minds: The Revolution in Information Management and Archives in the Post-custodial and Post-modern Era." *Archives and Manuscripts* 22 (1994): 300–29.

——. "Evidence, Memory, Identity, and Community: Four Shifting Archival Paradigms." *Archival Science*, DOI 10.1007/s10502-012-9180-7.

——. Foreword. "Archival Music: Verne Harris and the Cracks of Memory." In *Archives and Justice: A South African Perspective*, edited by Verne Harris, ix–xxviii. Chicago: Society of American Archivists, 2007.

——. "It's 10 O'Clock–Do You Know Where Your Data Are?" *Technology Review* 98 (1995): 48–53.

——. "Macroappraisal in Theory and Practice: Origins, Characteristics, and Implementation in Canada, 1950–2000." *Archival Science* 5, nos. 2–4 (2005): 101–61.

——. "'We Are What We Keep: We Keep What We Are': Archival Appraisal Past, Present and Future." *Journal of the Society of Archivists* 32, no. 2 (2011): 173–89.

——. "What Is Past Is Prologue: A History of Archival Ideas Since 1898, and the Future Paradigm Shift." *Archivaria* 43 (Spring 1997). http://www.mybestdocs.com/cook-t-pastprologue-ar43fnl.htm.

——, and Eldon Frost. "The Electronic Records Archival Programme at the National Archives of Canada: Evolution and Critical Factors of Success." In *Electronic Records Management Program Strategies: Archives and Museum Informatics Technical Report 18*, edited by Margaret Hedstrom, 38–47. Pittsburgh: Archives and Museum Informatics, 1993.

——, and Joan Schwartz. "Archives, Records, and Power: From (Postmodern) Theory to (Archival) Performance." *Archival Science* 2 (2002): 171–85.

Cortada, James W. *Archives of Data-Processing History*. New York: Greenwood Press, 1987.

Couture, Carol, and Daniel Ducharme. "Research in Archival Science: A Status Report." *Archivaria* 59 (2005): 41–67.

Cox, Richard J. *The First Generation of Electronic Records Archivists in the United States: A Study of Professionalization*. New York: Haworth Press, 1994.

——. "The Record in the Information Age: A Progress Report on Reflection and Research." *Records and Retrieval Report* 12 (1996): 1–16.

——. "The Record: Is it Evolving?" *Records and Retrieval Report* 10 (1994): 1–16.

——. "Re-discovering the Archival Mission: The Recordkeeping Functional Requirements Project at the University of Pittsburgh, A Progress Report." *Archives and Museum Informatics* 8 (1994): 279–300.

——, and Wendy Duff. "Warrant and the Definitions of Electronic Records: Questions Arising from the Pittsburgh Project. *Archives and Museum Informatics* 11 (1997): 223–31.

Crooke, Elizabeth. "The Politics of Community Heritage: Motivations, Authority and Control." *International Journal of Heritage Studies* 16 (January–March 2010): 16–29.

Cuddihy, Elisabeth F. "Aging of Magnetic Recording Tape." *IEEE Transactions on Magnetics* 16 (July 1980): 558–68.

Cullen, Charles T., Peter B. Hirtle, David Levy, Clifford A. Lynch, and Jeff Rothenberg. *Authenticity in a Digital Environment*. Washington, D.C.: Council on Library and Information Resources, 2000. http://www.clir.org/pubs/abstract/pub92abst.html.

Cumming, Kate. "The Work of Peter Scott: An Overview." *Recordkeeping Roundtable*, November 16, 2011. http://recordkeepingroundtable.org/2011/11/16/the-work-of-peter-scott-an-overview-2/.

Cunningham, Adrian. "The Archival Management of Personal Records in Electronic Form: Some Suggestions." *Archives and Manuscripts* 22, no. 1 (1994): 94–105.

——, ed. *The Arrangement and Description of Archives amid Administrative and Technological Change: Essays By and About Peter J. Scott*. Brisbane: Australian Society of Archivists, 2012.

——. "Commentary: Journey to the End of the Night: Custody and the Dawning of a New Era on the Archival Threshold." *Archives and Manuscripts* 24, no. 2 (1996): 312–21.

——. "Digital Curation/Digital Archiving: A View from the National Archives of Australia." *The American Archivist* 71 (Fall/Winter 2008): 530–43.

Curry, Andrew. "Piecing Together the Dark Legacy of East Germany's Secret Police." *Wired Magazine* 16 (January 2008). http://www.wired.com/politics/security/magazine/16-02/ff_stasi?currentPage=all

Daniel, Dominique. "Documenting the Immigrant and Ethnic Experience in American Archives." *The American Archivist* 73 (Spring/Summer 2010): 82–104.

Daniels, Maygene F., and Timothy Walch. *A Modern Archives Reader: Basic Readings on Archival Theory and Practice*. Washington, D.C.: National Archives and Records Service, 1984.

Data Intensive Cyberinfrastructure Foundation. "Introduction to iRODS and Data Management." http://diceresearch.org/DICE_Site/Introduction.html.

Davis, Watson. *Science News Letter*. October 9, 1937, 230.

——. *Science Service Document #45*. Washington, D.C.: Documentation Institute of Science Service, July 11, 1935.

Day, Michael. "CEDARS: Digital Preservation and Metadata." Paper presented at 6th DELOS Workshop: Preservation of Digital Information, Tomar, Portugal, June 17–19, 1998. http://www.ukoln.ac.uk/metadata/presentations/delos6/cedars.html.

——. "Metadata for Digital Preservation: A Review of Recent Developments." In *Proceedings of the European Conference on Digital Libraries, ECDL 2001* (2001), 161–72.

Day, Ronald E. *The Modern Invention of Information: Discourse, History, and Power.* Carbondale, Ill.: Southern Illinois University Press, 2008.

Derrida, Jacques. *Archive Fever: A Freudian Impression.* Translated by Eric Prenowitz. Chicago: University of Chicago Press, 1996.

DigCCurr: Preserving Access to Our Digital Future: Building an International Digital Curation Curriculum. http://ils.unc.edu/digccurr/.

Digital Curation Centre. http://www.dcc.ac.uk/.

Digital Preservation Testbed. *Preserving Email.* The Hague: ICTU, 2003. http://en.nationaalarchief.nl/sites/default/files/docs/kennisbank/volatility-permanence-email-en.pdf.

Digital Repository Audit Method Based on Risk Assessment (DRAMBORA). "DRAMBORA: About." http://www.repositoryaudit.eu/about/.

Divine, William R. "The Second Hoover Commission Reports: An Analysis." *Public Administration Review* 15 (Autumn 1955): 263–69.

Dollar, Charles M. *Authentic Electronic Records: Strategies for Long-Term Access.* Chicago: Cohasset Associates, 2000.

——. *The Impact of Information Technologies on Archival Principles and Method.* Macerata, Italy: University of Macerata Press, 1992.

Donaldson, Devan Ray, and Paul Conway. "Implementing PREMIS: A Case Study of the Florida Digital Archive." *Library Hi-Tech* 28, no. 2 (2010): 273–89.

Dubester, Henry. "The Role of the American Documentation Institute in International Documentation." *American Documentation* (January 1962): 115–17.

Dubrow, Aaron. "Behind the Scenes: A Glimpse to the Archives of the Future." *Live Science.* March 24, 2011. http://www.livescience.com/13406-glimpse-archives-future-bts-110325.html.

Duff, Wendy. "Harnessing the Power of Warrant." *The American Archivist* 61 (1998): 88–105.

——, and Verne Harris. "Stories and Names: Archival Description as Narrating Records and Constructing Meanings." In *Archives and Justice: A South African Perspective,* 131–56. Chicago: Society of American Archivists, 2007.

——, and Sue McKemmish. "Metadata and ISO 9000 Compliance." *Information Management Journal* 34 (2000). http://infotech.monash.edu/research/groups/rcrg/publications/smckduff.html

Duranti, Luciana. "Archival Legislation for Engendering Trust in an Increasingly Networked Digital Environment." Paper presented at International Congress on Archives, Brisbane, August 2012.

——. "Archives as a Place." *Archives and Manuscripts* 24, no. 2 (1996): 242–55. Republished in *Archives and Social Studies: A Journal of Interdisciplinary Research* 1, no. 1 (2007). http://tinyurl.com/2dbasvb.

——. *Diplomatics: New Uses for an Old Science.* Lanham, Md.: Society of American Archivists, Association of Canadian Archivists, and Scarecrow Press, 1998.

——. "From Digital Diplomatics to Digital Records Forensics." *Archivaria* 68 (Fall 2009): 39–66.

——. "Protecting Electronic Evidence: A Third Progress Report on a Research Study and Methodology." *Archivi and Computer* 6, no. 5 (1996): 343–404.

——. "Reliability and Authenticity: The Concepts and Their Implications." *Archivaria* 39 (1995): 5–10.

——, Terry Eastwood, and Heather MacNeil. *Preservation of the Integrity of Electronic Records.* Dordrecht, Neth.: Kluwer Academic, 2002.

——, and Heather MacNeil. "The Protection of the Integrity of Electronic Records: An Overview of the UBC-MAS Research Project." *Archivaria* 42 (1996): 46–67.

——, and Randy Preston, eds. *International Research on Permanent Authentic Records in Electronic Systems (InterPARES) 2: Experiential, Interactive and Dynamic Records.* Padova, Italy: Associazione Nazionale Archivistica Italiana, 2008. http://www.interpares.org/ip2/book.cfm.

——, and Kenneth L. Thibodeau. "The Concept of Record in Interactive, Experiential and Dynamic Environments: The View of InterPARES. *Archival Science* 6, no. 1 (2008): 13–68.

Eastwood, Terry. "Should Creating Agencies Keep Electronic Records Indefinitely?" *Archives and Manuscripts* 24 (November 1996): 256–67.

——, Eastwood, Terry, Hans Hofman, and Randy Preston. "Part Five–Modeling Digital Records Creation, Maintenance and Preservation: Modeling

Cross-domain Task Force Report." In *International Research on Permanent Authentic Records in Electronic Systems (InterPARES) 2: Experiential, Interactive and Dynamic Records*, edited by Luciana Duranti and Randy Preston. Padova, Italy: Associazione Nazionale Archivistica Italiana, 2008. http://www.interpares.org/display_file.cfm?doc=ip2_book_part_ 5_modeling_task_force.pdf.

Eaton, Fynnette. "Electronic Media and Preservation." *IASSIST Quarterly* 181 (1994): 14–17. http://datalib.library.ualberta.ca/publications/iq/iqvol18.html.

Elsen, Marie K. "SPINDEX in a University Archives." *The American Archivist* 45, no. 2 (1982): 190–92.

Encoded Archival Description Working Group of the Society of American Archivists and the Network Development and MARC Standards Office of the Library of Congress. *Encoded Archival Description Tag Library, Version 2002*. Chicago: Society of American Archivists, 2002.

European Commission. *Requirements for the Management of Electronic Records (MoReq Specification)*. Brussels and Luxembourg: Cornwell Affiliates, 2001.

Faniel, Ixchel M., and Ann Zimmerman. "Beyond the Data Deluge: A Research Agenda for Large-scale Data Sharing and Re-Use." *International Journal on Digital Curation* 1, no. 6 (2011): 58–69.

Farkas-Conn, Irene Sekely. *From Documentation to Information Science*. New York: Greenwood Press, 1990.

Faulkhead, Shannon. *Narratives of Koorie Victoria*. PhD diss., Monash University, 2009.

Fear, Kathleen. "'You Made It, You Take Care of It': Data Management as Personal Information Management." *International Journal of Digital Curation* 2, no. 6 (2011): 53–77.

First Archivist Circle. *Protocols for Native American Archival Materials* (2007). http://www2.nau.edu/libnap-p/.

Flinn, Andrew. "Archival Activism: Independent and Community-led Archives, Radical Public History and the Heritage Professions." *InterActions: UCLA Journal of Education and Information Studies* 7, no. 2 (2011). http://escholarship.org/uc/item/9pt2490x.

———. "Independent Community Archives and Community-Generated Content: 'Writing, Saving and Sharing our Histories.'" *Convergence: The International Journal of Research into New Media Technologies* 16, no. 1 (2010): 39–51.

——, Mary Stevens, and Elizabeth Shepherd. "Whose Memories, Whose Archives? Independent Community Archives, Autonomy and the Mainstream." *Archival Science* 9 (2009): 71–86.

Foscarini, Fiorella. "Diplomatics and Genre Theory as Complementary Approaches." *Archival Science.* Preprint.

Foucault, Michel. *The Archaeology of Knowledge and the Discourse on Language.* New York: Pantheon, 1972.

Frusciano, Thomas J. "Automation Programs for Archival and Manuscript Repositories." *Library Hi Tech* 1, no. 2 (1983): 72–77.

Galloway, Patricia Kay. "Archives, Power, and History: Dunbar Rowland and the Beginning of the State Archives of Mississippi (1902–1936)." *The American Archivist* 69, no. 1 (2006): 79–116.

——. "Preservation of Digital Objects." *Annual Review of Information Science and Technology* 38 (2004): 549–90.

Gavrel, Katharine. *Conceptual Problems Posed by Electronic Records: A RAMP Study.* Paris: UNESCO, International Council on Archives, 1990.

Geller, Sidney B. *Care and Handling of Computer Magnetic Storage Media.* NBS Special Publication 500-101. Washington, D.C.: Institute for Computer Sciences and Technology, National Bureau of Standards, 1983.

General Notes, *Popular Astronomy* 45 (1937): 345–46.

Giddens, Anthony. *The Constitution of Society: Outline of the Theory of Structuration.* Berkeley: University of California Press, 1984.

Gilliland, Anne J. "Afterword: In and Out of the Archives." In *Interdisciplinary Essays on European Knowledge Culture, 1400–1900,* edited by Randolph Head, special issue *Archival Science* 10, no. 3 (September 2010): 333–43.

——. "Contemplating Co-creator Rights in Archival Description." *Knowledge Organization,* 39 no. 5 (2012): 340–346.

——. "Neutrality, Social Justice and the Obligations of Archival Educators and Education in the Twenty-first Century." *Archival Science* 11 nos. 2-4 (2011).

——. "Reflections on the Value of Metadata Archaeology for Recordkeeping in a Global, Digital World." *Journal of the Society of Archivists* 32 (April 2011): 97–112.

——. "Setting the Stage." In *Introduction to Metadata: Pathways to Digital Information, Version 3.0,* edited by Murtha Baca. Los Angeles: J. Paul Getty Trust, 2008. http://www.getty.edu/research/publications/electronic_publications/intrometadata/setting.html.

——. "Synergy and Symbiosis: Archival Practice and Academic Digital Repositories." In *Proceedings of the International Council on Archives Section on University and Research Institution Archives (SUV) Conference and the Fourth Conference on Scientific Archives: A Natureza dos Arquivos Universitários e de Instituições de Pesquisa, Perspectiva Internacional, 8-11 September, 2009, Rio de Janeiro,* Brazil, 164-72. Rio de Janeiro: ANAIS, 2009.

——, Lori Lindberg, Victoria McCargar, Alison Langmead, Tracy Lauriault, Monique Leahey-Sugimoto, Joanne Evans, Joe Tennis, and Holly Wang. "Part 6–Investigating the Roles and Requirements, Manifestations and Management of Metadata in the Creation of Reliable and Preservation of Authentic Electronic Entities Created by Dynamic, Interactive and Experiential Systems: Report on the Work and Findings of the InterPARES 2 Description Cross Domain Group." In *International Research on Permanent Authentic Records in Electronic Systems (InterPARES) 2: Experiential, Interactive and Dynamic Records,* edited by Luciana Duranti and Randy Preston, 261-307. Padova, Italy: Associazione Nazionale Archivistica Italiana, 2008. http://www.interpares.org/ip2/book.cfm.

——. Introduction and "Building an Infrastructure for Archival Research." *Archival Science* 4, nos. 3-4 (2004): 143-47, 149-99.

——. "Pluralising the Archives in the Multiverse: A Report on Work in Progress." *Atlanti: Review for Modern Archival Theory and Practice* 21 (2011): 177-85.

——. "Recordkeeping Metadata, the Archival Multiverse, and Societal Grand Challenges." In *Proceedings of the International Conference on Dublin Core and Metadata Applications 2012, Kuching, Malaysia, September 2012,* 106-115. http://dcpapers.dublincore.org/pubs/article/view/3661.

——, Nadav Rouche, Joanne Evans, and Lori Lindberg. "Towards a Twenty-First Century Metadata Infrastructure Supporting the Creation, Preservation and Use of Trustworthy Records: Developing the InterPARES2 Metadata Schema Registry." *Archival Science* 5, no. 1 (2005): 43-78.

Gilliland-Swetland, Anne J. "Automated Archival Systems." In *Encyclopedia of Library and Information Science,* edited by Allen Kent. Vol. 48. New York: Marcel Dekker, 1991, 1-14.

——. *Enduring Paradigm, New Opportunities: The Value of the Archival Perspective in the Digital Environment.* Washington, D.C.: Council on Library and Information Resources, 2000.

——. "Management of Electronic Records." *Annual Review of Information Science and Technology (ARIST)* 39 (2005): 219-53.

——. "Popularizing the Finding Aid: Exploiting EAD to Enhance Online Browsing and Retrieval in Archival Information Systems by Diverse User Groups." *Journal of Internet Cataloging* 4, nos. 3–4 (2001): 199–225.

——. "Social Science Data Archives in the New World?" In *For the Record*, edited by Rena Lohan et al., 54–63. Dublin, Ire.: Institute of Public Administration, 1996.

——. "Testing Our Truths: Delineating the Parameters of the Authentic Archival Electronic Record." *The American Archivist* 65, no. 2 (2002): 196–215.

——, and Philip B. Eppard. "Preserving the Authenticity of Contingent Digital Objects: The InterPARES Project." *D-Lib Magazine* 6 (2002). http://www.dlib.org/dlib/july00/eppard/07eppard.html.

——, and Carol Hughes. "Enhancing Archival Description for Public Computer Conferences of Historical Value: An Exploratory Study." *The American Archivist* 55 (Spring 1992): 316–30.

——, and Gregory T. Kinney. "Uses of Electronic Communications to Document an Academic Community: A Research Report." *Archivaria* 38 (Fall 1994): 79–96.

——, Robin L. Chandler, and Layna White. "MOAC II User Evaluation: Making Museum Content Useful." In *Proceedings of the 66th Annual Meeting of the American Society for Information and Technology—Humanizing Information Technology: From Ideas to Bits and Back, Long Beach, California, October 20–23, 2003.* Medford, N.J.: Information Today, 2003.

——, Carina M. MacLeod, M. Kathleen Svetlik, and Layna White. "Evaluating EAD as an Appropriate Metadata Structure for Describing and Delivering Museum Content: MOAC II Evaluation Study." In *Proceedings of the 2004 International Conference of Digital Libraries, February 24–27, 2004, New Delhi, India.* New Delhi, India: The Energy and Resources Institute, 2004, 504–12.

——, Layna White, and Robin L. Chandler. "We're Building It, Will They Use It? The MOAC II Evaluation Project." In *Proceedings of Museums and the Web 2004, Arlington, Virginia, March 31–April 3, 2004.* http://www .museumsandtheweb.com/mw2004/papers/g-swetland/g-swetland.html.

Giri, Ananta Kumar. "Cosmopolitanism and Beyond: Towards a Multiverse of Transformations." *Development and Change* 37 (November 2006): 1277–92.

Gorman, Michael. *The Enduring Library: Technology, Tradition, and the Quest for Balance.* Chicago: ALA Editions, 2003.

——. "RDA: The Coming Cataloguing Debacle." http://www.slc.bc.ca/rda1007.pdf.

Graham, Peter S. *Intellectual Preservation: Electronic Preservation of the Third Kind*. Washington, D.C.: Commission on Preservation and Access, 1994. http://www.clir.org/pubs/reports/graham/intpres.html.

Green, David. "Cyberinfrastructure for All of Us: An Introduction to Cyberinfrastructure and the Liberal Arts." *Academic Commons*, December 16, 2007. http://www.academiccommons.org/commons/essay/cyberinfrastructure-introduction.

Greene, Mark A. "MPLP: It's Not Just for Processing Any More," *The American Archivist* 73 (Spring/Summer 2010): 175–203.

——, and Dennis Meissner. "More Product, Less Process: Revamping Traditional Archival Processing." *The American Archivist* 68, no. 2 (2005): 208–63.

Gross, David. *Lost Time: On Remembering and Forgetting in Late Modern Culture*. Amherst: University of Massachusetts Press, 2000.

Grossman, Ruth. "Our Expectations about Archives: Archival Theory Through a Community Informatics Lens." http://ccnr.infotech.monash.edu/conferences-workshops/prato2006papers.html.

Ham, F. Gerald. "Archival Strategies for the Post-custodial Era," *The American Archivist* 44 (Summer 1981): 207–16.

Harris, Verne. "The Archival Sliver: Power, Memory, and Archives in South Africa." *Archival Science* 2 (2002): 63–86.

——. "Law, Evidence and Electronic Records: A Strategic Perspective from the Global Periphery." *Comma, International Journal on Archives* 1–2 (2001): 29–44.

Heazlewood, Justine, Jon Dell'Oro, Leon Harari et al. "Electronic Records: Problem Solved? A Report on the Public Record Office Victoria's Electronic Records Strategy." *Archives and Manuscripts* 27, no. 1 (1999): 96–113.

Hedstrom, Margaret L. "Recordkeeping Metadata: Presenting the Results of a Working Meeting." *Archival Science* 1 (2001): 243–51.

——. "Understanding Electronic Incunabula: A Framework for Research on Electronic Records." *The American Archivist* 54 (Summer 1991): 334–54.

Henry, Linda J. "Schellenberg in Cyberspace." *The American Archivist* 61 (Fall 1998): 309–27.

Hensen, Steven L., comp. *Archives, Personal Papers, and Manuscripts*. Chicago: Society of American Archivists, 1983.

——. "Squaring the Circle: The Reformation of Archival Description." *Library Trends* 36 (Winter 1988): 539–52.

Hickerson, Thomas H. "Archival Information Exchange and the Role of Bibliographic Networks." *Library Trends* 36 (Winter 1988): 553–71.

——. *Archives and Manuscripts: An Introduction to Automated Access.* Chicago: Society of American Archivists Basic Manual Series, 1981.

Higgins, Sarah. "The DCC Curation Lifecycle Model." *International Journal of Digital Cutation* 1, no. 3 (2008): 134–40.

——. "The Digital Curation Life Cycle Model." In *Proceedings of the 8th ACM/IEEE-CS Joint Conference on Digital Libraries, Pittsburgh, Penn., 2007,* 453.

——. "Digital Curation: The Emergence of a New Discipline." *International Journal of Digital Curation* 2, no. 6 (2011): 78–88.

Higham, J. "The Ethnic Historical Society in Changing Times," *Journal of American Ethnic History* 13, no. 2 (1994): 30–44.

Hillman, Diane, Karen Coyle, Jon Phipps, and Gordon Dunsire. "RDA Vocabularies: Process, Outcome, Use." *D-Lib Magazine* 16 (January/February 2010). http://dlib.org/dlib/january10/hillmann/01hillmann.html.

Hirtle, Peter B. "Archival Authenticity in a Digital Age." In *Authenticity in a Digital Environment.* Washington, D.C.: Council on Library and Information Resources, 2000. http://www.clir.org/pubs/abstract/pub92abst.html.

——. "Atherton Seidell and the Photoduplication of Library Material." *Journal of the American Society for Information Science* 40 (1989): 427.

Hodge, Gail M. "Best Practices for Digital Archiving: An Information Life Cycle Approach." *D-Lib Magazine* 6 (2000). http://www.dlib.org/dlib/january00/01hodge.html.

Hollier, Anita. "The Archivist in the Electronic Age." *EP Libraries Webzine* 3 (March 2001). http://library.web.cern.ch/library/Webzine/3/papers/5/.

Home Movie Day Initiative, http://www.homemovieday.com/about.html.

Honhart, Frederick L. "The Application of Microcomputer-based Local Systems with the MARC AMC Format." *Library Trends* 36 (Winter 1988): 585–92.

——. "MicroMARC:amc: A Case Study in the Development of an Automated System." *The American Archivist* 52 (Winter 1989): 80–86.

Hurley, Chris. "Parallel Provenance (If These Are Your Records, Where Are Your Stories?)," 6. http://www.infotech.monash.edu.au/research/groups/rcrg/publications/parallel-provenance-combined.pdf.

——. "Parallel Provenance: (1) What, If Anything, Is Archival Description?" *Archives and Manuscripts* 33, no. 1 (2005): 110–45.

——. "Parallel Provenance: (2) When Something Is *Not* Related to Everything Else." *Archives and Manuscripts* 33, no. 2 (2005): 52–91.

——. "Strength Below and Grace Above: The Structuration of Records." Presentation at "Hacking the Archives: Archival Description in an Online World," Recordkeeping Roundtable, September 2011. http://recordkeepingroundtable.org/2011/09/02/report-on-hacking-the-archives-archival-description-in-an-online-world/.

International Association for Social Science Information Services and Technology. "About IASSIST." http://www.iassistdata.org/about/index.html.

International Council on Archives, http://www.ica.org/3/homepage/home.html.

International Council on Archives. Committee on Electronic Records. *Guide for Managing Electronic Records from an Archival Perspective.* Paris: International Council on Archives, 1997.

International Council on Archives. *General International Standard Archival Description.* 2nd edition. Paris: International Council on Archives, 1999.

——. *International Standard for Describing Functions.* Paris: International Council on Archives, 2008.

——. *ICA-ISDIAH, International Standard for Describing Institutions with Archival Holdings.* 1st edition. Paris: International Council on Archives, 2008.

International Federation of Library Associations (IFLA). "Functional Requirements for Authority Data—A Conceptual Model." http://www.ifla.org/publications/ifla-series-on-bibliographic-control-34.

——. *Statement of International Cataloguing Principles.* http://www.ifla.org/files/cataloguing/icp/icp_2009-en.pdf.

International Federation of Library Associations (IFLA) Working Group on Functional Requirements for Subject Authority Records (FRSAR). *Functional Requirements for Subject Authority Data (FRSAD) A Conceptual Model.* Draft report. June 10, 2009. http://nkos.slis.kent.edu/FRSAR/report090623.pdf.

The Internet Archive. http://www.archive.org/.

Jones, Steve. *Virtual Culture: Identity and Communication in Cybersociety.* Thousand Oaks, Calif.: Sage Publications, 1997.

InterPARES Project. *The Long-term Preservation of Authentic Electronic Records: Findings of the InterPARES Project* (2002). http://www.interpares.org/book/index.htm.

Inter-University Consortium for Social and Political Research (ICPSR). "Glossary." http://www.icpsr.umich.edu/icpsrweb/datamanagement/support/glossary#D.

Jimerson, Randall. "American Historians and European Archival Theory: The Collaboration of J. F. Jameson and Waldo G. Leland." *Archival Science* 6 (December 2006): 299–312.

JISC. *Digital Preservation Briefing Paper.* http://www.jisc.ac.uk/publications/ briefingpapers/2006/pub_digipreservationbp.aspx.

Johnson, Richard K. "Institutional Repositories: Partnering with Faculty to Enhance Scholarly Communication." *D-Lib Magazine* 8, no. 11 (2002). http://www.dlib.org/dlib/november02/johnson/11johnson.html.

Joint Steering Committee for the Development of RDA. "A Brief History of *AACR.*" http://www.rda-jsc.org/history.html.

——. "Resource Description and Access." http://www.rda-jsc.org/rda.html.

Kakali, Constantia, Irene Lourdi, Thomais Stasinopoulou, Lina Bountouri, Christos Papatheodorou, Martin Doerr, and Manolis Gergatsoulis. "Integrating Dublin Core Metadata for Cultural Heritage Collections Using Ontologies." In *2007 Proceedings of the International Conference on Dublin Core and Metadata Applications,* 129–39.

Kaye, Joseph "Jofish," Janet Vertesi, Shari Avery, Allan Dafoe, Shay David, Lisa Onaga, Ivan Rosero, and Trevor Pinch. "To Have and to Hold: Exploring the Personal Archive." *CHI 2006* (April 22–28, 2006). http://alumni.media.mit. edu/~jofish/writing/tohaveandtohold.pdf.

Ketelaar, Eric. "Archivalisation and Archiving." *Archives and Manuscripts* 27 (1999): 54–61.

——. "Archival Temples, Archival Prisons: Modes of Power and Protection." *Archival Science* 2, nos. 3–4 (2002).

——. "Sharing: Collected Memories in Communities of Records." *Archives and Manuscripts* 33 (2005): 44–61.

Kirschenbaum, Matthew G. "Extreme Inscription: The Grammatology of the Hard Drive." *Text Technology* 13, no. 2 (2004): 91–125.

——. *Mechanisms: New Media and the Forensic Imagination.* Cambridge, Mass.: MIT Press, 2008.

Klaebe, Helen, and Marcus Foth. "Capturing Community Memory with Oral History and New Media: The Sharing Stories Project." In *Proceedings 3rd International Community Informatics Research Network (CIRN) Conference,* edited by Larry Stillman and Graeme Johanson. Prato, Italy: Monash University, 2006. http://eprints.qut.edu.au/4751/.

Koorie Archiving: Trust and Technology Project, Final Report. http://infotech. monash.edu/research/centres/cosi/projects/trust/final-report/.

Koorie Heritage Trust. http://www.koorieheritagetrust.com/collections.

Kothari, Rajni, D. L. Sheth, and Ashis Nandy, eds. *The Multiverse of Democracy: Essays in Honour of Rajni Kothari.* Thousand Oaks, Calif.: Sage Publications, 1996.

Kragh, Helge. "Contemporary History of Cosmology and the Controversy over the Multiverse." *Annals of Science* 66 (October 2009): 529–51.

Kuhn, Thomas S. *The Structure of Scientific Revolutions.* Chicago: University of Chicago Press, 1962.

Kurtz, Matthew. "A Postcolonial Archive? On the Paradox of Practice in a Northwest Alaska Project." *Archivaria* 61 (2007): 63–91.

Langmead, Alison. "Moving beyond Polemics: The Ramifications of Reintegrating Archives and Records Management." Master's thesis, University of California, Los Angeles, 2007.

Lau, Andrew, Anne Gilliland, and Kim Anderson. "Naturalizing Community Engagement in Information Studies: Pedagogical Approaches and Persisting Partnerships." *Information, Communication and Society* 15, no. 7 (2012): 991-1015.

Lavoie, Brian F. *The Open Archival Information System Reference Model: Introductory Guide.* Digital Preservation Coalition Technology Watch Series 04-01. January 2004.

Leahy, Emmett. "Records Administration and the War." *Military Affairs* 6 (Summer 1942): 97–108.

Lee, Christopher A., ed. *I, Digital. Personal Collections in the Digital Era.* Chicago: Society of American Archivists, 2011.

——. Digital Preservation Management. "Timeline." http://www.icpsr.umich.edu/ dpm/dpm-eng/timeline/index.html.

——, Matthew Kirschenbaum, Alexandra Chassanoff, Porter Olsen, and Kam Woods. "BitCurator: Tools and Techniques for Digital Forensics in Collecting Institutions," *D-Lib Magazine* 18 (May/June 2012). http://www.dlib.org/dlib/may12/lee/05lee.html.

——, and Helen Tibbo. "Where's the Archivist in Digital Curation? Exploring the Possibilities through a Matrix of Knowledge and Skills." *Archivaria* 72 (2011): 123–68.

Lee, Tim Berners. "Information Management: A Proposal." WC3. http://www.w3.org/History/1989/proposal.html.

Lefcowitz, M. J., and R. M. O'Shea. "A Proposal to Establish a National Archives for Social Science Survey Data." *American Behavioral Scientist* 6 (1963): 27.

Leland, Walter Gifford. "Some Early Recollections of an Itinerant Historian." *Proceedings of the American Antiquarian Society* (October 1951).

Lesk, Michael. *Preservation of New Technology: A Report of the Technology Assessment Advisory Committee to the Commission on Preservation and Access.* Washington, D.C.: Commission on Preservation and Access, 1992. http://www.clir.org/pubs/reports/lesk/lesk2.html.

Levy, David. "Where's Waldo? Reflections on Copies and Authenticity in a Digital Environment." In *Authenticity in a Digital Environment*, 24–31. Washington, D.C.: Council on Library and Information Resources, 2000. http://www.clir.org/pubs/abstract/pub92abst.html.

Library of Congress National Union Catalog of Manuscript Collections. "*NUCMC* Timeline." http://www.loc.gov/coll/nucmc/timeline.html.

Lord, Philip, and Alison Macdonald. *e-Science Data Curation.* Briefing paper, JISC, 2004. http://www.jisc.ac.uk/publications/documents/pub_escience.aspx.

Lynch, Clifford. "Repatriation, Reconstruction, and Cultural Diplomacy in the Digital World." *EDUCAUSE Review* 43 (January/February 2008): 70–71. http://net.educause.edu/ir/library/pdf/ERM08110.pdf.

Ludaescher, Bertram, Richard Marciano, and Reagan Moore. "Towards Self-validating Knowledge-based Archives." In *11th Workshop on Research Issues in Data Engineering (Ride), Heidelberg, Germany, IEEE Computer Society, 2001.* http://www.sdsc.edu/~ludaesch/Paper/ride01.html.

Lyotard, Jean-François. *La Condition Postmoderne: Rapport sur le Savoir [The Postmodern Condition: A Report on Knowledge].* Paris: Editions de Minuit, c. 1979.

MacNeil, Heather. "Contemporary Archival Diplomatics as a Method of Inquiry: Lessons Learned from Two Research Projects." *Archival Science* 4, nos. 3–4 (2004): 199–232.

——. "Providing Grounds for Trust: Developing Conceptual Requirements for the Long-term Preservation of Authentic Electronic Records." *Archivaria* 50 (2000): 52–78.

——. "Providing Grounds for Trust II: The Findings of the Authenticity Task Force of InterPARES." *Archivaria* 54 (2002): 24–58.

Marciano, Richard. "Archivists' Workbench: A Framework for Testing Preservation Infrastructure," 2004. http://www.interpares.org/display_ file.cfm?doc=ip2_dissemination_cs_marciano_us-interpares_symposium_ 2004.pdf.

Markey, Karen, Elizabeth Yakel, Jihyun Kim, Yong-Mi Kim. *Census of Institutional Repositories in the United States MIRACLE Project Research Findings.* Washington, D.C.: Council on Library and Information Resources, February 2007.

Martin, Lyn. "Viewing the Field: A Literature Review and Survey of the Use of U.S. MARC AMC in U.S. Academic Libraries." *The American Archivist* 57 (Summer 1994): 482–97.

McClure, Charles R., and J. Timothy Sprehe. *Analysis and Development of Model Quality Guidelines for Electronic Records Management on State and Federal Websites: Final Report.* Washington D.C.: National Historical Publications and Records Commission, 1998. http://www.mybestdocs.com/ mcclure-sprehe-nagara5.html.

McDonald, John. "Information Management and Office Systems Advancement." In *Information Handling in Offices and Archives*, edited by Angelika Menne-Haritz, 138–51. New York: K. G. Saur, 1993.

———. "Managing Information in an Office Systems Environment: The IMOSA Project." *The American Archivist* 58 (Spring 1995): 142–53.

———. "Managing Records in the Modern Office: Taming the Wild Frontier." *Archivaria* 39 (1995): 70–79.

McKemmish, Sue. "Are Records Ever Actual?" In *The Records Continuum: Ian Maclean and Australian Archives First Fifty Years*, edited by Sue McKemmish and Michael Piggott, 187–203. Clayton, Aus.: Ancora Press in association with Australian Archives, 1994.

———. "'Constantly Evolving, Ever Mutating:' An Australian Contribution to the Archival Metatext." Ph.D. diss., Monash University, Melbourne, 2001.

———. "Evidence of Me . . ." *Archives and Manuscripts* 29, no. 1 (2001). http://www.mybestdocs.com/mckemmish-s-evidofme-ch10.htm.

———. "Placing Records Continuum Theory and Practice." *Archival Science* 1 (2001): 333–59.

———. "Traces: Document, Record, Archive, Archives." In *Archives: Recordkeeping in Society*, edited by Sue McKemmish, Michael Piggott, Barbara Reed, and Frank Upward. Wagga Wagga, Aus.: Centre for Information Studies, Charles Sturt University, 2005.

———. "Understanding Electronic Recordkeeping Systems: Understanding Ourselves." *Archives and Manuscripts* 22 (1994): 150–62.

———, Glenda Acland, and Barbara Reed. "Towards a Framework for Standardising Recordkeeping Metadata: The Australian Recordkeeping Metadata Schema." *Records Management Journal* 9 (1999): 177–202.

———, Glenda Acland, Nigel Ward, and Barbara Reed. "Describing Records in Context in the Continuum: The Australian Recordkeeping Metadata Schema." *Archivaria* 48 (Fall 1999): 3–42.

———, Shannon Faulkhead, and Lynnette Russell. "Dis-trust in the Archive: Reconciling Records." *Archival Science* 11, nos. 3–4 (2011): 211–39.

———, and Anne J. Gilliland. "Archival and Recordkeeping Research: Past, Present and Future," in *Research Methods: Information Management, Systems, and Contexts*, edited by Kirsty Williamson and Graeme Johanson, 80–112. Prahan, Vic: Tilde University Press, 2012.

———, Anne Gilliland, and Eric Ketelaar. "'Communities of Memory': Pluralising Archival Research and Education Agendas." *Archives and Manuscripts* 5 (2005): 146–75.

———, Livia Iacovino, Eric Ketelaar, Melissa Castan, and Lynnette Russell. "Resetting Relationships: Archives and Indigenous Human Rights in Australia." *Archives and Manuscripts* 39, no. 1 (2011): 107–44.

———, and Dagmar Parer. "Towards Frameworks for Standardising Recordkeeping Metadata." *Archives and Manuscripts* 26 (1998): 24–45.

———, and Frank Upward. "Somewhere Beyond Custody." *Archives and Manuscripts* 22, no. 1 (1994): 138–49.

Menand, Louis. *The Metaphysical Club: A Story of Ideas in America*. New York: Farrar, Strauss, Giroux, 2001.

Miksa, Shawne D. "Resource Description and Access and New Research Potentials." *Bulletin of the American Society for Information Science and Technology* 35 (June 2009). http://www.asis.org/Bulletin/Jun-09/JunJul09_Miksa.pdf.

Mims, Christopher. "Digital Archaeologists Excavate Chips, Not Dirt." *MIT Technology Review*, July 19, 2011. http://www.technologyreview.com/blog/mimssbits/27013/.

Minnesota Historical Society State Archives Department. *Electronic Records Agenda Project Final Report* (June 2003). http://www.mnhs.org/preserve/records/docs_pdfs/eragenda_main_june03.pdf.

MINOM. Annual Conference Cape Verde 2011. http://www.minom-icom.net/ index.php?option=com_content&view=category&id=28:cape-verde-2011&Itemid=4&layout=default.

Monash Country Lines Archive. http://www.infotech.monash.edu.au/research/ projects/independent/countrylines-archive/

Moore, Reagan. "Building Preservation Environments with Data Grid Technology." *American Archivist* 69 (Spring/Summer 2006): 139–58.

——, Chaitan Baru, Arcot Rajasekar, Bertram Ludaescher, Richard Marciano, Michael Wan, Wayne Schroeder, and Amarnath Gupta. "Collection-based Persistent Digital Archives: Part 1," *D-Lib Magazine* 6 (2000). http://www.dlib.org/dlib/march00/moore/03moore-pt1.html.

——, Chaitan Baru, Arcot Rajasekar, Bertram Ludaescher, Richard Marciano, Michael Wan, Wayne Schroeder, and Amarnath Gupta. "Collection-based Persistent Digital Archives: Part 2. *D-Lib Magazine* 6 (2000). http://www.dlib.org/dlib/april00/moore/04moore-pt2.html.

Model Requirements for Electronic Records (MoReq) Collateral. http://www.moreq2.eu/home.

Muller, Samuel, Johan Adriaan Feith, and Robert Fruin. *Manual for the Arrangement and Description of Archives.* Archival Classics Series. Translated by Arthur Leavitt. Introduction by Peter Horsman. Chicago: Society of American Archivists, 2003.

National Academy of Public Administration. *The Archives of the Future: Archival Strategies for the Treatment of Electronic Databases. Report to the National Archives and Records Administration.* Washington, D.C.: National Academy of Public Administration, 1991.

——. *The Effects of Electronic Recordkeeping on the Historical Record of the U.S. Government: A Report for the National Archives and Records Administration.* Washington, D.C.: National Academy of Public Administration, 1989.

The National Archives Public Record Office. *ERM Systems Evaluation Scheme Functional Requirements and Testing of Electronic Records in Management Systems,* December 21, 2000. http://www.21cfrpart11.com/files/library/ government/uk_erecsystemsevaluationscheme.pdf.

National Archives and Records Administration. *Managing Electronic Records.* Washington, D.C.: National Archives and Records Administration, 1990.

——. *A National Archives Strategy for the Development and Implementation of Standards for the Creation, Transfer, Access, and Long-term Storage of Electronic Records of the Federal Government.* National Archives Technical

Information Paper 8. Washington, D.C.: National Archives and Records Administration, 1990.

National Archives and Records Service. *Spindex II: Report and Systems Documentation*. Washington, D.C.: National Archives and Records Service, 1975.

National Archives of Australia. *The DIRKS Manual: A Strategic Approach to Managing Business Information* (2007).

National Archives of Canada. *Managing Information in Office Automation Systems: Final Report on the FOREMOST Project*. Ottawa: National Archives of Canada, 1990.

National Archives of Canada and Canadian Workplace Automation Research Centre. *IMOSA Project: Functional Requirements: Corporate Information Management Application (CIMA)*. Ottawa: National Archives of Canada and Canadian Workplace Automation Research Centre, 1991.

National Archives of Canada and Department of Communication. *The IMOSA Project: An Initial Analysis of Document Management and Retrieval Systems*. Ottawa: National Archives of Canada, Department of Communications, 1993.

National Association of Government Archives and Records Administrators. *A New Age: Electronic Information Systems, State Governments, and the Preservation of the Archival Record*. Lexington, Ky.: NASIRE/The Council of State Governments, 1991.

National Center for Research Resources. *Recovery Act 2009 Limited Competition: Enabling National Networking of Scientists and Resource Discovery (U24)*. http://grants.nih.gov/grants/guide/rfa-files/RFA-RR-09-009.html.

National Historical Publications and Records Commission. *Research Issues in Electronic Records: Report of the Working Meeting*. St. Paul: Published for the National Historical Publications and Records Commission by the Minnesota Historical Society, 1991.

National Institute of Standards and Technology. *Framework and Policy Recommendations for the Exchange and Preservation of Electronic Records, Prepared for the National Archives and Records Administration*. Washington, D.C.: National Institute of Standards and Technology, 1989.

National Research Council. *Building an Electronic Records Archive at the National Archives and Records Administration*. Washington, D.C.: National Academy Press, 2003.

——. *Preserving Scientific Data on Our Physical Universe: A New Strategy for Archiving the Nation's Scientific Information Resources.* Washington, D.C.: National Academy Press, 1995.

——. *Study on the Long-term Retention of Selected Scientific and Technical Records of the Federal Government: Working Papers.* Washington, D.C.: National Academy Press, 1995.

National Science and Technology Council Interagency Working Group on Digital Data. *Harnessing the Power of Digital Data for Science and Society.* Washington, D.C.: National Science and Technology Council, 2009.

National Science Board and National Science Foundation. *Long-lived Digital Data Collections: Enabling Research and Education in the 21st Century.* Washington, D.C.: National Science Foundation, 2005.

National Security Archive. "White House Email." http://www.gwu.edu/~nsarchiv/white_house_email/index.html.

Negroponte, Nicholas. *Being Digital.* London: Vintage Books, 1995.

Nesmith, Tom. "Still Fuzzy, But More Accurate: Some Thoughts on the 'Ghosts' of Archival Theory." *Archivaria* 47 (Spring 1999): 136–50.

Network Development and MARC Standards Office, Library of Congress, in cooperation with Standards and Support, National Library of Canada. *MARC 21 Format for Bibliographic Data: Including Guidelines for Content Designation.* Washington, D.C.: Library of Congress, Cataloging Distribution Service, 1999.

Newton, S. C. "The Nature and Problems of Computer-generated Records." In *Computer Generated Records: Proceedings of a Seminar,* edited by Michael Cook, 1–4. Liverpool, U.K.: University of Liverpool, 1987.

New York State Department of Education. *Building Partnerships: Developing New Approaches to Electronic Records Management and Preservation: Final Report.* Albany: New York State Department of Education, 1994.

——. *Building Partnerships for Electronic Recordkeeping: The New York State Information Management Policies and Practices Survey: Summary of Findings.* Albany: New York State Department of Education, 1994.

Niles Maack, Mary. "The Lady and the Antelope: Suzanne Briet's Contribution to the French Documentation Movement." *Library Trends* 53 (Spring 2004): 719–47.

Nora, Pierre. *Rethinking France: Les Lieux de Mémoire,* vol. 1, translated by David P. Jordan. Chicago: University of Chicago Press, 2001.

OCLC/RLG Working Group on Preservation Metadata. *Preservation Metadata and the OAIS Information Model: A Metadata Framework to Support the Preservation of Digital Objects, A Report.* (June 2002). http://www.oclc.org/research/pmwg/pm_framework.pdf.

Oliver, Gillian. "Investigating Information Culture: Comparative Case Study Research Design and Methods." *Archival Science* 4, nos. 3–4 (2004): 287–314.

Olson, David. "'Camp Pitt' and the Continuing Education of Government Archivists, 1989–1996." *The American Archivist* 60, no. 2 (1997): 202–14.

O'Shea, Greg, and David Roberts. "Living in a Digital World: Recognizing the Electronic and Post-custodial Realities." *Archives and Manuscripts* 24, no. 2 (1996): 286–311.

Park, Eun Gyung. "Understanding 'Authenticity' in Records and Information Management: Analyzing Practitioner Constructs." *The American Archivist* 64 (2001): 270–91.

Patton, Glenn E. "From FRBR to FRAD: Extending the Model." Report *of the IFLA Working Group on Functional Requirements and Numbering of Authority Records*, December 8, 2009. http://conference.ifla.org/past/ifla75/215-patton-en.pdf.

Pearce-Moses, Richard. *A Glossary of Archival and Records Terminology.* Chicago: Society of American Archivists, 2005. http://www.archivists.org/glossary/index.asp.

Personal Digital Archiving 2013. http://mith.umd.edu/pda2013/.

Portuondo, Maria. *Secret Science: Spanish Cosmography and the New World.* Chicago: University of Chicago Press, 2009.

PREMIS: Preservation Metadata Maintenance Activity. http://www.loc.gov/standards/premis/.

Price, Derek J. de Solla. *Little Science, Big Science.* New York: Columbia University Press, 1963.

Prom, Christopher. "Making Digital Curation a Systematic Institutional Function." *International Journal of Digital Curation* 1, no. 6 (2011): 139–52.

Public Record Office Victoria. *Victorian Electronic Records Strategy Final Report.* Melbourne: Public Records Office Victoria, 1998.

Pyenson, Lewis, and Christophe Verbruggen. "Ego and the International: The Modernist Circle of George Sarton." *Isis* 100 (2009).

Ramani, Rehka. "Note and Comment: Market Realities v. Indigenous Equities," *Brooklyn Journal of International Law* 26 (2001): 1147–76.

Rayward, Warden Boyd. "The International Federation for Information and Documentation." In *Encyclopedia of Library History*, edited by Wayne Wiegand and Don G. Davis, 290–94. New York: Garland Press, 1994.

——. *Paul Otlet, Internationalist and Bibliographer*. PhD diss., University of Chicago, June 1973.

RDA Toolkit. http://www.rdatoolkit.org.

Recordkeeping Metadata Schema (RKMS). http://infotech.monash.edu/research/groups/rcrg/projects/spirt/deliverables/austrkms-techintro.html.

Reed, Barbara. "Electronic Records Management in Transition." *Archives and Manuscripts* 22, no. 1 (1994): 164–71.

——, and David Roberts, eds. *Keeping Data: Papers from a Workshop on Appraising Computer-based Records*. Sydney: Australian Council of Archives and the Australian Society of Archivists Incorporated, 1991.

Reith, Mark, Clint Carr, and Gregg Gunsch. "An Examination of Digital Forensic Models." *International Journal of Digital Evidence* 1, no. 3 (2002): 1–12.

Resource Description and Access. http://www.rda-jsc.org/docs/rdabrochureJanuary2010.pdf.

Rhoads, James B. "The Historian and the New Technology." *The American Archivist* 32 (July 1969): 211.

Rice, Paul R. *Electronic Evidence Law and Practice*. Chicago: American Bar Association, 2005.

Richards, Thomas. *The Imperial Archive: Knowledge and the Fantasy of Empire*. New York: Verso, 1993.

Ricoeur, Paul. *Memory, History, Forgetting*. Chicago: Chicago University Press, 2004.

Ridener, John. *From Polders to Postmodernism: A Concise History of Archival Theory*. Duluth, Minn.: Litwin Books, 2009.

Rieger, Morris. "Archives and Automation." *The American Archivist* 29, no. 1 (1966): 109–11.

——. "The Fifth International Archives Congress." *The American Archivist* 28, no. 1 (January 1965): 31–37.

Roberts, David. "Defining Electronic Records, Documents and Data." *Archives and Manuscripts* 22, no. 1 (1994): 14–26.

Robertson, Roland. "Comments on the 'Global Triad' and 'Glocalization.'" In *Globalization and Indigenous Culture*, edited by Inoue Nobutaka. Institute for Japanese Culture and Classics, 1997. http://www2.kokugakuin.ac.jp/ijcc/wp/global/15robertson.html.

———. "The Conceptual Promise of Glocalization: Commonality and Diversity." *ART-e-FACT: Strategies of Resistance* 4. http://artefact.mi2.hr/_a04/lang_en/theory_robertson_en.htm

Robu, Valentin, Harry Halpin, and Hana Shepherd. "Emergence of Consensus and Shared Vocabularies in Collaborative Tagging Systems." *ACM Transactions on the Web (TWEB)* 3, no. 4 (2009).

Roque Ramirez, Horacio. "A Living Archive of Desire: Teresita la Campesina and the Embodiment of Queer Latino Community Histories." In *Archive Stories: Facts, Fictions, and the Writing of History*, edited by Antoinette Burton, 111–35. Durham, N.C.: Duke University Press, 2005.

Ross, Fiona, Sue McKemmish, and Shannon Faulkhead. "Indigenous Knowledge and the Archives: Designing Trusted Archival Systems for Koorie Communities." *Archives and Manuscripts* 34, no. 2 (2006): 112–49.

Ross, Rodney A. "Waldo Gifford Leland and Preservation of Documentary Resources." *Federalist* (Summer 1986).

———. "Waldo Gifford Leland: Archivist by Association." *The American Archivist* 46 no. 3 (Summer 1983): 264–76.

Ross, Seamus, and Ann Gow. *Digital Archaeology? Rescuing Neglected or Damaged Data Resources: A JISC/NPO Study within the Electronic Libraries (eLib) Programme on the Preservation of Electronic Materials, February 1999*. London: British Library and Joint Information Systems Committee, 1999. http://www.ukoln.ac.uk/services/elib/papers/supporting/pdf/p2.pdf.

Ruffins, Faith Davis. "Mythos, Memory, and History: African-American Preservation Efforts, 1820–1990." In *Museums and Communities: The Politics of Public Culture*, edited by Ivan Karp, Christine Mullen Kreamer, and Steven D. Lavine. Washington, D.C.: Smithonian Institution Press, 1992.

Russell, Lynette. "Indigenous Records and Archives: Mutual Obligations and Building Trust." *Archives and Manuscripts* 34, no. 1 (2006): 32–43.

Ruusalepp, Raivo. *Infrastructure Planning and Data Curation: A Comparative Study of International Approaches to Enabling the Sharing of Research Data, Version 1.6*. London: JISC, 2008.

Samuels, Helen Willa. *Varsity Letters: Documenting Modern Colleges and Universities*. Metuchen, N.J.: Scarecrow Press, 1992.

Sawyer, Steve, and Howard Rosenbaum. "Social Informatics in the Information Sciences: Current Activities and Emerging Directions." In "Information Science Research," special issue, *Informing Science* 3, no. 2 (2000): 89–95. http://www.inform.nu/Articles/Vol3/v3n2p89-96r.pdf.

Schama, Simon. *Landscape and Memory.* New York: Vintage Books, 1995.

Schwartz, Joan M., and Terry Cook. "Archives, Records and Power: The Making of Modern Memory." *Archival Science* 2 nos. 1–2 (2002): 1–19.

Scheindlin, Shira E., and Daniel J. Capra. *Electronic Discovery and Digital Evidence: In a Nutshell.* Sedona Conference: West Nutshell Series, 2009.

Schellenberg, Theodore R. "A Nationwide System of Controlling Historical Manuscripts in the United States." *The American Archivist* 28 (July 1965): 409–12.

———. *Modern Archives: Principles and Techniques.* Chicago: University of Chicago Press, 1956.

Schultz, Claire K., and Paul L. Garwig. "History of the American Documentation Institute—A Sketch." *American Documentation* 20 (April 1969): 152–60.

Scott, Peter J. "The Record Group Concept: A Case for Abandonment." *The American Archivist* 29, no. 4 (1966): 493–504.

Sentilles, Renée M. "The Archives of Cyberspace." In *Archive Stories: Facts, Fictions and the Writing of History*, edited by Antoinette Burton, 136–56. Durham, N.C.: Duke University Press, 2005.

Shankar, Kalpana. "Recordkeeping in the Production of Scientific Knowledge: An Ethnographic Study." *Archival Science* 4, nos. 3–4 (2006): 367–82.

Shepherd, Elizabeth, and Geoffrey Yeo. *Managing Records: A Handbook of Principles and Practice.* London: Facet Publishing, 2003.

Sickinger, James P. *Public Records and Archives in Classical Athens.* Chapel Hill: University of North Carolina Press, 1999.

Sinn, Donghee, S. Syn, and S. Kim. "Personal Records on the Web: Who's in Charge of Archiving, Hotmail or Archivists?" *Library and Information Science Research* 33, no. 4 (2011): 320–30.

Slosson, Edwin Emory, and Watson Davis. "Plan for Film Record Prepared by Science Service." Science Service Document 1. Washington, D.C., June 5, 1926.

Smith, Graham. "The Making of Oral History: Sections 1–2." In *Making History: The Changing Face of the Profession in Britain* (London: Institute of

Historical Research, 2008). Making History, http://www.history.ac.uk/makinghistory/resources/articles/oral_history.html.

Smith, Linda Tuhiwai. *Decolonizing Methodologies: Research and Indigenous Peoples.* London: Zed Books, 1999.

Smith, Wilfred I. *Archives: Mirror of Canada Past.* Toronto, Ont.: University of Toronto Press, 1972.

Smorul, Mike, Joseph JaJa, Yang Wang, and Fritz McCall. *PAWN: Producer–Archive Workflow Network in Support of Digital Preservation.* Institute for Advanced Computer Studies, University of Maryland. UMIACS-TR-2004, 2004.

Society of American Archivists. *Describing Archives in Context: A Content Standard.* Chicago: Society of American Archivists, 2004.

——. *SAA Description and Brief History.* n.d.

South African History Archive. http://www.saha.org.za/.

Srinivasan, Ramesh, Robin Boast, Katherine Becvar, and Jonathan Furner. "Blobgects: Digital Museums and Diverse Cultural Knowledges." *Journal of the American Society of Information Science and Technology* 60, no. 4 (2009).

——, Alberto Pepe, and Marko A. Rodriguez. "Eliciting Cultural Ontologies: A Comparison between Hierarchical Clustering Methods and Participatory Design Processes." *Journal of the American Society of Information Science and Technology* 60, no. 2 (2009).

Stevens, Mary, Andrew Flinn, and Elizabeth Shepherd. "New Frameworks for Community Engagement in the Archives Sector: From Handing Over to Handing On. *International Journal of Heritage Studies* 16 (January–March 2010): 59–76.

Stoler, Ann Laura. *Along the Archival Grain: Epistemic Anxieties and Colonial Common Sense.* Princeton, N.J.: Princeton University Press, 2009.

Stories for Change. http://storiesforchange.net/.

StoryCorps: Every Voice Matters. http://storycorps.org/.

Stuckey, Steve. "Keepers of the Fame? The Custodial Role of Australian Archives—Its History and Its Future." *Archives and Manuscripts* 22, no. 1 (1994): 35–48.

Svärd, Proscovia, and Anneli Sundqvist. "IT, the Most Revolutionary Issue Globally: But Is It for All?" *INFOtrend: Nordic Journal for Information*

Specialists 62, no. 3 (2007): 71–78. http://www.sfis.nu/sites/default/files/dokument/infotrend/2007/IT307.pdf.

Taylor, Arlene G., and Barbara B. Tillett. *Authority Control in Organizing and Accessing Information: Definition and International Experience.* Vol. 1. Hove, U.K.: Psychology Press, 2004.

Taylor, Diana. *The Archive and the Repertoire: Performing Cultural Memory in the Americas.* Durham, N.C.: Duke University Press, 2003.

Temple-Raston, Dina. "Predicting the Future: Fantasy or a Good Algorithm?" National Public Radio, October 8, 2012. http://m.npr.org/news/U.S./162397787.

Thibodeau, Kenneth. "Building the Archives of the Future: Advances in Preserving Electronic Records at the National Archives and Records Administration." *D-Lib Magazine* 7 (February 2001). http://www.dlib.org/dlib/february01/thibodeau/02thibodeau.html.

———. "To Be or Not to Be: Archives for Electronic Records." In *Archival Management of Electronic Records,* edited by David Bearman, 1–13. Pittsburgh: Archives and Museum Informatics, 1991.

———, and Darryl Prescott, D. "Reengineering Records Management: The U.S. Department of Defense, Records Management Task Force," *Archivi and Computer* 6, no. 1 (1996): 71–78.

Tibbo, Helen R., and Christopher A. Lee. "Closing the Digital Curation Gap: A Grounded Framework for Providing Guidance and Education in Digital Curation." In *Proceedings of Archiving 2012,* 57–62. Springfield, Va.: Society for Imaging Science and Technology, 2012.

Tillett, Barbara. *What Is FRBR? A Conceptual Model for the Bibliographic Universe.* Washington, D.C.: Library of Congress Cataloging Distribution Service, 2003. http://www.loc.gov/cds/downloads/FRBR.PDF,

Tonkin, Emma et al. "Collaborative and Social Tagging Networks." *Ariadne* 54 (January 2008). http://www.ariadne.ac.uk/issue54/tonkin-et-al.

Tooby, Paul. "Award-Winning TPAP Digital Preservation Prototype Keeps Growing." *D-Lib Magazine* 13 (July/August 2007). http://www.dlib.org/dlib/july07/07inbrief.html.

Turner, Deborah A. *Conceptualizing Oral Documents.* PhD diss., University of Washington, 2009.

Twain, Mark. *Following the Equator: A Journey around the World.* Hartford: American Publishing Company, 1897.

United Nations Advisory Committee for the Co-ordination of Information Systems. *Management of Electronic Records: Issues and Guidelines.* New York: United Nations, 1990.

——. *Strategic Issues for Electronic Records Management: Towards Open Systems Interconnection.* New York: United Nations, 1992.

United States Assistant Secretary of Defense for Networks and Information Integration/Department of Defense Chief Information Officer. *DOD 5015.2-STD, Design Criteria Standard for Electronic Records Management Software Applications, rev. April 2007.* http://www.dtic.mil/whs/directives/corres/pdf/501502std.pdf.

United States Congress. Sarbanes-Oxley Act of 2002. Pub. L. No. 107-204, 116 Stat. 745.

United States House of Representatives Committee on Government Operations. *Taking a Byte Out of History: The Archival Preservation of Federal Computer Records.* House Report 101-978. Washington, D.C.: Committee on Government Operations, U.S. House of Representatives, 1990.

United States National Archives and Records Administration Electronic Records Archive (ERA). http://www.archives.gov/era/.

Upward, Frank, "Cloud Computing and the Post-custodial Archive." Workshop presented at AERI 2012, Los Angeles, July 2012.

——. "Modelling the Continuum as Paradigm Shift in Recordkeeping and Archiving Processes, and Beyond–A Personal Reflection." *Records Management Journal* 10, no. 3 (2000): 115–39.

——. "Structuring the Records Continuum Part One: Postcustodial Principles and Properties." *Archives and Manuscripts* 24 (1996): 268–85.

——. "Structuring the Records Continuum Part Two: Structuration Theory and Recordkeeping." *Archives and Manuscripts* 25 (1997): 10–35.

——, Sue McKemmish, and Barbara Reed. "Archivists and Changing Social and Information Spaces: A Continuum Approach to Recordkeeping and Archiving in Online Cultures." *Archivaria* 72 (Fall 2011): 197–238.

Van den Broek, Jan. "From Brussels to Beijing." In *Proceedings of the 13th International Congress on Archives, Beijing, 2–7 September 1996. Archivum: International Review on Archives* 43 (Munich: K. G. Saur, 1997): 31–62.

Voutssas, Juan. "Long-term Digital Information: Challenges in Latin America." *Aslib Proceedings: New Information Perspectives* 64, no. 1 (2012): 83–96.

WC3. "Facts about W3C." http://www.w3.org/Consortium/facts#process.

W3C. "W3C Semantic Web Activity." http://www.w3.org/2001/sw/.

W3C Semantic Web. "RDFa Applications Working Group." http://www.w3.org/2010/02/rdfa/.

Walch, Victoria Irons. "Automated Records and Techniques Curriculum Development Project. Committee on Automated Records and Techniques." *The American Archivist* 56, no. 3 (1993): 468–505.

———. "Innovation Diffusion: Implications for the CART Curriculum." *The American Archivist* 56, no. 3 (1993): 506–12.

———, comp., with contributions from Marion Matters. *Standards for Archival Description: A Handbook*. Chicago: Society of American Archivists, 1994. http://www.archivists.org/catalog/stds99/index.html.

Wallace, David A. "Metadata and the Archival Management of Electronic Records." *Archivaria* 36 (1993): 87–110.

———. "Preserving the U.S. Government's White House Electronic Mail: Archival Challenges and Policy Implications." Paper presented at the Sixth DELOS Workshop: "Preserving Digital Information," Tomar, Portugal, June 19, 1998. http://www.ercim.eu/publication/ws-proceedings/DELOS6/wallace.pdf.

White, Kelvin L. "*Meztizaje* and Remembering in Afro-Mexican Communities of the Costa Chica: Implications for Archival Education in Mexico." *Archival Science* 9, nos. 1–2 (2009).

———, and Anne Gilliland. "Promoting Reflexivity and Inclusivity in Archival Education, Research and Practice." *Library Quarterly* 80 (July 2010): 231–48.

White, Layna, and Anne J. Gilliland-Swetland. "Museum Information Professionals as Users and Providers of Online Resources: Museums and the Online Archive of California II Study." *ASIST Bulletin*, June/July (2004): 23–26.

Williams, Kate, and Joan Durrance. "Community Informatics." In *Encyclopedia for Library and Information Science*. 3rd ed. New York: Taylor and Francis, 2009.

Winget, Megan A., and William Aspray, eds. *Digital Media: Technological and Social Challenges of the Interactive World*. Lanham, Md.: Scarecrow Press, 2011.

Woods, Kam, and Christopher A. Lee. "Acquisition and Processing of Disk Images to Further Archival Goals." In *Proceedings of Archiving 2012*, 147–52. Springfield, Va.: Society for Imaging Science and Technology, 2012.

Wosh, Peter J., ed. and intro. *Waldo Gifford Leland and the Origins of the American Archival Profession.* Chicago: Society of American Archivists, 2011.

Wurl, Joel. "Ethnicity as Provenance: In Search of Values and Principles for Documenting the Immigrant Experience." *Archival Issues* 29, no. 1 (2005): 65–76.

Yakel, Elizabeth, Soo Young Rieh, Beth St. Jean, Karen Markey, and Jihyun Kim. "Institutional Repositories and the Institutional Repository: College and University Archives and Special Collections in an Era of Change." *The American Archivist* 71 (Fall/Winter 2008): 323–49.

——, Seth Shaw, and Polly Reynolds. "Creating the Next Generation of Archival Finding Aids," *D-Lib Magazine* 13 (May/June 2007). http://www.dlib.org/dlib/may07/yakel/05yakel.html.

Young, Arthur P. "Aftermath of a Prediction: F. W. Lancaster and the Paperless Society." *Library Trends* 56 (April 1, 2008): 843–58.

Your Archives. http://yourarchives.nationalarchives.gov.uk/index.php?title=Home_page.

Zinn, Howard. *A People's History of the United States.* New York: Harper and Row, 1980.

Index

NISTF Data Elements Dictionary, 94–95
noncustodial approach, 179, 180
Norton, Margaret Cross, 148
NSF. *See* National Science Foundation
NUC. See National Union Catalog
NUCMC. See National Union Catalog of Manuscript Collections

O
OAIS. *See* Open Archival Information Systems (OAIS)
obsolescence, 184, 204
Office of Scientific Research and Development (OSRD), 134
Online Computer Library Center (OCLC), 188
Open Archival Information Systems (OAIS)
    Information Model, 188
    Reference Model, 167, 176, 188, 225–26, **225f**, 228
Open Library, 202
oral history, 45
original order, 13, 206
O'Shea, Robert, 136
Otlet, Paul, 62–63, 64, 68–69, 75

P
paperless office, 238
paradigms
    modern archival, 6–10, **7–8t**, 104
    traditional, 32
    Western-centric, 42
"Parallel Provenance" (Hurley), 215
Paris Principles, 88, 91, 114
partnerships, 21, 232
pattern analysis, 122, 142
people's history. *See* social history
Persistent Archives Technology, 122–23, 178, 189
personal digital archives, 202–4
Personal Digital Archiving Conference, 202–3
personal digital assistants (PDAs), 238
physical archives, 13, 15–16
physicality
    of archives, 47, 249–50
    of digital infrastructure, 47
    of records, 174–75, 256
Pitti, Daniel, 97

About the Author

Dr. Anne Gilliland is professor and director of the archival studies specialization, Department of Information Studies, and director of the Center for Information as Evidence, at the Graduate School of Education and Information Studies, University of California, Los Angeles. Her teaching and research interests relate to the design, evaluation, and history of recordkeeping, cultural and community information systems and practices, metadata creation and management, community-based archiving, and archival pluralization. Gilliland is a Fellow of the Society of American Archivists.